ama omnēs

THIS BOOK IS SENT AT
THE REQUEST OF

SUMNER J. SMITH

for your examination and consideration as a text.

D. C. HE

MONEY, BANKING, AND ECONOMIC ACTIVITY

MONEY

BANKING

AND

ECONOMIC

ACTIVITY

GEORGE G. SAUSE

Lafayette College

D. C. Heath and Company / Boston

PREFACE

A book about money at first may seem superfluous. We encounter money so frequently that we may feel we know all that we need to know about it. Surely, we understand that a serious problem arises if we are without it, and that many opportunities for enjoyment and useful activity exist if we possess it in sufficient quantities. No doubt, we also realize that it is a powerful motivating device as the common expressions, "money talks," and "the love of money is the root of all evil," indicate.

However, the discussion of money need not be so superficial. All of us have heard people comment that the dollar is now worth fifty cents. We do not accept this expression literally, but it does indicate that the value of money changes. Most people realize that this change in value creates social and economic problems. The ordinary citizen is aware of the gold outflow and the balance of international payments difficulties of the United States. He also concerns himself with the question of achieving economic growth and avoiding instability. These are problems which involve monetary factors. If we wish to analyze these and similar problems and to make intelligent policy decisions regarding them, a study of money is essential.

Even a brief reading of the history of the United States and other nations will indicate the importance of money. In the case of the United States, monetary policy has been an important political issue in almost every decade. The issuance of paper currency to finance the Revolutionary War, the controversy over the Second Bank of the United States, the post-Civil War problem of deflation, the gold standard controversies of the 1890's and 1930's, and the current debate concerning the balance of payments deficit are examples of political issues of a monetary nature. A knowledge of monetary economics contributes to an understanding of these events and the policies developed in an effort to solve them.

It is our purpose, therefore, to examine the way in which the use of money affects the economic welfare of human beings. In pursuit of this objective, we shall have occasion to concentrate on banks, other financial institutions, credit instruments, abstract theories, and several other topics, but our purpose always will be the same.

The book has been designed for a one-semester course; however, it can be used as the basis for a two-semester course by assigning appropriate supplementary reading. I have written for the student, not for my colleagues. More specifically, I have assumed that the student using this book has completed the principles course but has not had a course in either intermediate economic theory or national income analysis.

I am indebted to many people for assistance in the preparation of this volume. In particular, I should mention the students at Lafayette College, before whom and with whom I have covered the subject matter. My chief obligation, however, is to my wife, Evelyn, who typed the manuscript and served as volunteer copy editor.

CONTENTS

LIST OF TABLES

LIST OF FIGURES

I

MONEY AND
THE ECONOMIC SYSTEM

1

THE CONCEPT OF MONEY

The basic function of money is the facilitation of the exchange of goods and services. Exchange makes it possible for individuals to specialize to a high degree, and this specialization, in turn, leads to increased output and a higher standard of living.

THE ROLE OF MONEY

It is possible to conceive of a society without specialization. Such a society would have a low level of subsistence. Each family unit would produce all the necessities and comforts of life which it consumed. The individual would be forced to turn his hand to a large number of tasks and would have little chance of becoming an expert in any of them. Furthermore, there are many useful products which are too large or too complicated for production by an individual, or even by a family unit. The human race, at an early date, learned that production is greater and the standard of living is higher if individuals specialize in producing a single good or a service, or possibly just a portion of a good or a service. A society of specialists, however, must make provision for the exchange of the surplus of one individual for that of another. Money has been developed to facilitate this process of exchange.

A Barter System

Money facilitates exchange but trading may take place without it. A group may use direct exchange, known as barter, although it is most inefficient. In fact, it is so inefficient and so cumbersome that no society relies upon it exclusively. Hence, the main benefit derived from an examination of a barter system is the insight gained regarding the use of money rather than an understanding of a system currently in operation.

A primary defect in a system of barter is the absence of a standard of value. There is no common denominator in which to express the value of products. In trading commodity *A* for commodity *B*, it is

3

necessary to determine the number of units of A to surrender for a B unit. This entails expressing the value of commodity A in terms of the value of commodity B and *vice versa*. The determination of the value of A in terms of the value of B involves mental calculations by the owner of each commodity, in addition to the haggling and bargaining maneuvers employed. This can consume a considerable portion of the participants' time and energy, and it is necessary to repeat the process when trading A for C, D, E, and so forth. Exchanging B, in turn, for C, D, or E necessitates determining its value in terms of these commodities. This valuation process must be accomplished for each pair of commodities traded. This is not too difficult if the society uses and trades few commodities, but the number of combinations mounts as the variety of items exchanged increases. Thus, for a system with five commodities there are 10 combinations. For 10 commodities, there are 45 combinations; and for 100, there are 4,950.[1] The system obviously becomes impossible when expanded to include the thousands of items traded in a highly developed economy.

Furthermore, the lack of a standard of value means that there is no common unit in which to keep accounts. Even in the absence of trading, a firm or a household encounters difficulty in ascertaining whether its assets are increasing or are decreasing, or in comparing its current income with that of a previous year. For example, General Motors Corporation may know that this year it has produced more Chevrolets but fewer diesel locomotives than it did last year. This knowledge, however, will not permit General Motors Corporation to analyze its relative prosperity unless there is some common unit of account in which to express the costs of production and the values of the two products.

A second major defect in a barter system is the necessity for the existence of a double coincidence of wants before an exchange is possible. If a person wishes to acquire a pair of shoes and is willing to give several bushels of corn in exchange, he must find someone who not only wishes to acquire corn but who has surplus shoes which he is willing to surrender. Searching for this ideal partner entails a great deal of time and effort. A primitive society with few commodities and a limited number of possible combinations may be able to exist under such a system. It is obviously impractical in a society which trades in a large variety of products.

[1]The number of combinations is determined by the formula $nCr = \frac{N!}{r!(n-r)!}$, where C = the number of combinations, n = the number of commodities, and r = the number of commodities included in each combination. Thus, for ten commodities $C = \frac{10 \times 9}{(2 \times 1)}$ = 45.

Two other defects of the barter system result from these short-comings. There is no standard of deferred payments or common unit in which to express promises to pay at a future date. Although this may not make a credit system impossible, it does create great difficulties. Debt, or credit, must be expressed in terms of goods and services. We shall see in later chapters that a credit system which uses financial assets can contribute substantially to a nation's development. Finally, a barter system fails to provide a means for storing value in the form of general purchasing power. It is true that certain commodities can be stored; but there is the danger of spoilage, the inconvenience of storage, and, more important, the likelihood that the need to be satisfied in the future demands different commodities. Hence, a barter system does not encourage saving.

Specific Services of Money

Having described the defects of a barter system at some length, we can cover quickly the specific services of money. The statement, "money overcomes the defects of barter," summarizes these specific services.

First, money serves as a standard of value. Instead of thinking of the value of a good or a service in terms of all the other goods and other services, we express its value in money, using the terms *dollars, pounds,* or some other monetary unit. Closely connected to money's service as a standard of value is its use as a unit of account. By expressing all costs and inventory values in dollars, General Motors Corporation overcomes the problem previously cited. The use of credit cards is another example of money serving as a unit of account. If an individual possesses the appropriate cards and if he or his employer regularly deposits his salary in the bank, the employee will have little use for money in its physical form. This is possible because money is the common denominator in which we express all values.

The second major service of money is its use as a medium of exchange. It avoids the need for finding trading partners with a double coincidence of wants. The man with surplus corn can trade it for money and then can exchange the money for shoes from a third party. In simpler terms, he sells the corn and uses the money to buy shoes. Thus money, serving as a medium of exchange, enables man to expand the size of markets in terms of the variety of products traded and the number of people involved. This larger market, in turn, permits greater specialization and productivity.

Because it is a standard of value and a medium of exchange, money serves as a standard of deferred payment and as a means of storing general purchasing power. Contracts for future payment call for settlement in monetary units. This overcomes the problem of storage and allows the creditor options with regard to the commodities he receives at the time of settlement. The creditor exercises these options by spending the money he receives in any way he chooses. Money, therefore, permits debt contracts of greater length and in greater numbers and is the basis of our system of credit.

Finally, money is a means of storing generalized purchasing power. When used for this purpose, it permits a time option in the consumption of an individual's current production. A man may elect to save a part of his income for his retirement or for some other purpose. Money renders a distinctive service in permitting the individual to postpone his decision regarding the use of his saving until a later date. This is almost impossible if saving takes the form of specific commodities being kept in storage. Consequently, money increases the utility of saving and increases the incentive to save. Increased saving, in turn, can lead to economic growth; but it also creates problems, as we shall see in later sections.

MONEY DEFINED

Having noted the services money performs, we may define it. Money is anything which is accepted generally as a standard of value and a medium of exchange. Note that we have defined it by describing the work it performs, but that we can define it also as general purchasing power or as a debt which society owes to the holder. It is sometimes defined as, "that which buys things." The preceding statements define money in abstract terms. In Chapter 2, we shall define it in more specific terms and as it applies to the United States.

From this comparison of a barter system with a monetary system, it should be apparent that money increases in importance as civilization develops. A primitive society with few consumption items and a low rate of per capita output may use barter, but we could not have achieved our present standard of living without the use of money.

MONEY—CONSEQUENCES OF ITS USE

The main consequence of the use of money is the one we have just described. It facilitates exchange and increases the trading area in terms of the goods and services handled and the number of people involved. Therefore, specialization may be more highly developed, output increased, and the standard of living raised.

Most persons are aware of this service but generally do not realize the contribution money makes to an individual's freedom. We recognize that self-sufficient family units are impossible except at an extremely low standard of living. We also agree that barter is impractical. Accordingly, we must devise some method for co-ordinating the specialized production and distribution of goods and services within a society. Direct controls by the government are a possibility. Under such a system, each individual has a task assigned to him and he receives a portion of the commodities produced. Or custom and tradition, perhaps reinforced by a caste system, may take the place of the government as a co-ordinating device. In neither case is the individual free to choose his occupation nor the composition of his consumption.

Money allows individuals to be free by making possible a system of co-ordination based on prices operating in free markets. The individual may choose the occupation he wishes to follow and the products he utilizes. Also, the actions of individuals in our society are interrelated through the use of money. The effects of actions by an individual or an area are transmitted to other persons and to other areas through the system of markets and prices mentioned in the preceding paragraphs.

Not all the consequences of using money are beneficial, however. Its use involves overhead costs. If money takes the form of *Overhead costs* precious metal, labor and material must be used to extract and to refine the ore. In using paper money there is the much lower cost of printing, while a system based on bank deposits and checks requires considerable clerical expense.

A much more serious consequence of the use of money is the danger that the system will not function properly. There are times when money serves poorly as a standard of value and causes inconvenience and even hardship. Thus, inflation, which is a decrease in the value of money, may dispossess certain people of their wealth; likewise, it may relieve others in a very real sense of their obligations to pay their debts.

Finally, money has become so dominant in our society that it may influence us in other ways. This is a relatively new point of view, and we can introduce it by quoting the older concept.

It must be evident, however, that the mere introduction of a particular mode of exchanging things for one another by first exchanging a thing for money, and then exchanging the money for something else, makes no difference in the essential character of transactions. It is not with money that things are really purchased. Nobody's income (except that of the gold or silver miner) is derived from the precious metals. The pounds or shillings which a person receives weekly or yearly, are not what constitutes his income; they are a sort of tickets or orders which he can present for payment at any shop he pleases, and which entitle him to receive a certain value of any commodity that he makes choice of. The farmer pays his labourers and his landlord in these tickets, as the most convenient plan for himself and them; but their real income is their share of his corn, cattle, and hay, and it makes no essential difference whether he distributes it to them directly, or sells it for them and gives them the price. . . . There cannot, in short, be intrinsically a more insignificant thing, in the economy of society, than money; except in the character of a contrivance for sparing time and labour. It is a machine for doing quickly and commodiously, what would be done, though less quickly and commodiously, without it: and like many other kinds of machinery, it only exerts a distinct and independent influence of its own when it gets out of order.[2]

In this passage, Mill notes that money facilitates exchange and is useful, but he proclaims its neutrality. He claims that money does not affect the motives of producers nor the rate at which various goods and services are exchanged for each other. Modern economists challenge this point of view. We now believe that money has become so dominant in our pattern of living that it serves as a motivating factor. To some extent, people strive to acquire money as an end in itself rather than as a means for securing goods and services. If everyone is producing in order to acquire money to build up a bank balance rather than to purchase goods and services, it is impossible to sell the commodities produced and depressed business conditions will be the result.

A disadvantage of an economic system based on money is the danger that the system will experience these periods of business depression. It should be understood that these depressions are not the same as the lean years to which Biblical history refers. Societies that are more primitive than ours suffer want because weather and other conditions of nature prevent them from producing the necessities of life. In a highly developed economic system, the problem is one of "want in the midst of plenty." The physical capacity for production is not the problem. We shall examine the extent to which money causes this problem in later chapters.

SUMMARY

The primary function of money is to facilitate exchange. Barter is impractical for this purpose because of the lack of a standard of value and the need for a double coincidence of wants. Money, which serves as a standard of value and a medium of exchange, overcomes these defects. In addition, money serves as a standard of deferred payments and as a convenient means of storing value. The use of

[2]John Stuart Mill, *Principles of Political Economy*, ed. Sir W. J. Ashley (New Impression; London: Longmans, Green and Co., 1929), pp. 487–88.

money creates certain problems. By acting as a motivating device it may be the cause, at least to some extent, of unemployment and depressions.

QUESTIONS

1. Name three current political issues in which the monetary system is an important factor.
2. Why do many colleges present a course in "money," although they do not present courses in housing, the steel industry, and other aspects of economic life?
3. List examples of the use of barter in the United States today.
4. What is the meaning of the term "Money is a unit of account"? Can you think of an example not cited in the text?
5. The disadvantages of barter as opposed to the use of money have been described. What, if any, are the advantages of barter?
6. Do people work to acquire money or to acquire the goods and services money will buy? Relate this question to the quotation from J. S. Mill.

SUGGESTED READINGS

Halm, George N. *Monetary Theory.* 2d ed. Philadelphia: The Blakiston Company, 1946. Chapter 1.

Robertson, D. H. *Money.* Chicago: The University of Chicago Press, 1959. Chapters 1, 2, and 3.

SOURCES OF CURRENT DATA

(These references apply to the entire book)

Board of Governors of the Federal Reserve System. *Annual Reports.*

_____. *Federal Reserve Bulletin* (monthly).

Federal Deposit Insurance Corporation. *Annual Reports.*

International Bank for Reconstruction and Development. *Annual Reports.*

International Monetary Fund. *Annual Reports.*

U.S. Department of Commerce. *Survey of Current Business* (issued monthly).

U.S. Government Printing Office. *Economic Report of the President* (issued annually).

2

TYPES OF MONEY—ITS EVOLUTION

We have seen the services money performs and have noted some of the problems connected with its use. We now turn to the question: What is used as money? In answering this question, we shall trace the development of money and shall obtain a knowledge of its characteristics.

The list of things that the human race has used as money is impressively long. Among others, it includes:

beads	debt	metals
beaver skins	dogs' teeth	paper
cattle	feathers	rice
cigarettes	fish hooks	stones
corn	grain	tobacco
cotton	hides	wampum
cowry shells		

The variety of items leads to confusion rather than clarity when one is attempting to isolate the characteristics of money. Accordingly, let us consider the question: What characteristics should an ideal money have?

CHARACTERISTICS OF AN IDEAL MONEY

Money should be durable if it is to serve as a store of value. Since we transfer it from place to place, portability is a second characteristic which money should possess. An item used as money should be divisible into small units, and the individual units should be uniform in quality. Finally, money should be easy to recognize, difficult to counterfeit, and relatively inexpensive to produce.

These are characteristics which we find in the circulating media of most modern monetary systems. If we take the American dollar as an example, we note that it is easy to transport, is divisible into cents in a routine fashion, is easy to recognize, and is difficult to counterfeit. It has limited durability, but the ease and slight cost of replacing

10

worn out units balances this defect. These characteristics, which were difficult to achieve in earlier times, are now largely taken for granted.

Stability of Value

One characteristic, however, is missing from the preceding requirements. This is stability of value. Its importance is apparent if we recall that money serves as a standard of value. To examine this characteristic, we must expand our study and consider the entire monetary system rather than simply the currency component. We may note that our concern with inflation should make obvious the fact that modern monetary systems have not solved the problem of developing money with this characteristic. In later chapters, therefore, we shall emphasize the attempt to achieve stability of value. For most of this chapter, however, we shall concern ourselves with the evolution of money and the attainment of such characteristics as portability, divisibility, and so forth.

EVOLUTION OF MONEY—COMMODITY MONEY

The first type of money of which we have knowledge is commodity money. The inconvenience resulting from the lack of a standard of value and a medium of exchange provided the incentive for developing a monetary system. In a primitive society, where few goods were available, all individuals used some basic commodity. It was quite natural to begin to use this commodity as money. Since it was a common item, it was convenient to think of the value of other things in terms of units of this item. Thus, it served as a standard of value. Again, because everyone used it, an individual was willing to accept it in trade. He could easily dispose of it for something which was of value to him if he did not need it.

In societies that lived mainly by hunting, there is evidence that furs and skins were the dominant types of money. In fact, this practice continued into relatively modern times in certain areas, such as Northern Canada. The domestication of animals brought them into the market and caused their widespread use as money. Cattle particularly were popular for this purpose, and their use as a unit of value continued long after man had become acquainted with metals. Other agricultural products frequently served as money in both ancient and modern times.[1] All these commodities retained the characteristics of a commodity while serving as money. The key to the use

[1]For an interesting and revealing description of the use of cigarettes as money in a World War II prison camp, see R. A. Radford, "The Economic Organization of a P.O.W. Camp," *Economica*, XII, No. 48, New Series (November, 1945), 189–201.

of any item as money is its general acceptability. General acceptability refers to the public's willingness to surrender valuable goods
and services and to receive the item used as money in return. The
utility of an item as a commodity insures this acceptability. Agricultural products, however, have obvious defects when used as money.
The units are not durable, are not easy to transport, are not divisible
into smaller units in many cases, and are not uniform in quality.

Metal, particularly precious metal, possesses many of the characteristics desired in money. Man has known of gold and bronze
from the fourth millennium B.C. In addition, he has had a knowledge of silver, iron, and copper from very early times. Archaeological
studies indicate that all of these metals have had a monetary use
from the period of their first discovery.

When used as money, metal may take the form of ingots or irregular shapes that must be weighed and tested for quality for each
transaction. It is more convenient, however, to use units of uniform
shape and size that are easy to recognize as possessing a certain
weight and quality. Some of the earliest metallic monetary units are
shaped like miniature weapons or implements. These shapes indicate that the monetary unit originated as a commodity. There also is
a record of metallic money shaped like a miniature ox hide which
provides evidence of the original value of this standard unit.

Coins, whose contours symbolize nothing, appeared after the
above-mentioned shapes. Modern coinage began in the Eastern
Mediterranean about 800 years before the birth of Christ. Although
the methods of manufacture changed, the basic principle of the
commodity, or full-bodied coin, continued into the twentieth century. Metal, a commodity, is used as money. The government or
some other reliable institution[2] assumes the responsibility for putting
the appropriate quantity of metal of a certain quality into each unit.
Stamping or otherwise marking each unit, or coin, with a symbol
indicating its weight and quality relieves the user from the necessity
of weighing or testing the commodity.

The United States used such a system until 1933. Up to that
time, a $10 gold coin contained 232.20 grains of gold, nine-tenths
fine. There are 480 grains in an ounce, so that the coin contained
approximately one half of an ounce of gold. The term nine-tenths
fine means that nine tenths of the coin is gold, and the remaining one
tenth is a cheaper metal added to the alloy to make the coin more
durable. The coin, therefore, contained 258 grains of metal. The

[2]Modern coins generally are issued by the government, but the earliest ones were
issued by merchants. Private persons continued to mint coins in the United States
during the nineteenth century. For examples of all types of coins, see the Chase
Manhattan Bank Museum of Moneys of the World, New York City.

inscription placed on the coin by the United States Mint simply proclaimed these facts about the coin's physical composition. It should be noted that the above comments apply only to <u>full-bodied</u> coins. (These are coins whose value as a commodity is equal to their monetary value.) <u>Token coins,</u> the only type of coins used in the United States today, <u>contain a quantity of metal whose value as a commodity is less than the face value of the coin.</u> They circulate at face value because they are exchangeable for full-bodied coins or because they are part of an abstract monetary system.

In the case of full-bodied coins, a commodity becomes money. The mint forms the commodity into uniform units for convenience in exchange. The development and the widespread use of coins is quite significant in monetary history. When people use coins instead of a commodity in bulk form, they are likely to consider the coins as monetary units rather than as metal with important uses as a commodity. This is especially true if the metal is gold, which has few uses except as money. Consequently, the use of coins helps to bring about a change in the mental attitude of the population. Technically, the public still uses a commodity as money but ignores its commodity value. Individuals feel that coins are valuable simply because people will accept them in payment for goods and services. The use of coins, therefore, represents a step toward the development of abstract money.

Representative Commodity Money — *Whse Receipt* / *Gold Certificate*

Use of a commodity as money involves inconvenience with regard to transportation and presents a problem if the commodity wears out quickly when handled. Consequently, it is much more satisfactory to leave the commodity in a place of safekeeping and to retain in its place a receipt or other proof of ownership. When the owner of the commodity wishes to trade it—that is, spend it as money—he may reclaim it from the warehouse. However, it is likely that his partner is willing to accept or even prefers to accept the warehouse receipt instead of the commodity. The new owner can take physical possession of the commodity at his convenience, or he can transfer the warehouse receipt to still another party. <u>Warehouse receipts used in this fashion are representative money.</u> Since they represent ownership of a commodity, the term representative commodity money more precisely describes them.

The earmarking of hides is an early example of representative money. The hides, which were the commodity money, remained in storage. An irregularly shaped patch of leather, cut from an ear of each hide, served as proof of ownership. These patches, or earmarks, were primitive warehouse receipts and circulated as money. A more modern example involves the use of written documents as receipts. In colonial Virginia, where tobacco served as money, the hogsheads of tobacco remained in a bonded warehouse while the warehouse receipts passed from hand to hand. The system was not perfect, for planters tended to take the poorer grade tobacco to the warehouse and to sell the better quality leaves on the market. This example illustrates a problem that must be faced when a commodity which cannot be classified precisely as to quality is used as money.

The United States relatively recently used representative commodity money. As we noted above, gold coins circulated in the United States as commodity money until 1933. Since it was inconvenient to carry gold coins in large quantities, the Government issued gold certificates which were warehouse receipts for gold stored in the Treasury's vaults. These warehouse receipts circulated as paper money, and the owner of a certificate could demand payment in gold at any time. The Treasury, in turn, had sufficient gold in its vaults to redeem all of the outstanding certificates.

The development of representative commodity money may seem of little significance upon casual study. It is merely a substitution of paper warehouse receipts for the commodity stored in a warehouse. This change, however, does more than simply make convenient the payment of money. People become accustomed to the use of paper as the hand-to-hand unit of exchange. They become less interested in the commodity which money redeems but with which they have few contacts. In brief, the mental attitude of the population changes. People consider money valuable because other people will accept it and not because it is a commodity. Thus, when representative commodity money becomes common, another step toward abstract money has been taken.

It may be noted also that the role of government increases in importance as various types of money develop. In a system where a crude commodity circulates as money, there is little for the government to do. For a system using coins, the government normally assumes the responsibility for their manufacture and regulation. The users of coins must have some confidence in the government's integrity if they accept coins at face value. It is not too difficult to check on the government's honesty, however, by weighing or otherwise testing the coins.

In a system using representative commodity money, the public must have confidence in the custodian of the warehouse. In recent times, this means that the public must believe that the vaults of the treasury contain enough precious metal to redeem all of the outstanding certificates. The role of the government, therefore, becomes more important, and the opportunity for the effective use of monetary policy increases.

Debt Money

A debt in the form of a promise to pay a commodity is the last of the several kinds of commodity money we shall examine. If an individual or an institution promises to pay a certain quantity of a given commodity, the written evidence of this right to collect the commodity may serve as money just as the commodity does. The extent to which evidence of debt is acceptable in exchange for goods and services depends upon the confidence the public has in the debtor's ability and willingness to pay the debt when it falls due. In recent times, debt money has taken the form of a written promise by the government or by a bank to pay on demand a certain quantity of a given commodity, usually gold. Anyone accepting this promise as payment for goods or services can redeem it by demanding the commodity. In practice, redemption seldom occurs because it is more convenient to transfer the debt to someone else in payment for goods or services received. The written evidence of a debt therefore becomes paper money.

Debt money and representative commodity money have some characteristics in common. Both take the form of paper which is redeemable in a commodity. However, they are not identical. First, let us note the legal difference. Representative money is a warehouse receipt and is proof of ownership of the commodity. There is in a warehouse or a vault a sufficient quantity of the commodity to redeem all the outstanding receipts. Debt money, on the other hand, is a promissory note. It represents the promise of the debtor to pay a commodity to the creditor; it does not represent ownership. The debtor must own a large enough quantity of the commodity to enable him to satisfy those creditors who demand payment; he need not hold sufficient quantities to make good on all of his outstanding promises. The practical difference between representative and debt money is a result of this legal difference. For representative money, there is a one-to-one ratio of paper certificates to commodity units. In the case of debt money, promises to pay exceed the means of paying.

The United States prior to 1933 serves as an example of this difference. Representative commodity money in the form of gold certificates was in circulation, and the gold stored in the Treasury's vaults was sufficient to redeem all the certificates. The banks and to some extent the Treasury issued debt money, but gold was available to pay only a fraction of these debts although all individuals who demanded payment were satisfied. A given quantity of gold, therefore, supported a larger volume of debt money than of representative money. Since the ratio of gold to money is not one-to-one when using debt money, the government or other monetary authorities have considerable power to regulate the quantity in circulation. These authorities must assume responsibility for the proper functioning of the monetary system.

Furthermore, it can be said that with the use of debt money the public's tendency to think of money in terms of a commodity weakens. Although the debt is legally redeemable in a commodity and is technically commodity money, it is paper which passes from hand to hand. The ordinary individual probably has no use for a commodity such as gold and does not force the redemption of the debt. Indeed, if every individual tries to do so, the system will collapse. Accordingly, we are at the stage in our study of monetary development where people are uninterested in the commodity underlying the system. Money can be redeemed in gold on demand, but its acceptability is not based on this feature. Instead, individuals accept paper money as payment for goods and services rendered because they are confident other people will accept it as payment for goods and services received. The stage is set now for the next type of money.

Abstract or Token Money

Abstract money is money which is not redeemable in a useful commodity and is valuable only because people are willing to accept it. This money has no use except as a standard of value and a medium of exchange.

The use of abstract money developed slowly. We have seen that the first money was a commodity. At a later stage, men stopped using the physical commodity and substituted paper which was redeemable on demand in the commodity. A system of abstract money came into existence when the government used its sovereign power to repudiate the promise to pay a commodity in exchange for paper money. The United States accomplished this by the passage of a law which relieved the banks and the Treasury of the obligation to redeem paper money in gold. Token coins became fiat money at the same time although they continued to possess some value as a commodity. It might be expected that a promise to pay would become valueless when it could no longer be enforced legally. This was not the case. People had been accustomed to using paper money and continued to do so after losing the right to redeem it in gold. Indeed, there was no alternative since barter was, and is, impractical.

Because of its origin as debt redeemable in a specific commodity, token money frequently retains the outward appearance of a debt. For example, the words, "will pay to the bearer on demand," appear on most United States paper money.[3] The term is meaningless, for the item paid on demand is another unit of paper currency. An abstract, or token, monetary system operates through a tacit agreement. Each individual agrees to accept certain pieces of paper or other tokens in return for the goods or the services which he sells. He does this because he is confident other people will accept the paper from him in exchange for the goods and the services he wishes to buy.

It might be suggested that the use of a commodity, like gold, as money is also based on a tacit agreement. Most individuals have little or no use for gold as a commodity. They accept it because they are confident that other individuals will accept it from them. What, then, is the practical difference between a monetary system based on a commodity and an abstract system if both rely on this tacit agreement? The answer lies in the physical restriction placed on the quantity of money in a commodity system as opposed to the lack of a physical limit on the amount of abstract money which may be created. This will be explored at greater length in the chapter on monetary standards.

ACCEPTABILITY—THE ROLE OF THE GOVERNMENT

Referring to our definition of money, we note that it is anything which is acceptable generally as a standard of value and a medium of exchange. We now ask: What is it that causes certain things to be acceptable and hence money?

The general acceptability of commodity money originally rested on the utility of the item as a commodity. In the later stages of the development of commodity money, this explanation is not valid since few people use gold as a commodity. Its acceptability then is simply an institutional fact explained by long-existing custom. This explanation applies also to representative and debt money since their original acceptability rested on the ability to redeem them in a commodity. In our examination of abstract money, we saw that its acceptability was the result of habits formed during the period when the monetary token was redeemable in a commodity. In none of the preceding cases does the government play a major role in establishing money's acceptability. However, all modern governments have adopted measures to make money more acceptable.

[3]This promise appeared on all Federal Reserve notes until late in 1963. At that time $1 Federal Reserve notes were issued for the first time. These bills simply state that they are $1 Federal Reserve notes.

Legal Tender

A government may declare that certain money is legal tender. For example, all coins and paper currency are legal tender in the United States. When money becomes legal tender, creditors must accept it for all debts. The penalty for nonacceptance varies for different nations and for different eras. In the United States, the refusal to accept legal tender causes the creditor to forfeit the right to collect interest or to take action to force payment in some other form. The creditor retains the right to collect the debt at a future date but only in legal tender. However, the penalty may be more severe. The refusal to accept paper assignats, the legal tender of the French Revolution, was punishable by twenty years in irons.

It is incorrect, however, to think that the government can cause money to be acceptable. Legal-tender provisions may force a creditor to accept payment in doubtful currency; they deny to him the use of the courts in forcing payment in another form. These provisions do not force people to sell goods and to accept payment in the doubtful currency nor do they force a creditor to make new loans. There are many cases where the public refuses to accept "money," despite energetic action by the government. Indeed, the very fact that the government is acting vigorously is evidence that the currency is not being accepted readily. The French assignats are an excellent example of the public's refusal to accept legal tender when the government issues excessive quantities of currency. In spite of the harsh penalty for nonacceptance, the assignats were not acceptable and were worth only a tiny fraction of their original value within a few years after their issue.

On the other hand, many types of money exist and the public accepts them readily without benefit of a legal-tender provision. Prior to 1933, Federal Reserve notes were not legal tender, but they were the main component of the United States currency system. Only in rare instances did an individual refuse such a note and demand payment in a gold certificate. (At the present time, checks are not legal tender, but they account for over 90 per cent of the payments made in this country) Thus, the legal-tender provision may contribute to an item's acceptability as money, but it does not guarantee it.

Discussions concerning the acceptability of items used as money are related to the problem of the value of money; however, the two terms are not synonymous. If an item called money is accepted in payment for goods and services, it is valuable by definition. Consequently, we may regard the question of the value of money as a question of the degree of its acceptability. However, it is customary to distinguish between the two terms since the practical problem of stabilizing the value of money leads to policies relatively unrelated to the problem of acceptability.

THE UNITED STATES MONEY SUPPLY

Having examined the types of money and its evolution, we shall look at the present United States money supply. This brief examination of United States money serves several purposes. It satisfies curiosity concerning what we use for money; and noting the quantities, we become aware of each of the several types of money. We also see that the supply of money changes, and we are able to understand the emphasis placed on banks and demand deposits. It serves to introduce monetary policy by noting the issuing agent for each type of money and the factors for determining the quantity issued. Although no attempt is made at this point to present a monetary history of the United States, the evolutionary process and the importance of political events are suggested by comments concerning the origin of the several types of money. Furthermore, the section serves to introduce terms, such as bank notes and "near-money," which we shall use in later chapters.

The money in circulation in the United States in 1955 and 1965 is shown in Table 2–1. The term "in circulation" refers to money in the possession of the public or in the vaults of commercial banks. Coins and paper currency which are held by the United States Treasury or the Federal Reserve banks are excluded.

Let us consider briefly the items labeled "in the process of retirement." Gold certificates, national bank notes, and Federal Reserve bank notes are in circulation officially since the records indicate that their issue exceeds the amount the Treasury has withdrawn. In reality, most of these items do not circulate. The outstanding units are lost, destroyed, or part of a collector's set.

Gold certificates. The Treasury Department issued gold certificates while the United States was on the gold coin standard. They were warehouse receipts for gold and were redeemable on demand. They have not been redeemable in gold since 1933, but anyone possessing these certificates may redeem them at the Treasury Department for other types of currency. The $30 million which the Treasury Department listed as "in circulation" in 1961 is, in reality, lost, destroyed, or on display as collectors' possessions.

National bank notes. National bank notes are still a legal type of currency and a few units circulate as money, but the Federal Reserve banks are withdrawing them whenever they come into their possession. A national bank note is a promissory note which any one of

Table 2−1

THE MONEY SUPPLY OF THE UNITED STATES

(In millions)

Kind of Money	Type of Money	Issued by	Amount in Circulation	
			1955	1965
Minor coins	Token coin	U.S. Treasury	$ 433	$ 782
Subsidiary silver	Token coin	U.S. Treasury	1,202	2,172
Standard silver dollars	Token coin	U.S. Treasury	223	482
Silver certificates	Representative token money	U.S. Treasury	2,171	1,120
U.S. notes	Debt	U.S. Treasury	319	289
Federal Reserve notes	Debt	Federal Reserve banks	25,617	33,585
Money in the process of retirement[a]	[a]	[a]	264	110
Total coin and currency			$ 30,229	$ 38,540
Demand deposits (adjusted)[b]	Debt	Commercial banks	105,100	124,200
Total money supply			$135,329	$162,740

[a]Money in the process of retirement includes gold certificates, national bank notes, and Federal Reserve bank notes. In 1961, the last year in which the *Federal Reserve Bulletin* lists the amounts separately, there were $30, $56, and $100 million of the respective kinds of money in circulation.
[b]This excludes deposits which one commercial bank maintains in another commercial bank.
Source: *Federal Reserve Bulletin,* August, 1955; August, 1961; and March, 1965.

several thousand national banks issued. In the nineteenth century, it was the normal practice for commercial banks to issue these notes. This type of bank debt served as a medium of exchange just as demand deposits do today. United States Government bonds backed the national bank notes which were redeemable in gold as long as the nation was on the gold coin standard. At present, they are redeemable in other currency. The origin of these notes will be more fully covered in Chapter 8.

Federal Reserve bank notes. These notes must not be confused with Federal Reserve notes. Both are promissory notes of the Federal Reserve banks, but Government bonds back the Federal Reserve bank notes whereas gold certificates and commercial paper[4] or gold certificates and Government bonds back the Federal Reserve notes.

Federal Reserve bank notes have been issued only in periods of emergency. Issues were made during and immediately after World War I, in 1933, and in 1942. In each case, the issue was withdrawn after the emergency had passed. The Federal Reserve banks have not had the right to issue these notes since 1945 and they are recalling those in circulation.

Standard silver dollar. Sizable quantities of two kinds of money, standard silver dollars and silver certificates, circulated until quite recently. The standard silver dollar is a famous coin in United States monetary history. It contains 371.25 grains of silver (about ¾ of an ounce), a figure that has not changed since 1792. The adjective "standard" generally means that money is full-bodied. For many years prior to 1963, however, the silver in the dollar was worth less than 100 cents. Consequently, the standard silver dollar was a token coin until the rising price of silver caused 371.25 grains of silver to be worth $1.

Silver dollars are legal tender which were obtainable in return for silver certificates. The number in circulation depended on the public's preference for them as opposed to its desire for paper currency. As you may note from Table 2–1, the quantity officially in circulation increased during the past decade; however, most of these coins serve as collectors' items rather than as currency. At the present time, the Government is not minting these coins. One must remember also that it will be profitable to melt these coins and to sell the silver as a commodity if the price of silver continues to rise.

Silver certificates. A silver certificate is a warehouse receipt for the precise amount of silver contained in a standard silver dollar. Therefore, it was representative token money for many years but can now be redeemed for a dollar's worth of silver. Since the Treasury's vaults contain 371.25 grains of silver for every $1 silver certificate in circulation, the Treasury can redeem the outstanding issue without difficulty. It had been customary for the Treasury to redeem silver certificates with standard silver dollars. The Treasury stopped doing

---

[4]The term commercial paper refers to promissory notes, drafts, and acceptances which have been created to finance the needs of various forms of business. See Chapter 5 for a more detailed description.

this, however, when it ceased minting the coins. Consequently, silver certificates currently in circulation are redeemable in Federal Reserve notes, granules of silver, or metal ingots.

Acts of Congress, which directed the Treasury to purchase silver, determined the quantity issued.[5] For many years, the price of silver was so low that silver producers were eager to sell to the Government; accordingly the Treasury bought so much silver that all $1 bills and some $5 and $10 bills were silver certificates. In recent years, the price of silver rose to the point where the Treasury stopped buying the metal. The price continued to rise until, as noted in the preceding section, the silver content of the dollar was worth 100 cents. Since that time, the Treasury has been selling silver and has been retiring silver certificates. As this process continues, Federal Reserve notes will replace silver certificates, and the latter units which are officially in circulation will in reality be collectors' items.

Minor coins. The term minor coin covers coins made of metal other than silver, such as the one cent and the five cent pieces. This is token money whose commodity value is but a small fraction of its face value. Table 2–2 shows their composition. The United States Mint produces all coins and the Treasury deposits them in the Federal Reserve banks, which are the issuing agents. The Government receives the monetary, or face, value of these coins when it deposits them and, therefore, it makes a profit called seigniorage.

The quantity issued, however, is not influenced by any desire to make a profit but is determined, instead, by public demand for small change. Steps are taken by the Government and other monetary authorities to control the overall money supply, but the portion of this total which is held in the form of minor coin is determined by the public. The public exercises its right to make this decision by withdrawing minor coins from or depositing them in the banks. The public's need for coins for vending machines, parking meters, piggy banks, sales taxes, *et cetera*, in turn, affects its decision. Hence, the Government must vary the supply of coins as these underlying factors change.

Subsidiary silver. The Treasury Department classifies the silver dime, the quarter dollar, and the half dollar as subsidiary silver. Table 2–2 indicates that they are token coins. They are in fact "minor coins" made of silver instead of copper and nickel, and they possess the same characteristics as the minor coins. The history of subsidiary silver is different from that of minor coin, and this may

[5]See Chapters 4 and 23 for details of the silver policy of the United States.

Table 2–2

COMPOSITION OF UNITED STATES COINS
AND THEIR COMMODITY VALUES[a]

Coin	Weight[b] (in grains)	Composition	Value in cents (as of August, 1965)
Cent	48.00	95 % Copper 5 % Tin, zinc	.2
Five cent	77.16	75 % Copper 25 % Nickel	.4
Dime (pre-1966)	38.88	90 % Silver 10 % Copper	9.4
Dime (1966 and later issue)	—	$87\frac{1}{2}$% Copper $12\frac{1}{2}$% Nickel	—
Quarter dollar (pre-1966)	96.45	90 % Silver 10 % Copper	23.6
Quarter dollar (1966 and later issue)	—	$87\frac{1}{2}$% Copper $12\frac{1}{2}$% Nickel	—
Half dollar (pre-1966)	192.90	90 % Silver 10 % Copper	47.1
Half dollar (1966 and later issue)	—	40 % Silver 60 % Copper	—
Dollar	412.50	90 % Silver 10 % Copper	100.0

[a]Based on daily reports of commodity markets.
[b]480 grains equal one ounce.

explain the separate listing. Until 1853, the United States attempted to keep full-bodied silver coins in circulation in denominations of fifty cents and lower. At that time, it reduced their silver content and the silver coins which were smaller than one dollar became token coins. Note, however, that the seigniorage for subsidiary silver is much smaller than that for minor coins. As a result of the Act of 1853, the silver content of a dollar in subsidiary silver is less than that of the standard silver dollar. For this reason, it is not profitable to melt the coins in order to obtain commodity silver at this time. If silver prices continue to rise, however, these coins might disappear from circulation. To insure the nation of a supply of coins, the Government has reduced the silver content of the half dollar to 40 per cent and has eliminated all silver from dimes and quarter dollars issued after 1965.

Both minor coins and subsidiary silver are legal tender. For many years, the legal-tender characteristic limited minor coin to 25 cents and subsidiary silver to $10. Legal experts disagree regarding whether legislation in the 1930's eliminated the legal-tender provision. The courts have not rendered a definitive decision.

United States notes. This paper currency accounts for a relatively small portion of the nation's supply of money. Some $5 and most $2 bills are United States notes. They can be identified quickly by the red seal and the words "United States Note" printed at the top of the bill. The United States Treasury first issued these notes, frequently called "greenbacks," during the Civil War. They are promises of the United States Government to pay $2 or $5 to the bearer on demand. At one time, these promissory notes were redeemable in gold and the promise was meaningful in a material sense. Now they are redeemable in lawful money which includes United States notes as well as other types of currency. While these units are listed as Treasury liabilities, to speak of them as promises to pay, or as debts, may be misleading, although it is correct in a technical sense. A United States note is abstract money. Like other abstract money, it is redeemable in a very real sense for whatever it will purchase or for the debt it will satisfy when used as legal tender.

It was intended originally that the United States notes should be redeemed and should be withdrawn from circulation as soon as possible after the Civil War. Political opposition to this practice developed, however, and there is still $320 million of these notes in circulation. This amount is only slightly less than the $379 million in circulation in 1865. Hence, greenbacks serve as an example of how government debt, issued to finance a war, can become a permanent part of the monetary system.

Federal Reserve notes. Federal Reserve notes are promissory notes which the twelve Federal Reserve banks issue. Each note is an obligation of the issuing bank. They constitute the main component of our currency supply, and the amount in circulation fluctuates with business conditions.

Federal Reserve notes first were issued in 1914, the year in which the Federal Reserve system was organized. At that time, the notes were backed by gold and commercial paper and could be redeemed in gold on demand. The issuing banks were required to keep a reserve of gold in order to honor this obligation and to meet the legal requirement. The Federal Reserve banks have not had the legal right to pay gold to note holders or to own gold since 1933. Federal Reserve notes are now legal tender, and they are redeemable in lawful money. Federal legislation does not define the term lawful money, but the expression is understood to encompass the several kinds of money just described. The experience of a Cleveland citizen sheds additional light on the question of the redemption of modern United States money. This individual noted on a $10 Federal Reserve note the words, "This note . . . is redeemable in lawful money at the United States Treasury or at any Federal Reserve Bank." He sent the $10 bill to the Treasury with a request that the Treasury send him $10 in lawful money. The Cleveland citizen received two $5 United States notes in return along with an explanation of the term lawful money.[6] Thus, Federal Reserve notes, like the other components of the United States money supply, are redeemable in other currency to pay a debt or for whatever they will buy on the open market.

When the Federal Reserve banks stopped redeeming their notes in gold, they turned over their gold reserve to the Government in return for gold certificates. At the present time, the Federal Reserve banks must hold a minimum of 25 cents in gold certificates in addition to sufficient commercial paper or government bonds to equal 100 cents for every dollar of Federal Reserve notes they issue. The gold reserve is not used to redeem Federal Reserve notes but is held as backing for the notes. The term "backing for paper currency" can be misleading. Traditionally, "backing" means that the reserve is available and is for use in redeeming paper currency. The gold certificate reserve held by the Federal Reserve banks is not, and in fact legally cannot be used for this purpose, except on an international basis. It does serve as a restrictive device to prevent excessive note issue. However, the Federal Reserve banks currently hold gold certificates well in excess of the legal requirements; hence it is obvious that factors other than the size of the gold certificate reserve determine the quantity of Federal Reserve notes issued. The leaders of the Federal Reserve System determine the quantity issued. The needs of the national economy, in turn, influence their decision.

The Federal Reserve banks issue these notes in denominations of $1, $2, $5, $10, $20, $50, $100, $500, $1,000, $5,000, and $10,000. Surprising as it may seem, there are between four and five hundred $10,000 notes in circulation. Theories vary as to why the public uses these large notes instead of bank checks. In some cases, people may use them for illegal transactions to avoid the tracks checks leave as they go through the clearing process. In other cases, the transactions are legal but the individuals involved have a preference for currency as opposed to checks.[7]

[6]The complete correspondence is reproduced in, Lawrence S. Ritter (ed.), *Money and Economic Activity* (2d. ed.; Boston: Houghton Mifflin Company, 1961), p. 45.
[7]In a recent commercial aircraft accident, rescue workers discovered that one of the victims was carrying a $10,000 bill neatly folded in a money clip. A business associate explained its presence by stating that his friend was an impulse buyer. A number of editorial writers expressed suspicion that this was not the true reason.

Demand deposits. Up to this point, we have discussed only currency; that is, coins and paper money that pass from hand to hand when monetary transactions occur. Payments of large sums of money, however, usually take the form of a check drawn on a commercial bank. In fact, estimates indicate that 90 to 95 per cent of all dollar payments in the United States are by check. Our next task, therefore, is the examination of this "checking account" money, which we shall call by its proper technical name, demand deposits. This represents the most important component of our money supply. Table 2–1 shows that demand deposits are equal to approximately 3½ times the value of all coin and paper currency.

The common statement that a man has money on deposit in a bank is somewhat misleading since the word deposit suggests that physical items are being stored. This is not the case. When a bank declares that it holds deposits of $10 million for its depositors, it does not mean that it has $10 million in coin or paper currency in its vaults. To have a deposit in a bank simply means that the bank owes money to the depositor. Accordingly, a bank deposit is a debt which the bank owes to a depositor.

Some of the debts owed by banks are in the form of savings, or time deposits. These debts cannot be transferred by check, so we do not include them in the money supply. We shall postpone our discussion of them until we reach the section on near-money. The remainder of the deposits are of the demand type.

Demand deposits, as the name suggests, are debts which the bank must pay to the depositor whenever he requests his money. The depositor can pay money to another individual by signing a written order which directs the bank to pay to this person the debt which the bank owes to its depositor. This payment is accomplished by the familiar process of writing a check. When money is paid by check, neither coin nor paper currency is exchanged. Instead, the right to collect a debt is transferred from the writer of the check to the payee. In this way, demand deposits become media of exchange and hence money.

Demand deposits and the checks drawn against them are not legal tender nor are they as readily acceptable as coins and paper currency. Checks may be refused as payment for goods or services under certain circumstances, and payment, pending an investigation of the identity of the signer and his possession of an account, may be delayed. Thus, it may be argued that demand deposits generally are not accepted as a medium of exchange and should not be classified as money. (If we refuse to classify demand deposits as money, however, we are stating, in effect, that 90 to 95 per cent of the dollars paid in the United States are not money.) Consequently, it is customary to consider demand deposits as part of the money supply even if the decision is a bit arbitrary.

Check writing is an ancient custom. We can trace its origin as far back as the ninth century B.C., but the widespread use of checks did not occur until the nineteenth century. Transfer of demand deposits by writing checks became the most popular method of paying money in the United States after the Civil War. The practice is still growing.

The use of checks is growing because they have several advantages over currency. The canceled check serves as a receipt. Checks may travel by ordinary mail since there is no monetary loss if a check is lost or stolen. In addition, a precise amount can be paid without the problem of "change." Checks drawn against a deposit in a specific bank can usually be cashed at any bank in the United States.[8]

The nation's monetary authorities control the size of demand deposits in the United States. Accordingly, they indirectly control the money supply since demand deposits are its largest component. The term "monetary authorities" refers to the leaders of the Federal Reserve System and the Treasury Department. A more thorough understanding of the meaning of this term and the manner in which these authorities control demand deposits must await Chapter 10.

An Overall View

Now that we have considered the various kinds of money in use in the United States, we may draw some conclusions concerning the system. It should be noted that only a small portion of the total money supply has been issued by the United States Government. The Treasury Department issues minor coins, subsidiary silver coins, standard silver dollars, silver certificates, and United States notes. The quantity of money accounted for by all these items amounts to only $4,845 million, which is 3 per cent of the money supply.[9] The Federal Reserve banks, which are privately owned institutions that have close ties with the Government, account for $33,585 million, or 21 per cent. The remaining $124,200 million, or 76 per cent, of the total money supply consists of demand deposits which commercial banks issue. Consequently, a discussion of banking occupies a sizable portion of any course of study dealing with money and its effect on the economic system. One cannot study money and banking separately.

It should be noted also that the composition of our money supply is unnecessarily complicated. All of the coins which the Treasury Department issues are token coins, but the conditions for issuing

[8]To understand the check clearing process, see Chapters 5–7.
[9]All figures are for 1965.

standard silver dollars are different from those applying to minor coins and subsidiary silver.[10] Both the Federal Reserve banks and the Treasury Department issue paper currency; the latter agency issues both silver certificates and United States notes.

The complexity of the money supply is the result of a series of financial crises, each of which has caused the nation to issue fresh supplies of money. This new money frequently supplements but does not supplant the kinds of money previously in existence. At least to some extent, the present system is a historical accident and the result of past monetary crises. We have seen an example of this in the case of United States notes, and we shall see further evidence of the validity of this statement in the historical section. If a new system based entirely on reason were to be adopted, it no doubt would consist only of token coins which the Treasury Department issued, Federal Reserve notes which the Federal Reserve banks issued, and the demand deposits of commercial banks.

Students and others who wish to understand its technical features find the present system complicated, but this is not true for the person who simply uses the money. The several kinds of money are interchangeable, and the different issuing agents do not affect the operation of the system.

Near-Money

Financial assets, such as time (saving) deposits or Series E and H United States Savings Bonds, are known as near-money. Time deposits are not transferable by check; consequently they do not serve as a medium of exchange. Nor can a United States Series E bond serve as a medium of exchange since it is not transferable. Both of these financial assets serve as a store of value, however, and both can be turned into money on a moment's notice.[11] If these assets are not money, they are almost money, or near-money. Also note that near-money, like money, takes the form of a debt. What is the distinctive characteristic that causes us to class certain assets as money while we class others, with similar characteristics, as almost money? An examination of liquidity supplies the answer.

We have defined money as anything which is generally acceptable as a medium of exchange and a standard of value. We could refer to it as the most liquid of assets. (The question whether or not a given item is money hinges upon the relative degree of liquidity it possesses.)

---

[10]The standard silver dollar had been a token coin for approximately 90 years prior to 1963. The section on this kind of money (p. 21) discusses its present classification.
[11]A bank has the legal right to require that a depositor notify it of his intention to withdraw a time deposit, but it normally waives this right.

Liquidity. Liquidity refers to the speed and the certainty with which one can turn assets into money. Coin and paper currency are money by definition and thus are the most liquid of assets. One can turn demand deposits into currency without loss, but there is the possibility of delay in establishing identity or in waiting for a bank to open. Neither Series E and H bonds nor time deposits suffer a loss of principal, but the delay in redeeming these items may be longer. Other financial assets possess liquidity to a lesser degree. The owner of short-term United States obligations (91-day bills) can turn them into cash by selling them on the open market, but there is a danger that the price he receives will be less than the price he paid for them. By waiting until maturity, one achieves certainty of payment but at the cost of a delay in time. Accordingly, these short-term securities have a high degree of liquidity, but it is not so high as that possessed by Series E and H bonds. United States securities with more distant maturity dates are even less liquid. Debts of private corporations with high credit standings are rated regarding liquidity in the same fashion. This principle is illustrated in the following list of assets which is arranged in order of decreasing liquidity.

Coin and currency
Demand deposits
United States Series E and H Savings Bonds
Time (savings) deposits
United States short-term marketable debt
United States long-term obligations   *Less Liquid*
Corporate bonds
Corporate preferred stock
Corporate common stock
Real estate

All of these assets represent a claim that the owner holds against society if a market exists and he can dispose of them. In other words, the assets differ because their liquidity differs.

The first item, coin and currency, is 100 per cent liquid. As we move down the list, each item becomes less liquid: there is a greater likelihood that a delay will occur in changing the asset into money or there is less certainty that the owner will receive its face value. The owner of a debt normally receives compensation for illiquidity in the form of interest or some other return on his investment. Note also that coins, paper currency, and demand deposits do not earn interest. Time deposits, bonds, *et cetera*, yield a return to the owner.

It now should be clear why the position of the line drawn between money and near-money is arbitrary. We agree that demand deposits are money even though they are not 100 per cent liquid.

Logically, we could go one step further and include Series E and H bonds and time deposits which are almost as liquid as demand deposits. The same reasoning could be used to include the next item on the list. If we continued the process, we eventually would declare that all assets are money. Arbitrary though it may be, it is customary at the present time to include only currency and demand deposits as money. Customs change and the time may come when economists will label as money some of the assets we now call near-money.

At this stage in our study, the contemplation of the distinction between money and near-money helps us to understand the concept of money. At a later stage (Chapter 14), we shall see that possession of near-money may influence an individual's desire to hold or to spend money. When one is considering monetary theory or policy, near-money becomes a legitimate area for study.

SUMMARY

Man has used many items in his attempt to find an ideal money. The characteristics of an ideal money are: portability, durability, divisibility, cognizability, and stability of value. Modern money possesses all of these characteristics except the last one; consequently current monetary problems center around the stability of value.

The first money was a commodity which people used as a standard of value and a medium of exchange. The development of coins eliminated the need to weigh the commodity for each transaction. Representative commodity money, a warehouse receipt for a commodity, and debt money, a promise to pay a commodity on demand, provide the convenience of a paper money while retaining the other characteristics of commodity money.

Abstract, or token, money has no utility except as a medium of exchange. We accept it because we believe that we can pass it on to others.

The government may help to make money acceptable by declaring it legal tender. However, such action by the government does not guarantee acceptance nor does the absence of a legal-tender provision prevent certain items from becoming money.

The United States money supply consists of coins which the Treasury issues, currency which both the Treasury and the Federal Reserve banks issue, and the demand deposits of commercial banks. The several kinds of currency vary as to origin and the legal basis for issue, but all are interchangeable one with another and are acceptable to the users of money. Demand deposits are not legal tender, but they are acceptable as money and account for 90 to 95 per cent of all payments in the United States.

Financial assets which are highly liquid are near-money. Like money, these assets are debts. They are exchangeable for money without loss of value and with little or no delay.

QUESTIONS

1. What are the defects in a system which uses cattle as money? What are the virtues of such a system?
2. "Any item may be used as money if it is accepted generally." What is the meaning of this statement?
3. Explain the difference between representative and debt money.
4. What are the significant differences between abstract and commodity money?
5. Are you willing to accept money which is not legal tender? How much use have you for currency which is legal tender but otherwise is unacceptable to the general public?
6. In your opinion, what changes would be necessary in order to change United States Savings Bonds from "near-money" to money?

SUGGESTED READINGS

Angell, Norman. *The Story of Money.* New York: Frederick A. Stokes, 1929.

Burns, Arthur R. *Money and Monetary Policy in Early Times.* New York: Alfred A. Knopf, Inc., 1927.

Carothers, Neil. *Fractional Money.* New York: John Wiley and Sons, Inc., 1930.

Einzig, Paul. *Primitive Money.* London: Eyre & Spottiswoode, 1948.

Shaw, W. A. *The History of Currency, 1252 to 1894.* 3d ed. New York: G. P. Putnam's Sons, 1896.

3

MONETARY STANDARDS

Beginning with the colonial period, almost every generation of Americans has participated in sharp controversy concerning the nation's monetary standard. In the nineteenth century, the issue was whether we should use a gold standard or a bimetallic standard of gold and silver. In the 1930's, the continuation of the gold standard was the point at issue. A paper standard was the alternative. In the early 1960's, the United States faced the problem of a loss of gold while it joined the other nations of the free world in a search for a monetary standard which would be international in character but which would allow for considerable management by individual nations.

What is the reason for monetary controversy? What objectives do the advocates of a given standard hope to achieve? In general terms, economic welfare is the answer. More specifically, the proper choice of a monetary standard leads to a stable price level, economic growth, and a high level of employment. Also, the choice of a monetary standard affects international economic relations. Certain standards tend to promote one of these specific goals more than another; and, with the passage of time, opinions pertaining to the relative importance of the several goals change. For example, in the United States, there have been periods when the nation felt that the achievement of full employment was more important than the maintenance of a stable price level or the encouragement of international trade. At other times, the stabilization of the price level and the stimulation of economic growth have rated top priority. Opinions concerning monetary standards change as the priorities assigned to the goals change. Furthermore, there is room for honest differences of opinion regarding the effectiveness of a given monetary standard in promoting these goals. Monetary standards, therefore, are legitimate topics of controversy.

In this chapter, we shall examine the main types of monetary standards. We shall see how they function and how they affect our economic welfare. We shall note, too, that government and political decisions play a more important role in a modern monetary system than the reader may have inferred from the preceding chapters. Even though money may exist without legal support, its use is so vital to a nation's well-being that all governments have adopted policies to regulate and to support the system.

TYPES OF STANDARDS   *COMMODITY - GOLD* *ABSTRACT*

There are two basic types of monetary standards: a standard based on a commodity and an abstract, or inconvertible paper, standard. Of the commodity standards, the one most recently used is the gold standard. We shall concentrate on it.

The standard money is the unit in which all other currency is redeemable. This standard money may circulate as a medium of exchange along with other currency. This was true in the United States prior to 1933. At that time, the standard money was gold, and gold coins circulated along with paper money and token coins. All the nongold money was redeemable in gold on demand.

In some systems, the standard money does not circulate. The English system between the years 1926 and 1931 is an illustration. During that period, only paper currency and coins of silver and copper circulated. Nevertheless, England was on the gold standard; all currency was redeemable in gold but only in large quantities.

GOLD STANDARDS

The traditional gold standard exists in several forms. They are: a gold coin standard, a gold bullion standard, and a gold exchange standard. All the forms possess the common characteristic of keeping the monetary unit constant in terms of gold. To do this, the government declares that the unit is equal to a certain quantity of gold and provides for a mechanism that insures that the value of the monetary unit in practice is the same as the legal definition.

We shall look at the gold coin standard in detail. It is a simple type which clearly illustrates the principles, the advantages, and the disadvantages of the system. The United States used the gold coin system until 1933. Congress defined the dollar as equal to 23.22 grains of gold. Congress also provided for free and unlimited coinage at this rate by the Mint. There were no restrictions on the export or other use of gold. Hence, the owner of coins could treat his stock of money as a commodity if he so desired. Paper currency and token coins circulated as money along with gold coins, but all money was redeemable in gold.[1]

[1] Under a "pure" gold coin standard, gold coins and only gold coins circulate as money. Such a system illustrates the characteristics of a metallic monetary standard very clearly; however, the difficulties encountered in using only gold as money are so great as to make it impractical in modern times.

A moment's examination of these provisions shows us that the value of the dollar was constant in terms of gold. Any person holding a dollar in the form of a gold coin obviously had 23.22 grains of gold, the amount of gold used by the Mint in producing it. An owner of a paper dollar could redeem it for a gold coin. Consequently, the dollar could not be worth less than 23.22 grains of gold. Nor could it be worth more—for example, 25 grains of gold—for the owner of 25 grains of gold could receive a gold coin worth $1 by taking only 23.22 grains of gold to the Mint.

This sytem stabilizes the value of money in terms of gold, but we are interested in the value of money in terms of its ability to purchase a wide variety of goods and services. Stabilization in terms of gold does not guarantee stabilization of value in this broader sense; the value of gold relative to other commodities can vary as market conditions change. A shortage of gold relative to other products will cause the value of gold and the value of money to rise. The reverse, of course, is possible and we can cite historical examples where this has happened.

Nevertheless, the advocates of a gold standard cite stability of the value of money as the main advantage it possesses over the inconvertible paper standard which, in modern times, has been the alternative system. When using a paper standard, the government may print excessive amounts of money which then will decline in value. Under a gold standard, the quantity of gold limits the quantity of money which the government can create.

Gold and only gold circulates as money under a pure gold standard. Consequently, the quantity of money is equal to the gold supply. When paper currency and token coins circulate in addition to gold, the government has some power to control the money supply but its management potential is limited. If the government or the monetary authorities issue an excessive amount of paper money, public confidence will decline and individuals will redeem their currency in gold. The possibility, or even probability, that this demand for redemption will arise forces the government to restrict the money supply to a small multiple of the gold supply.

Hence, the gold standard provides little opportunity for the government to manage the money supply. The government originally defines the value of money in terms of gold but once established the system runs with little governmental control. Adjustments occur automatically without government interference as gold flows into or out of the nation. This is especially true if a pure gold coin standard is in operation. However, the government's role is small even when paper currency and token coins circulate since the ratio of gold to other kinds of money is subject to only minor variations.

The gold coin standard, therefore, appeals to those persons who believe in keeping government participation in the economic system to a minimum. It should not surprise us to find that it was the dominant system in an era when most people agreed with Thomas Jefferson that, "that government is best which governs the least."

Limitation of the supply of money, and, hence, a guarantee of its continued high value, is the main argument in favor of the gold standard. In addition to this, gold was the international currency since every nation adopted it as its standard money. It thus provided the world with a common monetary system. We have indicated that the United States dollar contained 23.22 grains of gold. The English pound sterling contained 113.0016 grains of gold during this same period. Simple arithmetic indicates that the pound was equal to $4.86656. An individual possessing dollars could acquire pounds at the above rate by demanding gold for his dollars, shipping the gold to England, and turning it into pounds. Since the reverse was true also, pounds and dollars always were exchangeable at this rate with minor fluctuations caused by shipping costs. Opinions vary regarding the desirability of this worldwide monetary system. It facilitated international trade and investment, but it also caused close economic relations among the various nations. This function, serving as the basis for a system of international payments, was an important feature of the traditional gold standard. At the present time, nations have abandoned this type of standard and have severed the direct ties between gold and the domestic monetary system. However, gold continues to be the most reliable basis for international payments and plays an important role as an international monetary standard.

Use of the gold standard involves a number of disadvantages. It is an illogical method for determining the money supply. As production and national income increase, the number of transactions rises. Consequently, there is a need for an increase in the quantity of money in circulation. Under the gold standard, an increase in the money supply depends upon an increase in the gold supply. There is no reason to assume that the discovery and the exploitation of gold deposits will occur at a rate which will lead to an ideal increase in the stock of money. The discovery of rich gold deposits may increase the money supply at too rapid a rate and may cause money to decline in value. Or the reverse may happen. Economic activity may grow at a faster rate than the gold supply and thus may create a shortage of money. The government has the power to manage money to a limited extent and to alleviate the problem by changing the ratio of paper and other currency to gold. Because of the limit placed on the government's ability to change this ratio, this action will not be successful if the problem is acute.

Previously we noted that the use of the gold standard ties each nation's economic system closely to the rest of the world. The gold standard now becomes a vehicle for the transmission of prosperity or depression from one nation to another. A desire to avoid this effect was the main reason for the abandonment of the gold standard by the United States in 1933. The Roosevelt administration was about to launch a program of federal spending designed to bring back prosperity and full employment. We were unwilling to have the effect of this spending dissipated by its transmission to the rest of the world. Abandonment of the traditional gold coin standard was necessary if we were to achieve economic isolation.

Gold Bullion Standards

The gold coin standard which had been adopted by all the important commercial nations in the nineteenth century was abandoned during the first World War. When most of these nations reestablished the gold standard in the 1920's, they adopted the gold bullion type; the United States, which retained the gold coin standard, was an exception.

The gold bullion standard, like the gold coin standard, stabilizes the value of money in terms of gold and facilitates international trade. However, it achieves these objectives by a more efficient use of gold than does the gold coin standard.

Gold bullion standards of the full, or unlimited, type differ from gold coin standards in two ways: (1) The government does not mint gold coins nor does it permit them to circulate as money. The government or central bank is willing to buy unlimited quantities of gold at a fixed price, thus ensuring that the value of money does not appreciate in terms of gold. (2) Money is redeemable in gold but only in quantities sufficient to purchase a bar of gold of a certain minimum weight. For example, in Great Britain, which used this system in the 1920's, the minimum amount of gold purchasable cost approximately $7,500.

A gold bullion standard, therefore, provides for the redemption of paper money in gold on demand and allows for the conversion of gold into money in unlimited quantities. The English type gold bullion system is in effect a gold coin standard where the smallest "coin" is worth $7,500. Since persons or agents who export gold or use it for industrial purposes normally deal in sizable units, the monetary and market value of the metal will be the same despite the limit on redemption and purchase.

What, then, is the real difference between these two standards? The gold bullion standard uses gold more efficiently. By removing gold from circulation as media of exchange and by keeping it in the vaults of the treasury or the central bank, it becomes the basis for a larger issue of paper currency. Hence, the statement that a gold bullion standard conserves gold or that it uses gold more efficiently. In the 1920's, when the world's economic activities were growing more rapidly than the gold supply, this type of standard became very popular. We should note also that a gold bullion standard permits, and in fact requires greater management of the monetary system by the government than the gold coin standard does. The individual, however, can defend his position against what he considers improper management or the excessive creation of paper money by demanding the redemption of this currency in gold. This is possible, of course, only for those people who possess $7,500 or multiples thereof in cash. Many criticize the system as a "rich man's" standard for this reason. Advocates of the system defend it with the claim that the threat of demands for redemption forces the government to exercise restraint in creating money and thus provides for a stable currency. Note that a shift from a gold coin to a gold bullion system does not affect the position of gold as the basis for international payments. Consequently, the significance of gold in the field of international relations is the same for either a gold coin or a gold bullion standard. As an additional consequence, the use of the gold bullion standard eliminates gold coins from the money supply and makes possible a later transition to a system which restricts the use of gold more severely or which eliminates gold as the base of the money supply.

The preceding paragraphs describe a full, or unlimited, gold bullion standard. It is unlimited in that gold can be turned into money and *vice versa* with no restrictions other than the requirement that the units of the transactions at least be equal to a certain minimum size. However, the right to change other money into gold may be restricted. This practice leads to modification of the gold bullion standard.

The United States at the present time is on a modified, or limited, gold bullion standard. The Treasury is willing to buy all gold offered to it at $35 per ounce; that is, owners of gold can convert it into money at this rate in unlimited quantities. However, the Government restricts the right to redeem United States dollars in gold to industrial users and foreign governments or central banks for legitimate monetary purposes. This limitation permits even greater management of the monetary system by the Government. It does not tie the quantity of money so closely to the supply of gold. Nevertheless, gold is still an important factor in international monetary relations. We see evidence of this in the concern of the United States over the decline in its gold supply since 1958.

Gold Exchange Standard

A nation is on the gold exchange standard if its monetary unit is redeemable in a foreign currency rather than in gold while the foreign currency is redeemable in gold. The Philippine Islands was an example of this system for many years. The peso was redeemable in United States dollars at a given rate at a time when the dollar was equal to 23.22 grains of gold. The Philippine Government maintained a reserve of dollars in the form of deposits in United States banks rather than gold reserves stored in treasury vaults. Members of the British Empire used a similar system for many years.

The nation using a gold exchange standard stabilizes the value of its money in terms of gold without incurring the expense of acquiring and maintaining a supply of gold. The system has its disadvantages. The foreign currency used to redeem the money may change in value, or the foreign country may refuse to permit the withdrawal of bank deposits in gold. Stability of the value of the national currency thus depends upon favorable action, or at least an absence of unfavorable action, on the part of a foreign country.

The country whose currency serves as a reserve, the United States in the preceding example, faces the danger of a gold outflow. Nations with reserves on deposit in the United States may decide to redeem them in gold because they fear that the United States dollar will depreciate in value or for some other reason. Co-operation, therefore, is essential if a gold exchange standard is to be successful.

At the present time, many nations of the free world are on a "mixed" gold exchange standard. The bulk of their monetary reserves is in the form of dollar deposits in United States banks or deposits in pounds sterling in English banks. However, they hold some of their reserves in the form of gold in which they can redeem their currency, at least to a limited extent. Nations following this practice are on a mixed gold exchange and limited gold bullion standard.

The advantages and the disadvantages of the gold exchange standard, which we cited in the preceding paragraphs, are applicable to this mixed system. In fact, the recent loss of gold by the United States is traceable, in part, to the decision of these nations to change the proportions of the mixture. They have decided to increase the size of their gold-bullion holdings relative to their holdings of dollars deposited in United States banks. This example illustrates the present importance of gold as well as the need for international co-operation if a gold exchange or a "mixed" gold exchange system is to be successful.

Concluding Comments on the Gold Standards

The several forms of the gold standard all keep the value of money stable in terms of gold, but they vary in the specific role assigned to gold. Gold may circulate as money as it does under the gold coin standards. If the unlimited gold bullion standard is in use, gold remains in the vault as a reserve. The treasury will pay gold on demand but only in large amounts. With a limited gold bullion standard, money is redeemable in gold for legitimate industrial uses or for export for legitimate monetary purposes. The government, however, may adopt a narrow definition of legitimate in these cases. Finally, a nation may adhere to a gold exchange standard even though it does not possess any gold.

At this point, the student may legitimately question the development of the many variations of the gold standard. What is the difference among the several forms in terms of their effect on the monetary system? One finds the answer first in the degree to which government plays a role in managing the money supply. At one extreme, the pure gold coin standard makes no allowance for management. Here the supply of gold automatically determines the amount of money in circulation, and the supply varies as gold flows into or out of the country. The other gold standards allow for the circulation of other types of money and thus provide for increasing degrees of management. For example, with a gold bullion standard, the money supply will be some multiple of the gold supply. Policy decisions of the treasury, the central bank, or other monetary authorities will lead to a change in this ratio through actions we shall examine in later chapters. Because of this management, gold reserves do not determine the money supply precisely although the size of these reserves will influence monetary policy. The desire to manage the money supply caused nations to shift from the gold coin standard to the gold bullion standard. It should be obvious from the foregoing discussion that the influence of changes in the supply of gold decreases as the degree of management of the monetary system increases.

The preceding discussion applies to the traditional gold standard in which gold had a direct influence on a country's domestic money supply. All nations have abandoned this traditional type in favor of a modified system which allows for greater management of money. The governments define the monetary unit in terms of gold but do not permit redemption for domestic monetary purposes. Therefore, there is no direct tie between gold and the domestic supply of money. Gold continues to play an important international role, however. The official rate of exchange between the various national currencies are fixed in terms of gold, and gold is used to settle international balances. Hence, gold is significant today, chiefly as an international monetary unit; but it does retain an indirect influence on the domestic system because of this international role.

OTHER METALLIC STANDARDS — SILVER

Silver has not played an important role as a monetary standard for approximately one hundred years, although it has had a role in monetary history since ancient times. Since the basic principles are the same as for gold, we shall discuss silver standards briefly.

The value of money is stabilized in terms of silver, first, by defining the monetary unit as equal to a certain quantity of silver. Provision is made for the free and unlimited coining or buying of silver at that rate, and no restrictions are placed on the exporting of silver or the melting of coins for use as a commodity. All nonsilver currency is redeemed in silver on demand in a nation using the silver standard.

The criticisms of the gold standard are applicable to the silver standard. Under this system, the rate of silver production affects the size of the nation's money supply and the output of the mines may be too large or too small to care for a growing economy. In the case of silver, the world was less fortunate than in the case of gold. During the latter half of the nineteenth century, silver production was so high that it endangered the value of money based on this metal. This phenomenon, along with other factors, led to the abandonment of silver as a monetary standard.

Bimetallic Standards

As the name suggests, a bimetallic standard involves the use of two metals as standard money. History provides us with a number of examples of attempts to establish and to use a gold and silver standard. In the United States, some of the most intense political controversies over monetary policy concerned the bimetallic standard.

In a bimetallic standard, the monetary unit is defined in terms of gold and in terms of silver. For example, in the United States in 1834, the dollar was defined as equal to 371.25 grains of silver or to 23.22 grains of gold. Provision was made for free and unlimited coinage of both metals and no restrictions were placed on the exporting, melting, or other use of the coins. If the system had worked satisfactorily, these provisions would have stabilized the value of the dollar in terms of both gold and silver.

A bimetallic standard possesses several advantages. Full-bodied coins of both gold and silver circulate. This eliminates the necessity for token coins except for extremely small transactions. In a period when some nations are on the gold standard and others are on the silver standard, a bimetallic standard facilitates trade with each group and stabilizes the rate of exchange between the countries using silver and those using gold. Finally, and perhaps most important, it stabilizes the value of the dollar in terms of general purchasing power. We have noted the danger that the exchange value of a single metal may vary because of fluctuations in its supply relative to the number of transactions taking place. If a nation uses two metals, however, it is unlikely that both will change in value at the same time. If only one changes, the change in the value of money will be small because of the cushioning effect of the metal which remains stable in value.

No nation has realized these benefits because none has been able to retain two metals as standard money for a prolonged period. The basic defect of a bimetallic standard has been the tendency for one metal to disappear from monetary use, leaving the nation on either a gold or a silver standard.

The United States was formally on a bimetallic standard from 1792 to 1873, and its history illustrates the problems encountered when using this system. The Coinage Act of 1792 defined the dollar as equal to 371.25 grains of silver or 24.75 grains of gold. It applied free and unlimited coinage to both metals and placed no restrictions on the export or other use of coins. We can avoid the use of the unfamiliar term "grains" by expressing the value of the metals in terms of dollars per ounce (480 grains equal one ounce). We then note that an ounce of silver entitled the owner to $1.29 in silver coins when he delivered it to the Mint; an ounce of gold yielded $19.40 in gold coins. The Coinage Act, therefore, declared that an ounce of gold was equal in value to 15 ounces of silver $\left(\frac{19.40}{1.29}\right)$. This was the mint ratio. Both metals, however, were commodities. Dealers traded gold and silver in the world's markets, and foreign countries which were on the bimetallic standard accepted both metals. The foreign treasuries were simply part of the world market from the point of view of the United States. The relative values of gold and silver when used for purposes other than coinage at the United States Mint is the market ratio. This market ratio was approximately 15½ to 1 during the period when the mint ratio of the United States was 15 to 1.

Under these circumstances, an owner of gold or silver found it profitable to dispose of the gold on the world market, where one ounce of gold was the equivalent of 15½ ounces of silver. If the owner of the gold had delivered it to the Mint for coinage, it would have yielded the equivalent of 15 ounces of silver. Furthermore, owners of gold coins already in existence could sell them as a commodity at a profit. Using a similar process of reasoning, we can see that an owner of silver would have brought it to the Mint for coinage. The individuals possessing gold or silver simply disposed of the metal on the market or at the Mint, depending on whichever yielded the higher price. As a result, gold disappeared from monetary use and silver remained as the monetary standard.

The United States, therefore, was on a bimetallic standard *de jure* but a silver standard *de facto*. In 1834, Congress attempted to correct this condition by reducing the gold content of the dollar to 23.22 grains. The result was the politically famous mint ratio, gold to silver, of 16 to 1. Since the market ratio remained at 15½ to 1, the discrepancy did not disappear. It simply reversed its direction. Silver disappeared from circulation, and the United States was on a *de facto* gold standard.

The ancient world had noted this phenomenon; for example, Aristophanes referred to it about 400 years before the birth of Christ. Sir Thomas Gresham, a sixteenth century London merchant and government adviser, analyzed and described the principle involved. Succeeding generations have referred to the principle as Gresham's law in the mistaken belief that Sir Thomas was the first to note the phenomenon. In its briefest form, Gresham's law states that bad money drives good money out of circulation. This implies that either gold or silver is bad money. It is more accurate to state that money which the Mint overvalues relative to the world market drives out of circulation money which the Mint undervalues. In addition to helping us to a better understanding of monetary problems, Gresham, by formulating his law, gave the world a figure of speech which is applicable to many nonmonetary discussions.

Bimetallic standards proved a failure and it is unlikely that any nation will attempt them again. The system could operate successfully, however, under certain conditions. International co-operation to ensure common mint ratios by the several nations using this standard would be a first requirement. This mint ratio should be equal to the market ratio, and sizable reserves of both gold and silver would be necessary in order to absorb changes in the supply and the demand for these metals in the commodity market.

COMMODITY STANDARDS—NONMETALLIC *not used in modern times*

No nation in modern times has used a nonmetallic commodity standard, and it is unlikely that any nation will adopt such a standard. A brief description of such a proposed standard is useful, however, for it illustrates certain monetary principles. We noted these principles in our discussion of metallic monetary standards, but our habit of thinking of gold and silver as money may partly obscure them.

In covering the gold standard, we saw that this system fixed the value of money in terms of gold but permitted fluctuations in the purchasing power of money. This defect is unavoidable because we do not use money to buy gold; we spend it to purchase ordinary goods and services.

Logically, therefore, the value of money as general purchasing power will be stabilized if the monetary unit is defined in the terms of the goods and the services which are commonly purchased instead of in the terms of a single metal. Such a system, which is known as the commodity reserve plan, has been proposed by Benjamin Graham.[2] Under this plan, the gold in our monetary system would be replaced by a commodity complex consisting of fixed amounts of commonly used storable commodities. For example, the commodity complex might be composed of 10 yards of a standard woolen cloth, 10 pounds of sugar, 5 pounds of copper, *et cetera*. A value, say $10, would be assigned to this "bundle" of goods. Such a bundle of commodities could be brought to a government warehouse and "sold" for $10 by anyone possessing it. All money would be redeemable in these commodities at the rate of $10 per complex unit. This is the equivalent of the free coinage and the redeemability features of the gold standard.

The ability to change money into the commodity complex at a fixed rate and *vice versa* stabilizes the value of money in terms of these commodities. If the commodities in the complex are typical regarding the type and concerning the amount of the items normally purchased with money, the value of money will be stable in terms of general purchasing power. The plan possesses an additional advantage, for it provides for an increase in the money supply as the production of commodities increases.

There are defects in this system, too. First, we can include only easily stored commodities in the complex. This being so, the complex cannot be truly representative of a nation's buying habits. This problem will become more acute as the importance of services as opposed to goods increases. Furthermore, customs change and adjustments will be necessary if the complex is to remain representative of buying habits. Secondly, for this system to operate, it will be necessary to immobilize a considerable quantity of useful goods in order to provide for a supply of money. We do not avoid this by using

[2]See Benjamin Graham, *Storage and Stability* (New York: McGraw-Hill Book Company, Inc., 1937.

a gold standard, but we tend to overlook it because we are accustomed to thinking of a vault as the proper place for gold. The amount of national resources needed to acquire a gold reserve, however, is probably just as great as the amount needed to produce a reserve for the commodity reserve plan.

The commodity reserve plan has much to recommend it if one compares it with a gold standard on strictly logical grounds. Nevertheless, no nation has seriously considered adopting it. If we are to use a commodity standard, gold seems to be the international choice because of its past history. If a nation abandons the gold standard, an inconvertible paper standard seems to be a more logical replacement than a commodity reserve plan.

INCONVERTIBLE PAPER STANDARDS

From a rational point of view, any monetary standard based upon a stored commodity is open to criticism. We noted this in the foregoing example of the commodity reserve standard. Critics of the gold standard poke fun at this system which uses labor and other resources to mine gold and to rebury the gold in a vault at the cost of an additional expenditure of human and other resources. In the course of this mining and reburying of gold, the monetary authorities print paper money and place it in circulation. Since paper currency is to be the medium of exchange, these critics suggest that we simply print money and conserve the resources used in mining and storing gold. They are, in effect, advocating an inconvertible paper standard.

The term inconvertible paper standard applies to a variety of systems. The key characteristic of this standard is the failure to fix the value of the monetary unit in terms of gold or some other commodity. Some types provide for the purchase of gold at a fixed price to prevent the appreciation of money in terms of gold; none of the types provides for unlimited redemption of money in gold. Consequently, money may depreciate in terms of gold. One may claim that the United States is on an inconvertible paper standard, but we have placed it in the limited gold bullion group in this text because the Treasury redeems the dollar in gold for any legitimate export purpose.

Since paper money is not redeemable in gold, we cannot explain its value in terms of this commodity. Instead, we must cite the traditional use of the monetary unit as a standard of value and a medium of exchange. Money is valuable because it is an institutional fact. We must rely upon a limited supply and the legal-tender provisions to stabilize the value of money.

An inconvertible paper standard is desirable for a number of reasons. It lends itself to management of a thorough type because of the lack of a tie to a commodity. It is possible to use this manageability to keep the quantity of the circulating media at a level which stabilizes prices. On the other hand, misuse of this ability results in the printing of excessive amounts of currency.

The record of nations using an inconvertible paper standard has not been good. There has been a tendency to print excessive quantities of money which the government then spends. Thus, the printing of money becomes a substitute for taxation at the cost of creating inflation. This poor record does not prove that an inconvertible paper standard must lead to inflation nor that it is necessarily inferior to a gold standard. Most nations have adopted the system in time of war or other crisis when the gold standard has failed. The inflation and the other undesirable consequences are the result of the war or the other conditions which caused the adoption of the paper standard. In contrast with the metallic standards, the paper standards rely entirely upon the good judgment of the monetary authorities to keep the appropriate amount of money in circulation. There is no reason to assume that human judgment will be inferior to the chance factors of the gold market in determining a nation's money supply. For an inconvertible paper standard to be successful in a democracy, the public and the political leaders must realize the consequences which follow an excessive issue of paper money. The public must exercise will power and must avoid pressuring the political leaders to substitute the issuance of paper money for taxation. It follows from the preceding discussion that advocacy of an inconvertible paper standard is consistent with a philosophy which holds that a considerable amount of government participation in the economic affairs of a nation is desirable.

THE UNITED STATES AND THE MONETARY STANDARD

We have noted already that the United States is on a limited gold bullion standard. Private persons or corporations may own gold only for legitimate industrial purposes and as collector's items or museum pieces. Hence, the Government owns the entire monetary stock of gold in the nation and stores it in Fort Knox. This stock of gold serves as the basis for the United States money supply and places a legal limit upon the quantity of currency which the monetary authorities can create. However, we did not approach this limit for many years. When the monetary system did approach the limit, the nation modified the gold reserve requirements to permit further expansion. Consequently, we must conclude that gold has not affected and will not affect our domestic money supply directly.

The international role of gold is far more significant. The stock of gold of the United States is available for the purchase of goods and services from other countries. It follows that a change in the size of the gold reserve is of concern to the United States. Furthermore, policies designed to protect the gold reserve have an indirect effect upon the domestic money supply.

Many nations of the free world have adopted a "mixed" standard of which the gold exchange standard is a part. These nations maintain large dollar balances in the United States and use these dollars in making international payments. Or they may withdraw these balances in the form of gold. Consequently, the gold in Fort Knox plays an important role as the basis for international payments even though its significance in the domestic monetary system is limited.

The United States faces a number of problems because of this position of world leadership. In managing our money supply, we must consider the effect on other countries as well as the domestic results. There is also the danger that other nations will change large quantities of their dollar balances into gold, thereby depleting our gold supply. We shall discuss these problems in some detail in Chapter 25. At this time, however, it should be clear that the choice of a monetary standard and a monetary policy by one nation affects the rest of the world. International co-operation is a necessity.

SUMMARY

Monetary standards are important since they are the method by which we determine as well as maintain the value of money. Commodity and inconvertible paper are the two basic types of monetary standards. Under the gold standard, which is the most common example of a commodity standard, the quantity of gold in reserve fixes or at least influences the quantity of money in circulation. This limits the area in which human judgment operates.

In an inconvertible paper standard, the government or other monetary authorities determine the quantity of money. This involves human judgment. Consequently, the choice of a monetary standard depends upon the extent of our confidence in the ability of the government to manage the money supply.

QUESTIONS

1. What objectives did a nation hope to achieve when it adopted the international gold standard? When it abandoned the gold standard?
2. A monetary system based on labor has been proposed. Certificates would be issued for each unit of labor supplied. These certificates would then be

used as money to purchase the products created. Is such a monetary standard practical?

3. Assume that a bimetallic standard based on gold and silver is functioning in a satisfactory fashion. What would happen to the system if large deposits of rich silver ore were discovered?

4. What is the significance of the term "a worldwide shortage of gold"?

5. What do we mean when we speak of using gold in an efficient fashion? What are the dangers which must be faced when gold is used "efficiently"?

SUGGESTED READINGS

Crutchfield, James A., Henning, Charles N., and Pigott, William. *Money, Financial Institutions, and the Economy.* Englewood Cliffs, N. J.: Prentice-Hall, Inc., 1965. Chapter 2.

Graham, Benjamin. *Storage and Stability.* New York: McGraw-Hill Book Company, Inc., 1937.

Gregory, T. E. *The Gold Standard and Its Future.* 2d ed. London: Methuen & Co. Ltd., 1932.

Hawtrey, R. G. *The Gold Standard in Theory and Practice.* 5th ed. London: Longmans, Green and Co., 1947.

Kemmerer, Edwin W. *Gold and the Gold Standard.* New York: McGraw-Hill Book Company, Inc., 1944.

Ritter, Lawrence S. (ed.). *Money and Economic Activity: Readings in Money and Banking.* 2d ed. Boston: Houghton Mifflin Company, 1961. Chapter 2.

4

U. S. MONETARY STANDARDS
PRIOR TO 1914

We begin the study of American monetary history at this point even though we have not considered the principles of banking. We do this for several reasons. The study of monetary history enables us to understand better the concept of money. It presents factual material which will add meaning to the discussion of monetary theory, it suggests to us that monetary theory is problem-oriented, and it shows us the origins of the United States coinage system and therefore explains its "untidy" features.

COLONIAL PERIOD

Money was scarce in the American colonies relative to the amount needed to serve as a medium of exchange. There is, however, a ready explanation for this scarcity. It was a period when full-bodied gold and silver coins were money. Since the colonies did not possess gold or silver mines, they obtained the metals only in receipt of payments for exports. Although the colonists exported primary goods, such as tobacco and foodstuffs, they imported finished manufactured products and tended to have an import surplus. Hence, the acquisition and the retention of coins were difficult.

We can describe this condition in more direct terms. The colonies were rich in raw materials but were poor in capital goods and other manufactured products. The English and the European merchants accepted in payment for manufactured commodities the full-bodied coins the colonies earned from their export activities. The fact that the colonists sent their coins abroad indicated that they preferred to own manufactured goods rather than precious metal. This choice illustrates a point made in the preceding chapter: there is a cost involved in acquiring a medium of exchange. This cost is relatively high for a poor country if a precious metal is the monetary standard. The colonists, wisely choosing not to pay the high cost for an adequate supply of gold and silver specie, had to develop other media of exchange.

There was another defect in the monetary system: the coins which circulated in the colonies were not uniform in weight, metallic content, or national origin. Export trade was the source of the colonial money supply; consequently, the coins in circulation had their origin in the several nations to which the colonists sold commodities. Although the colonists kept accounts and quoted prices in terms of English shillings and pence, which was the unit of account, Spanish coins from the West Indies were the most common circulating media. In addition to the Spanish coins, Dutch, French, Portuguese, English, and a few domestically minted coins were in circulation. The variety of coins was greater than a list of the nations which minted them suggests. The colonial mints deliberately produced lightweight shillings in the hope that they would not be acceptable outside the colonies. Foreign coins of a single denomination and origin varied in weight because of wear, or because of clipping, or debasement.[1] Because of this lack of uniformity, persons accepting coins had to weigh them and had to make some test of their metallic content. Obviously this was time-consuming and interfered with trade.

Attempted Solutions: Commodity Money

The first approach to the shortage of circulating media was the use of domestically produced commodities of the several regions as money. Foodstuffs, tobacco, and even Indian wampum circulated. Although the practice of trading in commodities developed without official encouragement, the nation needed a uniform standard as the economy grew and trading became more widespread. The colonial governments tried to provide a monetary standard by accepting the commodity in payment, declaring it legal tender, and fixing its official value in silver. For example, Virginia set the rates at three shillings for first-grade and one and one-half shillings for second-grade tobacco. These rates, overvaluing tobacco officially compared with its market price, favored the tobacco growers. This practice provided an incentive to grow more tobacco, and the consequent increase in supply further depreciated its value. A similar instance occurred in Massachusetts where Indian wampum was acceptable at fixed rates. However, the white man learned to produce large quantities of wampum cheaply and its value depreciated. These cases show that

[1]Clipping is the practice of shaving the edge of coins to remove some precious metal. Governments practice debasing by substituting a cheap metal for some of the precious metal in a gold or a silver coin. In most cases governments attempt to conceal the fact that they are practicing debasement.

the official monetary policy may encourage the allocation of resources to the production of the medium of exchange rather than to the production of goods and services. We may also regard them as examples of Gresham's law. The tobacco grower disposed of his leaf on the market or converted it to money, whichever use was more profitable.

Despite these expediencies, the colonists continued to suffer from a shortage of money. Useful commodities, such as agricultural products, were not satisfactory circulating media and their use declined as the colonies matured economically.

Attempts to Coin Money and to Attract Foreign Coins

One of the colonies, Massachusetts, operated a mint from 1652 to 1684, when the British Government forced its abandonment. The shillings, half shillings, and quarter shillings produced contained approximately thirty per cent less silver than the English coins. The colonies hoped that foreign merchants would find these coins unacceptable and that this would prevent their export. They achieved this goal only in part because the foreign merchants accepted the coins at a discount. All the colonies tried to attract Spanish coins from other countries and neighboring colonies by officially overvaluing them in terms of English shillings. Since every colony was able to compete in this overvaluation, none was successful. The British Government prohibited the practice in 1704.

Paper Money

After attempts to attract and to retain an adequate stock of metallic money were unsuccessful and the use of agricultural commodities proved unsatisfactory, the colonists turned to paper money. At that time England and the nations of Continental Europe were beginning to use credit instruments as money, and it was natural that the colonists should regard this type of money as a solution to their problems. Accordingly, the governing bodies of the several colonies and later private banks began to issue paper currency.

Although recognized as a solution to monetary difficulties, a fiscal crisis was the cause of the first issue of paper money. In 1690 Massachusetts with an empty treasury faced the problem of paying the soldiers returning from an expedition against Quebec. The Colony issued one-year bills of credit redeemable in coin from tax receipts in the amount of £7,000. In origin these bills were tax anticipation notes which circulated, pending redemption, as money. Since the colonists did not like to pay taxes, however, they issued new bills to retire the old ones. This seemed a painless way to finance government, and Massachusetts and the other colonies issued more bills. As the prospects for redemption dimmed, bills of credit became outright fiat money which was valuable because of its monetary use and not because it was redeemable in coin or another specified commodity. The basic principle was sound: use fiat paper money as a medium of exchange and avoid the need to invest in gold and silver. The system worked satisfactorily in those colonies which practiced restraint and did not issue quantities of bills in excess of the needs of trade. In other colonies the issuing of excessive amounts led to a decline in value. Blaming this decline in value on the failure to redeem the bills in full-bodied coin is a mistake. There were many instances where paper currency circulated and did not depreciate in value even though there were no prospects for redemption. However, the failure to redeem the bills in coin was responsible indirectly for the decline in value since this removed a limit on the quantity issued.

By 1764 the British Parliament had prohibited the issue of legal-tender bills in all the colonies. This anti-inflation policy of the British Government may have simply been the result of a desire to concentrate all monetary power in Parliament, or its adoption may have been attributable to the influence of London merchants who were unwary enough to accept bills of credit which then depreciated in value. In any event the colonists, who felt that it impaired their ability to import goods and retarded economic development, resented the restriction.

Although economic conditions in the colonial period were quite unlike those in which our present monetary system operates, several points are worth noting. The colonial experience shows that a circulating medium which is uniform, generally accepted, and present in adequate quantities for the needs of trade is not achieved easily. A uniform medium is something Americans today take for granted. Also, during the colonial period, we may trace the process by which money developed from a useful commodity to something close to outright fiat money. In addition, we should note the ties between monetary policies and politics. Colonial governments first issued paper currency in response to a political crisis. The British anti-inflationary measures were a factor that helped to destroy American confidence in and loyalty to the mother country.

THE PERIOD OF THE AMERICAN REVOLUTION

From the beginning of the Revolution, the Continental Congress and the thirteen states faced the problem of financing the war. Some means of reallocating a larger share of the country's output to each of the several units of government was necessary, and Congress and the state assemblies had to devise a financial system which would accomplish this. Taxation would have been a logical and straightforward solution to the difficulty, or borrowing through the sale of securities would have achieved the same result. For the Continental Congress, neither of these methods was possible. First, it did not have the legal power to tax, nor was it in a position to acquire this power in the face of the prejudice against taxation. Even if this power had been available, it was unlikely that Congress could have exercised it effectively considering the economic upheavals caused by the war. Congress could not borrow because the colonists lacked capital funds for investment and, without tax revenue, the credit rating of Congress was poor. These difficulties forced Congress to issue paper money. The thirteen states possessed taxing powers but preferred not to use them to finance the entire cost of the war. Hence, the states also relied upon issues of paper currency.

The Continental Congress began the process with a modest issue of bills of credit equal in value to two million Spanish dollars. These bills paid the Army and bought supplies. It was assumed that the war would be brief and that the thirteen states would levy taxes to pay the requisitions that the Congressional Treasury made upon them to redeem the bills. The states, however, did not contribute large sums to Congress and the war proved to be lengthy. Consequently, Congress was forced to issue more bills. As the quantity issued became excessive, the value of the notes depreciated. The purchase of a given quantity of supplies then necessitated the issuance of a larger volume of notes and accelerated their decline in value.

The thirteen states repeated this pattern with the result that paper currency had lost all of its value by 1780. After that date, loans and subsidies from abroad permitted both monetary reform and a different system of war finance. Later generations have criticized the issuing of paper currency to finance the war, but there was little else that the Congress or the state governments could do under the circumstances. As we shall see, succeeding generations used the same method in a modified form to finance later wars and national emergencies.

The use of paper currency to pay for the war affected the distribution of the burden. When using this method, the government printed money and used it to buy the supplies it needed and to meet the payroll. The government paid soldiers or civilians who, in turn, spent the money for consumer goods. As the amount issued increased, persons receiving paper currency found that it had depreciated before they could spend it. An individual whose stock of money had declined in value in such a fashion made an involuntary contribution to the war effort. It was a substitute for taxation, and the burden fell on those persons holding money or assets with a fixed monetary value. We should note, however, that few people held assets of fixed value or had fixed incomes in that period. Hence, the hardship and the inconvenience were less than would be true today.

Financing the government by note issue instead of by taxation is open to question on grounds of effectiveness as well as equity. The public is likely to accept the first issue of notes, but it may resist later issues if it knows from experience that the value of the notes will depreciate. Because of the colonial and Revolutionary experiences, the nation emerged from the war with a lasting mistrust of government-issued paper currency.

The practice of issuing paper currency to reallocate resources is not unique to the American Revolution. We find it in other nations and in other times. Most nations which are born in war have the same experience as the United States. Underdeveloped nations in the mid-twentieth century are using this method to allocate resources to capital projects. It is an attempt to avoid the pain of withdrawing resources from the consumption sector of the economy by taxation or saving. An increased money supply accomplishes the reallocation and inflation is the price paid.

THE ADOPTION OF THE CONSTITUTION TO 1860

The financial strain on the central Government eased when hostilities ceased, but the Government was unable to establish a sound monetary system because of its limited power under the Articles of Confederation. The Constitution, adopted in 1788, granted Congress the right ". . . to coin Money, [and to] regulate the Value thereof, . . ." Court decisions have interpreted this clause to mean that the Federal Government has very broad powers although originally there was some question concerning the right to issue paper currency. The Constitution denies the states the power to coin money, issue paper money, or declare anything but gold and silver legal tender. This effectively prevented the states from issuing paper currency; nevertheless, as we shall see, state banks were able to issue bank notes.

Bimetallism: 1792 – 1834

Alexander Hamilton, who became the first Secretary of the Treasury in 1789, prepared a comprehensive plan for the nation's monetary system. He proposed to fund the public debt. In accordance with his funding proposal, the Treasury would issue long-term, interest-bearing securities in exchange for the bills of credit and other short-term liabilities issued during the Revolution. This would permit the Treasury to operate in an orderly manner and also would provide for a supply of financial assets in the country and thus would create a money market. He further proposed the establishment of a national bank. The bank would have close ties with the Government and would issue bank notes. Hence, paper currency would circulate but the notes would be liabilities of a bank and not of the Government. Also, he proposed that the United States define the monetary standard and establish a mint.

After considerable discussion, Congress adopted with some modification all of his proposals. It provided for the funding of the debt, but the opponents of funding won important concessions since the Government repudiated most of the original issues of Continental currency by redeeming them at one per cent of face value. In addition, Congress granted a charter to the First Bank of the United States in 1791 and passed the Coinage Act in 1792 establishing the Mint.

The Coinage Act was to provide for a sound and uniform national currency. The first step involved the definition of the monetary standard. The most commonly used coin in the United States was the Spanish 8-*real* piece, also known as the Spanish dollar. Since it was already the basic unit in circulation, the United States accepted it as the standard and the Spanish dollar became the United States dollar. These Spanish coins varied in weight, however, so it was necessary to choose the average or typical dollar. After a study of a number of units chosen at random, the Treasury estimated that the average Spanish dollar contained 371.25 grains of silver, and this became the official weight of the United States silver dollar. Since Hamilton and the Congress accepted the principle of a bimetallic standard, it was necessary to define the dollar in terms of gold. Hamilton, familiar with Gresham's law, realized that the official or mint ratio of gold to silver had to correspond to the commercial ratio which he estimated to be 15 to 1. Therefore, the United States set the gold grains in a dollar at 24.75, or $\frac{1}{15}$ of the number of silver grains. Congress authorized the minting of the coins shown in Table 4–1.

The lack of trust in government issues of paper currency extended to the coins. Originally the government issued only full-bodied token coins. The huge copper cents and half cents that resulted were impractical, however, and authorization for token one cent and one-half cent pieces followed a year later.

The estimated market ratio of 15 to 1 may have been accurate in 1792, but the value of silver relative to gold declined in succeeding

Table 4–1

UNITED STATES COINS, 1792

Metal	Denomination	Weight in Grains	
		Gross	Fine
Gold	Eagle, $10	270.0	247.5
	Half eagle, $5	135.0	123.75
	Quarter eagle, $2.50	67.5	61.875
Silver	Dollar	416.0	371.25
	Half dollar	208.0	185.625
	Quarter dollar	104.0	92.8125
	Dime	41.6	37.125
	Half dime	20.8	18.5625
Copper	Cent	264.0	264.0
	Half cent	132.0	132.0

Source: A. Barton Hepburn, *A History of Currency in the United States* (New York: The Macmillan Company, 1915), p. 43.

years. Consequently, gold became overvalued at the Mint and while the Mint produced some gold coins the public exported them. Hence, United States gold coins did not circulate as money, and the United States was on a *de facto* silver standard.

Another problem arose. Despite the attempt to make United States dollars equal in weight to the Spanish units, the coins of the United States Mint were slightly lighter than the Spanish dollar. The West Indies, however, accepted newly minted United States coins by tale; i.e., by counting them. Accordingly, it was profitable to export the United States silver coins. The owners of the heavy Spanish coins which entered the United States took them to the Mint and made a profit while abraded or lightweight foreign coins circulated as the media of exchange. Of necessity, the United States continued to recognize these foreign coins as legal tender. Thus, the Government was in the embarrassing position of operating a mint to supply coins for other countries while foreign coins continued to circulate at home. The exportation of United States coins stopped in 1806 when President Jefferson suspended the coinage of United States dollars, but foreign coins continued to circulate as legal tender. The operation of Gresham's law had practically put the United States Mint out of business.

During this period of a *de facto* silver standard, the Treasury issued a small quantity of paper currency. The reason for the issue of paper currency was a familiar one in American history: financial crises caused by war. The Treasury financed the War of 1812 in part by issuing short-term notes in small denominations. These notes were not legal tender, but they were acceptable in payment of taxes and other public charges. Some of them circulated as money until the Treasury withdrew them after the war.

Bimetallism: 1834–1860

The nation's leaders understood why gold coins did not circulate in the United States, and they made several attempts to change the mint ratio of gold to silver to correspond to the world-market ratio. All attempts to change the ratio failed until 1834. In that year Congress reduced the gold content of the dollar to 23.22 grains. Since the silver content of the dollar did not change, the mint ratio became 16 to 1. This mint ratio overvalued gold, a fact the Government seems to have realized at the time. Motives for overvaluing gold apparently were mixed. Some persons felt that bimetallism was impossible and preferred a gold standard if the nation was to use only one metal. Also the 16 to 1 ratio favored the domestic gold mining interests in Georgia and the Carolinas by raising the price of their product.

Since the Mint overvalued gold and undervalued silver, it was profitable to export silver coins or to treat them as a commodity; consequently the United States was on a *de facto* gold standard after a few years. Gold coins circulated but the absence of silver left the nation without a supply of currency of small denominations. Bank notes and even postage stamps filled the void, but these were not durable enough to be satisfactory for amounts of fifty cents and lower.

Issuing token coins would have solved the problem, but the nation delayed taking this step until 1853. By that date, the acute shortage of small coins had caused so much inconvenience that Congress reduced the silver content and stopped the free coinage of the half dollar, quarter, dime, and half dime. The Mint produced the new lightweight coins in amounts deemed necessary for small transactions and the reduction in weight was sufficient to insure their circulation as token coins. For all practical purposes, the United States was on a gold standard with subsidiary silver coins. The system worked so well that the Government terminated the legal-tender provisions for foreign coins. More than sixty years had passed since the passage of the first Coinage Act to the time when the country at last developed a national coinage system with uniform coins of relatively stable value. The position of the silver dollar remained a strange one. Officially, the United States was on a bimetallic standard, using a silver dollar which contained and was worth 371.25 grains of silver. However, no silver dollars were coined nor had they been coined for many years. This anomalous position of the silver dollar was to cause trouble for a later generation.

CIVIL WAR MONETARY DEVELOPMENTS

With the outbreak of the Civil War, the United States Government faced the same problem that had confronted the Continental Congress. The nation had to reallocate larger shares of output to the Government and to the war effort. In 1861 the Congress possessed powers unavailable to the Revolutionary body, but it made the same basic mistake in a less extreme form. It underestimated the length and the severity of the war and it, therefore, misjudged the cost. Consequently, plans for financing the war were inadequate.

The war cost the Federal Government approximately $3⅓ billion. This represented expenditures for goods and services over and above the regular expenditures by private persons and businesses. The United States used three methods to finance the war. Congress increased taxes to some extent but was unwilling or perhaps felt that it was politically impractical to enact the heavy taxes which modern economists feel it should have levied. Current taxes covered slightly less than one fourth of the cost of the war. The Treasury sold bonds but many of the issues went to commercial banks who paid for them by issuing bank notes or by creating deposits. This increased the money supply, and the economic effect was the same as if the Government had issued paper currency. In addition the Government issued paper currency. These noninterest-bearing promissory notes in small denominations bore the official title United States notes, but they became known popularly as "greenbacks." Approximately $430 million of these notes were issued, and they circulated as money along with the notes issued by the state and later by the national banks.

The results were not entirely satisfactory. As the public noted the increased quantities of paper money and anticipated still further issues as well as a rise in the price level, it hoarded gold. By the end of 1861, gold withdrawals forced the banks and the Government to cease paying liabilities in specie; i.e., gold. With this suspension of specie payment, the United States temporarily replaced the gold standard with one of inconvertible paper. During the war, the quantity of money increased by over 100 per cent, and the wholesale price level in terms of paper currency more than doubled. The price of silver rose to the point where token coins were worth more as a commodity than as money and the silver coins disappeared from circulation. There were then no monetary units between the one cent copper coin and the paper dollar. This void in the circulating media was a nuisance rather than a major problem; fractional bank notes soon appeared to fill the void. More important, however, were the shifts in wealth and income which occurred during the period of inflation.

What was the cause of the inflation? Some historians have placed the blame on the $430 million greenbacks in circulation, but the real cause was the excessive demand for goods and services. The Government's purchases of goods and services increased several fold, and any method of finance that did not reduce substantially the effective private demand would have led to the same result. In practice, private demand did not diminish; the creation of extra money accomplished the reallocation of the national output. The Government used the newly created money to outbid the private sector for the nation's resources. With this approach inflation was inevitable. The Civil War inflation was the result of the public's unwillingness to face an unpleasant fact: if additional resources are allocated to the Government, the private sector of the economy must make sacrifices. The refusal to pay taxes which were high enough to finance the war was an attempt to escape this sacrifice. Substituting newly created money for taxes allowed individuals to think that no sacrifice occurred. This practice has been repeated in the United States and in other nations for military and other purposes, as we shall see in later chapters.

POST-CIVIL WAR MONETARY PROBLEMS

By the end of the war, the national debt had grown to $2¾ billion, prices had become inflated, and the nation was on an inconvertible paper standard. These conditions are interrelated, and we shall approach the problems they raised by concentrating on the monetary standard. The possibility that the nation might remain on a paper standard was not seriously considered. Accordingly, the United States decided to return to a metallic standard and the chosen metal was gold. This return took the form of a resumption of the practice of paying the interest on bonds in gold and redeeming United States notes and the notes and deposits of commercial banks in gold on demand. However, resumption at 23.22 grains of gold to the dollar was not possible at once because of the inflation that had occurred during the war. The prices of goods in the United States in terms of paper currency were so high compared with prices in the rest of the world that it would have been profitable for persons to

redeem dollars in gold and to buy abroad. Any attempt at the resumption of specie payment, therefore, would have quickly exhausted the nation's gold supply.

There were two possible solutions to this problem. First, the
nation could recognize that the dollar had lost one half of its
purchasing power, and it could reduce the gold content of the dollar
to one half of its prewar figure. Redemption of paper currency in
gold on these terms would have been possible since the incentive to
persons to export gold and to buy abroad would be eliminated. We
apply the term devaluation to this solution but this is misleading. It
would be more accurate to say that we were admitting that devaluation in terms of the purchasing power of the dollar had occurred
already and that we were reducing the gold content to conform to
this lower value. The nation rejected this solution. Many considered
it unethical since the Government had sold bonds and other agencies
had borrowed money on the assumption that the postwar dollar
would contain 23.22 grains of gold. Opponents of devaluation argued
also that the nation would encourage saving, investment, and economic growth if it assured savers that the dollar's value would be
stable in the long run. While this confidence might survive a temporary decline in the value of the dollar caused by the wartime emergency, it was necessary to restore its purchasing power as soon as
possible. Also, national pride became involved. After most wars
there is a tendency to try to restore conditions to their prewar position.

Deflation was the alternative solution. The price level would
have to decline to the point where it was no longer profitable to
redeem paper dollars in gold to finance imports. Unfortunately,
deflation imposes hardships on certain classes because it involves
depressed business conditions and unemployment. There is also the
ethical problem of the debtor who is forced to pay creditors in hard
funds for the loans advanced to him in depreciated currency. The
nation could have avoided these hardships through devaluation. It
rejected this solution, however, and deflation began to run its pre-
dictable course.

There were several possible methods for lowering the price
level. The Government could levy taxes in excess of expenditures
and then could use the surplus to retire greenbacks or bonds held by
commercial banks.[2] The combination of a tax surplus and a reduction
in the supply of money would lead to depressed prices and probably
unemployment also. Secondly, the Government could sell bonds and
use the proceeds to retire paper currency. This, of course, would

[2]Chapter 6 explains the way in which the retirement of bonds held by banks causes a
reduction in the money supply.

have a very limited effect if commercial banks purchased the bonds. Thirdly, the Government could hold the supply of money relatively constant until the nation's economy expanded. In time the available money supply would be insufficient to finance the expanded trade at the high price level and deflation would occur.[3]

The United States used all of these methods to some degree. Its tax receipts exceeded expenditures in the postwar years, and it sold bonds. The combination of budget surpluses and bond sales reduced the currency supply, even though the growth of demand deposits and the use of checks as a means of payment led to a net increase in the money supply. Nevertheless, the nation's output and need for circulating media grew so rapidly that prices fell and the Treasury was able to resume the payment of its obligations in gold by 1879. While achieving this goal of a return to the gold standard, two interesting monetary developments occurred.

Greenbacks Continued in Circulation

The Government expected to retire the United States notes it had issued as soon after the war ended as possible. Such action would have been in keeping with the tradition that the Treasury issued only full-bodied money. When the war ended, the Government began to retire the greenbacks, but it quickly changed its policy in the face of political opposition. As could be expected, prices were falling and debtors were experiencing difficulties. The farm areas particularly were hard hit because many farmers who had contracted mortgages during the war now encountered falling agricultural prices. Groups adversely affected by low prices and depressed economic conditions blamed their problems on the reduced money supply. Accordingly, these groups regarded an increase in the currency in circulation as a solution to their difficulties. This provided the motive for a greenback political party. The party did not have an important effect on national elections, but this group and its allies did have sufficient influence to prevent the retirement of the United States notes. When the nation returned to the gold standard in 1879, and persons holding the United States notes redeemed them in gold, the Treasury reissued the notes. As a result, the quantity of United States notes in circulation today is approximately the same as it was one hundred years ago.

The anti-inflationists might have pressed their demands for an increase in paper currency more vigorously if they had not found a better cause in which to enlist.

[3]Part IV discusses the relationship of the price level to the money supply.

The Silver Problem

You will recall that an Act of Congress in 1834 placed the United States on a bimetallic standard under which it accepted gold and silver for coinage at the respective rates of 23.22 grains and 371.25 grains per dollar, or at the ratio of 16 to 1. Expressed in different terms, every ounce of gold brought to the Mint became $20.67 in gold coins while each ounce of silver became $1.29. We have noted that this mint ratio undervalued silver relative to the market price. Expressed in market terms, an ounce of silver was worth $1.29 at the Mint but it sold for more than that figure on the commodity market. Therefore, persons owning silver did not take it to the Mint and silver dollars did not circulate.

The Coinage Act of 1873 eliminated the silver dollar from the list of coins the Mint had authority to produce. Although Congress did not repeal bimetallism officially, this Act, in effect, eliminated silver as a monetary standard. There was no immediate opposition to the measure; it appeared to harm no one for, as we have seen, owners of silver had not found it profitable to bring silver to the Mint for many years. Soon after the passage of the Act, however, several events occurred which led to a decline in the price of silver. India and some other Eastern Nations stopped or reduced their imports of silver because of an unfavorable balance of payments. Several European countries, including Germany and France, adopted a monometallic gold standard. Consequently, the demand for silver fell and, as the nations abandoning the silver standard sold their silver reserves, the supply increased. Even more important was the enormous increase in the production of silver resulting from the discovery of silver deposits in the western section of the United States. By 1874 the price of silver had fallen below $1.29 per ounce, and producers realized the importance of the Act of 1873 which they now called the "Crime of '73." If Congress had not passed the Act, the United States Treasury would have been buying all silver offered to it at $1.29 per ounce. Consequently, the silver interests demanded the resumption of the practice of minting silver dollars for reasons that are easy to understand. They wanted a subsidy in the form of government price supports which would establish a floor under the price of the product they produced. There were not enough silver miners to determine government policy, but they found powerful allies.

In examining the issues of the silver controversy, we should note first that the public did not recognize the Government's support of the price of silver as a subsidy so easily as would have been true if another commodity, such as steel, had been involved. People had been using gold and silver as money for so many centuries that they felt that this was the natural and designated use for these metals. Many regarded the demonetization of silver as unethical and almost sacrilegious.

Keeping this in mind, we can examine the position of the antideflation groups. It may be logical for modern monetary theorists to recommend the issuance of paper currency, such as greenbacks, to overcome deflation; but in the nineteenth century this procedure would have appeared radical and unsound. Inconvertible paper had a bad reputation. In America it had declined in value whenever the Government issued it. Hence, the Greenback Party seemed to be advocating an irresponsible policy in suggesting the running of the printing presses and the issuing of paper dollars. But by joining the silver interests, the Party had an opportunity to achieve the objective of an increased money supply in a legitimate and respectable fashion. In adopting silver, antideflationists were demanding a return to the traditional American system.

The extreme position of the combined silver and antideflation forces called for free and unlimited coinage of gold and silver at the previous ratio of 16 to 1. If the United States had adopted the policy recommended by the silver interests, officially we would have had a bimetallic standard but actually we would have been on a silver standard since the Mint would have been overvaluing silver. A more moderate position called for substantial government purchasing of silver at the market price and the turning of this silver into dollars containing 371.25 grains of silver. The silver dollar then would be a token coin even though its weight was the same as the old, full-bodied coin. The Government accepted these moderate demands to a limited extent.

The Bland-Allison Act of 1878 directed the Treasury to purchase $2 to $4 million worth of silver each month at the market price. Although this was not free coinage, the purchases by the Government increased the demand for silver and supported the price. The Government, in turn, made a profit (seigniorage) when producing coins; for it purchased the silver in a dollar for less than 100 cents. To the extent that silver dollars increased the supply of money, this policy eased the deflationary pressure. Therefore, it might appear that this operation would make everyone happy.

The results of the Bland-Allison Act, however, satisfied neither the silver advocates nor its opponents. The quantity of silver purchased was too small to prevent a decline in the price; it did lessen the decrease. On the other hand, the Treasury had difficulty keeping silver in circulation. It could not place the blame for this difficulty on the inconvenience of carrying silver dollars, for Congress allowed the Treasury to issue silver certificates. The Treasury found that the public returned the silver dollars or certificates it issued in exchange for gold. This practice made it difficult to retain a large enough reserve of gold to remain on the gold standard. The problem of staying on the gold standard became more acute because our purchases of silver and the possibility that the Treasury would buy even larger quantities undermined confidence in the value of the dollar. Hence, there was an incentive to redeem dollars in gold and to hoard the metal or to transfer it to another country.

The friends of silver scored one more victory. The Sherman Silver Purchase Act of 1890 repealed the Bland-Allison Act and directed the Treasury to purchase 4½ million ounces of silver per month at the market price. Treasury notes, redeemable in gold or silver at the discretion of the Treasury Department, paid for the silver. The silver was not to be coined but was to serve as a reserve for the silver certificates. Operation of the Sherman Act almost forced the nation off the gold standard. The Treasury notes issued to purchase silver gave the public a claim against the Treasury's gold reserves; a decision to redeem the notes exclusively in silver would have meant that the nation had abandoned the gold standard. After several crises in which the nation narrowly avoided the suspension of the gold standard, President Cleveland secured the repeal of the Sherman Act in 1893.

The final and also the most famous political controversy regarding the monetary standard in the nineteenth century occurred during the presidential campaign of 1896. The Democratic candidate, William Jennings Bryan, campaigned vigorously and spoke eloquently in favor of the free coinage of gold and silver at the traditional 16 to 1 ratio. He did not win the election and the United States remained on the effective monometallic standard as established in 1873. Defeat of the silver group appeared to be final with the passage of the Gold Standard Act of 1900. This Act established gold as the standard money of the United States, and it directed that the Treasury Department maintain other forms of currency at a parity with it. In a later chapter, however, we shall see that silver again entered our monetary system.

Evaluation of the Monetary Controversy

To evaluate the monetary controversy of the period 1860 to 1900, recognition of two separate questions is essential. The first concerned the choice between deflation or continued high prices; and the second, the choice of a monetary standard.

We shall look at the first question. The period following the Civil War was one of rapid economic growth; nevertheless the benefits of this increased wealth were not shared by all sectors of the economy. Farmers in particular did poorly. To blame all their troubles on deflation is an oversimplification. During this era agricultural output expanded rapidly but demand was relatively inelastic. Deflation, consequently, added to the farmers' problems but falling farm prices would have occurred in any case. It is more difficult to assess the effect of deflation on the rate of economic growth. Sound money encouraged saving and thus capital accumulation, but it also contributed to periods of unemployment and depressed business conditions. These conditions retarded growth in addition to causing hardship at that time. Two questions arise: Did unemployment and depressed business conditions caused by deflation retard growth more than sound money encouraged saving and capital formation? If growth was stimulated by monetary policy, was it worth the hardship which the monetary policy also caused?

Judgment concerning the silver controversy is easy if we apply present-day standards. Free coinage of silver, if adopted, would have placed the nation on a silver rather than a gold standard; but it is not certain that this would have damaged the national economy in the long run. The purchase of silver in order to support its price cannot be justified. It involves a misallocation of resources as the nation expends labor and material on the production of silver rather than on more useful commodities. If more money were desired, a government controlled quantity of paper currency would have been a better solution. Incidentally, silver producers were not the only beneficiaries of the United States policy of purchasing silver. Nations like Germany which were abandoning silver as a monetary standard faced the prospect of a sizable loss in disposing of their stock of silver. The United States Government, which held no silver at the beginning of the period, supported the price of silver and absorbed some of the loss.

In closing we should note that the supply of money increased during the period of the controversy. Coins and paper currency remained relatively stable but demand deposits and the use of checks as a means of payment grew rapidly. At the turn of the century, the volume of money changing hands by means of bank checks exceeded the volume of currency transactions.

With the development of demand deposits and payment by check, the United States completed the evolution of money from a useful commodity to figures in a bank ledger. We shall examine the development of banks and the money banks create in succeeding chapters.

SUMMARY

Attempts to establish a sound and uniform currency system marked American monetary history prior to the Civil War. Scarcity of circulating media and nonuniformity of coins with respect to origin and weight hampered the colonists. The scarcity occurred because the colonists were unable or unwilling to sacrifice "useful" goods in order to acquire coins. They tried paper currency as a substitute for metal, but despite the soundness of the theory mismanagement of the note issues led to failure in many colonies.

The Government financed the Revolutionary War with paper currency which depreciated until it was worthless. This did achieve the reallocation of resources which was necessary to prosecute the war, although later generations have criticized the method because of the way it distributed the burden.

With the adoption of the Constitution and the establishment of a strong government, the United States adopted a bimetallic standard. The Government tried to create a sound and uniform currency by using full-bodied coins exclusively. It did not issue paper money. The nation's experience with bimetallism serves as a classic example of the operation of Gresham's law. The Mint overvalued silver first and later gold. As a result of the operation of Gresham's law, the United States was on a gold standard without formally having adopted it. In time the nation overcame the prejudice against token coins and achieved a sound and uniform coinage with full-bodied gold and token silver coins.

During the Civil War, the Government issued paper currency, the national debt increased, and the price level doubled. These conditions led to prolonged monetary controversy in the post-war years. The deflation required to re-establish the prewar gold standard was painful to many persons who therefore advocated a larger money supply. Because of the political power of this group, the paper currency issued during the war remains part of our present money supply. When the price of silver fell, the antideflation group joined forces with the silver producers to demand the re-establishment of bimetallism with free coinage of silver at the old rate of 371.25 grains to the dollar. The advocates of silver money were unable to re-establish silver as standard money, but they achieved some success since the Government purchased large quantities of silver between 1878 and 1893. Free coinage of silver was a major issue in the presidential campaign of 1896. The opponent of silver, William McKinley, won the election, however; and Congress reaffirmed the United States gold standard in the Act of 1900. During the nineteenth century, the development of banks and the use of checking accounts made demand deposits the main component of the money supply.

QUESTIONS

1. Discuss the statement, "Money was scarce in the American colonies." What would have been the best method for overcoming this shortage?
2. Printing money was a substitute for taxation during the Revolutionary War. Discuss.
3. What were the conditions which would have led to the successful operation of a bimetallic standard in the early 1800's?
4. What were the arguments in favor of devaluing the dollar after the Civil War? Why didn't the United States officially devalue the dollar at that time?
5. In what way may the purchase of silver for monetary purposes serve as a substitute for printing paper money?

SUGGESTED READINGS

Dewey, Davis R. *The Financial History of the United States.* 9th ed. New York: Longmans, Green and Co., 1924.

Harrod, Roy. *The Dollar.* New York: Harcourt, Brace and Company, 1954.

Hepburn, A. Barton. *A History of Currency in the United States.* Rev. ed. New York: The Macmillan Company, 1924.

Laughlin, J. Laurence. *The History of Bimetallism in the United States.* New York: D. Appleton and Company, 1898.

Mitchell, Wesley C. *A History of the Greenbacks.* Chicago: University of Chicago Press, 1903.

Nussbaum, Arthur A. *A History of the Dollar.* New York: Columbia University Press, 1957.

Studenski, Paul, and Krooss, Herman E. *Financial History of the United States.* 2d ed. New York: McGraw-Hill Book Company, Inc., 1963.

II

THE COMMERCIAL
BANKING SYSTEM

5

DEBT AND CREDIT

In the preceding chapters, we noted that most of our money takes the form of a debt. In 1965, promissory notes of the Federal Reserve banks and the United States Government plus the debt commercial banks owe to the owners of demand deposits accounted for $158.1 billion of the $162.7 billion in the money supply. If we expand our definition of money to include items called near-money, the importance of debt used as money becomes more apparent. However, we are not presently interested in debt as a circulating medium but rather as the basis of the banking system.

NATURE OF DEBT

As everyone knows, a debt is an obligation to pay money or some good or service at a future date. We usually think of a debt in terms of money but other forms of debt are possible. A man may promise to perform a specific service in the future, or he may have an obligation to deliver a certain number of bushels of wheat or an intangible item like shares of common stock. Close followers of professional sports will be familiar with the practice of trading players' contracts with the provision that one club will send one minor league performer to another club at some future, specified date. Here the debt is not an obligation to deliver money, a commodity, or the services of the debtor; it is the right to employ another party. Despite the many possibilities, however, most debt is an obligation to deliver money at a future time, and this is the only type of debt with which we shall concern ourselves in this study.

A second characteristic of debt that should be obvious is its identity with credit. One person incurring a debt automatically causes a second person to acquire a credit: the right to collect money at some future date. What one man regards as a debt another man considers a credit. Debt and credit are obviously the same thing observed from opposite points of view. We shall use the terms interchangeably in this chapter. We stress this rather obvious relation to remove any tendency to disapprove of debt on an ethical basis. The general public often thinks of debt as undesirable, or at least feels that an expansion of the amount of debt in existence is harmful. At the same time, we regard credit as a blessing. Certainly the public feels that a plentiful supply of credit is desirable and is good for the economy. Recognizing the identity of debt and credit, we obviously cannot maintain these opposing attitudes. Accordingly, we shall avoid statements to the effect that credit or debt is bad or good. In future chapters, we shall see that credit affects the development of the economic system. This effect, depending upon the amount of credit in existence, the rate at which the total is increasing or is decreasing, and the manner in which its creation is occurring, may be negative or positive. It is most difficult to determine the proper amount of credit for the well-being of a society, and experts frequently disagree on this point. We shall examine the issues involved in the section on monetary policy, but there are some elementary points we can note at this time.

Credit, and hence debt, has a number of useful functions. It enables an individual to adopt an advantageous consumption pattern that need not be the same as his income pattern with respect to time. Some individuals borrow and spend the proceeds for consumption goods, thereby consuming in advance of income; others save, postponing consumption of their income. Since each individual chooses to become a borrower or a saver, we assume that the consumption pattern which results yields more satisfaction to the group than one which is identical with current income. Incidentally, once again this demonstrates the equivalence of credit and debt: one individual saves; another consumes in advance of his income.

More important, credit contributes to a high rate of production. Many modern production processes require such large investments in plant and equipment that a single individual cannot save enough to acquire or to build the facility. A credit, or debt, system allows many individuals to save and to pool their savings for investment purposes.

TYPES OF DEBT

Many types of debt exist and there frequently is more than one name for each type. For this reason, it is easy to become confused by the multitude of terms we use to describe the major types and their subdivisions. In this section, we shall simplify the problem of terminology by classifying debt according to the reasons for its creation, the type of debt, the likelihood of repayment, and the maturity date of the debt.

Debt arises because certain individuals and institutions wish to purchase and to use goods and services before they pay for them. The seller of goods may agree to accept payment at a later date, or the purchaser may borrow money in order to purchase goods and services. In either case the purchase of goods and services leads to the creation of debt. The use made of the goods and the services purchased provides one basis for classifying debt. If the debtor incurs a liability to purchase household furnishings, an automobile, or other consumer goods, it is consumer debt. Individuals and business firms purchasing plant, equipment, and materials for manufacturing or other productive uses incur much larger debts. In addition, the several levels of government borrow sizable amounts of money which they spend for public purposes. Therefore, if we classify debt according to its use, we have consumer, productive, and public debt.

The extent to which a creditor accepts promises to pay in place of cash depends upon his estimate of the ability and the willingness of the debtor to pay the debt when it becomes due. Because of the varying degrees of uncertainty regarding the repayment of debt, we classify indebtedness according to quality. Thus, we rate debt instruments Aaa, Baa, and so forth. Or classification of the risk may be according to the number of signatures on the debt instrument. For example, a promissory note may be a "one-name" or a "two-name" paper. The likelihood of debt repayment is obviously of extreme importance to a creditor, and a number of specialized institutions have come into existence to analyze the credit worthiness of "would-be" debtors and to inform creditors of their findings. Classifying debt according to quality automatically results in a classification of debtors, or, more precisely, the credit rating of debtors. The determination of the credit rating of an individual or a corporation involves the use of techniques and analytical procedures which are beyond the scope of this book. Note, however, that the determination includes a study of the debtor's character, capital, collateral, and capability.

The length of time until maturity is another basis for classification. There is long-term debt which has a maturity date five or more years in the future. Corporate or government bonds are debt instruments which are evidence of the existence of long-term debt. Intermediate-term debt has a maturity date one to five years in the future, and short-term debt is due within a year. In addition, a debt may be of the demand type; that is, the debtor must make payment whenever the owner or creditor demands it.

EVIDENCE OF DEBT: DEBT INSTRUMENTS

A debt contract may be oral. In this case, human memory is the only evidence of its existence. Debt also may be of the open-book type, or proof of its existence may be a written document. Oral debt contracts usually are for small amounts, and they have no significant effect on the monetary system. For this reason, we shall confine our discussion to the open-book type and to the type which credit instruments represent.

There are a great many examples of open-book credit. On the consumer level, it is common practice for retailers to maintain charge accounts which allow the customers to purchase an article without paying for it immediately. At the end of the billing period, the retailer sends a statement calling for payment to the debtor. This practice is growing. Nonretail businesses have established this practice to an even greater extent. They normally allow their customers thirty days, or possibly a longer period, to pay for the goods purchased. Until settlement is made, evidence of the debt exists in the form of entries in the accounts receivable ledgers of the creditor.

There are a number of advantages connected with this practice. On the wholesale and the retail levels, it reduces sales resistance. It even may be necessary to use this system to meet competition in the market. The simplicity of this method allows for the rapid completion of transactions with a minimum of overhead expense.

Unfortunately, there are also disadvantages to this type of credit. Because of the informality of the transaction, disagreements arise over the exact terms of the contract. The creditor may experience delay and difficulty in collecting the debt for any of several reasons. The debtor may claim that the creditor did not fulfill his portion of the contract and may refuse to pay the debt. This occurs if the debtor feels that the goods which he purchased when incurring the debt do not meet the specifications promised by the creditor. Or the debtor may admit his obligation to pay a specific debt but may claim that a debt which the creditor owes to him cancels in whole or in part the debtor's debt.

These possible legal defenses against payment indicate that the creditor's claim is not of high quality. Although the system works well most of the time and this is the most common form of debt in the United States, there are situations in which it is not appropriate. The inappropriateness of open-book debt is most apparent when a creditor wishes to liquidate some of his assets by selling to another creditor his right to collect money. The potential buyer of accounts receivable is reluctant to purchase them at their face values because of the low quality of the claims. He bases his reluctance on his fear that the debtor will refuse to pay and will defend this position on the legal grounds just described. Hence, open-book credits are difficult to sell except at a considerable discount.

This, in turn, leads to a misallocation of resources: it forces the specialist in manufacturing or retailing to serve as a creditor. He loans a portion of his capital to his customers, and he devotes some of his time and his energy to credit analysis. Experience has shown that a society operates more effectively when producers are highly specialized, so that a manufacturer devotes all of his resources to manufacturing while another specialist serves as a lender of money.

Negotiable Instruments

In order to facilitate the transfer of debt, traders developed a document known as a negotiable instrument. Note that owners of debt instruments can sell them even if the instruments are not negotiable in the technical, legal sense. Merchants frequently sell the open-book credits described in the preceding section. The seller, however, can only assign to the buyer his right to collect from the debtor. We have seen that this right to collect may be of low quality. By contrast, the purchaser buying a negotiable instrument receives a very high-quality claim since most of the legal defenses a debtor may make against the original creditor are not valid against a new creditor who has purchased the instrument in good faith.

A typical use of a promissory note, which is one type of negotiable instrument, illustrates the principle. In our previous example, the seller of merchandise might have insisted that the customer sign a promissory note. If the merchant had done so, he now could sell the promissory note to a bank or to any other creditor. The buyer of the promissory note would have the legal right to collect the debt even though the debtor might prove that the merchandise he bought was not as warranted or that the merchant owed him a debt in return. In brief, the debtor must honor a negotiable instrument. The customer may sue the merchant because of poor quality goods, but he has no legal alternative except to pay the rightful owner of a negotiable instrument. Use of a negotiable instrument, therefore, enables a creditor to transfer to another person a near-perfect right to collect money. It is this attribute of negotiable instruments that causes them to be highly marketable. The holder in due course (legitimate purchaser) has a valid claim even if the original owner did not.

To be negotiable a credit instrument must meet certain criteria. It must be:
1. Written.
2. Signed by the maker.
3. Definite concerning the amount payable.
4. An unconditional order or promise to pay.

5. Definite regarding the maturity date or payable on demand.

6. Payable to order or to the bearer.

This list of requirements may at first seem formidable, but a negotiable instrument is a simple document, as the specimen promissory note in Figure 5–1 shows. It is a written, signed, and dated document. It is an unconditional promise or order to pay (a promise in this example); it is definite about the amount payable, the time, and the place of payment; and it names the payee.

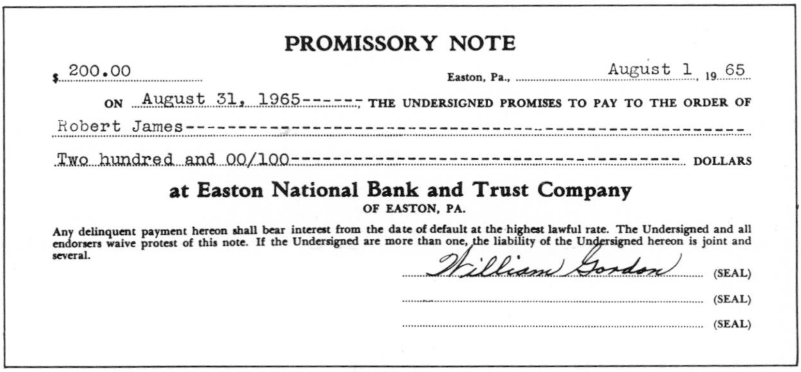

PROMISSORY NOTE

$ 200.00   Easton, Pa.,   August 1 19 65

ON August 31, 1965------ THE UNDERSIGNED PROMISES TO PAY TO THE ORDER OF

Robert James--

Two hundred and 00/100----------------------------------- DOLLARS

at Easton National Bank and Trust Company
OF EASTON, PA.

Any delinquent payment hereon shall bear interest from the date of default at the highest lawful rate. The Undersigned and all endorsers waive protest of this note. If the Undersigned are more than one, the liability of the Undersigned hereon is joint and several.

William Gordon   (SEAL)
    (SEAL)
    (SEAL)

(Courtesy of Easton National Bank and Trust Company, Easton, Pa.)

Figure 5-1.   A Promissory Note

Types of negotiable instruments. One type of negotiable instrument is the promissory note which Figure 5–1 shows. In this case, the instrument takes the form of a promise to pay, as the name promissory note suggests. A negotiable instrument may be an order to pay rather than a promise to pay. Orders to pay are drafts, or bills of exchange. In the case of a draft, one party (the maker or drawer) orders a second party (the drawee) to pay a definite sum of money to a third party (the payee). A check drawn on a bank holding demand deposits is an example of a draft. The person signing the check is the drawer who orders the bank (the drawee) to pay a definite amount of money to the payee (the person in whose favor the check is drawn).

When a check involves only two persons, the payee and drawer is the same party, or the drawee and payee is the same party. An illustration of the first case is a check payable to the person who signs it. The drawee and payee is the same party when a check is payable to the bank on which the drawer has drawn it. It should be obvious that an order to pay does not automatically oblige the drawee to pay. The bank will not honor the check illustrated in Figure 5–2 unless the drawer has at least $100 on deposit.

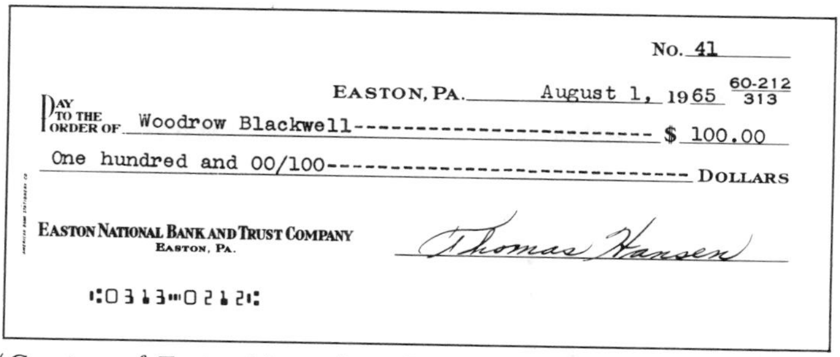

No. 41

EASTON, PA. August 1, 1965 60-212/313

PAY TO THE ORDER OF Woodrow Blackwell $ 100.00

One hundred and 00/100 DOLLARS

EASTON NATIONAL BANK AND TRUST COMPANY
EASTON, PA.

Thomas Hansen

⑆0313⑈0212⑆

(Courtesy of Easton National Bank and Trust Company, Easton, Pa.)

Figure 5-2. A Check

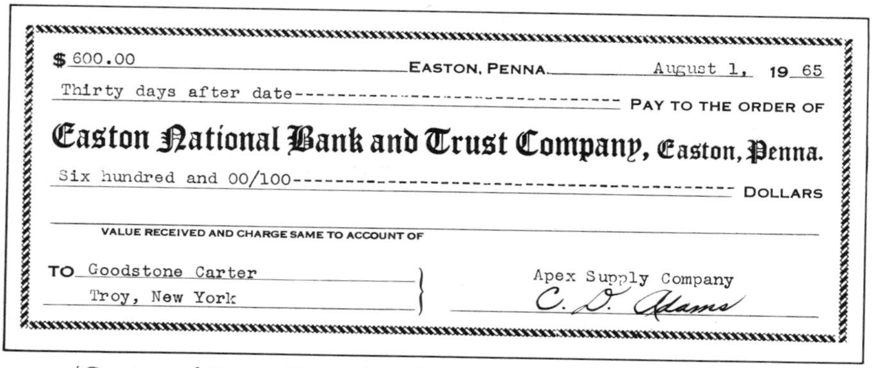

$ 600.00 EASTON, PENNA. August 1, 19 65

Thirty days after date PAY TO THE ORDER OF

Easton National Bank and Trust Company, Easton, Penna.

Six hundred and 00/100 DOLLARS

VALUE RECEIVED AND CHARGE SAME TO ACCOUNT OF

TO Goodstone Carter
Troy, New York

Apex Supply Company
C. D. Adams

(Courtesy of Easton National Bank and Trust Company, Easton, Pa.)

Figure 5-3. A Time Draft

In another example of a draft (Figure 5–3), the fact that the Apex Supply Company has ordered Goodstone Carter to pay does not obligate him to do so. A draft becomes an unconditional obligation to pay, however, if the drawee "accepts" it. That is, if he writes "accepted" and the date across the face of the draft and signs his name. If the seller of merchandise draws a time draft on a charge customer, we refer to it as a trade acceptance. Figure 5–4 is an example of a trade acceptance.

There are three types of negotiable instruments: promissory notes, drafts or bills of exchange, and acceptances. Since it is customary to use terms which describe a specific instrument more precisely, a promissory note may be a demand note if it is payable upon presentation or a time note if it bears a future maturity date. Classifying drafts, according to maturity dates, there are demand or sight drafts, time drafts, and arrival drafts. Sight drafts, of which a check is an

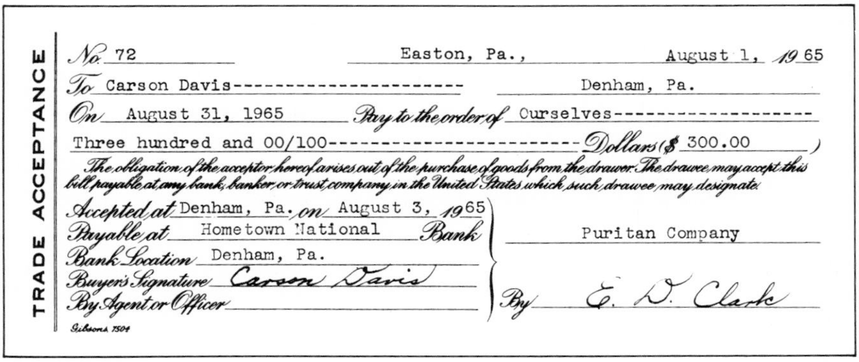
TRADE ACCEPTANCE

No. 72 Easton, Pa., August 1, 1965

To Carson Davis---------------------- Denham, Pa.

On August 31, 1965 Pay to the order of Ourselves-------------------

Three hundred and 00/100------------------------ Dollars ($ 300.00)

The obligation of the acceptor hereof arises out of the purchase of goods from the drawer. The drawee may accept this bill payable at any bank, banker or trust company in the United States which such drawee may designate.

Accepted at Denham, Pa. on August 3, 1965

Payable at Hometown National Bank

Bank Location Denham, Pa.

Buyer's Signature Carson Davis

By Agent or Officer

Puritan Company

By E. D. Clark

Gibsons 7504

Figure 5-4. An Honored Trade Acceptance

example, are payable on demand. Time drafts are payable at a future, specified date. These drafts become acceptances when presented for acceptance prior to maturity. Arrival drafts, used in connection with the shipment of merchandise, are payable when the goods reach their destinations.

Dealers in credit classify drafts according to the parties involved. Bankers' bills are drafts drawn by one bank against another bank. A draft drawn by a nonbank-type business on a bank is a trade bill; commercial bills are drafts drawn by one nonbank-type business firm on another nonbank. If the drawee accepts any of these drafts, they become bank, trade, or commercial acceptances.

When drafts are used in connection with the sale of goods across national boundaries, they frequently have attached to them documents which convey title to the goods in transit. The purchaser then can be required to accept the bill before receiving the documents which enable him to claim the goods from the freight company. Drafts with these documents attached are called documentary bills. If no documents are attached, they are known as clean bills.

Transfer of ownership. We have noted that a person who buys a negotiable instrument has a nearly perfect claim to the collection of a debt. The only defense against payment is evidence that the instrument is not genuine. The signature may be a forgery, someone may have altered the amount to be paid, or the maker may be a minor or otherwise legally incapacitated. A person who acquires a negotiable instrument in a legitimate fashion is "a holder in due course." Specifically, a holder in due course acquires the instrument under the following conditions:

1. The instrument is complete and is regular upon its face.
2. He became the holder before the instrument was overdue

and without knowledge that it had been dishonored, if such was the case.

3. He took it in good faith and for value.
4. At the time he acquired the instrument, he had no notice of any infirmity in the instrument or defect in the title of the person negotiating it.

If a negotiable instrument if "payable to bearer" it is transferable from one party to another simply by delivery; however, the buyer may ask for an endorsement. Endorsement is necessary also to transfer an instrument payable to a specified person or "to his order."

A person who gives an unqualified endorsement to a negotiable instrument warrants that:

1. The instrument is genuine and valid in all respects.
2. He has good title to it.
3. He has no knowledge of any fact which would impair the validity of the instrument.
4. If dishonored by the debtor when presented for payment, the endorser will pay the holder or any subsequent endorser who may have had to honor the instrument.

Several classes of endorsement are illustrated in Figure 5–5. It is assumed that these endorsements are placed on the reverse side of a note or a check payable to James Black.

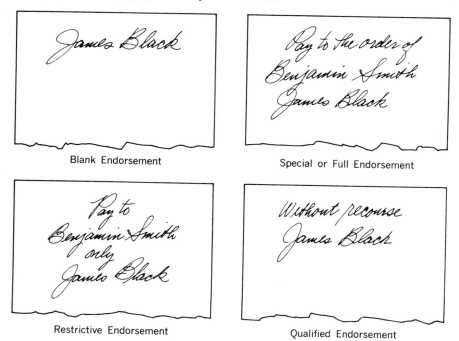

Blank Endorsement

Special or Full Endorsement

Restrictive Endorsement

Qualified Endorsement

Figure 5-5. Types of Endorsements

The first type illustrates the ease with which ownership of a negotiable instrument is transferable. James Black can transfer ownership to anyone he chooses by blank endorsement. The new owner, which may be a bank, a retail establishment, or another individual, can transfer ownership by endorsing the instrument in his turn. Only the person named, who is Benjamin Smith in the preceding illustration, can cash or can transfer an instrument with a special endorsement. A restrictive endorsement prevents further negotiation of the instrument, as the term indicates. It is a safe type to use when sending checks through the mail. An endorsement "without recourse" means that the endorser does not guarantee to honor the instrument if the original maker defaults. It is used only under special circumstances.

Uses of negotiable instruments. Sight, or demand drafts, in the form of bank checks are in common use to transfer funds. On occasion creditors use drafts to prod a tardy debtor. For example, a retail merchant may buy goods on open-book credit from a manufacturer in a distant city. If the manufacturer, who is the creditor, is unable to collect the debt on the day agreed upon in the terms of sale, he may draw a draft on the delinquent debtor and send it to a bank in the debtor's area for collection. If the bank, acting as the creditor's agent, is unable to collect, the debtor's credit rating suffers in his home area. Since the loss of a customer is the usual result of this method, creditors seldom use it.

Time drafts come into use in connection with the sale of goods. Competition among sellers causes wholesalers and manufacturers generally to allow customers thirty or sixty days after delivery before payment is due. During that period, the seller may need money to finance his own operations. He may receive immediate payment and still extend credit to his customer by using a documentary draft. He sends this draft, drawn on the buyer, to a bank which acts as the seller's agent. The buyer must accept the draft before receiving the bill of lading which enables him to claim the goods from the freight company. Because of the negotiable character of the acceptance, the seller of the goods now can transfer it to a bank or other lending institution in return for cash. In this fashion, the buyer of goods acquires credit; the seller receives immediate payment minus a small discount to allow for interest until the acceptance matures. This type of operation is quite common in transactions outside the borders of the United States; domestically, the tradition of open-book credit and the pressure of competition combine to limit its popularity.

Promissory notes are in common use when borrowing money for a relatively short period. They provide the creditor with proof of his claim against the debtor. Because they are negotiable, the first creditor can sell them if he desires cash. Promissory notes are a substitute for open-book credit. In this case, the buyer of merchandise signs a promissory note, which the creditor can sell to any lending agency. This is a common practice in consumer installment buying. The retailer transfers to a bank or finance company the notes signed by the customers. The endorsement from the seller of goods to the lending agency is frequently "without recourse," but the seller usually agrees to repurchase any consumer goods which a bank or a lending agency must seize on account of nonpayment.

Credit instruments make it easy to transfer funds and thus lead to greater specialization. More important, they facilitate the flow of credit and make possible a better utilization of resources. Finally, these instruments provide the stock-in-trade for commercial banks. In the process of acquiring these instruments, banks create money as will be explained in Chapter 6.

SUMMARY

A debt is an obligation to pay something, usually money, at a future date. Credit is the right to receive payment. Consequently, debt and credit are equivalents when viewed by the payer and payee, respectively. It is illogical to consider credit socially beneficial and debt harmful. The existence of debt allows a consumer to adopt a time pattern for consumption that is different from his income pattern. Debt also permits individuals to pool their savings to acquire industrial and other productive facilities.

We classify debt according to the use made of the proceeds of the loan, the type of debtor, the risk involved, and the time to maturity. Debt contracts may be oral or written. If written, evidence of debt exists. This evidence may take the form of a promissory note, a draft, or an acceptance — all are negotiable instruments. The owner of a negotiable instrument has an almost-perfect legal right to collect, and he may transfer ownership by endorsement. We use negotiable instruments to finance commerce, and they are important components of the inventory of a bank.

QUESTIONS

1. How does the existence of an effective system of credit influence the allocation of resources?
2. Discuss the significant differences between negotiable and non-negotiable credit instruments.

3. List the ways in which a negotiable instrument can be endorsed. What is significant about each type of endorsement?
4. Define: promissory note, bill of exchange, and acceptance.
5. Why do non-negotiable forms of credit continue to exist despite the advantages of negotiable instruments?

SUGGESTED READINGS

American Institute of Banking. *Negotiable Instruments*. New York, 1941.

Federal Reserve Bank of New York. *Money Market Essays*, 1952.

Federal Reserve Bank of Philadelphia. *Uniform Commercial Code*, 1953.

Robinson, Roland I. (ed.). *Financial Institutions*. 3d ed. Homewood, Illinois: Richard D. Irwin, Inc., 1960. Chapters 9–12.

6

COMMERCIAL BANKING

Many financial institutions carry the term bank in their titles. There are investment banks, savings banks, industrial banks, and central banks, in addition to commercial banks. In the next two chapters, we shall consider only the commercial banks. These banks are the well-known and frequently visited institutions that receive, transfer, create, and extinguish demand deposits. Since we have defined demand deposits as money, we can describe these banks as institutions which transfer, create, and extinguish money. An institution is a commercial bank if it fits the preceding definition. It is easy to recognize these banks for they handle checking accounts while other types of banks do not. The presence of checking accounts, or demand deposits, is the characteristic which enables these banks to create and to extinguish money as well as to transfer it. Commercial banks originally specialized in lending money to merchants and other commercial establishments, and their name described their function. At present, they are engaged in a wide variety of activities, and the term commercial no longer describes their most significant characteristic. Checking account banks would be a more appropriate title at the present time, but we continue to use the original name.

Central banks can create credit and are important factors in our monetary system. They play an important role in the check clearing process, lend money to commercial banks, and hold deposits for these institutions. In addition, central banks influence the amount of credit which commercial banks can create. We shall examine the functions of central banks in more detail in Chapters 9 and 10.

Savings banks, investment banks, and industrial banks also play an important role in our monetary system and are beneficial to society. For many years, students of monetary affairs regarded these banks as financial intermediaries that transferred funds from one person to another but did not create money. A modern school of thought has challenged this definition, as we shall see in Chapter 21. For the time being, however, we shall accept the traditional point of view and shall consider commercial and central banks as the only institutions which create money. In fact, we shall confine the scope of our immediate study to this function of commercial banks.

STRUCTURE OF COMMERCIAL BANKING
IN THE UNITED STATES

There are approximately 13,750 commercial banks in the United States, ranging in size from very small to very large. Some of these banks operate branches; hence there are approximately 28,400 offices which perform banking functions. Nearly 11,000 of the banks are unit banks which do not have branches, however. By contrast, Canada has ten banks and Great Britain six major banks. In both these countries there are, of course, many branch offices. In a later chapter, we shall see the reason for the development of a unit banking system in the United States. At this point, it is sufficient to note that unit banking and the consequent large number of small banks is a distinctive feature of the United States banking system. Unit banking survives because of the legal framework within which banks operate.

Banking is a regulated industry. We have seen that the Government has an interest in the maintenance of the monetary standard and the management of the money supply. Since the demand deposits of commercial banks are the main component of the money supply, we should expect some government control. In fact, many government agencies play a role in the regulation of banks. These agencies serve as a basis for classifying banks.

Slightly more than one third (4,784 of 13,784) of the banks operate under corporate charters issued by the Federal Government. These are called national banks. The fifty states have chartered the remaining 9,000 banks which we call state banks. Classification becomes more complicated as we continue the process. All of the 4,784 national banks and 1,451 of the state banks, or a total of 6,235 banks, are member banks of the Federal Reserve System. The remaining 7,549 state banks are classified as nonmember banks. Although the nonmember banks outnumber the member banks, the latter institutions account for approximately 85 per cent of the banking business in the United States. Finally, 13,510 commercial banks have their deposits insured with the Federal Deposit Insurance Corporation and are called insured banks. The remaining 274 units are classified as noninsured banks. The existence of these categories causes writers to refer to terms which confuse foreigners. We have national, state, member, nonmember, insured, and noninsured banks. This also leads to legal complications. There are 53 legal entities which have authority over and some responsibility for banking in the United States. They are: the 50 states, the Federal Government, the Federal Reserve System, and the Federal Deposit Insurance Corporation.

ORIGINS OF COMMERCIAL BANKING

We can trace certain functions of commercial banking to very early times, but we shall concentrate on a relatively recent period. The seventeenth-century goldsmiths of London illustrate the development of the principles of modern banking.

Money in seventeenth-century England consisted of gold and silver coins. Merchants and other wealthy persons faced the problem of finding a safe place in which to store their wealth. Some of them entrusted their store of precious metal to the King for storage in the Tower of London. Since the King "borrowed" this money during a political crisis and did not return it, the depositors had to find another method for the safekeeping of their valuables.

The goldsmiths of this period possessed two characteristics that caused people to entrust their money to them. First, as workers in precious metals, they maintained an inventory of gold and silver and provided secure places for storage. Second, they were trustworthy. Recognizing these characteristics, persons of wealth began to leave their precious metal with a goldsmith and to accept a receipt in return. At first, the goldsmith, acting as a warehouse operator, placed this precious metal in sealed boxes. This was equivalent to storing money in a safe deposit box at a modern bank; and, like a modern bank, the goldsmith collected a fee for the service. In time, the goldsmith began accepting "deposits" of gold and silver coins. In the case of a deposit, the goldsmith's receipt guaranteed that he would return to the owner the same number of coins of equal weight as the owner left with him. He was not, however, required to return the identical items. A modern bank follows this principle when it accepts a deposit of $100 and promises to repay $100 on demand. It does not promise to return the same pieces of paper or coins. This change from a warehouse operation to a deposit-type operation may appear trivial. It is important. It is the key to the goldsmith's and the modern bank's ability to create money.

The next step followed naturally the development of the deposit concept. A merchant, wishing to spend money he had deposited previously with a goldsmith, could demand that the goldsmith return the metal to him. However, the person to whom the merchant paid the money would face the problem of storing it safely. In all likelihood, he would want to redeposit it with a goldsmith. Since the business community regarded a goldsmith's signature on a receipt as proof that he would pay money on demand, it became customary to transfer the ownership of the deposit receipt. Of course, the new owner or a subsequent owner of the goldsmith's receipt could demand payment in gold or silver; but in practice other persons depositing precious metal counterbalanced the few who made this demand.

At this point in the development of banking, the goldsmiths were not creating money. They were simply a means by which paper receipts, or promises to pay, circulated in place of coins. A statement of the contents of an imaginary goldsmith's vault and the outstanding promises to pay illustrates the point.

GOLDSMITH A
STATEMENT OF CONDITION

Contents of Vault	Promises to Pay on Demand or Paper Money
£10,000 deposited by Merchant X	£10,000 issued to Merchant X
£10,000 deposited by Merchant Y	£10,000 issued to Merchant Y
£15,000 deposited by Merchant Z	£15,000 issued to Merchant Z
£35,000	£35,000

In the course of normal business activity, merchants X, Y, and Z would transfer to others the promises to pay which they had received from the goldsmith. The persons receiving these promises would, in turn, pay them to still another group. Therefore, the goldsmith's promises, replacing coins which were inconvenient to handle and to store, became media of exchange. Of course, any holder of a goldsmith's promise could have demanded redemption in coin but few people did. Goldsmiths began to create money, or to expand the money supply, as a result of another activity in which they engaged. The goldsmiths owned gold and silver which they used for industrial purposes and, as men of wealth, they received frequent requests for loans. This was a profitable operation; the goldsmiths charged a high rate of interest.

Now let us assume that Goldsmith A is the owner of £20,000 of gold in addition to that which he holds for merchants X, Y, and Z. If one person or several persons borrow this money, we can assume that they will be willing to incur the high interest costs only if they wish to spend the money immediately. The borrowers may insist that they receive the proceeds of the loan in gold, but in this case others probably will deposit the money with a goldsmith as soon as the borrower spends the proceeds of the loan. Or the borrower may be willing to accept the goldsmith's promise to pay gold on demand since this promise circulates as money. In either case, the gold remains in the goldsmith's vault and the circulation of his promises to pay increases. The following statement illustrates this condition.

Let us assume that Goldsmith A receives additional applications

GOLDSMITH A
STATEMENT OF CONDITION
(after lending all the gold which he owns)

Contents of Vault	Promises to Pay on Demand or Paper Money
£35,000 deposited by Merchants X, Y, and Z	£35,000 issued as a result of deposits by Merchants X, Y, and Z
£20,000 owned by Goldsmith A	£20,000 issued as a result of lending operations
£55,000	£55,000

for loans. If he is extremely cautious or perhaps unimaginative, he may reply that he is unable to make more loans because he needs all his gold to honor outstanding promises. However, a more daring goldsmith, or one who is simply greedy, may lend money which he doesn't own. He has noted that persons holding his promises to pay can redeem them at any time but in practice few make demands for payment. Therefore, he reasons, why not make loans equal to another ten, twenty, or thirty thousand pounds and collect more interest? Legally the borrower or other persons who receive the promises to pay may demand that the goldsmith redeem his promises with gold. However, the goldsmith's experience causes him to be confident that the promises to pay will be satisfactory to the public. The statement of condition of Goldsmith A after he has loaned £50,000 in this fashion appears below.

GOLDSMITH A
STATEMENT OF CONDITION

Contents of Vault (Assets)	Net Worth and Liabilities
Gold	**Promises to Pay on Demand or Paper Money**
£ 35,000 deposited by Merchants X, Y, and Z	£ 35,000 issued as a result of deposits by Merchants X, Y, and Z
£ 20,000 original property of Goldsmith A	£ 70,000 issued as a result of lending operations
Securities	**Net Worth**
£ 70,000 promissory notes or other securities pledged by borrowers	£ 20,000
£125,000	£125,000

Since the operations of this fictitious goldsmith are becoming more complex, we must include items like securities and net worth (proprietor's capital) in order to keep the accounts in balance.

Note that the quantity of gold in existence is worth £55,000, but the supply of paper money, the goldsmith's promises to pay, equals £105,000. As a result of the goldsmith's lending operations, he has created £50,000. Expansion of credit or of money may be a better term for the process because, strictly speaking, the goldsmith did not create money where none existed. Instead, he expanded a small, original quantity into a larger amount.

Although the goldsmith does not have sufficient coin to redeem all his outstanding promises to pay, he does have assets in excess of these promises. The £70,000 in promissory notes left with the goldsmith by the borrowers more than balances the excess of the goldsmith's circulating promises over gold in the vault. In effect, the goldsmith monetizes—turns into money—the debt of those persons who borrow from him. He accomplishes this by accepting their promissory notes, payable at some date in the future, and by issuing promises payable on demand. The public treats these promises to pay on demand as money. Not all the holders of paper money can redeem it, but the goldsmith can accommodate any individual who wishes to do so. The system works so long as most people do not demand that the goldsmith honor his promises. On occasion, goldsmiths, like modern banks, through overissue of promises or for some other reason lose the confidence of the public which then demands immediate redemption of the notes. In this case, the system collapses; under normal conditions it works satisfactorily.

At first, the goldsmiths and the early banks which competed with them kept secret the fact that vault cash (reserves) was not equal to the outstanding promises to pay. Later, competition caused the goldsmiths to stop collecting fees and to start paying interest for the money the public left with them. This switch, no doubt, aroused suspicion concerning the disposition of money left with the goldsmiths. It was impossible to fool all of the people all of the time, and the public gradually became aware of the true state of affairs. By that time, however, the practice was recognized as socially beneficial. Today, individuals freely accept a bank's promises to pay with the full knowledge that the bank cannot honor the promises if all creditors demand payment immediately.

MODERN COMMERCIAL BANKS—CREATION OF CREDIT

Commercial banks operate on the same basic principles as the goldsmiths did. Balance sheets or bank statements customarily illustrate the results of the banks' operations. We already have followed this practice for the goldsmiths.

A modern commercial bank is a corporation. As a corporation, it raises capital by selling stock. If we organize a hypothetical bank and issue shares of stock which sell for $50,000, the bank's statement appears as follows:

ABC BANK

Assets		Net Worth and Liabilities	
Cash (reserves)	$50,000	Capital stock	$50,000

Now the bank begins to operate. It does this by announcing that it is open and is ready to receive deposits. Like the goldsmiths, this bank is inviting the public to deposit money which the depositor may reclaim whenever he desires. If the public deposits $20,000 with the bank, the bank statement reads as follows:

Assets		Net Worth and Liabilities	
Cash	$70,000	Capital stock	$50,000
		Deposits	20,000
	$70,000		$70,000

Money has not been created up to this point. Instead, money already in existence in the form of coins or paper currency has been placed in the bank. Since the deposits may be spent by writing checks, these coins and paper bills have been replaced as money by demand deposits.

We can simplify the demonstration of the creation of money by a bank if we make three assumptions. First, we assume that this bank is the only one in existence. Consequently, checks drawn against it will not be deposited in other banks. Second, we assume that there are no cash withdrawals from the deposit account. Third, and last, we ignore interest payments in handling the bank's statement. In a later section, we shall drop the first two of these unrealistic assumptions, but we shall retain the third one to avoid complicated accounting procedures. However, dropping this assumption would not alter the illustrated principles of bank operation.

Despite our dismissal of interest charges from the accounting process that leads to the bank statement, we must recognize that the collection of interest from loans provides the incentive for organizing and operating a bank. The bank accepts deposits only because they enable it to make additional loans. If our hypothetical bank is to prosper, it must lend money. In the process of lending, it creates money.

Like the goldsmiths, this bank can lend money without actually delivering coins or paper currency to the borrower. A loan applicant invariably plans to spend the money he receives by accepting a deposit in return for the promissory note or other evidence of debt which he surrenders to the bank. If the bank makes loans totaling $50,000, its statement is as follows:

Assets		Net Worth and Liabilities	
Cash	$ 70,000	Capital stock	$ 50,000
Loans and discounts	50,000	Deposits	70,000
	$120,000		$120,000

Total deposits of $70,000 represent the $20,000 in coin and paper currency accepted by the bank, plus the $50,000 granted to the debtors to whom the bank extended loans. The owners of these deposits transfer them by writing checks; since no withdrawals take place under assumption two, the total does not change. Checking account money, which is the debt of the bank, replaces another type of money.

The bank now has loaned its entire capital of $50,000; but, like the goldsmith, it can continue to extend credit. This occurs when the bank awards deposits to additional borrowers in return for their promises to pay in the future. If the bank makes additional loans equal to $100,000, its statement is as follows:

Assets		Net Worth and Liabilities	
Cash	$ 70,000	Capital stock	$ 50,000
Loans and discounts	150,000	Deposits	170,000
	$220,000		$220,000

The $170,000 in the checking accounts exceeds the $70,000 originally in existence; therefore, the bank has created money, or we may say that the bank has caused the $70,000 to expand to $170,000.

The process can be viewed as merely an exchange of promises to pay. By signing a promissory note, the borrower promises to pay money to the bank on some future date. In return, he receives a deposit, the bank's promise to pay on demand. Because of its excellent financial reputation, the bank's debts are acceptable as money; the debts of the borrowing public are not. Hence, the bank monetizes the debts of those who borrow from it. If the promissory notes or other debt instruments of the loan applicants were acceptable to the public as money, the bank would have no role to play. It may be more appropriate to say that the general public monetizes the borrowers' debts through its willingness to accept bank debt as money.

It should be apparent that the creation of demand deposits occurs regardless of the type of loans the bank makes. If the bank purchases bonds — that is, loans money to the government — the result is the same. Government bonds replace loans and discounts in the asset column, but this is the only change. In fact, any asset which the bank acquires and pays for with a demand deposit causes these deposits to increase. However, banks generally acquire only financial assets, such as promissory notes, acceptances, and government and corporate bonds.

THE HOMETOWN NATIONAL BANK AND TRUST COMPANY
REPORT OF CONDITION, AUGUST 31, 1965

Assets		Net Worth and Liabilities	
Cash on hand and due from banks	$ 1,675,684.20	Capital stock	$ 300,000.00
U. S. Government bonds	3,688,773.59	Surplus	500,000.00
Other bonds and securities	320,822.38	Undivided profits	194,656.86
Loans and discounts	6,561,048.64	Deposits	11,456,351.22
Banking house, fixtures, and miscellaneous assets	222,299.79	Other liabilities	17,620.52
	$12,468,628.60		$12,468,628.60

Figure 6-1.   Bank Statement

Figure 6–1 shows the statement of condition for a country bank. This statement, which a bank publishes several times a year, assures depositors that the bank is solvent and presents other pertinent information. On the asset side "cash on hand and due from banks" represents vault cash — i.e., currency and coin held by the bank — and deposits which this bank has in the Federal Reserve Bank and in other commercial banks. This item is also known as the bank's reserve, a term which refers to nonearning cash assets that are readily available. The next three items show the type of interest-earning assets which the bank has acquired and, therefore, the type of debt which the bank is monetizing. The biggest item, "loans and discounts," represents short-term credit granted to local firms and to individuals. It is the type of commercial credit in which banks traditionally specialize. Since loans and discounts account for 52½ per cent of the assets, we note that this bank is functioning primarily as a commercial bank, even though "United States Government bonds" and "other bonds and securities" account for 29½ per cent and 2.6 per cent, respectively. On the net worth and liabilities side, the first three items represent funds which the bank's owners have invested in the business either by purchasing stock or by reinvesting earnings. The reader may compare this statement with Table 7–3 to determine the extent to which this bank is typical of all United States banks.

Banks can extinguish money as well as create it. Having noted that the lending operations of a bank lead to the creation of money, one might suspect that the repayment of a bank loan would cause money to disappear. This is, in fact, what occurs. When the repayment date of a loan arrives, the debtor pays the bank by writing a check drawn against his demand deposit. The bank then cancels the promissory note which the debtor previously signed and deducts the amount of the check from his deposit account. The bank statement shows a reduction in the loans and discounts account on the asset side as well as a drop in the deposit accounts. Referring to our first hypothetical bank, we find the following changes when debtors repay $20,000 to the bank:

Assets		Net Worth and Liabilities	
Cash	$ 70,000	Capital stock	$ 50,000
Loans and discounts	~~150,000~~	Deposits	~~170,000~~
	130,000		150,000
	$200,000		$200,000

It is the reduction in deposits which interests us at this time because this indicates that money has disappeared. In this manner, banks create money through their lending operations; they extinguish it by reversing the process and by collecting outstanding loans.

Tracing the history of an imaginary bank loan, we can see the role of this process in the economic system. Retail shoe merchant Jones borrows $10,000 from his bank for the purpose of increasing his inventory. He signs a promissory note and delivers it to the bank, which credits him with a deposit of $10,000. Jones writes checks against this deposit transferring it to wholesale suppliers and shoe manufacturers who, in turn, transfer it by check to their employees and to other suppliers. The $10,000 is still on deposit with the bank; but the bank now owes this amount to a large group of people, not to Jones. Jones, in turn, receives merchandise which he proceeds to sell. By the time the loan matures, we assume that Jones has sold his stock of goods to the public and has received payment by checks. He deposits the checks in the bank and builds up his account to at least $10,000. Jones now repays the bank, losing his $10,000 deposit account in the process.

In this instance, the bank creates money and then extinguishes it. Between creation and extinction, this money, serving as a medium of exchange, allows Jones to trade his retail distribution service for the specialized services of others. In fact, the existence of this money enables each individual in the shoe industry to trade the specialized service he performs on many pairs of shoes for a smaller quantity of the finished product.

This is obviously an oversimplified example: the shoe industry does not exist by selling shoes exclusively to others in the industry. If we expand our example, the picture becomes more complex but the principle remains unchanged. Merchants and manufacturers in many industries borrow money from the bank. Payroll checks and payments for supplies and services transfer the demand deposits thus created to the general public. The public, the purchaser of the products of these industries, transfers the ownership of these deposits back to the merchants and the manufacturers who use them to repay their debts to the bank.

The week-to-week operation of a bank includes loans to many merchants, like Jones, and many repayments of loans. If loans exceed repayments, the resulting net increase in deposits creates money. There is a net reduction of money when repayments exceed loans. Table 2–1 in Chapter 2 shows an increase in demand deposits between the years 1955 and 1965. These were years of economic expansion in the United States. The simple example just presented indicates that expansion of deposits occurs during years of economic growth. If Table 2–1 had covered a period of economic decline, such as 1929 to 1933, it would have revealed a reduction in deposits and in the entire money supply. The quantity of bank-created money is changing constantly as the nation's economy grows and as we move through prosperity-recession cycles. In addition, seasonal patterns exist: deposits increase in the autumn and decline in the late winter and the spring of the year.

The discussion to this point emphasizes the tendency for changes in business conditions and in the level of deposits to occur together. However, this does not prove that a causal relationship exists. That discussion must await a later chapter.

Limits to Deposit Creation

Although we have ignored interest payments in order to simplify our balance sheet examples, we know that these payments exist and provide the bank with an incentive for making loans. Since the bank can lend money by creating deposits, what is to stop it from increasing its profits by expanding indefinitely its loans and deposits? The restraints imposed on the bank by the Government and the bank's fear of cash withdrawals provide the answer.

As noted previously, government regulation of banks is relatively strict when contrasted with other types of business. One of the regulations requires a bank to maintain reserves that are at least equal to a given percentage of its deposits. This is the minimum reserve requirement. Because of this, the size of the reserve[1] limits

[1]The reserve consists of cash and deposits in other banks. We shall examine this reserve in Chapter 7.

the size of the deposits. If the minimum reserve requirement is 20 per cent, a bank may hold up to $5 in deposits for every dollar in reserves, based on the formula

$$D = \frac{R}{r}$$

where D represents the maximum deposits; R, the reserves; and r, the reserve requirement expressed as a decimal of the deposits. Therefore, the bank in our previous illustration with reserves of $50,000 can expand deposits to, but not beyond, $250,000, if the reserve requirement is 20 per cent.

The Federal Reserve System, which draws its authority from the Federal Government, sets the reserve requirements for banks which are members of the System. Regulatory commissions of the individual states set the requirements for the remaining banks, but many state commissions have followed the lead of the Federal Reserve System. Reserve requirements for time deposits are different from those for demand deposits. These requirements also vary according to the type of city in which the bank locates. Country banks, which include banks in small- and medium-sized cities, currently must hold reserves equal to 4 per cent of their time deposits and 12 per cent of their demand deposits. For banks in larger cities, called reserve city and central reserve city banks, the ratios are 4 per cent and 16½ per cent, respectively.

Legal reserve requirements effectively limit deposit creation. However, a prudent banker would limit outstanding deposits to a reasonable multiple of reserves even if these requirements did not exist. He would practice restraint because of the fear of cash withdrawals, an external drain; or because of withdrawals by other banks, an internal drain.

External drain We now can drop the unrealistic assumption that no one withdraws money from a bank. In reality, of course, the public constantly is withdrawing cash from the bank, and the banker cannot be sure that redeposits will balance these withdrawals. The net withdrawal of cash by the public is an external drain (the money leaves the banking system.) A conservative banker would keep a substantial reserve in order to be able to meet these demands without being required to do so by the Government. Since there are minimum legal requirements, bankers must maintain a reserve in excess of this minimum in order to honor demands for withdrawals.

Net withdrawals in normal times do occur, but we must not exaggerate the amount of these withdrawals. The convenience and the safety of a checking account cause most people to prefer to keep their funds in the bank. Net withdrawals may seem large to an individual whose contacts with the monetary system are those of a wage earner and consumer who receives a regular pay check and just as regularly cashes it at the bank. He withdraws a sizable portion of his check or perhaps the entire amount. To this person, cash seems to be flowing from the bank in a one-way stream, and our assumption of no withdrawals appears to be ridiculous. If he traces the path of the cash he takes from the bank, however, he notes that it goes into the cash registers of local department stores, specialty merchants, restaurants, and so forth. These merchants, in turn, deposit the cash in a bank. Thus, there is a steady flow of cash into the bank to balance the withdrawals, and our assumption of no withdrawals for a monopoly bank is reasonably accurate if we change our assumption to no *net* withdrawals. The continued survival of banks is evidence that net withdrawals are small and usually are temporary; otherwise, a bank will expend its reserves quickly and it will be out of business.

For normal times, the assumption of no net withdrawals is reasonably correct; nevertheless abnormal times do occur. At such times, the public decides to make large net withdrawals of cash from the banks. A lack of public confidence in the banks' ability to meet demands for cash or some other cause may prompt these withdrawals. Regardless of the reason, a banker must keep sufficient reserves on hand to meet these demands if they arise.

Even in the absence of abnormal demands for cash, the assumption of no net withdrawals is accurate only if we use a relatively long time period for measurement purposes. In the short run, the bank may find that the public withdraws cash at the end of the week and redeposits it at the beginning of the following week. In addition, there are other seasonal patterns to consider. It follows that banks must limit deposits (liabilities) if they are to handle the expected temporary withdrawals with the available reserves.

Finally, net withdrawals must be anticipated if deposits expand. Even though net withdrawals do not occur so long as deposits do not expand, one must assume that the public will withdraw funds when its deposits increase. The public has accepted the custom of maintaining a certain ratio of currency and coin to demand deposits. The practice of making certain types of payments in currency and other payments by check determines this ratio, currently about 1 to 5. If demand deposits increase and people hold more money in the form of a bank account, they are likely to increase their spending, and some of the increased expenditures will require currency. There is also the likelihood that the individuals with larger checking accounts will desire the convenience derived from the holding of larger amounts of currency. For example, a man who maintains an average balance of $500 in his checking account may hold $50 in cash. If his bank account increases to $600, he probably will withdraw a portion of the extra $100 and will hold it as cash. Therefore, a bank must anticipate net withdrawals of cash whenever deposits expand. The net withdrawals will be less than 100 per cent of the added deposits, but in calculating the limit to which it can expand deposits following an increase in reserves the bank must take these anticipated withdrawals into consideration. The formula used to calculate the new deposits that an increase in reserves makes possible is:

$$\Delta D = \frac{\Delta R}{r + w}$$

where ΔR is the increase in reserves, ΔD is the maximum increase in deposits, r equals the reserve requirement, and w is the anticipated withdrawal of cash as deposits expand. According to this formula, deposits may increase $3.33 for every added dollar of reserves ($\Delta D = \frac{1}{.2 + .1}$, = $3.33), assuming r and w are 20 and 10 per cent, respectively. Nor is this a single-direction operation. If reserves are reduced, the required contraction of deposits is computed by using the same formula.

As noted, a prudent banker maintains reserves in excess of the legal requirements. Consequently, one cannot expect deposits to expand to the maximum limit indicated by this formula. Determining the safe limit to which deposits may expand is an art and not an exact science, but the formula serves as a guide and shows the relationship existing between deposit expansion and the size of bank reserves.

We now can drop the assumption that the single bank we are observing is the only bank in existence. In reality, if it is an American bank, it is competing with approximately 13,750 other commercial banks. An individual bank in this system may have continuous net withdrawals. The bank located in a residential district will have few retail firms making deposits of currency but will have many wage earners cashing checks. Such a bank must expect steady net withdrawals. Withdrawals from this bank and from other banks in a similar position are balanced by net deposits that are received by other banks. The banks sustaining net withdrawals receive many checks drawn on other banks. Note that in our example it is the cashing of pay checks which causes the withdrawals. The banks sustaining net withdrawals are able to replace the cash expended by presenting these checks to the banks which are the drawees.

The banks with net deposits of cash, in turn, must expect that their depositors will write checks which other banks will honor.

These banks, honoring checks drawn against them, must pay cash constantly to the banks experiencing net withdrawals. The cash rarely is sent from one commercial bank to another; the transfer is made through the Federal Reserve System.

Hence, the assumption of no net withdrawals is reasonably accurate if applied to the banking system, even though individual banks in the system experience net withdrawals or net deposits. The comments concerning the effect of the external drain in limiting bank deposit expansion are applicable to the banking system but are not pertinent to the individual bank in the system.

Internal drain. The process of "clearing" checks causes an internal drain of bank reserves. Since there are approximately 13,750 commercial banks in the United States, it is obvious that persons receiving checks drawn against an individual bank frequently deposit them in a different bank. All banks keep funds on deposit in the Federal Reserve bank or in other commercial banks (called correspondent banks) in order to clear these checks. Consequently, the bank receiving a check drawn on another bank can receive payment by forwarding the check to the Federal Reserve bank or the correspondent bank where the amount of the check is credited to the receiving bank's deposit account. The Federal Reserve bank deducts the amount of the check from the deposits it is holding for the drawee bank. Thus, the drawee bank is indirectly paying funds to the bank which has received the check.

A bank normally expects that the checks drawn on other banks that it receives will balance the checks presented to it for payment. On occasion, however, checks received for collection do not equal checks presented for payment and net payments are necessary to the other banks in the system. The bank making the payments obviously loses reserves. This is an internal drain. Or, we may call this an adverse clearing house balance. To the bank which is losing reserves, it is simply a drain. It is "internal" from the point of view of the system; other banks gain the reserves which one bank loses.

While an internal drain is of vital importance to an individual bank, it does not affect the amount of deposits which the banking system can create. The bank losing reserves must reduce its deposits; the bank or banks gaining reserves can increase deposits by the same amount. Dropping the assumption that only one bank exists, therefore, does not affect our conclusion that commercial banks can create deposits to the limit of their reserves. We simply modify our statement to say that the banking system, not the individual bank, creates and extinguishes money.

Diffusion of Bank Reserves

Further examination of the role of the individual bank in the credit-creation process reveals some interesting characteristics in the banking system. Let us look at the credit-creation process from the point of view of an individual banker whose bank has just received $1,000 in additional deposits in the form of cash which the bank has added to reserves. We find that he cannot think in terms of expanding deposits to some multiple of the newly acquired reserve funds.

With the present level of deposits, the checks drawn against this bank and presented to it for payment just balance the checks it received and presented to other banks. The banker must assume that any expansion of deposits will lead to additional checks drawn against his bank. This will disturb the balance of checks paid to checks received unless other banks are expanding deposits at the same rate. Since the banker has no reason to assume that other banks are expanding deposits, he must expect an internal drain whenever his own deposits expand. The occurrence of an internal drain is extremely likely if lending activities increase deposits.

The banker may assume that the $1,000 cash deposit will remain with his bank, but he must keep $200 as a legal reserve if we assume that the minimum reserve requirement is 20 per cent. This leaves the banker with $800 in excess reserves. We shall ignore the external drain in order to simplify the illustration.

Although the banker now has $800 in excess reserves, he cannot create deposits of $4,000 by lending this large amount. He knows that the owners of the additional deposits will write checks against them and that the other banks receiving these checks as deposits will present them for payment. Obviously, this bank cannot put itself in a position where it must pay $4,000 to other banks.

Instead, the banker feels that he can lend an amount equal to his excess reserves—a mere $800. This he does, and the bank statement appears as follows:

BANK A

Assets		*Net Worth and Liabilities*	
Reserves	$1,000	Deposits	$1,000
Loans	800	plus	800
	$1,800		$1,800

Now the person borrowing the money spends it by writing a check which he sends to a business associate who deposits it in Bank B which collects the $800 from Bank A. At the conclusion of the transaction, the bank statements are as follows:

BANK A

Assets		*Net Worth and Liabilities*	
Reserves	$200	Deposits	$1,000
Loans	800		

BANK B

Assets		*Net Worth and Liabilities*	
Reserves	$800	Deposits	$800

Following the same line of reasoning, banker B retains 20 per cent, or $160, as reserves for the $800 in deposits. He lends the remaining $640 to a loan applicant and creates a deposit in the process. The two bank statements now show:

BANK A

Assets		*Net Worth and Liabilities*	
Reserves	$200	Deposits	$1,000
Loans	800		

BANK B

Reserves	$800	Deposits	$ 800
Loans	640	plus	640

The borrower of the $640 from Bank *B* now sends a check for that amount to someone who deposits the money in Bank *C*, adding an additional link to the chain of credit creation. Table 6–1 shows the result if this process continues through all the banks in the system.

This example illustrates the manner in which one bank diffuses its newly acquired reserves throughout the system. It is unlikely, however, that this dispersion of reserves will occur in the precise pattern Table 6–1 indicates. If persons who borrow from Bank *A* pay money to other clients of this bank, the persons receiving checks drawn against the newly created deposits will redeposit them in Bank *A*. This will modify the dispersion of reserves because Bank *A*

Table 6–1

DIFFUSION OF BANK RESERVES

Bank	Reserves	Loans	Deposits
A	$ 200.00	$ 800.00	$1,000.00
B	160.00	640.00	800.00
C	128.00	512.00	640.00
D	102.40	409.60	512.00
E	81.92	327.68	409.60
F			
G			
–			
–			
–			
	$1,000.00	$4,000.00	$5,000.00

will retain some of the reserves which Banks *B, C, D,* and *E* acquired in our illustration. Bank *A* then will be able to make some of the loans listed for the other banks in Table 6–1. This fact explains the establishment of branch-bank offices and other competitive devices to attract depositors. These methods reduce but they cannot eliminate the diffusion of revenue so long as competing banks exist.

The emphasis placed on the dispersion of bank reserves must not divert attention from the more significant fact that the banks, viewed as a system, have new deposits equal to five times their newly acquired reserves. They have created deposits by lending money, $4,000 in this example, to the limit of their reserves.

We have stated that banks lend money in excess of their reserves. An individual banker denies that he lends money which he doesn't have, or that he makes loans of $4 for every $1 which depositors leave with him. On the contrary, he claims that he lends only a fraction, not a multiple, of his reserves. Banker *A* in our example can state that he makes loans of $800 on the basis of his $1,000 reserves, or on four fifths of his reserves rather than four times his reserves. Both claims are correct. The individual bank lends only a portion of its reserves; the banking system lends in excess of its reserves.

Understanding the principle of the diffusion of bank reserves, one gains insight into the individual banker's attitude toward profit. Table 6–1 indicates that the banking system holding $1,000 in reserves can make interest-producing loans of $4,000. Each bank, in turn, has this same ratio of $4 in loans to $1 in reserves. However, a banker receiving $1 in new deposits, which he adds to reserves, denies that he collects interest on $4 in outstanding loans. He claims that he must keep 20 per cent of the extra dollar as reserves so that only four fifths of a new deposit is income-producing. The diffusion principle explains the paradox of each bank's lending only four fifths of every dollar it receives but showing loans equal to four times its reserves.

SUMMARY

A commercial bank is an institution which creates and extinguishes money. It is able to do this because it holds demand deposits which its depositors transfer by check. Although these demand deposits are not legal tender, they generally are acceptable as money.

Modern commercial banking developed from the operations of goldsmiths of seventeenth-century London. The goldsmiths accepted money for safekeeping, and their written promises to repay the money on demand circulated as media of exchange. Since they received few demands for repayment, the goldsmiths began secretly to lend money and to issue promises to pay in excess of their cash reserves. They created credit which circulated as money.

Modern commercial banks openly follow the same practice as the goldsmiths did. Cash reserves are only a fraction of deposits. Banks acquire assets, usually debt instruments, and pay for them by creating deposits. The public accepts these deposits as money and transfers them by check.

The banking system cannot create deposits in unlimited amounts because of the legal requirement that each bank hold reserves equal to at least a stated fraction of its deposits. The expectation of an external drain also limits the banking system's ability to create deposits. The preceding factors plus the anticipation of an internal drain limit an individual bank's activities within the system.

QUESTIONS

1. Explain how a bank can create money by incurring liabilities. What prevents other persons or institutions from adopting this practice?
2. Were the goldsmiths described in this chapter practicing fraud or were they pioneers and innovators? Discuss.
3. A bank increases its reserves by one million dollars. Discuss the factors which limit the expansion of deposits.
4. A bank manager does not distinguish between external and internal drain. Discuss.
5. What factor forces a bank to share its newly acquired reserves with the other banks in the system?

SUGGESTED READINGS

Crosse, Howard D. *Management Policies for Commercial Banks.* Englewood Cliffs, N.J.: Prentice-Hall, Inc., 1962. Chapters I–III.

Prochnow, Herbert V. (ed.). *American Financial Institutions.* New York: Prentice-Hall, Inc., 1951. Chapters 1 and 2.

Richards, R. D. *The Early History of Banking in England.* London: Frank Cass and Company Ltd., 1958.

Robinson, Roland I. (ed.). *Financial Institutions.* 3d ed. Homewood, Illinois: Richard D. Irwin, Inc., 1960. Chapters 3–6.

7

BANK OPERATIONS
AND ECONOMIC ACTIVITY

Previous chapters have noted the important role of the commercial banks in the creation of the nation's money supply, in the transfer of funds, and indirectly in the allocation of resources. Proper operation of the system is necessary if the nation is to achieve economic progress. Hence, the problems of bank operation are not only a concern of the managers of banks but of the entire community.

THE PROBLEMS DEFINED

The bank manager must keep the bank in a profitable, solvent, and liquid condition. All business enterprises face the necessity of achieving these goals; however, the nature of the problem is different for commercial banks as compared with other businesses.

Profitability

A bank must have revenue or gross receipts in order to operate. It must pay salaries and other expenses. Nor is it sufficient simply to break even. A bank must have a net profit so that it can pay its stockholders a return on their investments and thus attract additional capital to the industry.

Solvency

An institution is solvent when its assets are equal to or in excess of its liabilities. Every business and every individual faces the problem of remaining solvent, but banks are different from nonfinancial enterprises in two respects. First, let us explore the cause of insolvency. Nonfinancial enterprises usually become insolvent because of a rise in liabilities. A commercial bank, along with other financial institutions, becomes insolvent because of a decline in the value of its assets. A bank holds financial assets which commit the borrower to pay specific sums of money on a future date. Thus, the debt contract fixes the apparent value of the bank's assets. However, the

101

market value of long-term debt instruments varies with the interest rate and conditions in the money market; for both long- and short-term assets the market value as opposed to the apparent, or face, value depends upon the debtor's ability to pay his obligation.

Consequently, bank assets which are sound may decline in value because of changes in money market conditions including the level of interest rates. In addition, bank assets decline if debtors fail to meet their obligations or if there is an expectation that debtors will be unable to pay. If the decline in the value of a bank's assets is sizable, the bank may become insolvent.

In the second place, bank failures have a more severe effect on the economy of the community than do insolvencies of other businesses. When a bank fails, the receiver freezes deposits pending liquidation of the assets. This curtails the business activity of the community, and there is usually a loss of a portion of the depositor's account.[1] This loss causes inconvenience or even hardship to the firms and the individuals involved. Furthermore, the forced liquidation of the bank's assets may create problems for those persons or business firms who are borrowers. The forced liquidation of notes and other credit instruments on their maturity dates causes distressed debtors to curtail their activities. If the bank was the only one in the area, there is the inconvenience of finding new methods of conducting financial transactions. When bank failures are widespread, the forced sale of assets may affect security and other markets adversely and further depress the economy. These conditions plus the losses suffered by the bank's stockholders cause a loss of business confidence and a further reduction of economic activity.

The special relationship of a bank to its creditors is worthy of note. Creditors of a manufacturing firm or other nonbank institution recognize the risk involved and foresee some inevitable losses. They have become creditors with this risk in mind and are generally in a position to evaluate the credit worthiness of the debtor. By contrast, a bank's creditors (its depositors) think of the bank as a safe repository for their assets, and the majority has neither the training nor the time and the facilities to determine the bank's credit rating. They regard the failure of the bank, therefore, as a breach of faith. Also, many depositors are persons of limited means who will suffer severe hardship from a loss of savings. Given the widespread use of checks as a means of payment, we must regard bank depositors as involuntary creditors. Accordingly, it is appropriate to offer special protection to a bank's creditors.

[1] Accounts in banks insured by the Federal Deposit Insurance Corporation are guaranteed up to $10,000. Losses may be sustained by owners of larger accounts and by depositors in uninsured banks.

Liquidity

As the term applies here, liquidity refers to the ability to meet liabilities as they become due. Maintenance of this condition presents a problem for any type of business. Even though a firm's assets exceed its liabilties, it requires time to turn the assets into cash, and during that time the payment of current liabilities may be difficult.

A bank's liquidity problem is unique. First, there is the nature of its liabilities. Demand deposits are due upon the demand of the depositor. Legally, the bank may require notice from time depositors before withdrawal, but widespread enforcement of this waiting period may cause the loss of public confidence in the bank. Consequently, a bank's liabilities are practically all of the demand type or, at the very least, of the type called current liabilities. In the bank statement shown on page 89, demand liabilities exceed cash assets by the ratio of 6.8 to 1. Hence, the simplest approach to a banker's liquidity problem is to state that he must be ready to pay $6.80 on demand while holding only $1 in cash assets. This contrasts with other types of business which generally show a current liability to a current asset ratio of less than 1.

Illiquidity becomes a reality during a bank "run," a phenomenon once common in the United States. Extra heavy withdrawals of deposits may start for any number of reasons, such as a rumor of insolvency. As news of the withdrawals spreads, depositors flock to the bank. When this happens, the bank may have to suspend operations even though the original rumor may have been false. If bank runs spread throughout the entire system, the attempted rapid liquidation of assets may depress the market prices of these assets to the point at which insolvency, in fact, does occur.

In addition to the condition just described, the bank has a liquidity problem of a different type. A nonbank enterprise with good assets may be short of cash without damage to its reputation as a successful and prosperous business. If the assets genuinely are sound and profit prospects are good, the business expects to be able to borrow from a commercial bank to meet demands for cash. The bank, in order to remain in business and to serve the community, must be ready to advance cash to these other enterprises. Therefore, it does not suffice for a banker merely to keep his bank liquid in a limited sense by meeting demands of depositors for cash. The bank also must be ready to solve the liquidity problems of the business community it serves. In brief, liquidity is what the bank has to sell. It must meet demands for withdrawals plus legitimate requests for new loans.

BANK POLICY

Bank management has followed certain policies in attempting to achieve profits without incurring insolvency or illiquidity. Since these policies have an effect on the nation's economy, they deserve some discussion along with the controls imposed by government to achieve the same end.

Banks have adopted certain generally accepted modern-office management procedures to keep overhead expenses to a minimum. These policies do not concern us particularly in our study of the monetary system. Nor do the charges levied by banks for the maintenance of checking accounts, safe deposit boxes, and other services present a problem to the student of monetary affairs. However, it is important for us to note that banks try to *maximize profits* by acquiring assets with high yields. As a general rule, a high yield is associated with long-term or risky loans and investments. Consequently, the profit motive conflicts with the objectives of safety (solvency) and liquidity.

Banks try to *achieve solvency* by holding only high-grade securities; yet we have noted that long-term, high-grade securities, such as United States Treasury obligations, do fluctuate in price as the market rates of interest change. Cash is obviously a safe asset; however a bank is reluctant to hold excessive quantities of it since the yield is zero. Accordingly, the bank must compromise. Some risk must be accepted in exchange for the prospect of earnings. The banks achieve both safety and earnings by carefully analyzing the credit worthiness of applicants before making a loan and by following generally accepted investment principles such as diversification. Nevertheless, the danger of failure remains. Analysis of risk involves some subjective evaluation and is never foolproof. A bank loan officer may be overly optimistic or he may allow the profit incentive to overcome his good judgment. In fact, a bank that suffers no losses is probably following a loan policy that is so conservative that the bank does not serve the community adequately.

Although it expects losses, a bank remains solvent by establishing reserves against which it offsets bad debts. The capital accounts further protect creditors against loss. As previously noted, capital accounts represent the stockholders' investment in the bank. The creditors' claims against a corporation have priority over the stockholders' claims; hence depositors will not suffer from a decline in the value of a bank's assets pending the exhaustion of the capital accounts. The ratio of deposits to capital accounts to this extent becomes a measure of the degree of solvency. There is no rigid ratio accepted generally as the proper or safe figure. The type of assets must receive consideration as well as the general business conditions. The ratio has varied over time as Table 7–1 indicates. Operating a bank with too low a ratio obviously courts disaster. On the other hand, insistence on too high a ratio restricts the bank's ability to expand deposits and to serve the community. A decline in the ratio generally occurs during periods of business expansion when loans and deposits grow rapidly. In Table 7–1, the period 1941–1945 illustrates this process. An improvement in the ratio usually occurs as a result of the capital accounts growing more rapidly than deposit liabilities. The bank may acquire additional capital by assessing stockholders or by selling more stock. However, most of the increase in the capital accounts is the result of retained earnings. Consequently, improvement in the ratio is likely to take place slowly.

Table 7–1

DEPOSIT TO CAPITAL ACCOUNT RATIOS
INSURED BANKS

Selected years, 1934–1965

Year	Deposits (In billions of $)	Capital Accounts (In billions of $)	Ratio of Deposits to Capital Accounts
1934	35.8	6.2	6.2–1
1937	47.8	6.4	6.4–1
1941	65.6	6.8	9.7–1
1945	147.8	8.7	17.0–1
1947	141.9	9.7	14.6–1
1951	162.9	11.9	13.7–1
1955	190.4	15.0	12.7–1
1959	218.5	19.2	11.4–1
1963	264.7	24.2	10.9–1
1965	272.9	27.7	9.9–1

Sources: Board of Governors of the Federal Reserve System, *Banking and Monetary Statistics* (Washington, 1943), and *Federal Reserve Bulletins.*

A severe liquidity problem will not occur so long as the depositors have confidence in the bank's ability to pay. Accordingly, a bank's first defense against illiquidity consists of measures designed to reassure the public that it is able to pay all demands made against it. In gaining and holding the confidence of the public, individual banks must consider their neighbor's reputation since the public may form an impression of banks as a group and not discriminate between separate institutions.

There are other approaches to the liqudity problem. Maintenance of large cash reserves is an obvious solution if illiquidity is the only problem requiring attention. It is equally obvious that such a policy conflicts with the need for earnings. Even in the absence of legal requirements, prudence requires the retention of some cash reserves. The proper size of reserves depends on economic conditions, the type of deposits, seasonal factors, location of the bank, and the type of depositors. Depositors with small accounts tend to maintain a more stable balance than do holders of large accounts; accordingly, banks frequently request clients with large accounts to notify them in advance of withdrawals. The United States Treasury complies with this request as do many other large depositors.

In the United States, where banks must meet legal minimum reserve requirements, the bank manager is in the odd position where he cannot pay to depositors the reserves, ostensibly held for liquidity reasons, without violating the regulations. Consequently, only the reserves in excess of legal requirements are truly available to him.

Since cash reserves are not the complete answer to the liquidity problem, the bank must use its earning assets as a second line of defense. The banker would like to acquire assets that have high earnings, never depreciate in value, and can be turned into cash at any time. He cannot find such ideal assets; hence he must compromise. Traditionally, banks regard short-term (less than one year) commercial paper as the best available earning asset for a bank. Since the loans which give rise to this paper are for productive purposes, such as manufacturing, selling goods, or harvesting crops, the debts are self-liquidating upon completion of the productive process. From the community's point of view, such a bank policy has the advantage that a corresponding change in production and output accompanies an increase or a decrease in bank deposits. Ideally, therefore, it serves as an automatic device to keep the money supply in balance with the quantity of goods and services on the market. However, strict adherence to such a policy deprives important segments of the community of the right to borrow from banks. The problem of bank profit also arises since competition for the self-liquidating debt lowers the interest rate.

This approach, known as the "real bills" doctrine, never enjoyed wide acceptance in the United States; and, at present, the supply of "real bills" is far from sufficient to support the banking system. Lacking a sufficient supply of short-term, self-liquidating commercial paper, the banker tries to hold assets that are shiftable; that is, readily marketable without undue loss of value. To be shiftable, an asset must be of high quality with a reasonably short time remaining until its maturity. The shiftability approach obviously rests on the assumption that other institutions or persons are always ready to buy.

There are defects in both these approaches. First, there is a limited supply of assets which qualifies for a bank's portfolio under these conditions. We have noted that competition lowers the yield. Accordingly, the need for a compromise with the profit motive arises once more. Second, and more significant, the assumption that some banks are willing to expand credit underlies the concept of a shiftable or a self-liquidating debt. If a single bank or only a few banks are experiencing liquidity problems, this assumption is valid. These banks can sell their assets to other banks and the debtors of the banks with liquidity problems can continue to sell their products to clients of other banks. However, if the liquidity crisis is widespread, buyers for the so-called shiftable assets are unobtainable and the self-liquidating character of commercial paper becomes an illusion.

We have reached the conclusion that an individual bank cannot guard against illiquidity by relying on its own resources. If the liquidity crisis is widespread, commercial banks must have access to another institution which can supply them with cash in exchange for illiquid assets like promissory notes. A central bank performs this function, as we shall see in Chapters 9 and 10. A commercial bank can satisfy its need for liquidity by borrowing from the central bank just as another business achieves liquidity by borrowing from a commercial bank. In summary, the first and best defense against illiquidity is the maintenance of confidence. This is to say, do not let the problem arise. If the problem does arise and becomes widespread, the commercial banks must receive help from another source—the central bank.

PUBLIC POLICY

This section deals with government regulation that is primarily designed to insure bank safety. We shall consider monetary policy, or control of the banking system, later. Since problems of bank failure or suspension involve the public welfare, both the Federal and the state governments have assumed responsibility for the regulation of banks. They have assumed this responsibility despite the nation's commitment to free enterprise and reliance upon competition as a regulating device. We find the explanation for this apparent inconsistency in the record of American banking. The nation justified government interference because bank failures occurred frequently and had adverse effects upon the public welfare. Furthermore, the monetary system traditionally has been a legitimate item for government control in an economy that is otherwise free.

Chartering

A few private, or nonincorporated, banks exist but these are not numerous enough to be significant. Control over the 13,750 incorporated banks begins with the granting of a corporate charter by the Federal or one of the state governments. At one time, only the privileged few received bank charters. There then followed a lengthy period during which the banking authorities granted charters freely. This practice led to the creation of a great many banks and, to the extent that excess banking facilities existed, competition removed the less competent or the unlucky.

In time, we recognized that this weeding out process was too costly in social and economic terms, and we returned to the practice of limiting the number of bank charters granted. At the present time, an applicant for a national bank charter must satisfy the banking authorities that a need for additional banking facilities exists. Requirements for the award of a state bank charter vary among the states but the number of banks granted charters usually is held to a minimum. This prevents "over-banking." It ensures the new bank of a sufficient volume of business to allow for success without endangering existing institutions. Other requirements designed to ensure the safety of a bank include provisions for adequate capital and an investigation of the character and the technical competence of the incorporators.

Regulation of Bank Operations

Control of a bank extends beyond the period of incorporation. The bank must maintain minimum cash reserves. Originally, reserves acted as a defense against illiquidity. This explanation for reserve requirements is not currently valid since the bank cannot pay "required" reserves to depositors. Reserve requirements now serve as a means of controlling the expansion of deposits.

Banks also are subject to control over their asset policy. They may not acquire assets, such as common stocks, whose values fluctuate freely. There are regulations regarding the types of loans they may grant and the investments they may acquire. The regulations restrict loans to bank officers and to other parties where a conflict of interest may arise. Through these regulations, the authorities attempt to insure bank safety by requiring careful credit analysis and diversification of assets.

There are indirect controls also. There is a ceiling on the interest rate banks may pay to depositors. The banks may not pay interest on demand deposits, although they may grant credit against service charges. Banks may pay interest on time deposits within the specified limits set by the regulations. In 1965, the limit for saving deposits was 4 per cent. For time deposits the limits were 4 per cent and 4½ per cent, respectively, for deposits held less than or more than ninety days. These limits eliminate an expensive form of competition within the system and reduce the incentive to acquire high-yield but risky assets. However, when competing with other financial institutions such as savings and loan associations, this regulation places commercial banks at a disadvantage.

Finally, there is a legal maximum to the interest rates which a bank or other lending agency may charge. These usury laws, or price ceilings, exist to protect the debtor from excessive costs and not to ensure the safety or liquidity of the bank or other lending agency. Their existence, like that of other government controls, implies a lack of confidence in the power of competition. These usury laws stem from ancient attitudes toward lending and lenders and are not unique to the American banking system.

Bank Examinations

In order to protect the public interest, the banking authorities examine banks periodically to insure that they are obeying the law. Agents of the Comptroller of the Currency, a Treasury official, examine national banks; state bank authorities examine state institutions. In addition, the Federal Reserve System examines state banks that are members of the System, and the Federal Deposit Insurance Corporation examines the nonmember state banks that it insures.

Bank examiners may attract attention by discovering fraud or embezzlement, but this is not the main purpose of their investigations. They wish to learn whether a bank is operating in a fashion that is consistent with the public interest. This involves the verification of the existence of assets and, more difficult, an appraisal of their value.

A bank must write off losses in asset value if the bank statement is to present an accurate picture. However, it is impossible to determine precisely the value of certain types of assets. Banks' assets are debt instruments. It is easy to ascertain the face value of these assets since it is the amount the debtor must pay at maturity. However, some debtors may be unable to pay their obligations on the due date. Accordingly, bank examiners reduce the present value of assets of questionable quality to allow for expected losses. For this reason appraising bank assets involves an evaluation of the credit worthiness of the bank's clients. The examiners check the diversity in assets and may explore the possibility that the bank has shown favoritism to officers and stockholders. The examiners may suggest that the bank increase certain types of loans or discontinue others which seem to be of poor quality. These suggestions can be of value to the bank manager because of the experience and the training of the examiners.

For many years critics of the system charged that bank examination policies aggravated business fluctuations. The examiners appraised assets at cost or the current market value, whichever was lower. Consequently, a fall in the market value of securities caused banks holding them to experience "book" losses even though the securities were sound. This rule applied even to government obligations. Furthermore, bank examiners tended to accept a bank's appraisal of its assets during periods of prosperity but insisted that the bank "write down," or depreciate, some items during periods of depression. The resultant paper losses decreased bank capital and tended to cause banks to contract deposits. This practice accentuated a depression. Presently bank examiners eliminate this apparent but unreal loss by valuing high-quality bonds at the price the bank paid for them. A few economists have suggested that bank examinations should serve as a stabilizing device. If this occurred, lax and severe examinations would alternate during recessions and prosperity. Such a system, however, might threaten the usefulness of examinations as a means of ensuring bank solvency and would not have an appreciable effect on the business cycle. The Government has a more direct approach to banking solvency: the creation of institutions such as the Federal Deposit Insurance Corporation.

Federal Deposit Insurance Corporation

Insurance as a means of eliminating many ill effects of bank failures is an old idea. In the United States the State of New York attempted to apply this principle as early as 1829 with a system to protect holders of bank notes. Several states developed methods of insuring bank deposits in the early years of the twentieth century; but these systems, like the New York Safety Fund, failed in periods of crises when bank failures became numerous. State governments could require only state banks to participate in their deposit insurance plans and since these banks tended to be the smaller and the weaker institutions, deposit insurance was impractical. An additional problem was a lack of diversity in assets when the state was dominated by a single industry, such as agriculture. Because of its record of failure, many bankers and legislators opposed deposit insurance. Furthermore, some critics felt that deposit insurance relieved bank management of close depositor scrutiny and in this way encouraged unsound practices. However, by 1933 bank failures had become so numerous and losses to depositors had become so serious that the opposition to deposit insurance was overcome. The Federal Government organized a temporary system in that year and replaced it with the permanent Federal Deposit Insurance Corporation (FDIC) in 1934.

Participation in the system is compulsory for all banks that are members of the Federal Reserve System; other banks may join if they qualify. The compulsory feature forces the large, strong banks to join and avoids the danger of insuring only poor risks. In 1965, 13,487 banks, or 98 per cent, of the total number of banks were members. Members of the FDIC held $291 billion, or 99½ per cent, of the nation's total bank deposits. Banks that are members of the System pay a premium equal to $\frac{1}{12}$ of 1 per cent of all deposits.[2] In return, the FDIC guarantees every deposit account up to $10,000.

When a bank fails the FDIC may use one of four methods to honor its guarantee. In each method the FDIC emphasizes quick settlement in order to reduce the depositors' inconvenience and to keep to a minimum the period of uncertainty. The FDIC may liquidate the bank. It pays the first $10,000 of every account in full. Those portions of deposit accounts that exceed $10,000 receive payment to the extent that assets permit. This method has several disadvantages. It leaves the community without banking services if the closed bank is the only one in the area. The large depositors sustain a loss, and the FDIC becomes involved in lengthy and perhaps costly liquidation proceedings.

In the second method, the FDIC sponsors a merger of the suspended institution with a sound bank. The remaining institution assumes the deposit liabilities and the assets of its suspended neighbor after the FDIC purchases the questionable assets. Purchase of the questionable assets allows the sound bank to acquire assets equal to the liabilities it assumes. After the merger, depositors may withdraw their accounts or maintain them in the sound bank. When the FDIC uses this method, neither large nor small depositors suffer a loss. Furthermore, the merged bank continues to offer banking services to the community. For the FDIC the loss sustained by purchasing the questionable assets of the closed bank may be smaller than the cost involved in liquidating the institution.

In the absence of a neighboring bank which is willing to merge, the FDIC may persuade the community to purchase shares of stock in a new bank which then assumes the assets and the insured deposit

---

[2]The FDIC reserve fund is now large enough to permit annual rebates of a large portion of this premium thus reducing the cost of insurance. The rebate takes the form of a credit toward the next year's payment. In recent years, this credit has been equal to approximately 60 per cent of the current year's premium. Therefore, the premium cost to the insured banks has been equal to $\frac{1}{30}$ of 1 per cent of the deposits.

liabilities of the suspended institution. The results are the same as in the merger method.

The FDIC may use a fourth method if the community does not subscribe to shares in the newly organized bank. The FDIC then administers the bank and limits its operation to a deposit business. It cannot make loans and may invest only in securities issued or guaranteed by the Federal Government. This type of bank must conclude its operations not later than two years after its organization. This method, therefore, does not provide banking services for the community. In recent years the FDIC has favored the second method: merger with a sound bank in the area.

The FDIC does more than simply alleviate the effects of bank failures. Its examiners visit member banks to insure compliance with the regulations. This examination and the advice of the examiners can be of great value to small banks. By refusing to guarantee more than $10,000 in a single account, the FDIC provides large depositors with an incentive to insist on sound banking practices. The FDIC and its supporters, therefore, claim that its inspection policy and its advice to bankers have prevented many bank failures. In addition, deposit insurance drastically reduces, if it does not eliminate, the danger of bank runs and the consequent forced liquidation of assets.

Table 7–2 shows the record of the FDIC. These data may be compared with those for the period 1920 to 1933 when 14,590 banks with deposits of $8½ billion failed.

Table 7–2

FAILURE OF INSURED BANKS

1934–1964

Period	Number of Banks Failing	Deposits (In thousands of $)
1934–1935	34	15,287
1936–1940	321	420,742
1941–1945	43	69,039
1946–1950	17	29,049
1951–1955	14	37,791
1956–1960	11	30,257
1961–1964	12	32,018
Total	452	634,183

Source: *Annual Report of the Federal Deposit Insurance Corporation for the Year Ended December 31, 1964.*

The deposit insurance system has not been free of criticism. Banks whose depositors have large accounts, usually the larger banks, object to paying premiums based on total deposits when the FDIC does not guarantee amounts in excess of $10,000. The FDIC claims that these more richly endowed depositors are in a position to judge a bank's quality. Since the insurance does not cover the full amount of these deposits, their owners must scrutinize bank operations closely. Hence, large depositors serve as informal "examiners." Strong, well-established banks object to paying the same rate as their weaker colleagues. To some extent the FDIC does charge the larger banks in order to protect depositors in smaller institutions. The size of the banks which have failed substantiates this claim. From 1934 to 1964, inclusive, the 452 banks which failed held average deposits of $1⅓ million.

The size of the FDIC reserves and indirectly the amount of premiums collected are open to question. On the one hand, the revenue seems excessively large: in thirty years of existence, disbursements to depositors of insolvent banks equal $30.5 million, or 1.2 per cent of the reserves. On the other hand, the reserves are equal to only 1.84 per cent of insured deposits, which seems small when considered in the light of pre-1933 history. A fair evaluation requires that we consider the changed asset structure of banks and their resistance to failure. For this change the FDIC has been responsible, at least in part. However, discussion of insurance reserves does raise a basic question: Is the risk of a bank sufficiently predictable for the insurance principle to be applicable?

BANK POLICY AND ECONOMIC WELFARE

We have completed our examination of the factors which influence bank operating policy. There is no set formula for acquiring assets which applies to all banks and to every time period. The banker must re-evaluate his position constantly and make necessary changes. How does the policy which results affect the public welfare? Previously, we noted that banks promote the general welfare by providing the nation with a medium of exchange. However, banks produce another effect on the public welfare through their lending policies. The firms, and in fact the entire industries, to which the banks extend credit, use this money to acquire resources. Consequently, these firms and industries are able to grow and to offer their products to the public. Firms and industries that are unable to secure bank credit are less able to acquire the factors of production. These latter industries can expand if they acquire capital from other sources, but they do not have access to bank credit which constitutes a large share of the money market.

The banks' lending policy, therefore, influences the allocation of resources and hence the pattern of economic activity. Industries

Table 7–3

ASSETS, LIABILITIES, AND CAPITAL ACCOUNTS
FOR ALL COMMERCIAL BANKS

June 30, 1964

ASSETS	Billions of Dollars		Per Cent of Total Assets	
Cash assets:				
Vault cash	4.5		1.40	
Deposits with F. R. banks	16.8		5.22	
Deposits with other domestic commercial banks	12.7		3.95	
Cash items in process of collection	19.2		5.96	
Total cash assets		53.2		16.53
Loans:				
Commercial and industrial	55.1		17.12	
Agricultural	7.7		2.39	
For purchasing or carrying securities	8.2		2.14	
To financial institutions	13.3		4.13	
Real estate	41.4		12.86	
Other (individuals)	37.6		11.68	
Other	4.4		1.37	
Total loans, net		164.5[a]		51.10[a]
Investments:				
U.S. securities	59.3		18.42	
State and local securities	31.4		9.75	
Other securities	5.0		1.55	
Total investments		95.7		29.73
Other assets: Bank premises, etc.		8.5		2.64
Total assets		321.9		100.00

Table 7-3 (continued)

LIABILITIES AND CAPITAL ACCOUNTS

	Billions of Dollars	Per Cent of Total Liabilities and Capital Accounts
Deposits:		
Demand	164.6	51.13
Time	120.3	37.37
	284.9	88.50
Other liabilities	10.2	3.17
Total liabilities	295.1	91.67
Capital accounts	26.8	8.33
Total liabilities and capital accounts	321.9	100.00

ªIndividual loan items are gross items and do not add to the net total from which valuation reserves have been deducted.

Source: *Federal Reserve Bulletin,* March, 1965, pp. 444, 448, and 449.

which bankers feel are bad risks receive fewer resources than the industries which enjoy the bankers' favor. We have seen that the profit motive combined with the need to remain solvent and liquid and not the desire to allocate resources forms the basis for the bankers' decisions. Nevertheless, these policy decisions influence the allocation of resources. Under ideal conditions, decisions based on the credit worthiness of the loan applicant should lead to the optimum allocation of resources. These ideal conditions may not prevail, however, and this has caused the Government to attempt to reallocate credit by organizing financial institutions which we shall examine in Chapter 20. These institutions are designed to channel funds to business activities which the nation has decided promote social welfare but which do not meet the bankers' loan criteria. Agriculture and residential real estate are probably the best present examples.

In Table 7-3 the statement for all commercial banks shows the major classes of bank borrowers and, therefore, suggests the channels into which bank policy allocates resources. Loans comprise 63 per cent of the total loan and investment accounts. In a general sense, loans represent short-term credit which banks furnish to their customers upon request. Investments represent credit which banks extend through the purchase of securities on the money market. Credit extended through the purchase of securities may be for a long or a short period of time. In the case of loans, the debtor takes the initiative. Banks take the initiative in acquiring securities. A high loan-to-investment ratio suggests that the banks are serving their local customers. The persons to whom the banks extend loans usually use the funds as working capital; hence there is a resource allocation implication.

The largest account in the loan category is "commercial and industrial." Table 7-4 presents the subcategories of this account for banks in large cities. Real estate loans and loans to individuals (purpose unspecified) are also large while agriculture and finance are relatively small.

Table 7-4

COMMERCIAL AND INDUSTRIAL LOANS
OF WEEKLY REPORTING MEMBER BANKS[a]

February 24, 1965
(In millions of dollars)

Type of Industry:		
Durable goods, manufacturing:		
Primary metals	661	
Machinery	2,371	
Transportation equipment	1,015	
Other fabricated metal products	1,017	
Other durable goods	1,200	6,264
Nondurable goods, manufacturing:		
Food, liquor, and tobacco	1,804	
Textiles, apparel, and leather	1,370	
Petroleum refining	1,170	
Chemicals and rubber	1,473	
Other nondurable goods	921	6,738
Mining, including petroleum and natural gas		3,284
Trade		6,522
Transportation		4,597
Construction		2,278
Other		6,479
		36,162

[a]Includes approximately 200 banks. These banks hold about 60 per cent of the loans held by all commercial banks.
Source: *Federal Reserve Bulletin*, March, 1965, p. 453.

United States securities and securities of state and local governments account for 95 per cent of the investment category. To summarize, therefore, we may say that the credit created by commercial banks enables commercial and industrial firms, real estate owners, other individuals, and the several levels of government to secure the use of the factors of production.

Commercial banks play a significant role in the allocation of resources, but we must not overemphasize their importance. The existence of other financial institutions permits a firm or an industry to secure funds for expansion even though commercial banks have refused its application for credit. Some students of finance claim that the relative importance of commercial banks in the money market is declining. If these persons are correct, the relative importance of banks in determining the allocation of the nation's resources is declining also.

SUMMARY

Banks play an important role in the economic system. Hence, the public as well as bank managers have an interest in their operations. The attempt to make a profit while keeping the bank in a solvent and a liquid condition serves as a guide to operating policy. Banks, like other businesses, must make a profit; however, banks' problems with regard to solvency and liquidity are not the same as those of nonbank institutions. If a bank becomes insolvent, the community usually suffers to a greater extent than occurs when other businesses become bankrupt. A bank's solvency, in turn, depends upon the continued solvency of the business community it serves. A bank has a unique liquidity problem because its liabilities payable on demand are several times the size of its cash assets. Also, a bank must stand ready to provide liquidity for the rest of the community.

Assets with high yields tend to be less liquid and more risky than assets with low yields. Consequently, the banker must follow an asset policy which is a compromise. The types of assets banks acquire depend on the judgment of bank managers and upon government regulations. Traditionally, banks favor short-term, marketable debt instruments as a defense against illiquidity. However, not all banks can "market" their assets at the same time. Accordingly, maintenance of liquidity requires the services of a central bank as well as the confidence of the public. Diversity and careful analysis of credit applications prevent bank insolvency.

The Federal Deposit Insurance Corporation guarantees deposits in insured banks up to $10,000 per account. This alleviates the hardships caused by bank failures. The FDIC helps to prevent bank failures by examining and advising insured banks.

Bank lending policies have an influence on the economic well-being of the community. The industries which have good credit ratings with banks receive loans and thus acquire resources for expansion and for productive activities. Consequently, resource allocation within the nation depends, in part at least, upon the policy decisions of bankers.

QUESTIONS

1. Are we correct if we describe the owner of a bank deposit as an involuntary creditor?
2. What is the significance of the statement, "Liquidity is the stock in trade of a bank"?
3. Can a bank be liquid and insolvent at the same time? Is the reverse condition possible? Discuss.
4. Should the Federal Deposit Insurance Corporation guarantee all the deposits of insured banks rather than the first $10,000 of each account?
5. Can a bank be certain of its liquid position in the absence of outside assistance?

SUGGESTED READINGS

Crosse, Howard D. *Management Policies for Commercial Banks*. Englewood Cliffs, N. J.: Prentice-Hall, Inc., 1962. Chapters IV–XII.

Crutchfield, James A., Henning, Charles N., and Pigott, William. *Money, Financial Institutions, and the Economy*. Englewood Cliffs, N. J.: Prentice-Hall, Inc., 1965. Chapter 3.

Federal Deposit Insurance Corporation. *Annual Reports*.

Reed, Edward W. *Commercial Bank Management*. New York: Harper & Row, Publishers, 1963.

Robinson, Roland I. *The Management of Bank Funds*. 1st ed. New York: McGraw-Hill Book Company, Inc., 1951.

Ritter, Lawrence S. (ed.). *Money and Economic Activity: Readings in Money and Banking*. 2d ed. Boston: Houghton Mifflin Company, 1961. Chapter 3.

8

UNITED STATES BANKING
PRIOR TO 1914

The history of banking in the United States will help us to understand our present banking system and to evaluate the current problems and suggested solutions. Furthermore, it will help us to realize that certain illogical or irrational features of our present system are the result of historical practices that were rational in their day. Present practices, therefore, will be understood although not necessarily justified. Finally, banking history is interesting in its own right.

EARLY BANKS

We have noted the shortage of currency in the American colonies and the attempts of the colonial assemblies to overcome the problem by issuing bills of exchange. Although Parliament prohibited legal-tender issues after 1764, it was still possible for privately owned banks to issue notes. These were not banks in the present sense of the word, for merchants in the normal course of their trading operations performed the deposit and the discount functions. To persons living in this period, a bank was simply a device for issuing paper money; it retained this reputation into the nineteenth century.

Colonial banks were frequently land banks which real estate landowners organized. These landowners mortgaged their land to these associations and received bank notes in exchange. These bank notes, promissory notes issued by the land banks, circulated as money. Hence, a land bank was a device designed to overcome the currency shortage by monetizing land. The colonists regarded land as the most permanent of assets and selected it for monetization. However, they did not neglect other assets completely. In 1733 Massachusetts organized a bank with power to monetize assets other than land. This "bank" was, in effect, a pawnshop which issued promissory notes redeemable in silver.

The usefulness of these bank schemes varied among the colonies. The record was good where moderation prevailed in the issuing of notes and rigid redemption policies existed. When the issues were larger than trade demanded, bank notes depreciated and the whole system acquired a bad reputation.

These banks and monetary policy in general played a role in the political events leading to the Revolution. As we have seen, the British Government, following an anti-inflationary policy, closed the colonial mints and prohibited the issuing of legal-tender notes by the several governing bodies. On the other hand, the American colonists favored paper money and other policies which tended to be inflationary. Each side had logical arguments to support its position. The British creditors objected to the depreciation of their claims against American debtors. To the extent that inflation encouraged American trade rather than agriculture, it conflicted with mercantilist philosophy. The Americans felt that imports would increase as paper currency replaced coins, and they argued that an adequate supply of money facilitated trade and led to a more rapid rate of economic growth.

The first bank, in the modern sense of the word, was the Bank of North America, chartered by the Congress of the United States in 1781 and located in Philadelphia. This bank, granted a Pennsylvania charter at a later date, is still in existence.[1] While the profit motive undoubtedly was present, the promoters of this bank presented it to the Congress as a device to assist the Government in financing the Revolutionary War. The acquisition of its original capital depended upon the receipt of specie from the French Government, which the Congress paid into the Bank, and on public subscriptions. The American banking system, therefore, was involved in politics from the date of its origin, and the favor of persons controlling the Government was vital to a bank's prosperity and even to its continued existence.

The Bank of North America facilitated the transfer of funds by issuing drafts. It loaned money to business and to the Government and issued bank notes which were redeemable in specie on demand. The Bank accepted deposits but its operation depended on bank notes rather than on deposit accounts. The issuance of notes rather than the acceptance of deposits continued to be the dominant item in the United States banking industry until the 1850's. Although the Bank of North America did not begin operating until the late stages of the Revolutionary War, it did assist the Congress in the prosecution of its war objectives. Through its financial operations, the Bank

[1] The First Pennsylvania Banking and Trust Company is the result of mergers which included the Bank of North America.

influenced the allocation of resources in the direction the Government desired. The Bank's success encouraged other states to organize banks; New York and Massachusetts both had chartered banks by 1785.

The system of state banks which developed had several defects when viewed by a modern observer. There was no fiscal agent of the central or national government; that is, no single bank was the logical depository for government funds. No single bank could act as creditor to the government or agent to assist the government in its borrowing from other sources. Since state banks did not have branches in other states, there was some difficulty in transferring funds to distant points. Too, there was no uniform standard for bank operations. The lack of uniformity was particularly dangerous with respect to bank notes. When state banks competed with each other, no single bank was responsible for the total notes issued. Hence, there was the danger of overissue and subsequent depreciation. In summary, there was no institution which performed the functions of a central bank. To a limited degree the Bank of North America performed these services. However, when it became a state bank it could no longer assume such responsibilities.

THE FIRST BANK OF THE UNITED STATES

Following the adoption of the Constitution, Alexander Hamilton in his role of Secretary of the Treasury proposed that the Federal Government charter a national bank. As used by Hamilton, the term national bank referred to an institution that received its charter from the Federal Government. Its operations were to be nationwide, and it was to have close relations with the Treasury Department. Hamilton argued that a national bank would help the Government to borrow money, facilitate the collection of revenue and the payment of funds by the Government, increase the nation's supply of productive capital, and aid trade. Although a modern monetary theorist would question some of these arguments, Congress accepted Hamilton's proposal over the opposition of Jefferson, who claimed such action was unconstitutional and represented a dangerous expansion of federal power.

The Bank received a twenty-year charter (1791–1811) (It was common practice at the time to limit the lifespan of corporations.) Congress set the capital at $10 million, of which the Federal Government subscribed one fifth and private investors provided the remainder. The stockholders chose the directors under a system of regressive voting; that is, the number of votes did not increase proportionately to the shares of stock owned. Foreigners could own

1st Bank of U.S. 1791–1811

Gov $2m   Priv $8m

stock but could not vote their shares by proxy. The Bank could issue notes, but its liabilities excluding deposits could not exceed its capital.

The Bank located its home office in Philadelphia and established branches in important cities throughout the nation. Apparently, it was well-managed. It transferred funds throughout the country by drafts drawn against its branches. It acted as fiscal agent of the Government, assisted the Treasury in managing the debt, and served as creditor to the Federal Government. In addition, it operated as a commercial bank, discounting paper and issuing bank notes in competition with state banks. In this latter capacity, it contributed to the stability of the entire banking system by setting standards and by restricting the number of notes issued. The Bank accomplished this function by accepting state bank notes in payment and promptly presenting them for redemption. A state bank's ability to issue notes, therefore, was restricted to a relatively small multiple of its reserves. The note-issuing ability of the First United States Bank, in turn, was limited by its charter. In summary, the First Bank of the United States served as a central bank. It was primitive by modern standards but adequate for its day. Despite its usefulness, it was not rechartered in 1811.

There were several reasons for its failure to win political favor:
1. The Federalists had created the Bank and men of that Party controlled it. Furthermore, there were charges of favoritism toward Federalists and of discrimination against Anti-Federalists in its lending policies. In 1811 the Federalists no longer controlled Congress.
2. Foreigners, notably Englishmen, had purchased bank stock. Therefore, the Bank's enemies charged that foreigners controlled the banking system. This was inaccurate since foreign stockholders could not vote by proxy. However, they did receive dividends, which the Bank's foes labeled "tribute."
3. The Anti-Federalists, basing their argument on the absence of specific provisions for bank charters in the Constitution, claimed the Bank was unconstitutional. The Constitution granted to Congress the exclusive right to coin money and to regulate its value, but there was some question whether this power applied to paper currency. Since the Bank issued paper currency and influenced the value of notes issued by state banks, the Federal Government indirectly regulated the value of the currency. To its opponents, the Bank represented a dangerous expansion of the power of the Federal Government.
4. A sizable portion of the population disapproved of paper

money whether issued by the Government or by banks and so opposed renewal of the charter. This was the "hard-money" faction.

5. The state banks and their advocates resented the restrictions on state bank note issues.

Despite this formidable array of opposition, the bank's recharter bill was defeated only after a 17 to 17 tie vote in the Senate was broken by the vote of Vice-President Clinton. Further discussion of the political implications will be postponed until the Second Bank of the United States is examined.

STATE BANKS, 1811–1816

With the demise of the Bank of the United States, state banks were able to expand note issues and new banks were formed for this purpose. Statistics of the period are not precise, but it appears that the note issue expanded from $45 million in 1812 to over $100 million by 1817. During the same period, the number of state banks increased from 88 to 246. The abuses and defects of a state bank system, examined in later pages, were all present during these years. By 1816 the notes of many banks were worthless and few were redeemable in specie. Also, the lack of a central bank and the consequent disorder of the monetary system intensified the problem of financing the War of 1812.

Reasons for the poor record of state banks included a shortage of specie, poor understanding of the principles of commercial banking, and a shortage of capital. The nation's supply of specie was sufficient to support a banking system, but the banks in the larger cities held most of it. Nevertheless, the newer communities insisted on having banks. These communities were short of real capital and the existence of a bank which issued bank notes appeared to be a method of creating capital without the inconvenience of saving. Many banks granted long-term loans and issued bank notes based on nonliquid assets. If noteholders presented the notes for redemption before the loans matured, the bank had to suspend payment. A conservative attitude on the part of the political and business leaders would have prevented this overexpansion. However, the leaders and the population of the frontier areas were not conservative. Instead, they tended to have unbounded faith in the future growth of their communities and the consequent profitability of investment schemes. Conditions improved as communities matured, but the problems reappeared in new areas as the border moved westward.

By 1816 a majority of the members of Congress realized that it was necessary to take some measures to restore order to the banking and currency system. Since Congress did not feel it had the power to regulate state banks, the only alternative was to establish a federal bank which would dominate the banking system.

1816-1836
Gov't.   Priv
$ 7m $28 m

THE SECOND BANK OF THE UNITED STATES

The Second Bank of the United States was given a twenty-year charter in 1816 by the Federal Government. Its capital was set at $35 million, of which one fifth was subscribed by the United States Government. The remaining $28 million was furnished by private persons, corporations, companies, and states; but no one unit was allowed to subscribe more than $300,000. The Government's subscription could be made in bonds. Private subscriptions had to be paid in at least 25 per cent specie and the remainder in Federal Government bonds. Of the twenty-five directors, one fifth were appointed by the President of the United States. The remainder were elected by the stockholders, using the system of regressive voting developed by the First Bank. Again, following the pattern of the First Bank, foreigners could not vote by proxy. The Bank acted as the fiscal agent of the Government and as a commercial bank. Note issues were redeemable in specie and were limited to the size of the bank's capital. A bonus of $1.5 million was paid by the bank to the Government.

In brief, the Second Bank of the United States was owned jointly by the Federal Government and private stockholders. Control of the bank was divided between these two groups, and precautions were taken to prevent domination by a few wealthy stockholders. Possession of the charter was considered a valuable asset as was shown by the willingness of the Bank to pay $1.5 million for the privilege of banking.

The Bank functioned as a commercial bank, making loans and accepting deposits from both governmental units and private persons. It dealt in foreign exchange, transferred funds, and issued bank notes. The Bank's significance in the development of the United States monetary system lies in its assumption of what we now consider central bank responsibilities. It served as fiscal agent of the Federal Government. It issued notes which, unlike state bank notes, circulated throughout the country, for they were redeemable at any of its twenty-five branch banks. These branches, accomplishing an objective now covered by the check-clearing system, facilitated the transfer of funds throughout the country. Most important, the Bank stabilized the monetary system — or more accurately the bank notes which accounted for a large portion of the system — by the same technique employed by the First Bank of the United States. When it received state bank notes in payment, the Second Bank could put them back into circulation or it could present them to the issuing bank for redemption in specie. If the United States Bank was expanding its loans, it paid the notes to the borrowers. On the other hand, if it was contracting loans, receipts of bank notes from current debtors exceeded the notes paid to new borrowers and the Bank redeemed the excess state bank notes. Thus, by contracting or expanding its own credit, the United States Bank increased or decreased the state banks' ability to issue notes and so controlled or at least greatly influenced the money supply.

We should note that any bank, state or otherwise, could have adopted the same practice. However, only the Second United States Bank was large enough to influence the monetary system of the entire nation. In the last half of its existence, there is evidence that the Second Bank recognized its power and also its responsibility to control money. It did not expand or contract credit on the basis of the profit motive alone but rather with a view to the condition of the national economy. In this respect, it acted like a modern central bank. In the process, it also gained the enmity of the state banks.

The question of whether or not to recharter the Bank became a major political issue by 1830. The re-election of its opponent, President Andrew Jackson, in 1832 was decisive; the Bank's charter expired in 1836. The Bank continued to exist for a few years under a Pennsylvania charter and then ceased operations. Thus, the first American experience with a central bank ended. The experience had been so painful and the political controversy so acrimonious that the Federal Government abstained from any formal attempt to regulate the banking system until 1863 and did not authorize a central bank until 1914.

Was the decision to eliminate the Bank a wise one? The evidence is difficult to evaluate since the debate that raged for many years was highly partisan. In fact, even some current writers become emotionally involved when treating this subject.

Some of the arguments against the Bank may be dismissed quickly. It was mismanaged in its early years, but this defect was corrected rather quickly and this alone cannot be used to explain the opposition to a central bank in general. The political activities of the Bank and particularly of its President, Nicholas Biddle, were criticized. Because of its position and responsibilities, the Bank could not avoid politics completely; however it is difficult to justify the partisan nature of its activities. Certainly the battle with President Jackson was a tactical error when examined after the fact.

There were more fundamental issues, however.

*Easy money.*Those persons who desired easy money and few restrictions on note issues opposed the Bank. These people were politically dominant in the West and in the South, the agricultural and relatively undeveloped areas of the nation. Bank notes represented a means of increasing capital resources to these people. They regarded tight money and restrictions on note issues as devices which favored the vested interests and the capital-rich sections. To the extent that easy money favors debtors and redistributes wealth, this group must receive credit for logically pursuing its self-interest.

Hard currency. Some of the population distrusted all paper money whether banks or the Government issued it. This hard-money group logically should have opposed state banks more vigorously than the United States Bank; but, in fact, its political force was arrayed against the Second Bank. The Bank was the unhappy target of both the easy-money and the hard-currency groups. The alliance of these two groups with opposing viewpoints was not so illogical as it may appear. The Second Bank stood for sound paper currency—a position midway between easy money and hard currency.

Constitutionality. Many opponents claimed the Bank was unconstitutional. Jefferson had opposed the First Bank on this premise, and President Jackson had cited it as his reason for vetoing a recharter bill. This question was part of a broader issue: Should the Federal Government or the states regulate banks? Since many of the states had indicated that they were unable or were unwilling to regulate banks effectively, this was not simply a question of abstract political theory but a question of whether banks should be regulated by any level of government.

State banks. State banks objected to the monopoly the United States Bank possessed with respect to holding government deposits. Many state banks also objected to the restrictions placed on their note issue by the United States Bank's redemption policy.

Concentration of financial power. The Bank was a financial giant which aroused the opposition of those who saw danger in the concentration of financial and economic power.

We have treated the issues raised by the Bank's opponents at some length because a number of the arguments continued to influence our monetary and financial decisions for many years. A fear of bigness and especially of monopolistic power has been a dominant theme. The sectional differences seen in the Bank controversy also have affected our policies. For many years, the Western and the Southern sections feared financial domination and exploitation by the financial powers of the Northeast. Finally, the hard- versus easy-money dispute continues to the present day. Coupled with the preceding fears is a distrust of human judgment as the means of regulating the monetary system. Consequently, we tend to seek solutions of a "structural" type, as we shall see in later sections.

STATE BANKING, 1836–1863

Removal of the restraining influence of the Second Bank of the United States and the failure of the Federal Government to regulate banking by other methods left the field to the state banks. The relationships of the state governments to banks varied. In some cases, the state did little more than issue a charter; supervision or regulation being almost nonexistent. Some states were strict in the regulation of banks, and in some cases the states operated the banking system. A system of state ownership usually occurred after flagrant abuses of the banking privilege by private persons. These state-owned banks were very successful in South Carolina and Indiana. In some other states, notably Mississippi, they became printing presses turning out bank notes to finance government deficits. This period of state banking, marked by many abuses, is regarded generally as a time of bad banking and monetary confusion.

The abuses and defects in the state banking system were serious and deserve condemnation, but this should not obscure the fact that there were many well-managed banks. The states that had fairly strict regulatory laws and a plentiful supply of capital had sound banks relative to other states. For example, banks in Massachusetts, New York, and Louisiana usually were sound. Their notes circulated at par and were redeemable in specie, with exceptions. This period was responsible for several developments which more modern banking systems have adopted.

Free banking. Until 1837, each bank charter was the result of a special act of the state legislature. This practice invited corruption on the part of "would-be" bankers in an effort to get a charter bill passed. Once established, banks enjoyed a monopoly and sometimes exerted political influence to defeat bills which would create competitors. In 1837 and in 1838 Michigan and New York, respectively, initiated a free-banking system. By this action they applied the principle of free entry to the banking business. Any group posting bonds or other security with the state comptroller received a charter. The state comptroller issued bank notes in exchange. Although the state comptroller issued these notes, they were liabilities of the individual banks and not of the state. Other states copied the system and it became the basis for granting charters under the National Banking Act. (See pages 130-37 following.) In some states, "free banking" was a mixed blessing since the authorities permitted the establishment of more banks than the area could support. However, with some modification "free banking" exists today.

New York Safety Fund System. Other potentially favorable developments included the creation of the New York Safety Fund System in 1829. Under this insurance system, the member banks paid premiums and the fund guaranteed bank noteholders and depositors against loss in the event of insolvency. The State amended the system to cover noteholders only after the panic of 1837 had exhausted the fund. It is of interest as an early example of special protection for a bank's "involuntary" creditors and as a forerunner of the Federal Deposit Insurance Corporation.

The Suffolk Banking System. The banks of Boston took steps in 1824 to stabilize the value of notes in New England. Notes of New England country banks had circulated at a discount in areas removed from their home offices. However, any country bank could have its notes redeemed by the Suffolk Bank of Boston by maintaining a deposit with that bank. Since notes redeemable in Boston circulated at par, this stabilized the value of the notes of all banks that joined the system. Pressure to join the system occurred when the Boston banks collected notes of nonmembers and presented them for redemption at the home office. In this instance, several large banks located in the financial center of New England co-operated and were able to force sound banking practices on the area. A sound currency resulted. This is an example of central-bank activity by commercial banks on a regional basis.

Clearing houses. During the later years of the state-bank era, clearing houses developed. New York banks organized the first one in 1853. It provided for daily meetings where representatives of the several banks exchanged checks drawn on other members of the clearing house association and their correspondent banks. Thus, it led to a more efficient transfer of funds. In addition, it performed certain regulatory functions such as establishing and enforcing ethical standards.

Defects of State Banking

The abuses of the state-chartered banks were numerous, and a discussion of their shortcomings helps us to understand the principles of sound banking. Furthermore, the banking practices of this period are interesting in their own right. The more serious were:

Inadequate capital. In some cases promoters organized banks without sufficient capital subscriptions. On occasion, subscriptions took the form of promissory notes of the stockholders. When this occurred, the capital of the bank appeared to be adequate; but its value depended on the credit of the stockholders. As one might suspect, the credit of stockholders resorting to such devices was unlikely to be of high quality. Without adequate capital, the bank's creditors were unprotected against even minor losses.

Poor asset and loan policy. Many banks made risky loans. In some cases promoters organized the bank for the purpose of financing a certain project. Consequently, loans to this project were large and bank officers were unlikely to evaluate its credit worthiness with care. Americans of the period tended to be overly optimistic with regard to the certainty of profits in real estate promotion and other development projects. Many examples of bad loans to such schemes are available.

Insufficient reserves. During the period deposits grew in importance but note issue remained the chief business of a bank. Since the note issue provided the basis for profit, banks were tempted to issue as large a number of notes as possible. The banks, therefore, kept reserves against notes and deposits to a minimum and discouraged redemption of these claims in specie. It was not uncommon to locate the bank offices in inaccessible places to avoid demands for redemption.

These defects led to a note issue which not only fluctuated rather severely over time but was also often excessive with regard to the needs of trade. Each of the state banks issued its own notes which, of course, varied in value according to the reputation of the bank. Furthermore, because of a lack of uniformity the system was ideal for counterfeiters and forgers. To protect themselves, business firms subscribed to a bank note register which listed the various genuine notes and their rates of discount, the counterfeit notes, the notes of insolvent banks, and the notes of fictitious banks.

The result of the system was a nonuniform currency which was obviously a hinderance in economic transactions. Equally serious were the recurrent losses suffered by noteholders or depositors of banks which became insolvent. The public tolerated the system for reasons discussed in the section on the First and Second United States Banks. Viewed from the twentieth century, the underlying cause for poor banking seems to have been a shortage of capital. Areas with inadequate capital resources felt that a local bank could correct this deficiency. Needless to say, banks founded on this basis were likely to be unsound. In relatively capital-rich areas banks generally were reliable.

What was the economic effect of this period of banking? We have already noted the disadvantages. Some modern historians, however, feel that the system fostered economic growth. Bank note issues certainly are not a substitute for real capital, but they may be the means of allocating resources to the noteholder. Therefore, the frontier banks by issuing notes and by lending them to developers may have influenced the allocation of resources in the direction of development and investment and away from other uses, presumably consumption. If this did occur, the "unsound" banking practices aided development but the nation paid a price. That price was the reduced consumption of persons holding notes or bank deposits when depreciation took place. Hence, it was a form of forced saving, if we define saving simply as reduced consumption. The questions raised here concern choice of objectives and problems of equity: who should make the decision and who should suffer the reduction in consumption?

THE NATIONAL BANKING SYSTEM

Although it had improved over the years, the state banking system was still unsound at the time of the Civil War. Proposals for improvement through action by the Federal Government invariably met with defeat. Policies with respect to banks had exhibited sectional divisions from the nation's origin and these differences continued. The Congressional representatives from the Northern and the Eastern states cast votes in favor of stronger central banking facilities and sounder currency while opposing votes came from the South and the West. However, when the Southern states seceded, the departure of Southern Congressmen altered the political balance; so that the forces which had recommended that the Federal Government curb the excesses of state banking were able to push their legislation through Congress. At the same time, Secretary of the Treasury Chase was anxious to create new markets for Government bonds. A financial crisis, therefore, was responsible for some of the immediate pressure for a new banking system.

Congress passed the National Banking Act in 1863. The provisions were so stringent that very few banks sought national charters. Congress liberalized the law and levied a two per cent tax on state bank notes in 1864. Although further amendments were enacted, the Act remained the basic bank legislation until 1913, and it is still the basic Act governing commercial banks. Congress hoped to achieve two objectives by passing the Act: (1) to establish a sound currency which would circulate at par and which would be redeemable on demand, and (2) to assist the Federal Government in financing the Civil War by providing a new source for loans. To achieve these objectives, Congress established a system of federally chartered banks with uniform standards.

Provisions of the National Banking Act

Structure. The National Banking Act adopted the free banking principle. Any group of at least five persons who could meet the requirements of the Act could obtain a charter. It also encouraged state banks already in existence to obtain a national charter. In addition it created a new office, the Comptroller of the Currency, in the Treasury Department. The Comptroller has responsibility for issuing charters, examining national banks, and administering the system in general.

Capital. As the following tabulation shows, the minimum capital requirements varied with the population of the city in which a bank located its office.

Population	Minimum Capital Required
Not over 6,000	$ 50,000
From 6,000 to 50,000	100,000
Over 50,000	200,000

During the period 1900–1933, an amendment permitted a minimum capitalization of $25,000 in places with a population of less than 3,000, but Congress repealed the amendment in 1933 and the preceding figures apply today.

To avoid the abuses of the state system, the Act required the payment of one half of the capital prior to a bank's opening and the payment of the remainder within five months. In an effort to protect a bank's creditors from loss, bank stock carried a double liability provision. Accordingly, a stockholder was liable for an additional amount equal to the par value of his stock. The provision did not accomplish its objective; it did lead to hardship and to some confusion. Congress repealed it in 1933.

Asset policy. Attempts to insure bank solvency did not stop with minimum capital requirements. Regulations governing a bank's lending policy and the acquisition of other assets were designed to prevent or at least to minimize losses. A national bank was required to purchase United States securities equal to one third of its capital or at least $30,000, whichever was larger. These assets were regarded as safe but the requirement was designed primarily to provide a market for Government bonds rather than to protect banks. Classes of loans that had been proven unsound in the past, such as those secured by real estate, were forbidden. Diversity in a bank's assets was encouraged and no more than 10 per cent of its capital could be loaned to a single borrower. The specific restrictions have been changed from time to time, but the general principle of regulation has been maintained.

Reserve requirements. At first a bank held reserves against the notes it issued and the deposits it held; however, an early amendment (1874) exempted the note issue from reserve requirements. The minimum reserve requirement varied with the classification of the bank. Central reserve city banks comprised banks in New York City, in Chicago, and for awhile in St. Louis. Reserve city banks included banks in relatively large cities, other than those just listed. The remaining banks were country banks. The reserve requirements were:

Class	Ratio to Deposits	Form of Reserve
Central reserve city bank	25%	Lawful money.
Reserve city bank	25%	At least one half in lawful money. Remainder might be a deposit in a central reserve city bank.
Country bank	15%	At least two fifths in lawful money. Remainder might be a deposit in a reserve or a central reserve city bank.

The system of reserves was proven to be defective and was changed when the Federal Reserve System was created. Varying reserves according to the classification of the bank has been continued, however, with one change: the central reserve city and the reserve city bank classes were combined in 1962.

Note issue. Creation of a sound and uniform currency was the primary reason for establishing the National Banking System. The preceding provisions by contributing to the solvency of banks were conducive to a sound note issue. Additional steps were taken. National bank notes could be issued up to 90 per cent of the par value

or the market value, whichever was lower, of the United States
bonds which the bank had purchased and had deposited with the
Comptroller of the Currency. In addition, a 5 per cent redemption
fund was held by the Comptroller. This counted as part of the bank's
reserves. Notes, redeemable at the bank of issue or at the Treasury,
could not be issued in excess of a bank's capital.

In the event of bank insolvency or redemption refusal, the
Comptroller redeemed the outstanding notes with the proceeds from
the sale of the bonds which he held. Thus, noteholders, whom the
Act regarded as involuntary creditors, received preferential treatment. Furthermore, the Act required each national bank to accept at
par the notes of all other national banks. The system became operational too late to assist the Government in its financing of the Civil
War, but it did achieve its primary objective. National bank notes
were sound. The public accepted them at par throughout the country, and they remained a significant element in our currency system
until the depression of the 1930's. A 10 per cent tax placed on notes
of state banks forced them out of circulation. Table 8–1 shows the
decline in the volume of outstanding state bank notes and the increase in the national bank note issue.

Table 8–1

DEPOSIT AND NOTE LIABILITIES OF
NATIONAL AND STATE BANKS

Selected Years, 1865–1900
(In millions of dollars)

Year	National Banks		State Banks		All Banks	
	Bank Notes	Deposits	Bank Notes	Deposits	Bank Notes	Deposits
1865	132	614	48	75	180	689
1870	291	706	45	70	336	775
1875	318	897	—	1,111	318	2,009
1880	318	1,085	—	1,137	318	2,222
1885	269	1,420	—	1,659	269	3,078
1890	126	1,979	—	2,598	126	4,576
1895	179	2,279	—	3,260	179	5,539
1900	265	3,621	—	5,301	265	8,922

Source: U.S. Bureau of the Census, *Historical Statistics of the U.S., Colonial Times
to 1957* (Washington: Government Printing Office, 1960), pp. 627 and 629.

The attempt to establish a banking system regulated by the
Federal as opposed to the state governments was only partially

successful. At the time of the passage of the National Banking Act, Congress felt that a bank could lend money profitably only if it issued bank notes. Therefore, it believed that restricting the note-issuing privilege to banks with a national charter would force state banks either to convert to national banks or to go out of business. In the early years, many state banks changed to national banks, as Table 8-2 shows. It soon became apparent, however, that the increasing importance of checking accounts enabled banks to lend money by expanding deposits rather than by issuing notes. Because of this change, state banks could operate profitably; they surpassed national banks in numbers after 1892. In this fashion, the "dual" system of banking arose. It is, to some extent, a result of historical accident rather than careful planning.

Table 8-2

NUMBER OF STATE AND NATIONAL BANKS

Selected Years, 1862 – 1900

Year	State Banks	National Banks
1862	1,492	—
1863	1,466	66
1864	1,089	467
1865	349	1,294
1870	325	1,612
1875	586	2,076
1880	650	2,076
1885	1,015	2,689
1890	2,250	3,484
1892	3,773	3,759
1893	4,188	3,807
1895	4,369	3,715
1900	5,007	3,731

Source: Board of Governors of the Federal Reserve System, *Banking Studies* (Washington, D.C., 1941), p. 418.

Defects of the National Banking System

We shall consider these defects at some length because a knowledge of these problems is of assistance in understanding the concept of a central bank. There were several defects in the National Banking System, and we may summarize them by stating that the system failed to perform the important functions customarily accomplished by a central bank. It was these defects, in fact, which forced the nation to create a central bank.

Inelastic currency. When applied to the National Banking System, this phrase refers to the fact that the quantity of national bank notes in circulation did not vary with the needs of business. Instead, the issue varied with the quantity of United States securities possessed by the banks. The amount owned, in turn, depended on the size of the United States debt and the price and the interest yield of the bonds. It was not profitable to issue notes if the bonds to secure them were selling at a high price or if the yield was low.

Table 8–1 shows that the note issue declined during 1870 to 1890, a period of rapid economic development. This inelastic, or more precisely perversely elastic, feature might have had more serious effects except for the growth of demand deposits which Table 8–1 also shows.

Defective reserve system. The reserve system combined with an inelastic currency led to recurrent liquidity crises. There were several defective features in the System. The dispersion of the nation's reserves among the several thousand banks in the System made it difficult or even impossible for banks which were experiencing a shortage of reserves to use the excess reserves of other banks. Instead, in times of trouble each bank, fearing that it might be the next one to suffer from the shortage, held its reserves and restricted its lending operations.

The presence of correspondent relationships between banks caused the apparently large reserve ratios of 15, 25, and 25 per cent to be partly fictitious. The development of a unit-bank system instead of branch banking in the United States had caused individual banks to maintain deposits in other banks, particularly those in large cities. The National Banking Act recognized and gave statutory approval to these correspondent bank relationships. Country banks with minimum reserve ratios of 15 per cent could keep three fifths of their reserves in reserve or central reserve city banks. Since the city banks paid interest on these deposits, there was an incentive to keep the bare minimum of three fifths of the reserves in the vault. Reserve city banks, in turn, could keep one half of their required reserves on deposit with a central reserve city bank and thus earn interest. As a result an individual bank's reserves were equal to 15 or 25 per cent of its deposits, but for the System the reserves of lawful money in the vaults of banks were smaller than these stated ratios.

This process led to the concentration of bank reserves in the financial district of the City of New York. City banks were competing for the deposits of country banks by paying interest. The city banks then sought a return on these funds by depositing the maximum portion allowed by law with the central reserve city banks, usually New York City banks. Banking was competitive in New York, so these banks paid interest to attract depositors. This system placed the New York City banks in a vulnerable position. Country and reserve city banks might demand the return of their deposits at any time. Therefore, substantial cash reserves were desirable if the banks were to honor these demands, but the profit motive and the rigors of competition made cash reserves unattractive. The demands of the securities market for credit provided an apparent solution to the problem. Sizable amounts were lent to buyers of securities as "call money;" that is, loans which are payable on demand. These loans financed the purchase of stocks on margin. The end result of this pyramiding was a series of liquidity crises. The banking system, prepared for "normal" withdrawals, found that abnormally large demands for currency occasionally occurred. Withdrawals occurred in the rural areas at harvest time. As country banks experienced demands for currency, they withdrew their deposits from reserve city banks and in this way started a chain reaction. The chain ended when demands for currency from all over the country confronted the New York City banks. Since these banks held little currency in excess of the minimum required, they had to demand payment of the call loans. Such action forced a decline in stock prices.

More serious, however, was the effect on the monetary system when the New York City banks could not meet the demands for cash. When this occurred, the nation experienced a liquidity crisis. Business firms, individuals, and banks might be solvent; but money in the form of currency was scarce or unobtainable. Those persons having cash jealously guarded it and in this way added to the crisis. Serious crises of this type occurred in 1873, 1884, 1893, and 1907.

Credit shortages that were not serious enough to be crises occurred in other years. Since banking systems with smaller reserve ratios operated successfully, the size of the reserve requirement did not cause these crises. Nor could the concentrating of reserves in the nation's financial center be responsible for a similar system worked satisfactorily in other nations. Crises arose because the banks holding the concentrated reserves—that is, the banks in the center of the monetary system—did not keep sufficient excess reserves in normal times. Therefore, they were unable to meet unusually heavy demands for currency. This is to say that the New York City banks did not fulfill the responsibilities which their central position demanded. It is worth repeating the principle: the bank or banks at the center of the banking system must hold excess reserves in normal times in order to protect the liquidity of all banks in abnormal times.

We should not criticize the individual banks in New York City for this failure. These banks existed in a competitive environment and were profit-motivated. To be successful in protecting the System's liquidity, a bank must have monopoly powers or be so large as to dominate the System. None of the New York City banks was in this position.

The check clearing system. The inefficient system for clearing checks made use of the deposits which banks maintained in correspondent banks in other cities. Following this practice, when a Philadelphia bank received a check drawn on a New York City bank, the Philadelphia bank sent the check to its New York City correspondent for collection. Difficulties arose, however, when a bank received a check drawn on a bank in a city where the receiving bank had no correspondent bank. In those cases, the receiving bank customarily sent the check to a correspondent bank which "might" have correspondent relations with the paying bank. If the second bank did not have the paying bank as a correspondent, it sent the check to a third bank, and so on. For example, if a bank in Harrisburg, Pennsylvania, received a check drawn on a bank in Grand Rapids, Michigan, it might send the check to a correspondent bank in Pittsburgh which might send it to New York City, then to Chicago, and finally to Detroit. Or the route might be more indirect. In an extreme example, cited by the Federal Reserve Bank of New York, a check drawn on a bank in Sag Harbor, Long Island, and deposited in Hoboken, New Jersey, passed through eleven banks and travelled 1,233 miles in eleven days before being presented for payment. Thus, delays in payment were frequent, transfer of currency occurred more often than was necessary, and needless expense resulted.

Attempted Solutions to the Problems

Other nations avoided these problems — liquidity crises, awkward check clearing, and lack of a fiscal agent — through the establishment of a central bank. Such a procedure would have solved the problems of the United States; however, the nation rejected this solution for reasons noted earlier in this chapter.

Substitutes for a central bank developed. The Independent Treasury System came into existence in 1846. The motivation for its creation was a desire to eliminate all contacts between the Federal Government and the banking system which, at that time, had a bad reputation. The Government kept its receipts in the Treasury vaults in the form of currency and made payments in the same form. This practice quickly proved to be impractical and the Treasury began depositing some of its cash in banks. With the passage of time, the

Treasury accepted some responsibility for the proper operation of the banking system. It varied the ratio of funds held in the Treasury vaults to those on deposit with the commercial banks. By withdrawing deposits or depositing currency with the banks, it increased or decreased bank reserves as economic conditions demanded. This form of monetary management, however, was not powerful enough to prevent liquidity crises.

New York established the first clearing house in 1853 and other cities quickly copied it. The main purpose of these institutions was check clearing but they attempted to perform other central-bank functions. In crises, they issued clearing house certificates. These certificates took the place of currency in the settlement of the claim of one bank against another bank. Clearing houses also served, and continue to serve, as a regulatory device maintaining minimum standards for members.

Economic effects. These substitutes for a central bank were inadequate; they did not correct the defects of the National Banking System. The inelastic currency of the period hindered commerce and would have had more serious effects except for the growth of demand deposits and checks as a means of payment. The use of checks, however, often led to delays in clearing and this, in turn, hampered trade. The effects of liquidity crises were more serious. They retarded economic growth and caused inconvenience and hardship to many persons. By 1913 the defects were serious enough to overcome the objections to a central bank and Congress passed the Federal Reserve Act.

SUMMARY

Prior to the Revolution, the American colonists recognized the advantages of paper currency and organized several banks. These banks were devices which monetized physical assets by issuing bank notes. This attempt to use paper currency was successful in the areas where the note issue did not exceed the volume needed for transaction purposes. In areas which issued excessive quantities of notes, the currency depreciated in value.

The first modern-type commercial bank was organized in 1781 in Philadelphia, and several additional banks were established in other cities within a few years. These banks were designed to perform the discount functions and to issue bank notes.

The United States Government realized the need for an institution which would perform the functions of a central bank and chartered the First and later the Second Bank of the United States.

These banks served as the fiscal agent of the Government, facilitated the transfer of funds throughout the nation, and regulated the volume of notes issued by all commercial banks. The Government failed to renew the charter of the Second Bank of the United States in 1836 and state banks existed alone until 1863.

The state bank system produced an unsound and unreliable currency and was generally unsatisfactory. The National Banking Act of 1863 and amendments to it gave the nation a sound and acceptable currency but the volume of notes issued did not vary with the needs of trade. Defects in the reserve system combined with the inelastic currency led' to recurrent liquidity crises and illustrated the need for a central bank.

National characteristics and attitudes developed during the period, and these attitudes continued to influence our monetary system. The nation distrusted large financial institutions and feared concentrated financial power. Because of this fear a unit banking rather than a branch banking system developed. We can also note a distrust of human discretion as a means of regulating the monetary system. This distrust helped to prevent the establishment of a central bank. We find another illustration of the distrust in the National Banking System. The size of the national debt determined the volume of bank notes issued. This method was not satisfactory but it avoided reliance on human judgment.

QUESTIONS

1. How did the early land banks differ from modern banks in their approach to the problem of achieving liquidity, solvency, and profitability? *issuing bank notes*
2. What services did the First and the Second Bank of the United States perform for the nation? Why did the Congress refuse to recharter these banks?
3. Which of the several principles of banking discussed in Chapters 6 and 7 were violated during the state bank era?
4. Do unsound banking practices always injure a nation? Can sound banking practices retard growth? Discuss.
5. What were the provisions in the National Banking Act which made liquidity crises possible and even probable?
6. Could the defects in the National Banking System have been corrected without establishing a central bank?

SUGGESTED READINGS

Barger, Harold. *The Management of Money*. Chicago: Rand McNally & Company, 1964. Chapter 2.

Board of Governors of the Federal Reserve System. *Banking and Monetary Statistics*. Washington, 1943.

————. *Banking Studies*, 1941.

Hammond, Bray. *Banks and Politics in America from the Revolution to the Civil War*. Princeton: Princeton University Press, 1957.

Smith, Walter Buckingham. *Economic Aspects of the Second Bank of the United States*. Cambridge, Massachusetts: Harvard University Press, 1953.

Studenski, Paul, and Krooss, Herman E. *Financial History of the United States*. 2d ed. New York: McGraw-Hill Book Company, Inc., 1963.

Trescott, Paul B. *Financing American Enterprise*. New York: Harper & Row, Publishers, 1963.

U.S. Bureau of the Census. *Historical Statistics of the U.S., Colonial Times to 1957*. Washington: Government Printing Office, 1960.

III

CENTRAL BANKING

9

THE FEDERAL RESERVE SYSTEM: STRUCTURE AND SERVICE FUNCTIONS

The Federal Reserve Act of 1913 created the first genuine central bank in the United States, although the Treasury Department had performed certain central-bank functions prior to this date as had the First and Second United States Banks. Americans had been debating banking policy for decades. Because we feared a concentration of financial power, the nation had attempted to achieve a sound monetary system without the establishment of a true central bank. We described the failure of the last such attempt in the discussion of the defects of the National Banking System. This system led to credit crises and after a particularly severe crisis in 1907 the need for improvement in the system became so apparent that the Congress overcame its opposition to a central bank.

Congress passed the Federal Reserve Act in 1913 after extensive study and debate, and the Federal Reserve System began operations in 1914. The functions which the System was to perform were those which central banks in other nations already were accomplishing. Hence, we adopted many principles developed by other banks, especially those of the Bank of England. There are many unique features, however, in the American system.

Instead of establishing a single bank with branches throughout the country, the Act divided the nation into twelve districts, each containing a bank. The size of the country and the diverse characteristics of the several regions explain the multiplicity of banks to some extent. A more realistic explanation lies in the long history of the fear of domination by the financial powers of the East and in the necessity to gratify local pride if Congress was to pass the Act. In this fashion, the controversy between President Jackson and the Second Bank of the United States influences twentieth-century banking. We may infer the importance of the need for satisfying local pride and for overcoming the fear of domination by the New York financial community by examining Figure 9–1, which shows the Federal Reserve Districts and the location of the Federal Reserve banks and their branches.

LEGEND

—— Boundaries of Federal Reserve Districts
—— Boundaries of Federal Reserve Branch Territories.
⊘ Board of Governors of the Federal Reserve System
⊙ Federal Reserve Bank Cities   • Federal Reserve Branch Cities

Figure 9-1   Boundaries of Federal Reserve Districts and
Their Branch Territories

STRUCTURE OF THE FEDERAL RESERVE SYSTEM

There are five major elements in the Federal Reserve System:
the Board of Governors of the Federal Reserve System, the twelve
Federal Reserve banks, the member banks, the Federal Open Market Committee, and the Federal Advisory Committee. The System
possesses great powers to influence the economy, and the Act provides safeguards against the abuse of this power or its concentration

in a few hands. The safeguards are of the type known as checks and balances in the political area. We shall observe the operation of these checks and balances as we examine the several elements in some detail.

The Board of Governors of the Federal Reserve System

The Board of Governors is the highest administrative unit in the System. The President of the United States appoints its seven members, subject to confirmation by the Senate, for a fourteen-year term. The President also appoints one of the members as chairman for a four-year term. Despite the fact that the President of the United States selects the Board of Governors, the Federal Reserve System is not an agency of the Government. Rather, it is an independent unit. As applied in this instance, independence refers to the Board's ability to reach decisions which may be distasteful to the President or to the other units of government. One should not interpret independence in terms of complete freedom, nor should one regard the Board as uninfluenced by the political administration. On the contrary, there are close ties between the Board and the Treasury Department; and one must bear in mind that an Act of Congress created the Federal Reserve System and that another act could terminate it or, more likely, could change its structure and powers. Therefore, the Federal Reserve System and the Board of Governors are definitely in the political arena, but the Board does have a degree of freedom and independence. We shall see that the provision for appointment to the Board of Governors and the tenure of that office assures this independence.

We have noted that the length of term is fourteen years. During his term in office, a governor is not subject to removal except for cause, and he is ineligible for reappointment after serving a full term. Safeguards against domination by one section of the country or an industrial group are found in the requirements: first, that no more than one member at a time serve from a single reserve district; and second, that in making appointments the President "have regard to a fair representation of the financial, agricultural, industrial, and commercial interests and geographical divisions of the country." A governor may not have any ties with a commercial bank or trust company, including stock ownership, during his tenure of office. If a member resigns before the expiration of his term of office, he may not hold any position with a member bank for a period of two years. The salary, incidentally, is quite modest—$20,000 per year, except for the chairman who receives $20,500—a sum considerably below that paid to the presidents of many member banks. The concern over possible conflict of interest situations or domination by a small section of the nation is understandable when one studies an enumeration of the powers and responsibility of the Board of Governors.

In addition to possessing overall supervisory responsibility for the System, the Board of Governors possesses other administrative powers. It appoints one third of the directors of each Reserve bank, approves the appointment and the reappointment of the president and the first vice-president of each Federal Reserve bank, and removes any Federal Reserve bank officer when necessary. It also requires the establishment or the discontinuance of Federal Reserve branches, and it must approve the merger of member banks.

Specific monetary powers of the Board of Governors include the right to set the minimum reserve requirements for member banks within the limits fixed by law, approve the discount rates set by the Reserve banks, and establish margin requirements for the purchase of securities in organized markets. The Board of Governors is the main body charged with the determination of monetary policy, and the automatic membership of each governor on the Federal Open Market Committee further increases its influence.

In the fifty years since the Federal Reserve System's creation, certain elements have declined in importance and authority while others have grown. The influence of the Board of Governors has increased during this period and it has become the dominant element in terms of control of the System. In some cases the increased dominance is the result of statutory change; in other instances it is the result of the Board of Governor's assumption of responsibilities unforeseen by the Congress which created the System.

The Twelve Federal Reserve Banks

Each Federal Reserve district contains a Federal Reserve bank. These institutions are federally chartered corporations. The original Act limited the charters to twenty years' duration, a further indication of the mistrust of central banking in America. Action by Congress at a later date made the charters of indefinite length.

Each Federal Reserve bank is owned by the member banks in its district. Each member bank is required to subscribe to stock equal in value to six per cent of the member bank's capital and surplus. Only one half of this subscription must be paid in cash. It is doubtful that the remainder will ever be demanded.

Since the capital of a Reserve bank is dependent upon the size of the capital accounts of the member banks, it varies as banks join or resign from the System and as the capital of the member banks grows or declines. With the exception of several years in the 1930's, Federal Reserve capital has grown steadily. The capital of the several banks varies as one expects. New York has the largest capital account with $419 million, followed by Chicago with $190 million. St. Louis and Minneapolis with $55 million and $36 million in capital, respectively, are the smallest banks. The consolidated statement on page 153 shows the capital accounts for the twelve banks.

Provisions have been made to insure broad representation in the control of each bank. Each of the nine directors is elected to a three-year term. Three of these directors are called Class A directors; they are elected by the member banks which have been divided into three groups, large, medium, and small, for the purpose. Class A directors may be chosen from the officers of commercial banks and a bank president is generally selected. Thus, the commercial banks are represented on the Board. The three Class B directors are elected in the same fashion as the Class A members. Class B directors, however, may not be officers, employees, or stockholders of commercial banks. They are considered the representatives of the commercial banks' customers, and they are chosen from persons engaged in commerce, industry, or agriculture. The three Class C directors are appointed by the Board of Governors. They are regarded as representatives of the general public, and like their Class B colleagues they may not have connections with commercial banks. One of the Class C directors is appointed as the chairman of the Board and Federal Reserve agent and another as the deputy chairman by the Board of Governors.

The directors appoint the president and other officers of a Reserve bank. As noted previously, the Board of Governors must approve the appointment of the bank president and the first vice-president. The appointments are for five years, a provision which increases the Board of Governor's influence over the System since the Board reviews each bank president's record prior to its approval of his reappointment.

Member Banks

Commercial banks which join the Federal Reserve System are called member banks. All national banks are required to become members by the Federal Reserve Act, thereby assuring a broad base for the System. State banks are permitted to become members if they can meet the eligibility requirements. In 1965 there were 4,784 national and 1,451 state member banks, a total of 6,235. There were 7,549 nonmember commercial banks at the same time. Consequently, a minority, 45 per cent, of the nation's commercial banks are members. Member banks, however, hold 83 per cent of the total deposits; therefore the System includes the major portion of the banking industry. These percentages increased during the early years of the System but have been fairly stable since 1945. Table 9–1 shows this stability. The ratios which Table 9–1 shows are averages for the entire nation. If we examine each state individually, we find sizable differences. In the urban states, which have relatively large banks, such as New York and Massachusetts, a large percentage of the commercial banks are members. In the Southern and the mid-Western states that are predominantly rural, member banks are a relatively small percentage of the total bank population. One should remember that although national banks must be members of the System it is relatively easy to shift from a national to a state chartered bank. Hence, one might say that no bank must be a member bank.

Table 9–1

NUMBER OF MEMBER AND NONMEMBER BANKS
AND SIZE OF DEPOSITS

Selected years, 1915–1965

	Number of Banks					
Year[a]	National Banks	State Member Banks	Total Members	Nonmember Banks	Total Banks	Member Banks as a % of Total
1915	7,598	17	7,615	18,260	25,875	29.5
1925	8,066	1,472	9,538	18,320	27,858	34.2
1935	5,425	985	6,410	9,068	15,478	41.4
1945	5,017	1,867	6,884	7,130	14,014	49.1
1955	4,744	1,867	6,611	7,173	13,784	48.0
1960	4,530	1,644	6,174	7,300	13,472	45.8
1965	4,784	1,451	6,235	7,549	13,784	45.2

	Deposits (in millions of dollars)			
Year[a]	Member Bank Deposits	Nonmember Bank Deposits	Total Deposits	Member Bank Deposits as % of Total
1915	8,894	9,099	17,993	49.4
1925	32,457	12,095	44,552	72.9
1935	34,938	6,381	41,319	84.6
1945	129,669	20,571	150,230	86.3
1955	154,670	26,870	181,540	85.2
1960	193,029	36,834	229,863	84.1
1965	242,781	49,019	291,800	83.2

[a]June 30. Sources: *Federal Reserve Bulletins* and *Banking and Monetary Statistics*.

Membership requirements. To become a member, a bank must meet the minimum capital requirements, which are the same as those of the National Banking System (see page 131). In addition, there are minimum reserve requirements. These requirements vary with the classification of the member bank. We shall examine the reserve requirement and its use as an implement of monetary policy in Chapter 10. For the present, we may note that the Board of Governors has the power to suspend the requirement in times of emergency and that it levies a tax on member banks which are deficient in reserves. The System classifies member banks as country or reserve city banks, a practice carried over from the National Banking System. Classification does not depend entirely upon the location of the bank but hinges upon the type of business conducted. We have noted that because of the lack of a central bank with its check clearing and other service facilities, American banks began the practice of keeping funds on deposit with correspondent city banks at an early date. This practice attained statutory recognition in the reserve requirements of the National Banking Act, and the Federal Reserve System sustains it. Correspondent banks holding these deposits and located in the larger cities, designated reserve cities, are reserve city banks. However, some banks in the outlying sections of reserve cities do not serve as correspondent banks and may, therefore, be classified as country banks. When one remembers that the type of business rather than the geographical location determines the classification of banks, the different minimum reserve requirements for the classes are understandable.

In addition to meeting capital and reserve requirements, member banks must purchase stock in the Federal Reserve bank of their district. They must abide by Federal Reserve regulations with regard to lending and investing policies and must *remit at par*. A bank which remits at par pays the full face value of checks drawn against it. "Nonpar" banks levy a charge—for example, one tenth of one per cent—when honoring checks drawn upon them or cleared through them. This requirement to remit at par does not prevent member banks from levying a service charge on checks presented to them for collection from other banks, nor does it prevent the levying of a service charge on checking accounts. Also, the member bank must abide by other Federal Reserve regulations designed to promote higher standards of banking.

A member bank has the privilege of discounting commercial paper with the Federal Reserve bank and of borrowing from the Federal Reserve bank directly. This is a very valuable privilege; it insures the member bank of liquidity as long as its assets are sound. Member banks may clear checks through the Federal Reserve banks without charge and may call upon Federal Reserve personnel for advice. In addition, the member banks receive a six per cent dividend on their subscription to stocks in the Federal Reserve bank.

Deterrents to membership. Why have less than half the commercial banks in the United States joined the System? In a few cases the capital requirements have been too high, and in certain states the regulations on bank acquisition of assets are less severe than the Federal Reserve regulations. Consequently, banks have more freedom if they do not join the System. The Federal Reserve requirement that members remit at par also has reduced the number of banks seeking membership.

The main cause of nonmembership, however, lies in the fact that banks can enjoy most of the benefits of membership without becoming members. This is especially true for small banks which have correspondent relations with large city banks. These nonmember banks may clear checks and may receive advances through their correspondents and thus indirectly from the Federal Reserve bank. In addition, nonmembers may clear checks directly through the Federal Reserve System if they maintain deposits with a Federal Reserve bank. These banks are "clearing" banks, and the "other deposits" account in Table 9–2 suggests their importance. We should note that although the correspondent bank relationship enables country banks to avoid membership it does serve as a means of indirectly tying these banks to the System.

Congress has never approved legislation which would force all the banks to join the System, nor has it approved legislation which would apply pressure upon them to join. The explanation probably lies in the fact that the presence of nonmembers does not hinder monetary policy so long as the banks holding most of the banking system's assets are members. Therefore, the need for compulsory membership is not acute. Congressional sympathy with nonmembers also reflects the traditional American admiration for the small unit bank and the suspicion of large banks, including Federal Reserve banks, despite their proven merit. Finally, it reflects the great influence country bankers exert upon state and federal legislators.

The Federal Open Market Committee

The functions and responsibilities of this element will be discussed at greater length in Chapter 10. At this point, it is sufficient to note that Federal Reserve banks increase their deposit liabilities when they acquire assets and decrease these accounts when they dispose of assets. This is the same principle discussed in Chapter 6 for commercial banks. Since the deposits of the Federal Reserve banks constitute a major portion of member bank reserves (see page

114), it follows that the acquisition or disposal of assets by the Federal Reserve banks affects the size of member bank reserves. By the early 1920's the effect of these transactions on the monetary system was noted as well as the fact that unco-ordinated action was unlikely to achieve the desired effect. A committee, which had been formed in 1923, to co-ordinate open-market sales and purchases was given statutory recognition by an Act of Congress in 1935.

The Federal Open Market Committee consists of twelve members. The seven members of the Board of Governors automatically become members of the Committee. Of the remaining five, elected annually, one represents the Federal Reserve Bank of New York, and the following groups of banks have one representative each: Boston, Philadelphia, and Richmond; Cleveland and Chicago; Atlanta, Dallas, and St. Louis; Minneapolis, Kansas City, and San Francisco. These five members must be either presidents or vice-presidents of their respective banks. The Board of Directors of the Reserve banks who elect them invariably choose the bank president. The New York Bank, because of its location in the nation's money market, acts as the agent of all the banks in purchasing and selling securities. It always has a representative on the Committee. The Open Market Committee makes decisions concerning acquisition or disposal of securities for all the banks. No bank may buy or sell on the open market except in accordance with Committee regulations.

The Committee meets regularly (every three weeks) with the presidents of the twelve Reserve banks. The manager of the System Account, located in the New York Bank, implements the decisions reached by the Committee. Additional conferences by telephone take place as conditions demand.

The Federal Advisory Council

Each of the Federal Reserve banks appoints a member to the Federal Advisory Council. The Federal Reserve banks usually appoint representatives of leading commercial banks or business leaders from their districts. The Council meets at least four times per year, and the Board of Governors may convene extra sessions. As the name implies, its functions are advisory in nature. It does not play a significant role in our monetary system.

There are units of importance in the System in addition to the five just covered. Unlike these five elements, however, an Act of Congress has not recognized them; therefore they are less formal in nature. The presidents of the twelve Reserve banks meet regularly to discuss common problems and to co-ordinate policy, and committees explore methods to improve operations.

SERVICE FUNCTIONS OF THE FEDERAL RESERVE SYSTEM

The main interest of students of monetary economics in the Federal Reserve System lies in its role in directing the monetary policy of the United States. This is a function which requires many decisions by the top-level personnel of the System and absorbs most of their time. We shall postpone discussion of monetary policy and the techniques used to implement it until later chapters of this text.

The Federal Reserve System has a number of functions also of importance to the welfare of the nation which do not require frequent decisions with regard to policy. Because of the routine, or mechanical, nature of these functions, they are called "chores," tasks, or service functions.

A Reserve bank operates as a "banker's bank." It holds deposits for commercial banks, clears checks, and stands ready to liquidate assets for a member bank which needs cash. These are the same functions commercial banks perform for their customers. In addition to furnishing these services, the Federal Reserve banks examine member banks, require reports, and compile statistics for the banking system. The Federal Reserve banks provide the nation with an elastic currency by issuing Federal Reserve notes. They also serve as the fiscal agent of the Federal Government.

The Federal Reserve Bank Statement

An examination of the combined statement for the twelve Federal Reserve banks serves as an introduction to their operations. Also, an understanding of the statement of the Federal Reserve banks is necessary if we wish to analyze monetary conditions.

Gold certificates. These certificates represent a claim against the gold held at Fort Knox by the Treasury Department. Originally, the Federal Reserve banks owned gold, but they had to relinquish it to the Treasury in 1933 in return for the certificates. For many years the law required that Federal Reserve banks hold gold certificates equal to at least 25 per cent of the combined total of Federal Reserve notes and deposits. This requirement, therefore, placed a limit on the Federal Reserve banks' ability to expand credit just as the reserve requirement restrains commercial banks. A 1965 change in the law eliminated the gold certificate requirement for deposits but not for Federal Reserve notes. However, it is probable that this remaining requirement will be removed in a few years. Since the Federal Reserve banks held gold certificates in excess of the minimum requirement, the liberalization of the law had no immediate effect on their credit policy. It did free the gold reserve for use in making international payments.

Table 9–2

CONSOLIDATED STATEMENT OF CONDITION
TWELVE FEDERAL RESERVE BANKS

February 24, 1965
(In millions)

Assets		*Liabilities*		
Gold certificates[a]	$14,641	Federal Reserve notes		$33,881
Other cash	164	Deposits:		
Discount and		Member banks	$16,883	
advances	187	U.S. Treasury	919	
U.S. securities	36,681	Foreign	134	
Uncollected cash		Other	209	18,145
items	5,829			
Other assets	551	Deferred availability		
		cash items		4,284
		Other liabilities		599
		Total liabilities		$56,909
		Capital Accounts		
		Capital accounts		1,144
	$58,053			$58,053

Float =	Uncollected cash items	$5,829
	− Deferred availability cash items	4,284
	Float	$1,545

[a]Gold certificates equal 43.2 per cent of Federal Reserve notes.
Source: *Federal Reserve Bulletin*, March, 1965, p. 438.

Other cash. Federal Reserve banks serve as the agent for the distribution of Treasury-issued currency to the member banks and thus indirectly to the public. They also receive and redistribute currency from member banks that have a surplus. That portion of their currency "inventory" which does not consist of Federal Reserve notes is an asset. They record it as "other cash."

Discounts and advances. Federal Reserve banks stand ready to discount eligible notes and drafts offered to them by member banks and to advance (loan) money to banks in need of cash or reserves. Member banks are able in this way to liquidate assets if the need arises. The Reserve banks have the lending capacity to extend credit because of their practice of holding gold certificates in excess of the minimum legal requirement for Federal reserve notes. The need for this service was the most pressing reason for the creation of the System. Federal Reserve banks need not wait for member banks to request an advance or to offer paper for discount. They may take the initiative by buying on the open market; they are more likely, however, to deal in United States securities. Students of monetary affairs watch for changes in "discounts and advances" since this item reflects changes in the reserve position, and hence the lending capacity of member banks.

United States securities. The Federal Reserve banks purchase or sell securities in order to manage the monetary system. We shall discuss this control in Chapter 10. In an emergency, the banks may purchase securities to aid the Treasury Department in managing the public debt. These changes in the holdings of United States securities are important to persons studying monetary conditions, and we shall discuss them in the section on techniques of monetary policy.

Uncollected cash items. The check clearing function of the Reserve banks causes this item to appear in the bank statement. It represents checks which member banks have sent to the Reserve banks for collection. The Reserve banks send these checks to the drawer's bank but do not charge the check against the paying bank's deposit account until certain that the check is valid. In the interim it appears in the bank statement as an "uncollected cash item." This item is of some significance to the monetary system when considered in conjunction with the "deferred availability cash item" on the liability side of the statement.

Other assets. Bank premises and holdings of foreign currency account for most of the "other assets."

Federal Reserve notes. Chapter 2 contains a description of these notes. They account for the major portion of our currency supply. The law requires that the issuing Federal Reserve bank hold gold certificates equal to at least 25 per cent of the value of its outstanding notes. United States securities or discounted commercial paper constitute the remaining 75 per cent of the backing for the notes.

Deposits. A study of the statement indicates that Federal Reserve banks accept deposits from a select group of clients. They will not normally accept deposits from individuals, businesses, or state and local governments. Member banks keep funds on deposit with the Reserve bank in their districts. These deposits serve as part (the main part) of the required legal reserves, and they are of service in clearing checks. A member bank may draw on these deposits whenever it needs currency.

The United States Treasury keeps funds on deposit with the Federal Reserve banks. It draws checks against these deposits just as private citizens draw checks against deposits held in commercial banks. Foreign banks, including central banks, and a few other agencies may also have deposits with Federal Reserve banks. Commercial banks which are not members of the System may clear checks through the Federal Reserve System if they have funds on deposit in a Federal Reserve bank. These clearing balances are the "other deposits."

The law does not require that the Reserve banks hold gold certificates as a reserve for their deposit liabilities. However, the banks must expect that the volume of Federal Reserve notes will vary with the size of deposits. Consequently, there is an indirect requirement for gold certificates.

Deferred availability cash items. These items, like "uncollected cash items," arise as a consequence of the check clearing function. Commercial banks which present checks to the Federal Reserve bank for collection do not receive immediate credit in their deposit accounts. Instead, they must wait for the paying banks to acknowledge the checks. In case of delay, the bank submitting the check receives credit after the elapse of a certain period of time which varies with the distance the check must travel. Until the member banks receive credit for these amounts, the bank statement carries them as "deferred availability cash items."

The excess of cash items in the process of collection over deferred availability cash items represents the amounts credited to the deposit account of one member bank but not yet charged (debited) to the paying bank. This "float," to call it by its proper name, is, in effect, an interest-free "loan," or extension of credit, by the Federal Reserve banks to member banks. The size of the float varies with weather conditions, holiday schedules, and other factors which interfere with the check clearing process. The float seldom has a significant effect on the monetary system.

Other liabilities. As the name implies, this is a catchall for miscellaneous items that do not fit elsewhere.

Capital accounts. The funds received from the sale of stock to member banks plus the retained earnings carried over to surplus constitute the capital of a Federal Reserve bank. Previously, we noted the importance of the capital accounts in protecting commercial banks against insolvency. For Federal Reserve banks these accounts are of little significance because of the high quality of Federal Reserve bank assets.

THE LENDER OF LAST RESORT

We shall understand the operations of Federal Reserve banks more clearly by referring to the items in the statement. Congress created the Federal Reserve banks to overcome the liquidity crises of the National Banking System. The statement shows that each member bank keeps the major portion of its reserve on deposit with the Federal Reserve bank in its district, thus concentrating reserves in a single bank. This is similar to the concentration of reserves in the New York banks under the National Banking System. There is an important difference, however. The Reserve banks maintain gold certificates in excess of the 25 per cent minimum requirement for Federal Reserve notes. Hence, in times of need, they are able to issue Federal Reserve notes and to supply currency to any member bank that requests it. Furthermore, the Reserve banks have the ability to expand credit and to make loans to member banks that need additional reserves. This practice is not unique to the Federal Reserve banks but is common to all central banks. In fact, we may consider it the distinguishing feature of a central bank. Briefly stated, the central bank holds excess reserves in normal times so that it may extend credit to commercial banks in time of credit stringency. Because of this practice, we sometimes define a central bank as "the lender of last resort."

If this system is to work properly, the central bank must base its lending and credit expansion policies on the needs of the nation's economy rather than on profit considerations of the bank. Federal Reserve banks receive interest on loans and advances they have made and on the acceptances and the United States securities which they own. The law limits dividends to stockholders, however, to a maximum of six per cent. The remaining profits go to the United States Government except for a contribution to the Reserve banks' surplus accounts. In their half century of existence, the Federal Reserve banks have paid to the United States Treasury approximately 50 per cent of their gross revenue.

Check Clearing

By keeping money on deposit in the Federal Reserve bank in its district, each member bank facilitates the check clearing process.

Thus, when the holder of a check drawn on a Buffalo, New York, bank presents it to a Newark, New Jersey, bank, the Newark bank sends the check to the Federal Reserve Bank of New York for collection. Collection occurs when the New York Federal Reserve Bank increases the deposit account of the Newark bank and decreases the deposit account of the bank in Buffalo. A slight complication occurs if the paying and the receiving banks are in different Federal Reserve districts; for example, Chicago and Newark. In that case, the Newark bank receives credit at the New York Federal Reserve Bank for the amount of the check, and the Chicago Reserve Bank decreases the deposit which it is holding for the Chicago bank. The Chicago Reserve Bank must now pay the New York Reserve Bank. The Interdistrict Settlement Fund, established in Washington, D. C., clears these debts by transferring gold certificates.

Although of minor interest in a study of monetary economics, the check clearing function and the other chores of the System constitute a sizable portion of the System's workload. In the New York Reserve Bank alone, 703 million checks were processed in 1964. The job required the services of a large work force despite the use of labor-saving devices. This example also shows how the Federal Reserve System facilitates the transfer of funds about the nation as economic conditions within the several districts change. Although the Federal Reserve System clears a large volume of checks each day, it does not handle all intercity clearing. The correspondent bank system which predates the Federal Reserve System continues to serve as a method for clearing checks and transferring funds.

Other Services

In addition to the preceding functions, each Federal Reserve bank examines the member banks in its district. From the Federal Reserve bank, member banks receive reports which keep them informed of events affecting the banking industry and the economy. Member banks may call upon the Federal Reserve banks for advice when needed.

The Federal Reserve banks are not only bankers' banks, they are government banks; that is, the System serves as fiscal agent to the United States Government. The Federal Reserve banks hold government deposits and redeem checks drawn against the United States Treasury. The Treasury Department has deposits at commercial banks also, but it transfers these deposits to a Federal Reserve bank before it draws checks against them. The Federal Reserve System stores and issues Treasury currency and withdraws worn currency units from circulation. It serves as the Government's agent in financial transactions with other countries. Finally, the System is the agent through which the Government issues and redeems its securities. The System performs these services, for the most part, without charging a fee although the cost to the System is substantial. Indirectly, the Government does pay for these services, for the chief source of revenue to a Reserve bank is the interest received on its holdings of United States securities.

Unlike the early central banks in this country and abroad, the Federal Reserve banks do not operate as commercial banks except under unusual circumstances. The Federal Reserve Act does authorize loans to private borrowers who have been unable to secure credit from other lending institutions. It has used this power sparingly in times of emergency, such as the depression of the 1930's and in wartime. At no time have these industrial loans been large enough to cause the commercial banks to feel that the Federal Reserve banks are competitors.

COMMENTS ON THE NATURE
OF THE FEDERAL RESERVE SYSTEM

The Federal Reserve System defies classification as either a public agency or a private institution. The Board of Governors is a public agency in terms of the method of appointment of its members by the President. However, the long term of office permits its members to be independent of political control to a large degree. The Federal Reserve banks are privately owned and the stockholders elect two thirds of the directors; however the method of selection insures that the public interest rather than stockholder interest motivates the directors. One may describe the System as an agency which operates in the public interest and which has some ties to the Federal Government.

The degree to which the Government controls the System is not always clear. Despite the suspicion many Congressmen feel toward a central bank, an Act of Congress did create it. Congressional critics of the System always are present and the threat of hostile legislation limits the Board of Governors and the other elements in the exercise of their independent positions. Since the basic objectives of the Federal Government and the Federal Reserve System are the same, co-ordinated action is desirable. However, there may be disagreement concerning the methods of achieving the objectives and regarding the priorities given to several of the objectives.

Although its position with respect to the Government is difficult to describe, the System generally has worked well. The division of the country into twelve districts with a Reserve bank in each plus the rather complicated provision for the selection of the Board of Governors show that Congress retained its fear of concentrated financial power. We see this again in the reluctance to adopt legislation which would force all commercial banks to join the System. While we may feel that the organizational structure of the System is unnecessarily complicated, complications have not interfered with its operation.

SUMMARY

The Federal Reserve System is the first true central bank in the United States, although the Second Bank of the United States was developing into such an institution prior to its liquidation. The Federal Reserve System consists of (1) the Board of Governors, which is the dominant decision-making element; (2) the twelve Federal Reserve banks, which carry out the function of a central bank; (3) the 6,235 member banks, which account for 83 per cent of the deposits held by commercial banks in the United States; (4) the Federal Open Market Committee, which determines the amount of securities the Federal Reserve banks will buy or will sell; and (5) the Federal Advisory Council, which has an advisory function only.

The System provides the nation with an elastic currency, stands ready to provide liquidity to member banks in case of need, clears checks, and serves as fiscal agent to the United States Government. All these functions, plus management of the nation's money supply, which we shall consider in a later chapter, are the functions normally performed by a central bank.

The United States Government created the Federal Reserve System and has close ties with it, but the System is not a government agency. Its top-echelon element, the Board of Governors, possesses a certain degree of independence. The Federal Reserve banks, which operate in the public interest rather than for profit, are privately owned.

QUESTIONS

1. Who controls the Federal Reserve System?
2. Why have many commercial banks refused to join the Federal Reserve System? Has this failure to attract a larger membership reduced the effectiveness of the System?
3. What limits the volume of Federal Reserve notes issued by the Federal Reserve banks? What limits the size of their deposit accounts?
4. What "price" does a member bank pay for the check clearing service of the Federal Reserve System?
5. What is the significance of the nonprofit characteristic of a Federal Reserve bank?

SUGGESTED READINGS

Board of Governors of the Federal Reserve System. *Banking Studies,* 1941.
_____. *The Federal Reserve System.* Washington, 1961.
Chandler, Lester V. *Benjamin Strong, Central Banker.* Washington, D. C.: The Brookings Institution, 1958.
Crutchfield, James A., Henning, Charles N., and Pigott, William. *Money, Financial Institutions, and the Economy.* Englewood Cliffs, N. J.: Prentice-Hall, Inc., 1965. Chapter 7.
Federal Reserve Bank of Philadelphia. *Forty Years of the Federal Reserve Act,* 1954.
New York Clearing House Association. *The Federal Reserve Re-examined.* New York, 1953.

10

INSTRUMENTS OF MONETARY POLICY

The service functions performed by the Federal Reserve System and described in Chapter 9 benefit the nation by facilitating the transfer of funds, which, in turn, enables us to trade goods and services. The System performs these important service functions so well that they appear as routine operations and would seem to call for little comment or discussion. However, our study of the conditions which existed prior to the creation of the Federal Reserve System indicated the importance of these functions. The Federal Reserve System performs an even more important service—the management of the monetary system. Management of the monetary system, or the more popular term monetary policy, refers to the control of the quantity of money in existence and to some extent to the use made of it.

The operation of the monetary system has an effect on the price level, the level of employment and output, and the rate of economic growth. This fact, recognized for many years, is implicit in the debates over monetary standards. By adopting a monetary standard, some degree of management of the monetary system is achieved automatically. The definition of the monetary standard sets limits to the expansion of the money supply and determines the conditions under which the banking system creates and extinguishes credit. Management by automatic methods has been found inadequate, however, and controls governed by human discretion have been added. It is these controls, or instruments of policy, which this chapter covers.

THE FEDERAL RESERVE SYSTEM'S IMPLEMENTS OF MONETARY POLICY

We can divide the Federal Reserve System's implements of monetary management into two classes. There are indirect controls, known also as quantitative controls, which enable the Federal Reserve authorities to regulate the quantity of money. A second group, called direct or selective controls, does not affect the quantity of money but does influence the allocation of credit among competitive applicants.

161

Indirect or Quantitative Controls

Discount rate. Although the discount rate is of minor importance as a control device today, it is the only indirect control specifically authorized in the original Federal Reserve Act. Hence, a discussion of the role of the discount rate is desirable. We noted previously that a member bank may discount eligible commercial paper with the Federal Reserve bank in its district. Since the commercial applicant for credit previously had discounted the debt instrument with the member bank, this second discount procedure was a "rediscount," a term which has survived for many years.

We noted the purpose of this rediscount procedure in Chapter 9: it prevents credit crises by enabling the commercial banks to liquidate assets quickly. If commercial banks could have turned assets into cash or reserves without restraint, they might have overexpanded credit. An individual commercial bank expanding deposits to the limits imposed by reserve requirements could have exchanged earning assets for additional reserves which would have been the basis for further credit expansion. Consequently, it was not sufficient for the Federal Reserve banks to lend to member banks in times of credit stringency. The Federal Reserve System also needed a means of restraining credit expansion by the commercial banks. The method of restraint should not be rigid or credit crises would arise as they did under the National Banking System. In brief, the Federal Reserve banks had to be ready to aid banks if illiquidity threatened—that is, be a lender of last resort—and had to possess the power to restrain banks from overexpanding credit.

An approach to this problem was made by allowing Federal Reserve banks to vary the discount rate (the interest) charged to member banks seeking credit. A low rate was expected to encourage banks to use the discount facility, to increase their reserves, and to expand their deposits. It was felt that a high rate would make it unprofitable for member banks to follow this procedure but would allow a bank to secure reserves needed to meet withdrawals.

An additional safeguard against the overexpansion of credit was built into the System. Only "eligible" paper could be discounted at a Federal Reserve bank. To be eligible for discount at a Federal Reserve bank, credit instruments had to be in the form of promissory notes or bills of exchange which had been used to provide working capital for business or agriculture. Acceptances were declared eligible for discount if they had been issued to finance the sale of goods and had been drawn against the buyer or, in the case of bank acceptances, against a bank. Debt instruments which had been issued to finance the purchase of fixed capital or securities were ineligible.

The maturity of eligible paper was limited according to the type of activity it financed to ensure further its use for working capital purposes only.

Through the use of eligibility requirements, the authorities assumed that an expansion of credit could occur only if the quantity of goods and services for sale increased. Thus, the quantity of credit adjusted automatically to the need for currency as measured by the transactions arising from the production of goods and services. The automatic feature appealed to those persons who did not wish to rely on the judgment and discretion of public officials for the management of money.

During World War I, Congress amended the Federal Reserve Act to permit "advances" to banks. An advance is simply a loan by the Federal Reserve bank to the member bank on the member bank's own promissory note. United States Treasury bills or eligible paper secured these promissory notes. During the depression of the 1930's, amendments simplified the process of procuring advances. Member banks in need of reserves frequently did not have sufficient Treasury bills or eligible paper to secure the needed advances. Congress amended the Federal Reserve Act to permit advances secured by assets other than United States securities or eligible paper at a rate one-half per cent above the discount rate. The difference between discounting at the Federal Reserve bank and securing an advance may appear slight. In both cases, member banks take the initiative in requesting credit. There is a basic difference, however. If discounts only are permitted, the quantity of eligible paper automatically controls the supply of money. With the use of advances, a member bank may secure additional reserves on the security of Treasury debt or other assets, such as corporate bonds and mortgages. Since World War II, commercial banks have held large quantities of United States securities. Member banks needing additional reserves use these securities as the basis for an advance from the Federal Reserve bank and avoid rediscounting eligible paper. Credit expansion is no longer tied automatically to the volume of business transactions. Therefore, other controls of the monetary system are needed and reliance on human judgment cannot be avoided.

Monetary management through variations in the discount rate follows the pattern established by central banks in other countries, particularly the Bank of England. However, the discount rate has been less effective as a control device in this country than in other countries because of the structure of the American banking system. American banks customarily borrow from the central bank to repair deficiencies in their reserve position. These deficiencies arise because of unexpected withdrawals caused by check clearing. They occur more frequently in the United States with its approximately 13,750 commercial banks than in foreign countries which have few banks with many branches. Since American banks borrow from the central bank to mend their reserve position and not to expand credit, changes in the discount rate are unlikely to affect the volume of bank borrowing. Furthermore, there is a tradition in the United States against a commercial bank being in debt to the central bank for an extended period.

The Federal Reserve system officially does not support the position that member banks which borrow from it should have a stigma attached to them. As early as 1923, however, it established the principle that borrowing is a privilege extended to a member bank and not a right which the member bank can demand. Reserve authorities may refuse a member bank's application for credit if they feel that granting the credit is against the public's interest. In practice, Reserve banks do not refuse to grant credit to a bank which needs additional reserves. Continued indebtedness to a Federal Reserve bank, however, causes the authorities to advise the member bank to dispose of assets or to eliminate the debt to the Federal Reserve bank in some other fashion. The threat of more forceful action if the bank ignores the advice is always present. The establishment of this principle increased the importance of administrative decisions in monetary management and decreased the importance of eligibility requirements and variations in the discount rate. The individual Reserve banks set the discount rates, subject to approval by the Board of Governors. The rates may vary between banks but this variance is seldom more than 1/2 of 1 per cent and is usually temporary. A record-high rate of 7 per cent was in existence during the inflationary period of 1920–1921. Rates of 31/2 to 41/2 per cent were common in the 1920's while rates of 1 to 2 per cent were the rule in the 1930's and the 1940's. In the decade of the 1950's, the discount rate rose slowly; and it has fluctuated around the 31/2 per cent level in recent years.

The member banks, however, are seldom in debt to the Federal Reserve bank for sizable amounts relative to total reserves, as Table 10–1 shows. Free reserves are equal to excess reserves minus borrowing from the Federal Reserve banks. Some member banks, deficient in reserves, may borrow from the Federal Reserve bank while others are holding excess reserves. Negative free reserves, indicating a deficiency of reserves for member banks treated like a unit, occur when borrowings are larger than excess reserves. This occurred in 1952, 1955, 1956, 1957, and 1959 in addition to the years shown in Table 10–1.

At this point, one may well ask: Just what effective role does the

Table 10-1

RESERVES AND BORROWINGS OF MEMBER BANKS

Selected years, 1929-1965
(Average daily figures; in millions of dollars)

| Period | Reserves | | | Borrowings at F.R. Banks | Free Reserves |
	Total Held	Required	Excess		
1929, June	2,314	2,275	42	974	-932
1933, June	2,160	1,797	363	184	179
1939, Dec.	11,473	6,462	5,011	3	5,008
1945, Dec.	16,027	14,536	1,491	334	1,157
1947, Dec.	17,261	16,275	986	224	762
1950, Dec.	17,391	16,364	1,027	142	885
1954, Dec.	19,279	18,576	703	246	457
1958, Dec.	18,899	18,383	516	557	-41
1960, Dec.	19,283	18,514	769	87	682
1963, Dec.	20,746	20,210	536	327	209
1964, Dec.	21,614	21,203	411	243	168
1965, Jan.	21,619	21,217	402	299	103

Source: *Federal Reserve Bulletin*, February, 1965, p. 264.

discount rate play in the management of money? The Reserve authorities apparently feel that it has some purpose, for they vary the rate at irregular and admittedly infrequent intervals. If member banks borrow only in emergencies, when their reserves otherwise will be deficient, a change in the discount rate will have little significance. We should interpret the term emergency with some flexibility, however. The discount privilege enables a member bank to lend more freely since it can remedy a deficiency in reserves more readily. The higher the discount rate, the greater is the cost to the bank which overexpands its deposits. Logically, therefore, a change in the discount rate should have some effect on a member bank's willingness to extend credit if the bank's deposits are near the limit imposed by reserve requirements. However, the discount rate is not punitive; that is, it is not higher than the rate a member bank receives on its earning assets. The tradition against borrowing from the Federal Reserve bank makes a punitive rate unnecessary but this tradition seems to be weakening.

Changing the rate may have psychological implications known as an announcement effect. A rise in the discount rate may provide a bank loan officer with an excuse for refusing credit to doubtful applicants. An upward movement of the rate also notifies the financial community that the Federal Reserve authorities believe that the banks are overextending or are about to overextend the supply of credit. Thus, it serves as a notice of the probable application of other controls. There is some disagreement concerning whether such action will induce restraint in anticipation of other Federal Reserve action. It is possible that a rise in the discount rate reinforces the community's anticipation of inflation and induces actions which increase rather than restrain the expansion of bank credit.

On balance, it appears that a rise in the discount rate restrains credit expansion whereas a reduction induces expansion, but the effect is not large. The discount facility, therefore, serves chiefly as a means whereby the Federal Reserve authorities can prevent credit crises. The authorities must seek more positive effects through other controls.

Change in the reserve requirements. Control of the monetary system by changing the reserve requirements of the member banks is an instrument developed by the Federal Reserve System. Under the present law, the Board of Governors may set the reserve requirements for member banks within the limits listed below:

	Reserve City Banks	Country Banks	Time Deposits All Classes of Banks
Minimum	10%	7%	3%
Maximum	22%	14%	6%

The Board of Governors received this authority in a 1935 amendment to the Federal Reserve Act. At that time, commercial banks, which had survived the crisis of the early 1930's, were accumulating large amounts of excess reserves. These excess reserves, resulting from gold movements to the United States, were too large for open-market selling to control them. Although the demand for bank credit was low so that deposits did not expand immediately to the limits permitted by these increased reserves, the Federal Reserve authorities were afraid that an expansion of credit which was not warranted by business activity might occur. After receiving the legal right to raise reserve requirements, the Board of Governors was able to reduce excess reserves.

The effect of the changes in the legal reserve requirements is obvious. When the Federal Reserve System raises reserve requirements, excess reserves, which formerly were available for lending, become required reserves. This increase, of course, reduces a member bank's ability to expand deposits with a given volume of reserves. The opposite effect occurs if the Federal Reserve System lowers the reserve requirements.

Changes in reserve requirements occur at infrequent intervals. Table 10–2 shows these changes. Recent changes are explained by special conditions. The two classes, central reserve city banks and reserve city banks, were merged into a single category in 1962. Hence, the reserve requirements of the central reserve city banks were reduced gradually in anticipation of this merger. Prior to 1959 all required reserves had to be kept on deposit in the Federal Reserve bank. In 1959 and again in 1960, this rule was relaxed so that vault cash could be considered a part of the legal reserves. The reserve position of country banks, in particular, was improved by this relaxation of the rule, and the reserve requirement was raised from 11 to 12 per cent as a countermeasure. The reserve requirement for time deposits was decreased in 1962 to improve the member banks' competitive position with respect to savings banks.

Although a change in the reserve requirements is a powerful weapon, the Board of Governors has used it sparingly. Its reluctance to use this weapon is understandable. Reserve requirements affect only member banks; they place them at a competitive disadvantage with nonmember banks in the case of an increase. Changing the reserve requirements affects member banks which are operating conservatively as well as those which are responsible for overexpansion of credit. For many years, the banking community regarded changes in the reserve requirements as a harsh implement of monetary policy because the Board of Governors had raised the requirements by several percentage points during the 1930's. Small changes, however, are possible and the Board has employed them more recently.

Credit restrictions through reserve requirement increases tend to be extremely unpopular with member banks. If a member bank is unable to extend credit because of an increase in the reserve requirements, it is easy to trace the reason for the reduced prospects for profit to the action of the Board of Governors. By contrast, open-market operations are less direct and create less ill will.

Open-market operations. The Federal Reserve authorities rely upon open-market operations as the main instrument for the management of the monetary system. We have seen that commercial banks create deposits when acquiring assets and extinguish deposits when disposing of assets. This principle applies to central banks also. However, the deposit which a Federal Reserve bank creates when it acquires an asset becomes a reserve for a member bank. Consequently, Federal Reserve banks can increase or can decrease

Table 10–2

RESERVE REQUIREMENTS OF MEMBER BANKS

1948–1965

(Per cent of deposits)

Effective Date[a]	Net Demand Deposits[b]			Time Deposits	
	Central Reserve City Banks[c]	Reserve City Banks	Country Banks	Central Reserve and Reserve City Banks	Country Banks
In effect Dec. 31, 1948	26	22	16	7½	7½
1949, May 1, 5	24	21	15	7	7
June 30, July 1	—	20	14	6	6
Aug. 1, 11	23½	19½	13	5	—
Aug. 16, 18	23	19	12	—	5
Aug. 25	22½	18½	—	—	—
Sept. 1	22	18	—	—	—
1951, Jan. 11, 16	23	19	13	6	6
Jan. 25, Feb. 1	24	20	14	—	—
1953, July 1, 9	22	19	13	—	—
1954, June 16, 24	21	—	—	5	5
July 29, Aug. 1	20	18	12	—	—
1958, Feb. 27, Mar. 1	19½	17½	11½	—	—
Mar. 20, Apr. 1	19	17	11	—	—
Apr. 17	18½	—	—	—	—
Apr. 24	18	16½	—	—	—
1960, Sept. 1	17½	—	—	—	—
Nov. 24	—	—	12	—	—
Dec. 1	16½	—	—	—	—
1962, Oct. 25, Nov. 1	—	—	—	4	4
In effect Feb. 1, 1965	—	16½	12	4	4
Present legal requirement:					
Minimum	10	7	3	3	
Maximum	22	14	6	6	

[a]When two dates are shown, first-of-month or midmonth dates record changes at country banks, and other dates (usually Thursday) record changes at central reserve or reserve city banks.

[b]Demand deposits subject to reserve requirements are gross demand deposits minus cash items in process of collection and demand balances due from domestic banks.

[c]Authority of the Board of Governors to classify or reclassify cities as central reserve cities was terminated effective July 28, 1962.

member-bank reserves by acquiring or disposing of assets. Any asset handled by the Federal Reserve banks leads to this result, but in practice the Reserve banks purchase only United States securities on the open market. In a few instances, the Reserve banks acquire commercial paper, however.

The open-market instrument was developed in the early 1920's, but assets were acquired by the Federal Reserve banks prior to that time. However, the acquisition was motivated at times by a need for earnings, so the actions of the twelve banks were unco-ordinated. The effect on member bank reserves was noted and an Open Market Committee was formed in 1923 to co-ordinate the transactions of the several banks. It was noted in Chapter 9 that the Open Market Committee was granted statutory status by the 1935 amendment to the Federal Reserve Act. The usefulness of this instrument is illustrated by the following sample open-market transactions.

Let us assume that the Federal Reserve authorities feel that bank credit is or is about to become overextended. A rise in the discount rate will not cause member banks to curtail the extension of credit if they are not in debt to the Federal Reserve banks. The Federal Reserve authorities consider an increase in reserve requirements too harsh at this time. They have an alternative. By selling United States securities on the open market, they can reduce commercial member bank reserves and so can force these banks to restrict credit. If the Federal Reserve banks sell United States securities worth $100 million, the following results occur:

A. A member bank purchases the securities.

FEDERAL RESERVE BANK

Assets		Liabilities	
U.S. securities	−$100,000,000	Deposits of member bank	−$100,000,000

MEMBER BANK

Assets		Liabilities
Reserves	−$100,000,000	
U.S. securities	+ 100,000,000	

TABLE 10–2:

NOTE: All required reserves were held on deposit with Federal Reserve banks, June 21, 1917, until late 1959. Since then, member banks have also been allowed to count vault cash as reserves, as follows: Country banks—in excess of 4 and 2½ per cent of net demand deposits effective December 1, 1959, and August 25, 1960, respectively. Central reserve city and reserve city banks—in excess of 2 and 1 per cent effective December 3, 1959, and September 1, 1960, respectively. Effective November 24, 1960, all vault cash.
Source: *Federal Reserve Bulletin,* February, 1965, p. 268.

Thus, open-market selling reduces the reserves of the member banks and the ability to create deposits. Case A requires that the member banks co-operate by purchasing securities. However, member banks are unlikely to do so if it will impair their lending ability. We then have Case B where the Federal Reserve banks sell the securities to a private individual, a nonbank corporation, or a nonmember bank. In brief, they sell the securities to whomever they can; hence we have the term open market.[1]

B. An agent other than a member bank purchases the securities. The effect on the Federal Reserve bank statement is the same as in Case A:

FEDERAL RESERVE BANK

Assets	*Liabilities*
U.S. securities −$100,000,000	Deposits of member banks −$100,000,000

The purchaser pays for the securities with checks drawn against a member bank. When the bank honors the checks, the member bank statement shows these changes:

MEMBER BANK

Assets	*Liabilities*
Reserves −$100,000,000	Deposits −$100,000,000 *Requ.*

— but by not as much, because of Req.

Either Case A or Case B decreases member bank reserves. If member banks buy the securities, there is no immediate decrease in deposits held by the public. If someone other than a member bank buys the securities, deposits held by the public decline immediately.

Without a detailed explanation, it should be apparent that open-market buying by the Federal Reserve banks would have the opposite effect from selling. It is obvious that member bank reserves increase when we reverse the minus and the plus signs in the preceding examples.

The Federal Reserve authorities can conduct open-market operations in large or small amounts and as frequently or infrequently as is desirable. Because of this flexibility this instrument is extremely valuable, and the System uses it to rectify temporary shortages or excesses of credit and as a policy instrument. Since the Open Market Committee does not publicize policy decisions until the Board of Governors publishes its annual report, there is no announcement effect. One can discover the extent to which open-market transactions have been taking place by checking the security

---

[1] In practice open-market transactions are conducted through established dealers in Government securities, some of whom are commercial banks.

holdings of Federal Reserve banks in the statements of condition they publish weekly. Like changes in the reserve requirements, this instrument becomes effective at the discretion of the Reserve authorities. They need not wait for member banks to take the initiative as they must in the case of the discount rate.

Other Federal Reserve Instruments of Monetary Management

The control measures we covered to this point concern the quantity of credit created by the banking system. Measures affecting member bank reserves indirectly control this quantity. Other methods of control are available, however.

[Moral suasion.] Strictly speaking this is not a control but is the use of persuasion by the Federal Reserve authorities. The Federal Reserve authorities attempt to persuade the commercial banks to operate in a fashion which the authorities feel will further the public interest. Moral suasion may take a mild, indirect form, such as providing member banks with up-to-date information concerning economic conditions in the nation. The Federal Reserve authorities assume that well-informed bank managers will make decisions which are correct from the point of view of the public welfare.

The authorities may use more forceful measures, such as appeals to reason, patriotism, and the need banks have for good public relations. Personal contacts or written communications serve to convey these appeals to the nation's bankers. In a few cases the System has instituted formal programs. The "voluntary" credit restraint programs of 1947 and 1951 which urged banks to curtail nonessential credit are examples of such measures.

It is difficult to assess the effectiveness of moral suasion. The prestige of the Board of Governors supports the program. Also member banks are aware that these "persuaders" have the power to use more forceful measures if necessary. On the other hand, the large number of banks in the United States presents a problem. An individual banker is likely to feel that his actions will not have a significant effect on the nation's economy. Countries with a small number of banks can use this method more successfully.

As a general rule, it seems that moral suasion is most effective in a time of national emergency. Banks are conscious of the need for a favorable public image. These emergencies are usually temporary, so that measures which restrict profits in the short run may have long-run benefits if banks create and maintain that favorable image.

Selective Controls

With the possible exception of moral suasion and eligibility requirements, none of the controls examined to this point has influenced directly the allocation of bank credit among the several sectors of the economy. Varying reserve requirements, changing the discount rate, and buying and selling on the open market control the amount of credit created; but the allocation of this credit is left to market forces. This is consistent with the belief that a free market leads to an allocation of resources in the public interest.

However, the Federal Reserve authorities feel that occasionally too much credit, causing undesirable results, is going to certain sectors of the economy; moreover they are reluctant to curtail the amount of credit being created since this will hinder development in other sectors of the economy. In brief, they deem improper the existing allocation of credit from the point of view of the public interest. Methods are available to modify the allocation.

Margin requirements. The previously stated condition existed in 1929. Speculators using bank credit in the stock market contributed to the rapid rise of security prices. At the same time, however, conditions in other sectors of the economy did not warrant a contraction of credit. The Federal Reserve authorities were unable to curtail credit in the securities market without hindering the other sectors of the economy.

Congressional action, following the stock market crash of 1929, remedied this situation. The Securities Exchange Act of 1934 gave the Board of Governors the right to set minimum margin requirements on loans made for the purpose of buying securities. In buying securities on an organized market like the New York Stock Exchange, it is common practice for large purchasers to pay in cash something less than 100 per cent of the purchase price. The purchaser borrows the remainder of the money from a commercial bank, and he pledges the stock as security for the loan.[2] The Board of Governors fixes the minimum margin requirement; that is, the percentage of the purchase price which the buyer must pay in cash. For example, if the minimum margin requirement is 70 per cent, the amount the purchaser may borrow in order to buy securities may not exceed 30 per cent of their purchase price. The use of the term selective, or allocative, control now should be obvious. If the Board of Governors raises the margin requirement, it reduces the allocation of credit to the securities market sector without restricting credit creation in general. Table 10–3 shows the margin requirements for the past twenty years.

[2] These loans are arranged by stockbrokers. In Chapter 8, we referred to this practice when discussing call loans in the New York money market.

Table 10–3

RECENT MARGIN REQUIREMENTS

Initial and Terminal Dates	Margin Required (% of market value)
July 5, 1945 – Jan. 20, 1946	75
Jan. 20, 1946 – Jan. 31, 1947	100
Feb. 1, 1947 – Mar. 29, 1949	75
Mar. 30, 1949 – Jan. 16, 1951	50
Jan. 17, 1951 – Feb. 20, 1953	75
Feb. 20, 1953 – Jan. 4, 1955	50
Jan. 4, 1955 – April 22, 1955	60
April 23, 1955 – Jan. 15, 1958	70
Jan. 16, 1958 – Aug. 4, 1958	50
Aug. 5, 1958 – Oct. 15, 1958	70
Oct. 16, 1958 – July 27, 1960	90
July 28, 1960 – July 9, 1962	70
July 10, 1962 – Nov. 5, 1963	50
Nov. 6, 1963	70

Source: U.S. Bureau of the Census, *Historical Statistics of the U.S., Colonial Times to 1957*, p. 659, and *Federal Reserve Bulletins*.

Consumer credit controls. In emergency periods, specifically during time of war, other selective controls have been employed by the Board of Governors. In World War II, for a brief period in the post-war years, and during the fighting in Korea, controls were placed on credit which was to be used for the purchase of consumer goods. These controls were utilized to serve several purposes. They reduced the demand for consumer goods and so restrained inflationary pressures during a period of scarcity. This decreased demand for consumer goods reduced the allocation of resources to the consumer sector and so made them available for essential war industries. Furthermore, they postponed the demand for consumer durables until the post-war period; thus they helped to avoid a recession.

The Board of Governors restricted consumer credit by setting minimum down payments for various classes of goods. This is the same principle as minimum margin requirements. The Board further discouraged borrowing for consumption purposes by limiting the time period allowed for repayment. It reasoned that the size of the monthly payment increases as the term of the loan decreases. Consequently, the number of people who can afford to buy on credit decreases as the time allowed for repayment decreases. By varying the conditions for different products, the Board achieved greater precision in allocating credit. Restrictions were more lenient on essential items than on nonessential items.

Real estate credit. The Board of Governors imposed controls on credit used for the purchase of real estate in the early 1950's. Fighting had broken out in Korea while the United States was experiencing a real estate boom. The restrictions were to control or at least to limit the speculative rise in price. Real estate controls were similar to those in the consumer field. The controls required minimum down payments and limited the length of time to maturity. These restrictions, varying according to the type and the value of the real estate purchased, were less severe on low-cost than on high-priced houses.

Evaluation of selective controls. Selective credit controls are examples of the use of monetary policy to influence directly the allocation of resources. Their use implies a lack of faith in the principle that free-market forces will bring about the optimum allocation of resources. Hence, selective controls are inconsistent with the basic principle underlying our economic system and have been criticized for that reason. The American experience with uncontrolled security markets, however, has not been a happy one and "interference" with market forces appears justifiable. Public opinion generally has supported the use of this selective control. We have used consumer and real estate credit controls in wartime and postwar periods only. During such times there is general agreement regarding the easily definable objectives of the economic system. A controlled or partially controlled economy may achieve these objectives more efficiently than a system directed by market forces, at least in the short run. Such selective controls, as part of a controlled economy, are in order but it is difficult to justify them except during such temporary periods. Congress apparently shares this opinion and has permitted the appliance of real estate and consumer credit controls only in emergencies. Selective controls which restrict consumer and real estate credit are unpopular with the sellers of these products who criticize the discrimination practiced against them.

While we might question the efficacy or the propriety of selective controls, changes in margin requirements do seem to have some effect on stock prices. This may be attributable to the psychological effect of the Board of Governor's announcement rather than to a change in the availability of credit. We must admit that loopholes exist whereby purchasers of securities obtain credit despite severe margin requirements. Securities which are not traded on an organized exchange are exempt from the regulations. For transactions on an organized exchange, margin requirements apply only to cases where the securities purchased provide collateral for a loan. A buyer may have other assets, including previously purchased securities, which he can use as collateral to obtain credit.

Consumer credit controls are more difficult to administer than margin requirements. Since many institutions in addition to commercial banks extend credit to consumers policing of all of them is necessary to ensure compliance with the regulations. Administration, therefore, requires a sizable labor force at an undesirable time since the emergency usually implies a labor shortage. The administrative difficulties cause consumer credit controls to be unpopular with many persons of authority in the Federal Reserve System. Many methods, such as inflated selling prices and trade-in values, by-pass the existing regulations. Controls on real estate credit were not particularly effective the one time the authorities used them because dealers were able to anticipate the imposition of the restrictions and thus were able to secure loan commitments in advance.

TREASURY INSTRUMENTS OF MONETARY POLICY

The Treasury no longer is responsible primarily for the nation's monetary policy. In the course of its normal activities, however, it performs certain operations which have an effect on the monetary system. The Treasury uses these operations to further the objectives of monetary policy wherever possible.

Treasury Currency Issues

At one time this was a major weapon of monetary policy, but it plays a minor and a passive role today. The Treasury issues coins and United States notes. We shall use United States notes to illustrate the effect of Treasury currency issues on the monetary system. The Treasury issues United States notes by depositing them with the Federal Reserve banks. It then spends money by drawing checks against these deposits. As the recipients of government checks clear them through commercial banks, the demand deposits of the public in commercial banks increase and the deposits of the member banks with the Federal Reserve banks increase. Treasury deposits in the Federal Reserve banks return to their original level as the Federal Reserve banks honor the checks. Thus, the money supply and member bank reserves have increased. Withdrawal of currency has the opposite effect with taxation or borrowing in place of government spending. If the Government issues coins, it must buy the metal but the monetary effect is similar to that which occurs when it issues United States notes.

A major instrument of monetary policy in the late nineteenth century was the issuance of United States notes and silver certificates. However, monetary effects arising from changes in the amount of currency issued by the Treasury Department have been slight in recent years and we can expect them to remain that way. The public's demand for small change determines the quantity of coins issued. Hence, the Treasury's role is a passive one. Congress has held the quantity of United States notes in circulation at approximately one third of a billion dollars for the last two decades, and it is unlikely to change this policy. The Treasury purchased silver and issued silver certificates in considerable quantities until quite recently, but it has been withdrawing these certificates from circulation since 1962. Since the price of silver as a commodity motivated the withdrawal, we cannot consider it a significant instrument of monetary policy.

Shifts in Treasury Deposits

The Treasury deposits the taxes and the proceeds of loans which it receives in Tax and Loan Accounts maintained by the Treasury at approximately 12,000 commercial banks. Payments by the Treasury take the form of checks it has drawn against its deposits in the Federal Reserve banks. Given these conditions, the Treasury obviously must transfer funds from its accounts with commercial banks to the Reserve banks. When such a transfer takes place, it reduces the deposit liability of the commercial banks to the Treasury; but it also reduces the commercial banks' deposits in the Reserve banks and hence member bank reserves by an equal amount. Transferring funds from the commercial banks to the Reserve banks is, therefore, a means of curtailing the commercial banks' ability to expand credit.

The Treasury spends money by drawing checks against its deposits in the Federal Reserve banks. The individuals who receive these checks deposit them in commercial banks thereby increasing the commercial banks' deposit liabilities. The commercial banks' reserves increase as soon as the Federal Reserve banks clear the checks. Consequently, the Treasury can increase member bank reserves by reducing its own deposits with the Federal Reserve banks. The process of collecting revenue, depositing it in Tax and Loan Accounts, transferring funds to the Federal Reserve banks, and spending money are continuous operations for the Treasury. The restrictions and the expansionary effects on the monetary system, therefore, cancel each other to a great extent. However, the Treasury does have some ability to vary the ratio of deposits in the Federal Reserve banks to deposits in commercial banks. If the Treasury increases the Tax and Loan Accounts in the commercial banks, these banks are able to expand credit. The reverse effect occurs if transfers to Federal Reserve banks are rapid so that they deplete the Tax and Loan Accounts. The transfer of currency from commercial banks to

Treasury vaults or the reverse produces the same effect as the transfer of deposits to or from the Federal Reserve banks.

Prior to the establishment of the Federal Reserve System, the accumulation or the disbursement of currency in Treasury vaults was a major instrument of monetary policy, as we noted in Chapter 8. The ability to shift cash balances is still of some value. It is the Treasury Department's major weapon; nevertheless, it is much less important than the instruments available to the Federal Reserve authorities. The Treasury can accumulate the cash balances which it shifts among the banks only if its tax receipts plus loan proceeds exceed expenditures. Government policy with regard to taxing, spending, and borrowing obviously must take into consideration objectives other than monetary management. Accordingly, the shifting of cash balances is a weapon of secondary importance. The Treasury uses it most frequently to neutralize the monetary effects brought on by the Treasury's practice of spending money evenly over time while it concentrates receipts in the months of March, June, September, and December.

UNCONTROLLED FACTORS AFFECTING MEMBER BANK RESERVES

A number of factors outside the control of Federal Reserve or Treasury authorities affects bank reserves. One of these factors is the supply of gold in the monetary system. The Treasury stands ready to buy gold at $35 per ounce. An owner of gold who surrenders it to the Treasury Department receives a check drawn against the Treasury deposits held by a Federal Reserve bank. When the check clears through a member bank, the quantity of money and the bank's reserves both increase. Changes in the bank statement illustrate this principle.

FEDERAL RESERVE BANK

Assets	Liabilities
	Deposits:
	Member bank ↑
	Treasury Dept. ↓

MEMBER BANK

Assets	Liabilities
Reserves ↑	Deposits ↑

The Treasury Department usually uses the gold as the basis for issuing a gold certificate to a Federal Reserve bank and receives a deposit credit in return. This exchange restores the Treasury's balance and, incidentally, increases the gold certificate holdings of the Federal Reserve bank. A decrease in the supply of gold has the opposite effect.

Indirectly the Treasury Department and Reserve authorities have some influence on the flow of gold into or out of the country, but they do not control this factor. Gold movements depend upon the conditions affecting the balance of payments, which we shall examine in Chapter 25. Consequently, monetary authorities use measures to offset the effects of gold movements rather than to control them.

Currency in Circulation

This item refers to that portion of the public's cash balance held as currency rather than as a demand deposit. The public, of course, determines the amount of currency it wishes to hold and the amount it deposits in a demand account. If the public changes the pattern by holding more currency, it withdraws deposits and indirectly reduces bank reserves. A change in the opposite direction has the reverse effect on the reserve position of commercial banks. Changes in the public's willingness to hold demand deposits as opposed to currency occur for several reasons. In fact, a recognized seasonal pattern was the cause of reserve difficulties prior to the Federal Reserve System. Open-market operations now serve to balance the effects of seasonal withdrawals. A less common reason for heavy cash withdrawals is a loss of confidence in the banking system. On the other hand, improved banking services and public education with regard to the use of checking accounts are long-range factors which favor demand deposits.

THE RESERVE EQUATION

Now we can assemble all the factors which affect directly the size of member bank reserves and thus affect indirectly the monetary system. Assemblying and arranging these factors in an orderly fashion helps us to understand the monetary system and the role of monetary policy.

The reserve equation lists all the factors which can create member bank reserves. These factors or sources can create money or a monetary base but the money so created need not become member bank reserves. The public may use it for other purposes. Hence, there is a second list of factors called "competing uses." It includes all dispositions of the monetary base other than allocation to member bank reserves. As a matter of simple logic, sources minus competing uses equal member bank reserves. The following is a list of sources and competing uses:

Sources	−	Competing Uses	=	Member Bank Reserves
1. Monetary gold supply		4. Currency in circulation		9. Member bank deposits with Federal Reserve banks
2. Treasury issued currency		5. Treasury vault cash		10. Vault cash of member banks

3. Federal Reserve credit
   a. Discounts
   b. United States securities
   c. Float
		6. Treasury deposits with Federal Reserve banks
		7. "Other" deposits with Federal Reserve banks
		8. Other Federal Reserve accounts		

We have just covered the manner in which an increase in items 1 or 2 can lead to an increase in member bank reserves. In an earlier portion of this chapter, we discussed the effect of Federal Reserve credit in the form of discounts or holdings of United States securities. Float is credit which the Federal Reserve banks inadvertently extend to member banks in the process of clearing checks. We also have described the manner in which money allocated to items 4, 5, and 6 reduces member bank reserves. The same principle applies to "other" deposits (item 7), a term which covers the deposits at Federal Reserve banks owned by "clearing" nonmember banks; certain agencies of the Federal Government, like the Export-Import Bank; foreign banks; and international agencies. Item 8, other Federal Reserve accounts, refers to miscellaneous liabilities and the capital accounts. An increase in this item, all other sources and competing uses held constant, causes a reduction in member bank reserves.

Table 10–4 shows the value of the factors.

Table 10–4

DETERMINANTS OF MEMBER BANK RESERVES

January, 1965
(In millions of dollars)

Sources:			
1. Monetary gold stock		15,258	
2. Treasury issued currency		5,395	
3. Federal Reserve credit:			
Discounts and advances[a]	435		
U.S. securities	36,684		
Float	2,126	39,245	
Total sources			59,898
Competing uses:			
4. Currency in circulation	35,400[b]		
5. Treasury vault cash	653		
6. Treasury deposits with F. R. banks	875		
7. "Other" deposits with F. R. banks	403		
8. Other F. R. accounts	949		
Total competing uses		38,280	
Member bank reserves:			
9. With F. R. banks	18,006		
10. Currency and coin	3,612		
Total member bank reserves		21,618	
Total competing uses and member bank reserves			59,898

[a]Includes industrial loans and acceptances held by Federal Reserve banks.
[b]Does not include currency and coin in the vaults of member banks as part of their reserves.
Source: *Federal Reserve Bulletin*, February, 1965, p. 262.

The reserve equation enumerates the determinants of member bank reserves. One might ask how do the reserves of nonmember banks fit into the equation? Some reserves of nonmember banks are vault cash and item 4, currency in circulation, includes them. Item 7, other deposits, includes that portion deposited with the Federal Reserve banks for clearing purposes. Nonmember banks deposit the remaining portion of their reserves with correspondent banks, usually member banks. The equation does not include this portion of nonmember bank reserves directly; these bank reserves do constitute a portion of member banks' deposit liabilities backed by items 9 and 10. Omission of nonmember banks from the reserve equation does not impair its use for monetary analysis so long as the ratio of members to nonmembers is stable.

Since monetary authorities may control the monetary system by influencing the volume of member bank reserves, they may achieve their policy objectives by varying one or several of the sources or competing uses. Upon examining the list, however, we note that neither the Board of Governors nor the Treasury authorities control the monetary gold supply, the currency in circulation, and the "other" deposits. Other factors are subject to some control by the monetary authorities, but tradition or the necessity for accomplishing other objectives limits this control. These latter factors include Treasury-issued currency, Federal Reserve discounts, float, Treasury vault cash, and Treasury deposits with the Federal Reserve banks. This leaves Federal Reserve credit in the form of holdings of United States securities the only factor over which the Federal Reserve authorities have complete control. Hence, open-market operations are the chief weapon of monetary policy.

SUMMARY

The operation of the monetary system has an effect on the economic well-being of the nation. At first the United States relied on automatic or structural controls to manage the monetary system; later it had to accept the principle that human discretion is necessary.

The primary responsibility for monetary management rests with the Federal Reserve authorities, which include the Board of Governors and the Open Market Committee. Instruments used to control the quantity of money are: changes in the discount rate, changes in the reserve requirements, and open-market operations. Moral suasion may have an effect on the quantity of credit created or on its allocation to the several sectors of the economy. Selective controls offset the allocation of credit, but the authorities confine them to the application of minimum margin requirements except in emergencies.

The Treasury Department, through its normal activities, has the power to influence the monetary system. However, its responsibility to finance the Government's operations restricts its use of these powers.

The reserve equation shows the relationship of all the factors which influence the size of member bank reserves. Federal Reserve credit, Treasury currency outstanding, and the monetary gold supply are sources which affect the relationship of the factors; for an in crease in any one of these items leads to an increase in member bank reserves, barring a balancing change elsewhere. Competing uses include those items in which an increase leads to a decline in member bank reserves, assuming that all other factors remain unchanged.

QUESTIONS

1. If the supply of money is to be increased, which of the instruments described in this chapter will be most effective? Defend your answer.
2. What were the defects in the eligible paper approach to monetary policy?
3. Are the objectives of a policy which employs selective controls different from the objectives of indirect controls?
4. Discuss the factors which limit the Treasury Department's ability to employ monetary policy.
5. Can you think of circumstances under which open-market operations would be ineffective?

SUGGESTED READINGS

Crutchfield, James A., Henning, Charles N., and Pigott, William. *Money, Financial Institutions, and the Economy.* Englewood Cliffs, N. J.: Prentice-Hall, Inc., 1965. Chapter 8.

Federal Reserve Bank of New York. *The Treasury and the Money Market,* 1954.

Fousek, Peter G. *Foreign Central Banking: The Instruments of Monetary Policy.* New York: Federal Reserve Bank of New York, 1957.

Ritter, Lawrence S. (ed.). *Money and Economic Activity: Readings in Money and Banking.* 2d ed. Boston: Houghton Mifflin Company, 1961. Chapters 7–11.

Robinson, Roland I. (ed.) . *Financial Institutions.* 3d ed. Homewood, Illinois: Richard D. Irwin, Inc., 1960. Chapter 7.

Roosa, Robert V. *Federal Reserve Operations in the Money and Government Securities Markets.* New York: Federal Reserve Bank of New York, 1956.

11

THE MONETARY SYSTEM—A SUMMARY

This chapter consists of a review of the principles governing the United States monetary system, which we discussed in the preceding chapters. In those chapters, we considered all the activities which create or extinguish money. Also, we saw that money in the United States consists of debt. Although anyone can go into debt, the public accepts the liabilities of only three institutions as money. They are: the United States Treasury, the Federal Reserve banks, and the commercial banks. Consequently, our study of the activities which create or extinguish money consisted of a study of the manner in which the Federal Reserve banks, commercial banks, and the Treasury Department acquired liabilities. However, not all the liabilities of these institutions serve as money. Therefore, we ignored the bonds and other interest-yielding debt instruments issued by the Treasury. We considered nonmonetary liabilities of the Federal Reserve banks and commercial banks, such as foreign deposits and time deposits, but we noted that they are not part of the money supply. The presence of these nonmonetary liabilities prevents us from calculating the money supply by the simple process of totaling the liabilities of the three money-creating institutions.

The problem is further complicated because the monetary debt created by the Treasury and the Federal Reserve banks serves either as the currency in circulation or as the reserve upon which member banks base their creation of monetary debt. Nonmember banks, in turn, use the monetary debts of the Treasury, the Federal Reserve banks, and correspondent commercial banks as a legal reserve in creating deposit liabilities. Calculating the potential or the maximum amount of money which banks may create is, therefore, a complicated operation. One must know the ability of the Treasury and the Federal Reserve banks to create monetary debt. One must then make assumptions concerning the extent to which this debt goes into commercial bank reserves or into circulation as money. Also, one must consider the ability of nonmember banks to use deposits in correspondent banks as the basis for further monetary expansion.

However, there is a method for combining the numerous determinants of the money supply into a single consolidated statement. This statement is based on the principle that assets equal liabilities plus capital accounts. Furthermore, it recognizes that an increase in liabilities accompanies an increase in assets for monetary institutions.

We construct this statement by using the consolidated balance sheet of the twelve Federal Reserve banks (Table 9–2) and developing similar statements for the commercial banks and the Treasury Department. In Chapter 7, Table 7–3 presents the assets, liabilities and capital accounts for all commercial banks. This is not a consolidated statement because certain items appear as both liabilities and

Table 11–1

CONSOLIDATED STATEMENT OF CONDITION FOR

ALL COMMERCIAL BANKS

As of June 30, 1964
(In billions of dollars)

Assets		
Cash items:		
Vault cash	4.5	
Deposits with F. R. banks	16.8	21.3
Investments:		
U.S. securities	59.3	
State and local securities	31.4	
Other	5.0	95.7
Loans		161.6
Other assets		6.6
Total assets		285.2
Liabilities and Capital Accounts		
Deposits:		
Demand	132.8	
Time	119.6	252.4
Other liabilities		6.0
Capital accounts		26.8
Total liabilities and capital accounts		285.2

Source: *Federal Reserve Bulletin*, March, 1965, pp. 448–449.

assets. For example, deposits of one commercial bank with a correspondent bank are part of the total deposit liabilities and the total cash assets. After eliminating these duplicate items, we have a consolidated statement for all commercial banks. This appears in Table 11–1.

As an initial approach to the development of a Treasury Department statement of condition, we might list its assets and liabilities. However, Treasury assets would not equal liabilities and we would not have a balancing net worth item. Furthermore, the Federal Government, and hence the Treasury Department, has many nonmonetary assets and liabilities which we should include if we were to calculate net worth. Such a balance sheet would be of little value in a study of money. Nevertheless, monetary statisticians have developed an "adjusted" statement using only monetary assets and liabilities of the Treasury Department.

Table 11–2

"ADJUSTED" TREASURY STATEMENT OF CONDITION

January 31, 1965
(In millions of dollars)

Assets		Liabilities	
Monetary gold stock	15,185	Gold certificates	14,906
Treasury currency		Treasury currency	
assets	5,400	issues	5,400
Federal Reserve notes	121	Treasury cash	400
Total assets	20,706	Total liabilities	20,706

Source: *Federal Reserve Bulletin*, March, 1965, p. 441.

These statisticians, admittedly, have made a number of rather arbitrary decisions in composing the statement. In Table 11–2, "adjusted" indicates that we have used some unusual definitions in estimating the monetary assets and liabilities of the Treasury Department. The statisticians have designed these definitions to achieve a balanced statement that fits into a consolidated statement of the monetary system. The reader may question the omission of deposits at the Federal Reserve and commercial banks from the asset side. We must remember, however, that we exclude as a Treasury liability the United States securities held by the Federal Reserve and the commercial banks. The monetary stock of gold held by the Treasury obviously is an asset as is the supply of Federal Reserve notes in treasury vaults, although the latter are liabilities from the Federal Reserve banks' point of view. To these items we add

Treasury currency assets. There is an arbitrary and somewhat fictitious element in this last item which consists of the silver bullion that backs silver certificates plus the face value of the coins and the United States notes issued by the Treasury. Since these coins and United States notes are not in the Treasury's possession, we may question their inclusion in the assets column. However, they do add to the monetary base and are monetary assets in this respect.

On the liability side, gold certificates represent claims against the Treasury. In this respect, they are liabilities. Treasury currency issued represents token coins and paper currency which the treasury has issued. Treasury cash is a balancing item. It takes the place of capital accounts in conventional balance sheets. Like Treasury currency assets, it is somewhat fictitious and arbitrary. It equals the difference between the monetary gold and the gold certificates outstanding plus the Federal Reserve notes held by the Treasury.

We are now ready to prepare a consolidated statement of the monetary system. This consolidated balance sheet combines the statements of the United States Treasury, the twelve Federal Reserve banks, and the commercial banks. Since it consolidates three statements, certain items "net out." For example, gold certificates are an asset item on the Federal Reserve statement and a liability item on the Treasury statement. Hence, they disappear from the combined statement. A similar situation prevails with respect to deposits of member banks with the Federal Reserve banks, member bank reserves, and loans and advances to member banks. We might prepare a consolidated statement for the monetary system by using data from Tables 9–2, 11–1, and 11–2. However, the monthly *Federal Reserve Bulletin* contains statistical information which allows us to prepare Table 11–3 directly. Table 11–3 includes some data from mutual savings banks, but the nonmonetary liabilities and capital accounts of these institutions cancel the assets so they do not affect the net monetary liabilities.

In Table 11–3 assets equal liabilities plus capital accounts even though we treat the three monetary agencies as a unit. Since we are interested in the money supply, we separate the nonmonetary from the monetary liabilities. Assets minus nonmonetary liabilities and capital accounts equal monetary liabilities, the nation's money supply.

This statement is superior to the three separate statements which serve as its base because of the "netting out" of matching assets and liabilities. By this process we overcome the difficulty raised by the fact that Federal Reserve bank liabilities may be member bank reserves or Federal Reserve notes circulating as currency. The portion of the Federal Reserve bank-created money which

Table 11–3

CONSOLIDATED STATEMENT OF THE MONETARY SYSTEM

As of February 24, 1965
(In billions of dollars)

Assets		
Monetary gold stock		14.9
Treasury currency assets		5.4
U.S. securities held by:		
F. R. banks	37.2	
Commercial and mutual savings banks[a]	66.5	103.7
Other loans and securities held by F. R. and commercial banks		257.7
Total assets		381.8[b]

Liabilities and Capital Accounts		
Nonmonetary liabilities:		
Time deposits	180.6	
Treasury deposits at F. R. and commercial banks	7.7	
Treasury cash holdings	.7	
Foreign deposits	1.5	190.5
Capital and miscellaneous accounts		35.2
Monetary liabilities (money supply):		
Currency outside banks	33.5	
Demand deposits	122.6	156.1
Total liabilities and capital accounts		381.8[b]

[a]Mutual savings banks account for a small portion of this item. An equal volume of the time deposits is attributable to these banks.
[b]Components do not equal totals because of rounding.
Source: *Federal Reserve Bulletin,* March, 1965, p. 443.

becomes member bank reserves is an asset to the member banks and a liability to the Federal Reserve banks. One item cancels the other. This is true also of Treasury-created money and commercial bank liabilities which serve as reserves for nonmember banks. The reader may regard the distinction between nonmonetary and monetary liabilities in the table as somewhat arbitrary, but it is consistent with our earlier definition of money.

The consolidated statement is valuable because it furthers our understanding of the factors affecting the money supply. Using the statement, we may trace the effect that changes in assets or nonmonetary liabilities have upon the money supply. Assuming all other determinants remain constant, the money supply will increase if there is an increase in:

1. The monetary gold stock.
2. Treasury currency assets.
3. United States securities held by the Federal Reserve and the commercial banks.
4. Other loans and securities held by commercial and Federal Reserve banks.

Other determinants remaining constant, the money supply will increase if there is a decrease in:

1. Time deposits.
2. Treasury deposits at the Federal Reserve and the commercial banks.
3. Treasury cash holdings.
4. Foreign deposits in United States banks.
5. Capital accounts and miscellaneous accounts.

It follows that a decrease in the items in the first list or an increase in the items in the second list has the opposite effect. It is unlikely that all but one of these determinants will remain constant. Nevertheless, the statement is useful for it guides us in our analysis of the monetary system and helps us to isolate the cause of a change in the money supply.

There are occasions when we are interested in the ability of commercial banks to create more credit rather than the quantity of money currently in existence. In these cases we concentrate on commercial bank reserves. The reserve equation in Chapter 10 shows the effect of the several determinants of member bank reserves. This equation is useful in analyzing the money supply and the factors influencing its size if we assume that commercial banks expand deposits to the limits imposed by reserves. Since commercial banks are profit-motivated, we generally make this assumption when analyzing our monetary system; yet, there are times when these banks hold heavy excess reserves. Furthermore, changes in reserve requirements and in the ratio of time to demand deposits allow for variations in the money supply which are independent of shifts in the level of member bank reserves. For these reasons, we find both the consolidated statement of the monetary system and the reserve equation useful.

Control of the Supply of Money

We have not discussed the precise relationship between the quantity of money and economic welfare; however, we have noted that changes in the money supply may produce significant economic effects. In addition, we have examined the institutions which create and extinguish money. Accordingly, it is appropriate for us to ask, what devices exist to ensure that these institutions control the money supply in the public interest? We approach this question by classifying the items in the consolidated statement of the monetary system (Table 11–3) as follows:

1. Items controlled by the Federal Reserve banks and the Board of Governors:
   a. United States securities held by the Federal Reserve banks.
   b. Other loans and securities held by the Federal Reserve banks.
   c. A portion of the capital and miscellaneous accounts.
2. Items controlled by the Treasury Department:
   a. Treasury currency issues.
   b. Treasury deposits at the Federal Reserve and commercial banks.
   c. Treasury cash holdings.
3. Items controlled by commercial and mutual savings banks:
   a. United States securities held by commercial and mutual savings banks.
   b. Other loans and securities held by commercial banks.
   c. A portion of the capital and miscellaneous accounts.
4. Items or factors which are "uncontrolled":
   a. Monetary gold stock.
   b. The division of Treasury, Federal Reserve and commercial bank liabilities among time deposits, demand deposits, and currency.
   c. Foreign deposits.

Beginning at the bottom of the list, we dismiss "foreign deposits" quickly since the quantity is too small to be significant. The next item, the division of Treasury, Federal Reserve, and commercial bank liabilities among time deposits, demand deposits, and currency, refers to a large volume of money and near-money. Also, a change in the ratio of nonmonetary to monetary liabilities has a significant effect on the money supply. Since no single individual or institution has the power to change this ratio, we have labelled it "uncontrolled." However, we could say that the public controls this division. Public control in this case is the result of decisions by millions of individuals. If concern that the control of the money supply may not operate in the public interest motivates our study, we can classify this item under public control and dismiss it.

We have included the gold stock in the "uncontrolled" category. This is an arbitrary decision in some respects. Accordingly, the role of gold in the monetary system of the United States requires further explanation. We have seen that the United States is on a limited gold bullion standard. This term may be misleading since gold has little significance as a direct control of the supply of money. The monetary gold stock does place a limit on the volume of Federal Reserve notes issued but the Reserve banks normally hold gold certificates in excess of the minimum requirement. Also experience indicates that the Congress repeals or modifies restrictions of this type when they become effective.

Nevertheless, the stock of gold is important. A change in this item reflects conditions in the balance of payments with other countries (see Chapter 25). A loss of gold indicates a deficit in the balance of payments and serves as a warning that corrective action is necessary. Consequently, the size of the gold stock affects the monetary system and the supply of money indirectly. A change in its size causes the monetary authorities to use open-market operations and other instruments of monetary control.

Commercial banks control items which account for over half the dollar volume of Table 11–3. The nation relies in part on competition to direct the activities of these profit-motivated institutions in the direction of the public interest. In addition, we have seen that government regulatory agencies and the Federal Reserve System influence the operations of commercial banks. Therefore, the items accountable to these institutions are controlled, at least in part, by the Federal Reserve System and the Government. In summary, we rely upon a combination of competition, government regulation, and Federal Reserve influence to direct commercial bank activities in the public interest.

The items controlled by the Treasury are small. Furthermore, the necessity of providing government services limits the Treasury's ability to use these items as monetary controls. The Treasury does influence the supply of money to some extent and the democratic process of government is the device which directs its activities in the public interest.

By a process of elimination we reach the conclusion that the Federal Reserve banks, the Board of Governors, and the Open Market Committee are the most important institutions controlling the money supply. We arrive at the same result if we begin at the top of the list. The Federal Reserve authorities, or more specifically the members of the Open Market Committee, have direct responsibility for a significant item, holdings of United States securities by the Federal Reserve banks. Indirectly, the Open Market Committee plus other components of the Federal Reserve System influence the size of the items which we list as "controlled by commercial and mutual savings banks." It follows that the Federal Reserve banks, the Board of Governors, and the Open Market Committee are very powerful institutions and the concern over safeguards to ensure that this power is used in the public interest is understandable.

SUGGESTED CHANGES

We examined the complicated structure of the System and noted that the framers of the Federal Reserve Act adopted this organizational pattern because they wished to prevent domination by special interests. This also implies that divided authority guarantees decisions in the public interest. A number of people challenge this assumption. They have misgivings concerning an institution with such great powers which is not subject to close public control.

We may classify the critics of the present system into three groups. One group recommends closer co-ordination between the Federal Reserve authorities and the Treasury Department. This group proposes a moderate structural change. Specifically, it recommends that the President of the United States designate the Chairman and the Vice-Chairman from among the membership of the Board of Governors to serve for a four-year period corresponding to his term of office. It also suggests a change in the terms of office of the members so that an incoming President would be able to appoint one new member soon after his inauguration. In addition, this group recommends an increase in the prestige of individual members by reducing the membership to five, raising salaries, and centering the powers of the System more fully in the Board. If the nation were to accept these suggestions, the System would remain independent but the executive branch of the government would have more influence within the System. A representative group consisting of leaders in government, finance, industry, labor, and education has endorsed these recommendations.[1]

A second group objects to the independent position of the Federal Reserve System. This group notes that the System is not controlled by Congress or any other elected body. The members of the Board of Governors are not elected nor are they subject to removal

[1]The Report of the Commission on Money and Credit, *Money and Credit, Their Influence on Jobs, Prices, and Growth* (Englewood Cliffs, N. J.: Prentice-Hall, Inc., 1961), chap. 3.

from office. Since the Reserve System is self-supporting, Congress does not have the control over this institution that it normally exercises through its power over appropriations. Quite logically, this group recommends that Congress exercise more direct control over the Federal Reserve banks and the Board of Governors. Political leaders supporting this position, of whom Congressman Wright Patman of Texas is the best known, follow in the tradition of Andrew Jackson, William Jennings Bryan, and others who distrusted banks in general and powerful central banks in particular. The statement that the Federal Reserve System is not responsible to any public body is correct. However, there remains the danger of an overexpansion of the money supply by a central bank subject to Congressional control.

A third group, or more precisely its spokesman Professor Milton Friedman,[2] presents a more basic criticism. He does not object to the independence of the Federal Reserve System; his criticism would be applicable even if the System were publicly controlled. Professor Friedman objects to the use of discretionary controls. He claims that their existence increases the factor of uncertainty in business. Furthermore, he notes that there is a time lag between the imposition and the effect of controls. During this period conditions may change and the influence on the economy may be the opposite of that desired. As a result, Professor Friedman urges the elimination of discretionary controls. In their place, the central bank would be given a mandate to increase the money supply at a fixed rate to be determined by the rate of economic growth. Further consideration of these criticisms and recommendations must await an examination of monetary theory and of the historical record.

SUMMARY

Several activities of the Treasury, the Federal Reserve banks, and the commercial banks influence the size of the nation's money supply. The consolidated statement of the monetary system combines the several factors which determine the money supply. By listing these factors as assets, monetary liabilities, and nonmonetary liabilities and capital accounts, we illustrate the effect of the activities of the three monetary institutions on the money supply.

The discussion of the instruments of monetary policy reveals the great power the Federal Reserve authorities possess. The complicated provisions which ensure that the system will have a broad base of control are, therefore, understandable. The Treasury also possess-

[2]Professor Friedman, a well-known economist, has presented many critical analyses of contemporary monetary institutions and policies. See Milton Friedman, *A Program for Monetary Stability* (New York: Fordham University Press, 1960).

es power to influence the monetary system. Hence, co-ordination between the Treasury Department and the Federal Reserve System is desirable. Critics of the present method of operation recommend either closer co-ordination of the Federal Reserve System and the executive branch of the Government, increased control by Congress, or the elimination of discretionary powers.

QUESTIONS

1. Compare Table 11–3 with Table 10–4. What is the purpose of each table? To what extent are they similar?
2. How does a consolidated statement of condition for all commercial banks (Table 11–1) differ from a combined statement (Table 7–3)? Under what conditions is each appropriate?
3. To what extent should the government control the central bank? Discuss.
4. How important a role does gold play in determining the money supply of the United States?

SUGGESTED READINGS

Barger, Harold. *The Management of Money.* Chicago: Rand McNally & Company, 1964. Chapters 10, 11, 14, and 15.

Commission on Money and Credit. *Money and Credit, Their Influence on Jobs, Prices, and Growth.* Englewood Cliffs, N. J.: Prentice-Hall, Inc., 1961.

Crutchfield, James A., Henning, Charles N., and Pigott, William. *Money, Financial Institutions, and the Economy.* Englewood Cliffs, N. J.: Prentice-Hall, Inc., 1965. Chapter 7.

U. S. Congress. "The ABC's of America's Money System," *Congressional Record,* 88th Congress, 2d Session. Speech of the Honorable Wright Patman, August 3, 1964. Washington: Government Printing Office, 1964.

Woodworth, G. Walter. *The Money Market and Monetary Management.* New York: Harper & Row, Publishers, 1965. Chapter 18.

IV

MONETARY THEORY

12

INTRODUCTION TO MONETARY THEORY

Monetary theory is a study of the relationship of the variables of the monetary system to certain economic objectives. In addition to studying relationships, monetary theory analyzes the determinants of the several monetary variables. In this chapter, we identify the variables and the economic objectives which are the subjects of monetary theory.

The most important variables in monetary theory are the quantity of money, the rate at which money circulates, and the volume of payments. The latter item obviously is related to the first two. Other important monetary variables are the rate of interest and the degree to which the public desires liquidity. These variables influence the entire economic system directly or indirectly. We shall study their influence by concentrating on the extent to which they affect the level of prices, the volume of employment and output, and the rate of economic growth.[1] A satisfactory price level, volume of employment and output, and rate of growth are objectives of the monetary system. We shall examine each of these objectives.

LEVEL OF PRICES

We define money as a standard of value, or as the device which measures the value of goods and services. Since we express the value of goods and services in terms of money, or price, we logically can express the value of money in terms of purchasing power or the amount of goods and services money will buy. Therefore, when we speak of the level of prices or of a change in the level of prices, we are speaking of the value of money. If one remembers that a change in the level of prices represents an opposite change in the value of money, the terms, level of prices and value of money, are interchangeable.

[1]The effect of these variables on the international balance of payments is important also. In Part VII, we shall consider this item.

197

The value of money does not change with every rise or fall in
the price of a good or a service. An increase in the price of one or
several commodities may balance a decline in other prices. The
value of money and the average price of goods then remain constant.
This is not to say that a change in the price of one commodity relative to another is unimportant. Such changes motivate necessary
adjustments in our economic system. They serve to encourage the
factors of production to move from areas where they are in surplus to
areas of scarcity, but the study of these changes traditionally is not
the concern of monetary analysts. There are occasions, however,
when the prices of a majority of the goods and services for sale move
in one direction. If this movement is upward, we say that the price
level is rising even though the price of certain items is declining.
When we speak of the level of prices in this fashion, we are speaking
of an average figure. Statisticians have developed index numbers to
measure this average change. Table 12-1 shows the changes, measured by index numbers, in the level of consumer prices in the
United States.

Table 12-1

CONSUMER PRICE INDEX

Selected years
(1957 – 1959 = 100)

Year	Index Number
1929	59.7
1933	45.1
1941	51.3
1945	62.7
1950	83.8
1955	93.3
1956	94.7
1957	98.0
1958	100.7
1959	101.5
1960	103.1
1961	104.2
1962	105.4
1963	106.7
1964	108.1

Source: U.S. Department of Commerce, Bureau of Labor Statistics. *Economic Report of
the President* (Washington: Government Printing Office, 1965), p. 244.

The United States Department of Commerce publishes index
numbers of wholesale prices and prices in other sectors of the econ-

omy in addition to the index of consumer prices. No single index measures the overall level of prices. We use the index of consumer prices as an example because it comes closer than any other series to measuring our concept of the price level, or the value of money. If we were to expand Table 12–1 to show the month-to-month index numbers, it would reveal minor fluctuations in addition to those appearing in the annual series. It is customary to interpret the term *stable price level* in such a way as to allow for small changes. We consider the price level to be stable if fluctuations remain within a narrow band; for example, 1 or 2 per cent. In the thirty-five years covered by Table 12–1, however, the changes are far too large for us to designate them as minor fluctuations. Prices fell drastically from 1929 to 1933. Since that time there has been an upward trend. The goal of a stable level of prices, therefore, has not been achieved.

A stable price level is not an end in itself, but it is desirable because of the consequences of instability. Changes in the level of prices affect the distribution of wealth, the distribution of income, and the level of output and employment. When an increase in the price level, known as inflation, occurs, the distribution of wealth is not affected if the prices of all assets change uniformly. However, this is an unlikely result. Prices of certain commodities change more than others, and the price of one particular class of assets remains constant. Bonds, promissory notes, nonparticipating preferred stock, as well as some other financial assets have constant redemption values in monetary terms. Therefore, their prices can change only to a very limited degree. It follows that members of the creditor class who are owners of these assets suffer a loss of real value when inflation occurs. Owners of commodities and other assets whose prices rise during inflationary periods gain. The chief beneficiary of the redistribution of wealth caused by inflation, however, is the debtor class which has fixed liabilities in monetary terms.

If the degree of inflation is modest, such as one per cent per year, the change in the pattern of wealth is small and may be offset by a higher yield on financial assets. On occasion, inflation may be so severe as to eliminate the real value of assets with a fixed price. This occurred in Germany after World War I when prices rose to a level over one trillion times as high as the prewar figure. As a consequence money and assets with a fixed monetary value became virtually worthless. This German case is a classic example, but many other nations have experienced inflationary periods which have eliminated the creditor class.

Inflation also affects income distribution. Certain types of incomes are constant in monetary terms. The most obvious examples are interest incomes and rental incomes fixed by long-term leases.

Other incomes react to inflation only after a time lag. Examples are the incomes of government workers and in general those of the salaried classes. These groups suffer a loss of real income. By contrast, persons with incomes based on profit or on commissions from sales gain. There is some disagreement as to the exact position of the hourly wage earner, but he seems to fall between the salaried groups and those who receive profits.

In surveying the effects of changes in the level of prices on the distribution of wealth and income, we have concentrated on inflation. We should note that deflation produces opposite results. We should also note that although we have treated income earners, owners of wealth, creditors, and debtors as distinct classes many individuals belong to several of these groups. An individual may belong to the salaried class and, by virtue of a mortgage on his home, to the debtor class. In addition he may have an interest in profits through ownership of shares of corporate stock, and he may have a bank account which makes him a creditor. Consequently, it is difficult to estimate the exact effect of inflation or deflation on any given individual.

The ultimate effect of price level changes on production and on the level of business activity is open to debate, but there is general agreement that mild inflation stimulates business activity in the short run. Production and the level of employment, therefore, tend to rise. It is more difficult to estimate the long-run effect of inflation on the level of business activity. The expectation of a prolonged period of price increases causes entrepreneurs to anticipate profits. This bright picture with respect to profit stimulates business expansion. However, the outlook is less bright for the saver who, in the absence of inflation, lends his savings to business and thus finances expansion. If the rise in the level of prices is severe, he may decide to buy tangible assets rather than to save and become a creditor. If this occurs business activity may be brisk but it may take the form of the production of consumer goods with little investment. The consequent lack of economic growth limits the level of economic activity from a long-run point of view. The tendency of deflation to have a depressing effect on business is less open to question. Depressed business conditions traditionally have accompanied periods of declining prices.

Causes of Price Level Changes

There are a number of theories concerning the cause of changes in the value of money, and the importance of monetary factors differs for the several theories. In the chapters which follow, we shall conçentrate on theories in which the monetary factors play a major role. In so doing, however, we should remember that nonmonetary factors are important also. Since the danger of a decline in the value of money has been a common problem, it is customary to present these ideas as theories of inflation. We shall follow this practice.

The traditional demand-pull theory of inflation. In this approach, we make use of the concept of aggregate demand and aggregate supply. Aggregate demand refers to the quantity of all goods and services which will be purchased at varying levels of price. Aggregate supply refers to the goods and services which will be offered for sale at different price levels. If we start from an equilibrium position with a price level p_0, we note from Figure 12-1 that the price level will rise to p_1 if aggregate demand increases from DD to $D'D'$. In the process the quantity exchanged rises from q_0 to q_1, indicating increased economic activity. We usually explain the change in aggregate demand in terms of a variation in one or more of the monetary variables. Because of the emphasis on monetary factors, we shall use this approach in the chapters which follow.

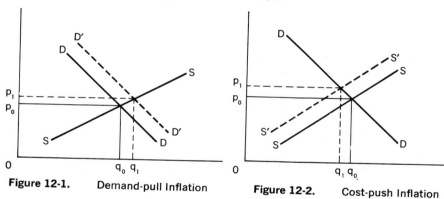

Figure 12-1.   Demand-pull Inflation   **Figure 12-2.**   Cost-push Inflation

Cost-push inflation. In recent years many analysts have challenged the traditional demand-pull theory of inflation. They admit its validity under certain conditions. Nevertheless, they claim that it does not adequately explain the most recent rise in the level of prices.

According to the cost-push theory of inflation, a shift in the aggregate supply curve causes the increase in prices. In Figure 12-2, we note that a shift from SS to S'S' leads to a higher price level and a reduction in the volume of transactions. It follows that the cost-push approach explains the simultaneous occurrence of higher prices and reduced economic activity. This ability to explain both inflation and unemployment has made the theory attractive.

The cost-push approach is significant to us because it eliminates, or at least de-emphasizes, monetary factors. Proponents of the cost-push theory point to noncompetitive conditions in certain sectors of the economy. In many instances they cite the apparent ability of powerful labor unions to demand wage increases in excess of the rise in productivity. If this occurs, the costs of production increase and the supply curve shifts as shown in Figure 12–2. Persons who are less critical of labor unions point to industries in which a small number of firms are able to control the supply and therefore the price of their products. In either case, the presence of noncompetitive conditions rather than the monetary factors is responsible for inflation.

Other Theories. There are a number of variations of the cost-push theory. Some observers of the economic system have noted the tendency of individuals and business firms to resist wage and price cuts and the relatively easy acceptance of rising price movements by the public. Accordingly, they claim that prices are flexible only in an upward direction. Behind this observation, there is an assumption that labor and business have the ability to resist downward pressure; that is, noncompetitive conditions exist. Another group cites the presence of administered rather than market determined prices. Like the preceding illustration, this condition can exist only in the absence of perfect competition.

FULL EMPLOYMENT

Idle capital equipment represents reduced production; hence, the desirability of fully utilizing capital and the other factors of production is obvious. In the case of labor, unemployment creates social problems in addition to its effect on production. Therefore, the goal of full employment is an end in itself.

The problem of determining the extent to which we fully utilize capital equipment is a difficult one. Custom and technological factors play a role. Forty hours a week represent full-time use for some items; twenty-four hours a day for others. There is also the question of how to treat obsolete plants and equipment that owners are maintaining in a standby capacity. Because of these difficulties, we shall not attempt a precise measurement of underutilization. However, there are periods when it is obvious that we are not fully utilizing our capital equipment.

Unemployed labor, by contrast, has been analyzed extensively, and the extent of unemployment is measured regularly by the Bureau of Labor Statistics. In defining full employment it is recognized that some persons will be unemployed because of job changes, because of the seasonal nature of their work, or for other reasons that are considered normal conditions. Hence, labor is considered fully utilized if no more than 3 to 4 per cent of the labor force is unemployed.

The exact degree of unemployment we must experience before we state that labor is underutilized is open to debate. Table 12–2 shows, however, that unemployment has been severe for certain years. Most economists agree that the level of employment in recent years is unsatisfactory.

Table 12–2

UNEMPLOYMENT RATE IN THE UNITED STATES

Selected years
(Per cent of civilian labor force)

Year	% Unemployed
1929	3.2
1933	24.9
1937	14.3
1938	19.0
1940	14.6
1945	1.9
1948	3.4
1950	5.0
1953	2.5
1955	4.0
1956	3.8
1957	4.3
1958	6.8
1959	5.5
1960	5.6
1961	6.7
1962	5.6
1963	5.7
1964	5.2

Source: U.S. Department of Commerce, Bureau of Labor Statistics. *Economic Report of the President* (Washington: Government Printing Office, 1965), p. 214.

Causes of Unemployment

Inadequate aggregate demand is an important cause of unemployment. Aggregate demand is inadequate if the total expenditure for goods and services is insufficient to purchase the output of an economic system operating at capacity. Since monetary factors are important determinants of aggregate demand, we shall analyze this cause of unemployment in the chapters which follow. However, we should remember that inadequate aggregate demand is not the only cause of unemployment.

Frictional Unemployment. In an earlier paragraph, we noted that workers in seasonal industries have periods of idleness. In addition, some people are temporarily idle because they are changing jobs and others are recent entrants into the labor force who have not yet found employment. We use the term *frictional unemployment* in describing the latter two groups. Frictional unemployment is not a major problem because it is likely to be of short duration for the individuals involved. Furthermore, some frictional unemployment is inevitable in a free economy. Since monetary factors do not influence this type of unemployment directly, we shall not consider it further.

Structural unemployment. Structural unemployment is a more serious problem. This type of involuntary idleness occurs when technological changes make certain skills obsolete. It also occurs when an industry moves to a different area. Aggregate demand may be high yet unemployment exists because the training or the location of the unemployed persons does not correspond to the requirements of modern industry. Monetary factors affect this problem only indirectly.

HIGH SUSTAINED RATE OF ECONOMIC GROWTH

Almost everyone agrees that a high sustained rate of economic growth is desirable. It enables us to raise the standard of living, to achieve other domestic social objectives, and to meet our international commitments. Unfortunately, we do not have a clear concept of economic growth that is acceptable to everyone. Some sectors of the economy are expanding while others are declining, and methods used to reach conclusions regarding the net change and to measure this change are subject to debate. If we are concerned with economic growth because it enables us to raise the standard of living, we should measure growth in terms of an increase in per capita output. Aggregate figures showing the increase in production by the entire nation are an appropriate measure if we are assessing our ability to meet international commitments. In either instance, the problem of whether to use gross output figures or net output figures, which allow for capital consumption, remains.

Gross national product data are used in the most widely accepted method of measurement. Since GNP is influenced by changes in the price level, adjustments must be made if the "real" rate of growth—that is, the increase in the production of goods and services—is to be measured. Such a figure, known as GNP in dollars of constant value, is computed by the United States Department of Commerce. The results of these computations, or more properly these estimates, are published in the United States Department of Commerce publication, *Survey of Current Business*, and in other statistical periodicals.

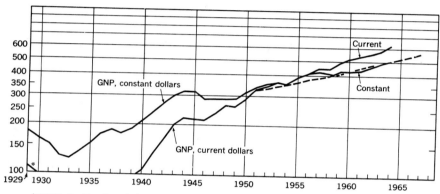

*GNP declined to $56.0 billion in 1933.

Source: U. S. Department of Commerce estimates. Board of Governors of the Federal Reserve System, *Historical Chart Book*, Washington, 1964.

Figure 12-3.   GNP in Current and Constant (1954) Dollars

Figure 12–3 shows the level of GNP measured in constant 1954 dollars and in current dollars for the period 1929 to 1964. The reference line indicates the level of GNP in constant 1954 dollars we would have experienced if the rate of increase beginning in 1954 had been a steady 3.5 per cent per year. This growth rate is in a sense an actual rate since the line representing it connects the GNP for 1954 and 1964. Critics of the present rate of growth claim that there is a greater potential for expansion in the nation. They claim that appropriate monetary policies plus other measures will lead to a better utilization of resources and consequently a higher rate of growth. The problem of deciding whether the growth rate is satisfactory is complicated by our inability to measure growth with complete objectivity. For example, the slope of the reference line in Figure 12–3 changes if we use different initial and terminal points.

Many factors influence the rate of economic growth. Natural

resources, the size and skill level of the labor force, institutional conditions, and the rate of capital formation are all important. However, capital formation is the only item in this group which is subject to change because of changes in the monetary system. Consequently, we shall concentrate on this item, also called investment, in our discussion.

PREVIEW OF MONETARY THEORIES

There is a reason for considering the goals of monetary policy before we examine monetary theories. Economists present monetary theories in an abstract form, but they generally develop these theories to justify specific policy recommendations or current practices. These theories explain the relationship between the monetary system and the rest of the economy. Several relationships are worthy of examination. There is the relationship between the quantity of money and the price level. We may expand the study of this relationship in order to include the rate at which money changes hands. The relationship of the level of employment and the level of economic output to the monetary system also demands examination. Until relatively recently we considered money and economic activity to be unrelated unless the monetary system was out of order. The quotation in Chapter 1 from J. S. Mill presents this idea. Nonmonetary factors determined the level of output and the allocation of that output among consumers and investors. Money was neutral, or passive, unless the monetary system had broken down, in which case it had a negative effect. We no longer feel that the monetary system is passive, but the belief that monetary systems can break down remains.

The earliest theory concerning the relationship of money to the price level regarded money as a commodity. The value of the commodity used as money determined the value of money and hence the level of prices. Economists rejected the theory many years ago, but vestiges of this type of thinking remain. For example, the law currently requires gold certificates as backing for Federal Reserve notes even though factors other than the gold supply limit the quantity of money. The recent use of silver as backing for certain types of money is another example of the reluctance of the United States to abandon the commodity theory.

The belief that there is a direct relationship between the quantity of money and the level of prices is a persistent one. There were theories which explained this relationship with some precision. The later versions of these quantity theories recognized the importance of the rate at which we spent money. The theory then considered not only the quantity of money but the rate of turnover of each unit. The quantity theories, however, still emphasized only one relationship—money and the price level. This was sufficient as long as the nation felt that the level of employment and output was satisfactory. When unemployment and a low level of economic activity were recognized as serious problems, these theories were of little use as policy guides.

Theories explaining the relationship of money to the level of employment and output as well as the price level have been developed. We refer to them as either the payments approach or the income and expenditure approach to monetary theory. In succeeding chapters, therefore, we shall examine two forms of the quantity theory as well as the income and expenditure approach. Of these several approaches, some form of the quantity theory dominated monetary thinking for several decades prior to the 1930's. Since that time, the income and expenditure form has overshadowed but has not replaced entirely these earlier approaches.

SUMMARY

Most economists agree that the objectives of monetary policy are a stable price level, a full utilization of resources, and a high rate of economic growth. We define price stability in nonrigid terms so that small fluctuations are acceptable. Full utilization of material resources is difficult to define, but we may relate it to the full utilization of labor. It is customary to consider labor fully utilized if the number of unemployed persons does not exceed 3 to 4 per cent of the labor force. Differences of opinion exist concerning the rate of economic growth which the nation should achieve and there is cause for honest debate regarding the rate we have achieved in the recent past. However, these differences of opinion need not deter us from considering the way in which the monetary system affects the rate of economic growth.

Monetary theory involves a study of the relationship between the monetary system and the goals we have just described. Of the two types of monetary theories, the quantity approach focuses attention upon the goal of price stability. The income and expenditure approach does not ignore the level of prices, but it does allow for consideration of the level of output and employment.

QUESTIONS

1. What is the difference between a stable price level and a system of rigid prices?
2. How does inflation affect the efficient operation of the production system? Discuss.
3. What does Figure 12 – 3 suggest to you concerning the level of prices in the United States?

SUGGESTED READINGS

Barger, Harold. *The Management of Money.* Chicago: Rand McNally & Company, 1964. Chapter 12.

Commission on Money and Credit. *Money and Credit, Their Influence on Jobs, Prices, and Growth.* Englewood Cliffs, N. J.: Prentice-Hall, Inc., 1961.

Woodworth, G. Walter. *The Money Market and Monetary Management.* New York: Harper & Row, Publishers, 1965. Chapter 11.

13

QUANTITY THEORY — EQUATION OF EXCHANGE

The desire to explain changes in the value of money motivated the development of the quantity theory of money. Economists long have recognized that some relationship existed between the quantity of money in circulation and the value of money. This recognition developed naturally from the commodity theory of money. In the period when a commodity served as money, the commodity theorists held that the value of money depended on the value of the commodity. We noted in an earlier chapter that the value of a commodity serving as money varied with the demand for this commodity for monetary purposes. Accordingly, a literal interpretation of the theory is invalid. However, since commodity theorists recognized that the value of this commodity varied according to its relative scarcity or abundance, there was an implicit acceptance of the theory that the quantity of money in circulation had an effect upon its value.

An example of this relationship was found in sixteenth-century Europe which used precious metals as money. The cause of the inflation which was occurring during that century was attributable to the increased quantity of money which, in turn, was the result of the importation of gold and silver from the Spanish possessions in America. Since gold and silver coins circulated as a medium of exchange, there was a close relationship between the quantity of money and the supply of the commodity. When a commodity like gold is the monetary standard, but debt redeemable in gold or both debt and gold coins circulate as money, variations in the quantity of money may be more drastic than fluctuations in the supply of the commodity. When this occurs, the commodity theory, modified to include considerations of variations in the supply of the commodity used as money, no longer is satisfactory. A theory applicable to either commodity or abstract money is required.

In its earliest and crudest form the quantity theory suggests that the price level and the quantity of money vary in direct proportion to each other. Thus, if the quantity of money doubles, prices double. As an expression of the relationship of money and the price level, this statement obviously is an oversimplification. No reputable theorist since the time of David Hume[1] (1711–1776) has accepted it although some relatively modern economists who emphasize the proper control of the quantity of money appear to do so.

THE EQUATION OF EXCHANGE

The quantity of money is not the only factor affecting the price level. We concern ourselves with the amount of money that we spend over a period of time to buy goods, services, securities, and other assets rather than with the quantity of money in existence. The amount of money we spend depends not only upon the quantity in existence but also upon the rate of circulation. Spending a $5 note twenty times in a month is equivalent to spending a $10 note ten times. In addition, the number of items being purchased with this flow of money has an effect on the price level. If, for example, the number of transactions increases while the amount of money being spent remains constant, the average price per unit declines. Consequently, we have three factors relating to the price level and to each other: the quantity of money; the rate of circulation, or the velocity of money; and the number of items exchanged for money, or the number of transactions. Note that this statement uses the phrase, "relating to the price level and to each other." We have chosen these words deliberately to avoid assumptions regarding causal relationships.

In the United States the statement of the relationship of these three factors and the level of prices usually takes the form of Professor Irving Fisher's[2] equation of exchange, $MV = PT$.

In the equation:

M = the average quantity of money in circulation during the period under consideration.

V = the velocity or average number of times each monetary unit is spent during the period.

P = the price level or average price per transaction.

T = the number of transactions or volume of trade during the period.

MV on the left side of the equation represents the total money expenditures for goods, services, securities, and other assets in a given period of time. The amount buyers spend obviously equals the

---

[1]David Hume, "Of Money," *Essays, Moral, Political and Literary*, Vol. III, *The Philosophical Works of David Hume* (4 vols.; Edinburgh: 1826), pp. 317–32.

[2]Irving Fisher, *The Purchasing Power of Money* (New York: The Macmillan Company, 1911). During his long career as an economist and a teacher, he discussed the relationship of the quantity of money to the price level with such thoroughness that his name is the first to come to mind when one mentions this theory.

amount sellers receive. The right side of the equation expresses receipts as the number of transactions that take place times the average Unit price, or PT.

The expression $MV = PT$ is not a true equation; it is an identity, or truism, which is valid by definition but is unlike a theory which may or may not be correct. The equation proper, therefore, is not the quantity theory of money. The theory develops when we make assumptions concerning the value and the behavior of certain factors in the equation. For example, we may have reason to believe that both V and T are constant or that they change together. When we insert these assumed values in the equation, the result is a theory concerning the value of money.

On occasion, economists have dismissed the equation of exchange because it is a truism. To discard it this casually is an error for it provides us with additional insight into the relationship of the several factors and is a useful tool in analyzing monetary conditions. The equation indicates that, other things remaining unchanged, the price level varies directly with the quantity and the velocity of money and inversely with the number of transactions. Other relationships, such as M and V, varying with T and the latter varying inversely with the price level are equally apparent.

Since the stabilization of the price level (P), one of the factors, is an important objective of monetary policy and another factor, the quantity of money (M), is subject to control by the monetary authorities, there is a temptation to use the equation as a guide to monetary policy. If we can assume that V and T are constant or that a change in one cancels the effect of a change in the other, the monetary authorities can stabilize the price level by controlling the money supply. In the pages which follow, we shall see that the assumption that V and T are constant is not justified. Nevertheless, there is some validity to the argument that on occasion we may ignore these factors when considering the effect of a change in the quantity of money on the price level. Several examples, such as the hyperinflation which Germany experienced in 1923 and the price increases which took place in this country during the Revolutionary War and the Civil War lend plausibility to the claim that we may ignore V and T.

When we accept the assumption that V and T are constant and passive, we have the crude, or rigid, form of the theory. We have also an excellent and simple guide to policy. During the period when the Fisher equation dominated monetary thinking in the United States, there was a tendency to accept these assumptions and thus to use the rigid form of the theory. Since these assumptions are open to serious question, it is necessary to precede an evaluation of the equation of exchange as a policy guide by an examination of the determinants of the several factors.

The Stock of Money

We shall adhere to the definition of money which excludes savings deposits and other near-money. Hence, the stock of money consists of currency and demand deposits which the public is holding. In Chapter 10 we discussed the methods by which the Federal Reserve authorities and the Treasury Department controlled the supply of money. Our discussion emphasized the determinants of the money supply, such as the stock of monetary gold, Federal Reserve credit, and the currency in circulation. At this point we must note that monetary gold supplies vary with changes in the balance of payments which the price level, in turn, influences. Thus, P, a passive variable according to our first assumption, influences the size of one of the other factors. The determinants affect commercial bank reserves and therefore the money supply. But their effect on the money supply depends upon the extent to which commercial banks are willing and are able to expand deposits to the limits reserves permit. From a long-run point of view, we may assume that banks will expand deposits to this limit because they are profit-motivated institutions. Nevertheless, in the short run the banks' willingness and ability to expand deposits depend upon the expectations of the banks and their customers regarding business conditions including the price level.

Accordingly, we may classify determinants of M as ultimate or immediate. The ultimate determinants are the supply of monetary gold and the other sources and the competing uses discussed in Chapter 10. Immediate determinants are the banks' willingness to lend and the public's desire to borrow. Conditions and expectations regarding interest rates, other prices, employment, and general business conditions, in turn, affect the immediate determinants and therefore the stock of money.

Thus, it is incorrect to assume that P in the equation of exchange is entirely passive. Changes and the expectation of changes in the price level influence the size of M. We may note the influence of the price level on the stock of money but we must not overemphasize it. Monetary authorities possess powerful weapons with which to counter the changes a variation in the price level causes.

Velocity

Velocity is the rate at which money changes hands. It is customary to express velocity in terms of the turnover per year. If each monetary unit changes hands through spending twenty-four times per year, the velocity is twenty-four. If velocity, V, is equal to twenty-four, there must be an average waiting period of one-half month between each turnover during which time some person or institution holds the money. Because of this inverse relationship of turnover to the average holding period, we may discuss the determinants of velocity in terms of reasons for holding money.

Money, unlike other assets for which it is exchangeable, does not yield a direct return to its owners. Accordingly, we assume the existence of other motives for holding it. There are two reasons for holding money: the transactions motive and the speculative motive. These terms first appeared when the quantity theories were declining in popularity, but they can be applied to an examination of velocity.

Persons holding money because of the transactions motive anticipate using it as a medium of exchange in the near future. Since the receipt of income does not coincide precisely with the schedule for necessary household expenses, people hold some money to pay the rent, the grocery bill, and other foreseeable expenditures. Business firms are in a similar position; they hold money to meet their payrolls and to honor other anticipated liabilities. Furthermore, money held for transactions reasons enables its owner to avoid inconvenience and embarrassment if unanticipated expenses arise. By holding money, households and business firms are in a position where they may buy on impulse or at a time and a place of their own choosing. In brief, the household or the business firm avoids embarrassment and gains freedom of action by holding cash. These are the obvious advantages to be gained by holding money for transactions reasons. Since the owner gives up an opportunity to earn interest or some other return, we must assume that he keeps these balances to a minimum consistent with his recognized needs.

The size of the cash balance which a prudent person holds for transactions reasons varies with the degree to which the community has developed credit institutions and an efficient system of payments. In a nation with a highly developed credit system, businessmen and householders are confident that they will be able to borrow money when they need it. Therefore, there is little cause for holding money and velocity rises. The extensive use of book credit, or "charging" purchases, as opposed to cash payments has a similar effect. Credit institutions also provide opportunities whereby persons with idle money may invest it profitably with confidence that they may liquidate their investments promptly and without loss.

The payments system of the community also influences velocity. If it is customary to make payments frequently, velocity will be high. A man paid once a week maintains lower cash balances on the average than one paid once a month. Hence, anything that increases the regularity and the frequency of payments tends to increase the rate of velocity. For example, an improvement in the check-clearing process enables the public to reduce the amount of money it is holding for transactions purposes.

If we take a long-range view of these influences upon the transactions motive, we can expect velocity to increase as the credit and the payment systems become more highly developed. This development is a gradual process, however, and one expects that the increase in V will be gradual. Consequently, V is unlikely to be constant in the long run but it will be stable.

Persons holding money for speculative reasons regard it as a store of value. This money does not yield an income, yet an individual may prefer to hold cash rather than another asset if he expects other assets to depreciate in value. Too, one holds money in preference to interest-earning assets if one anticipates higher yields on the assets he is planning to purchase. Consequently, expectations regarding the near future influence the amount of money being held for speculative reasons. An anticipated rise in interest rates is an incentive for holding larger amounts of money and for postponing its investment until the higher yield assets are available. Expected increases in the prices of tangible assets have an opposite effect. An expected rise in the price level leads persons anticipating the increase to buy immediately, thereby increasing their inventory of tangible assets and reducing their cash holdings to a minimum. Thus, an expected increase in the price level tends to increase V and vice versa. Finally, anticipated increases or decreases in personal income and in business receipts affect the public's willingness to hold cash. Since anticipation concerning the level of prices, interest rates, and income vary in the short run, velocity is not stable.

The results of this examination of the determinants of velocity are summarized in outline form:

I. Determinants which change gradually and which may be expected to increase the rate of turnover in the United States in the long run.

A. Development of credit institutions.
B. Expansion of book credit and installment buying.
C. Improvement of the payments system to provide for the rapid transfer of funds.

II. Determinants which change slowly, if at all. The direction of change is less certain than the determinants in group I.

A. Degree to which the schedule for income payments coincides with the schedule for expenditures.
B. Change in the regularity of income payments; for example, from monthly to weekly.
C. Change in the certainty of income payments.

III. Determinants which change rapidly, causing fluctuations in velocity.

   A. Expectations regarding the price level.
   B. Expectations regarding income.
   C. Expectations regarding the yield on financial assets.
   D. Direct controls of purchases imposed in time of war or national emergency.

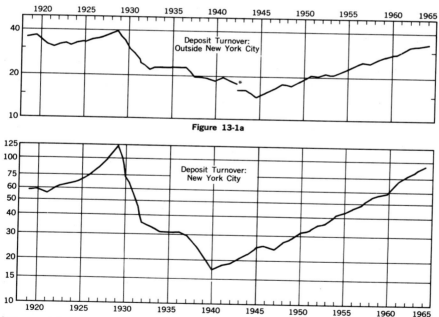

Figure 13-1a

*New series.

Sources: *Federal Reserve Historical Chart Book, Federal Reserve Bulletins.*

Figure 13-1b   Annual Rates of Deposit Turnover, 1919-1964

On the basis of this analysis, we reach the conclusion that V is stable in the long run but fluctuates in the short run. Unfortunately, the V to which we refer is a theoretical concept for which precise measurements do not exist. Consequently, empirical evidence to support or to disprove the preceding statements is not conclusive. We obtain an approximate measurement of V by taking the ratio of bank debits to average deposits. (A bank debit is the charge made against a deposit account when a bank honors a depositor's check or withdrawal slip.) Figure 13–1 on page 215 shows this ratio, or annual rate, of turnover of deposits.

The annual rate of turnover of deposits is not a precise measurement of V because it applies only to one component. It ignores the circulation of currency. Furthermore, these bank debits include payments made for purposes not included in our concept of transactions. These "extra" payments include repayments of loans, payments between branches of a single firm, and duplicate payments often made when settling real estate or security transactions. The data which the statisticians used in computing the ratios in Figure 13–1a exclude the deposits and debits of New York City banks. The ratios for these money-market banks are higher and are more volatile than those for the rest of the nation because of the influence of purely financial transactions. Figure 13–1b shows the rate of deposit turnover in New York City banks for selected years. This evidence, imperfect though it may be, lends support to the thesis that velocity is relatively stable in the long run. It also shows a definite upward trend for the years since 1944. Short-run fluctuations would be more apparent if we based Figure 13–1 on monthly rather than on annual data. Nevertheless, Figure 13–1 shows clearly the rapid decline in the rate of turnover during the depression of the 1930's. Figure 13–2 on page 217 shows the rate of turnover based on monthly data. Seasonal fluctuations are most apparent but we may also note other short-run changes.

Transactions

Transactions are the volume of trade accomplished with the stock of money. There are numerous determinants of the volume of trade. A portion of it arises from transactions involving currently produced goods and services. The quantity and the quality of a nation's human and material resources determine that nation's capacity to produce and thus fix an upper limit to transactions involving currently produced goods and services. Human resources are the labor force. The size of the labor force depends upon the population; its quality depends upon the development of skills and managerial

217

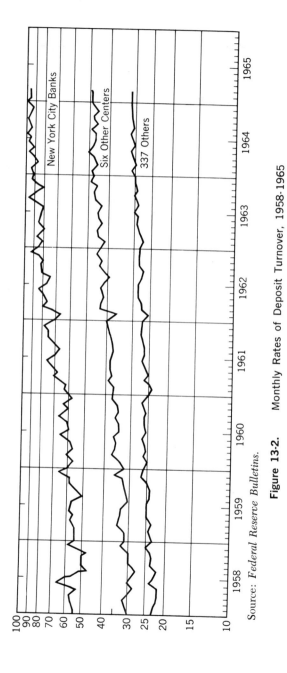

Figure 13-2. Monthly Rates of Deposit Turnover, 1958-1965

Source: *Federal Reserve Bulletins*.

ability. In the United States and in other nations, the population, and hence the labor supply, has increased in recent decades. The quality of the labor force also changes. In most countries we assume that the change is in the direction of improvement. Empirical studies seem to confirm this assumption.

The term material resources refers to capital equipment and natural resources. A nation constantly depletes its supply of high-grade natural resources. We counteract the effect of this depletion, at least in part, through new discoveries and technological improvements which allow us to use resources previously considered worthless. The supply of capital equipment declines because of depreciation; it increases as a result of new investments. Its quality improves when the new equipment is superior to that which it replaces. Experience indicates that a net increase in capital normally occurs. This net increase in the supply and the quality of capital more than balances the depletion of high-grade natural resources. Therefore, if one considers only the capacity to produce, one expects transactions to have an upward trend.

Unfortunately, the capacity to produce and the production of goods and services are not always equal. Nations frequently possess unused capacity in terms of unemployed workers and idle equipment. Since the volume of transactions depends upon output rather than the capacity to produce, we must consider the extent to which we fully employ labor and machinery. At this point we cannot discuss fully the reasons for changes in the level of employment. We can note, however, that the level of employment and output depends upon profit expectations. Profit expectations, in turn, have some relationship to anticipations regarding prices and to the anticipated demand for goods and services. Output and the volume of transactions fluctuate as these expectations concerning future business conditions change.

The industrial structure and the degree of specialization influence the volume of transactions arising from current output. In a nonintegrated industry, the process of creating the final product may involve several exchanges. Integration of the industry reduces the number of transactions; specialization of the productive process has the opposite effect for as specialization increases the number of exchanges is likely to rise. Changes in the structure of industry and in the degree of specialization, therefore, affect the volume of transactions. Structural changes take place gradually, however, and the effect on transactions takes the form of a trend rather than of short-run fluctuations.

Factors other than current production influence the level of T. One component of T is the volume of previously produced tangible assets which persons exchange in the current period. Real estate is an example of an asset in which transactions continue to take place long after the completion of production. Exchanges (sales) of intangible assets, such as newly issued securities or those already in existence, further increase the volume of transactions. The level of activity in these markets depends on expectations regarding the future price and the future earnings of the assets. Since these expectations vary with time, the volume of transactions traceable to these exchanges fluctuates.

We are now in a position to enumerate the determinants of the level of transactions.

I. Determinants with relative stability.
    A. Those which affect the capacity to produce.
        1. Population and the labor force.
        2. Extent of natural resources.
        3. Skill level of the labor force and the industrial management potential.
        4. Degree of development in capital equipment.
    B. Those which affect the number of exchanges that occur during the process of production.
        1. Degree of specialization.
        2. Business organization or the extent of business integration.
II. Determinants which fluctuate.
    A. Those responsible for the degree to which a nation utilizes its productive capacity.
        1. Price and profit expectations.
        2. Demand for goods and services.
    B. Those which affect the number of transactions involving intangible assets and assets produced in previous periods.
        1. New security issues.
        2. Activity in the market for old securities.
        3. Activity in the market for real estate and other previously produced tangible assets.

From the preceding discussion, we see that from a long-run point of view the volume of transactions is stable and tends to increase gradually. In the short run, we expect that T will fluctuate. These are the same conclusions we reached for V. Consequently, we may ask: Do changes in V on the left side of the equation counteract changes in T on the opposite side? If V and T do move together, P and M also will move together even though the assumption that V and T are constant is not valid. Our analysis indicates that velocity and the volume of transactions have some common determinants and the two factors generally move in the same direction. However, there is no reason to believe that the change in one factor is proportional to the change in the other. Accordingly, we conclude that changes in V and T in addition to changes in M influence the price level.

Price Level

The price level, P, is the average price of all the items exchanged for money. Some applications of the exchange equation to policy questions base their validity on the assumption that P is passive so that the other three factors determine its value. It is true that a change in P accompanies a change in one or more of the other factors, but this does not prove that P is passive. On the contrary, we have seen that a change in P or an expected change in P influences velocity, transactions, and even the money supply. Therefore, P can be a determinant of the other factors.

GUIDE TO MONETARY POLICY

A stable price level was at one time the main goal of monetary policy. It remains a major objective. Since the equation of exchange indicates the relationship between that goal and the quantity of money, it suggests that management of the money supply is a logical means of maintaining stable prices. But what about the other two factors in the equation, velocity and the volume of transactions? Ignoring these factors simplifies policy decisions since we can predict with accuracy the effect of changes in the supply of money on the price level. The usefulness of the equation as a policy guide, therefore, depends upon the extent to which we may ignore the behavior of V and T.

As long as we are concerned with the long-run equilibrium level of prices, we may consider both V and T to be relatively stable. In studying long-run equilibrium effects, we ignore fluctuations in V and T that are attributable to the several phases of the business cycle and to temporary conditions as the economy adjusts to changes in the money supply. We cannot assume that either factor will be constant for we have seen that economic growth, changes in the structure of industry, increased specialization of the productive processes, and changes in the methods of payments affect the volume of trade and the turnover of money. However, the changes will be gradual so that V and T are stable. They do not fluctuate. Since V and T are stable, the equation becomes a reasonable guide for long-range policy.

It is quite appropriate, therefore, that economists highly regarded the exchange equation in the period prior to the 1930's when they concerned themselves more with long-run than with short-run, or transitional, problems. Neither Fisher nor the other economists who advocated reliance upon the equation claimed that a change in M would cause a proportional change in P. They recognized that gradual changes in V and T could destroy the proportional relationship, but they asserted that the price level would change in the same direction as the money supply. The equation was an excellent means of illustrating the effect on prices of an excessive note issue or any other rapid increase in the money supply. Quantity theorists cited historical examples, such as the previously mentioned experiences of America in the American Revolution and Germany in 1923, as proof that inflation and an increase in the money supply had occurred simultaneously. Persons holding conservative views found the equation most useful since they could present it as proof of the unpleasant consequences they expected if the authorities adopted radical proposals for a change in the monetary system. One practical consequence of its wide acceptance was the added prestige it attached to the gold standard. The commodity theory had originally explained the value of money based on gold. By the nineteenth and the early twentieth centuries, this justification was no longer considered valid; the quantity theory led to the same practical recommendation that the traditional gold standard be retained. Adherence to the gold standard prevented a rapid increase in the money supply. Hence, the price level remained stable.

Use of the exchange equation is not restricted to a defense of the *status quo*. Since we can predict economic growth, and consequently a change in T, in an approximate fashion, some long-run adjustment in M is necessary to avoid deflation. The equation serves those theorists who claim that the money supply should increase at approximately the same rate as the nation's economic growth. Evidence of this type of thinking appears in the writings of modern economists who are not quantity theorists. For instance, it has led Professor Hansen[3] to warn the nation not to retire the national debt too rapidly since economic growth may require that we use it as a monetary base.

The equation of exchange has retained its usefulness as a device for explaining changes in the value of money from one generation to another and as a guide to long-run monetary policy. Its popularity declined in the depression of the 1930's when the interest of economists shifted from the consideration of long-run equilibrium conditions to concern over the short-run problems of deflated prices,

[3]Alvin H. Hansen, *Monetary Theory and Fiscal Policy* (1st ed.; New York: McGraw-Hill Book Company, Inc., 1949), pp. 197–98.

unemployment, and depressed business conditions. In the period following World War II, there was renewed concern over inflation as a problem and the equation of exchange regained some of its former popularity. Currently, however, economists make use of the quantity theory in the light of changed conditions and new policy goals.

When applied to short-run problems, the equation of exchange continues to be a valid truism. It has limited usefulness as a guide to policy. In the short run as in the long run, the quantity of money is the one factor subject to discretionary control. However, in stabilizing the price level by controlling the quantity of money, we must consider the short-run effect on V and T of changes in M. Fisher, incidentally, did not ignore these effects. He devoted a chapter[4] to the consideration of the effect of a change in M on velocity and the volume of transactions in the transition period. However, Fisher and his contemporaries felt that long-run rather than short-run problems were of major importance.

A hypothetical example illustrates the complications that arise when we use the equation of exchange as a policy guide in the short run. Let us assume that the price level has fallen and we propose to increase the quantity of money in order to raise P. How will velocity be affected? We may assume that an increase in the supply of money will lower the interest rate. The lower interest rate decreases the cost of holding idle cash and thus tends to lower velocity. However, the public may regard the measures taken to increase the money supply as inflationary in nature. If the public feels that prices will rise, it may act in such a fashion as to increase velocity. Thus, a change in V is likely as a result of the change in M, but the extent of the change and even its direction is difficult to predict.

The method employed to increase the money supply affects the extent and the direction of the change. Open-market buying by the Federal Reserve banks may have an immediate influence on interest rates. Since this buying involves the exchange of newly created money for existing securities, it is responsible for raising the price of securities and lowering the interest yield in the money market. It is probable that money created by commercial bank lending operations will have more effect on price expectations as the borrowers spend it for goods and services. The effect on V of the increase in the supply of money may not be the same in both instances.

It is not necessary for us to reach conclusions concerning the net change in V in specific instances at this point. It is sufficient to show that in the short run V may fluctuate in response to changes in M. Hence, an increase in the money supply may lead to an increase or a decrease in velocity. Inability to predict the behavior of V decreases

[4]Fisher, *op. cit.*, chapter IV.

the usefulness of the exchange equation as a guide to policy. We cannot assume that a specific change in the money supply will lead to a desired price level. Instead, the change in M may induce changes in V and T which we cannot predict with accuracy. Furthermore, we must consider autonomous variations in V and T.

Predicting the behavior of T in the transitional period is equally difficult. The actions which cause M to increase also may lead to a higher level of output and, hence, to a larger volume of transactions. This occurs if banks expand loans to finance the increased production of goods and services. A rise in output is possible only if the economy is operating at less than full production. However, an increase in the money supply under conditions of full employment may lead to a rise in transactions; the public, anticipating price increases, may engage in speculative transactions. In contrast to the preceding comments, evidence indicates that the supply of money may increase without an accompanying increase in output or in price expectations. An increased money supply may simply lower interest rates and lead to higher cash balances with no immediate effect on T. Thus, the behavior of T in a transitional period is unpredictable. It depends upon the psychological reaction of the public to changes in M and on the method employed in changing M.

During the transitional period, we must note that the conditions which bring about a change in the number of transactions are likely to affect velocity also. Improved business conditions and increased employment, which cause T to rise, tend to increase the rate of money turnover. Consequently, a rise in velocity may counteract the effect on the price level of an increased volume of trade. There is no guarantee that this action will occur or that V and T will rise to the same extent and nullify the effect on P.

In the discussion up to this point, we have considered the effects on V and T of an increase in M. We may apply the same analysis to a decline in the money supply. A shortage of money tends to raise interest rates and in this way increases the velocity of money. An expectation of lower prices, occasioned by a restrictive monetary policy, is likely to reduce velocity and the volume of transactions. Accordingly, the equation of exchange is not a simple policy guide in the short run.

In formulating monetary policy, it is incorrect to regard V and T as factors whose values change only in response to changes in the quantity of money. The discussions of the determinants of these factors show that any factor can change independently of the money supply. The need to counter these autonomous changes and their effects on the price level complicates the problems of the monetary authorities. Additional complications confront the persons formulating policy because it is necessary to achieve objectives other than the stabilization of the price level. Although the discussion up to this point has emphasized stable prices as an objective, the attainment and the maintenance of full employment are equally important.

Other Criticisms

One criticism of the equation of exchange is that it applies only to periods of full employment. This criticism is valid only in part. It is true that the equation lends itself more readily to service as a policy guide if full employment conditions prevail since we then have more reason to assume that T will be stable. If there is less than full employment of the factors of production, a low value of T reflects this condition although we must remember that current production does not affect some components of T. The equation is useful as a rough guide to a monetary policy designed to achieve full employment. By increasing M, we hope to raise T to the full-employment level. Unfortunately, as we have seen, the result is not certain. The extra money simply may lower interest rates and velocity, or it may raise prices but not the employment level. In dealing with the employment level, we concern ourselves with spending which creates income rather than with the stock of money or potential spending. Other analytical approaches have proven their superiority to the equation of exchange in relating monetary activity to employment.

There are other criticisms. The P in the equation has limited significance because it represents the average price level of dissimilar categories of assets and services. If stable prices are a policy goal, the question what prices shall we stabilize arises. In the Fisher equation, P is the weighted average price of all the items in which transactions occur. This includes: the price of labor, other services, consumer goods, wholesale goods, raw materials, new and old securities, and real estate. The price level of such a broad group is of little significance. Our concern is usually the value of money when we use it to purchase consumer and wholesale goods. The P in the equation of exchange may rise because of a boom in the securities market while the price of consumer goods and services remains steady. It is unlikely that we wish to change such a condition by lowering the price of all items to the point where P achieves its former level.

In concept, P is an index number. Unfortunately, P does not correspond to any of the published indices. In the published index numbers, consumer price levels, wholesale prices, security prices, and price levels of other categories appear as separate series. P in the

Fisher equation is an index number of all prices and no accurate measurement of its changes exists.

The same criticisms apply to T. The concept of T is so broad, including all types of transactions, that accurate data measuring changes in T do not exist. Because of this lack of statistical measurements for T and P, we are unable to test hypotheses concerning the extent to which the factors vary with each other. Even if we could measure changes in P and T, however, we have seen that the broad and all-inclusive nature of their bases restricts their usefulness.

OTHER USES

Although the applicability of the equation of exchange as a guide to policy has limits, it has other uses. It helps us to understand the relationship of the monetary system to economic activity. If the equation does not enable us to predict the result of policy measures with accuracy, it does help us to explain past events. These insights, in turn, help us to formulate current and future policy. Several examples are appropriate at this point.

We have noted already that the rise in the level of prices which Europe experienced in the sixteenth century may have been caused by the influx of gold and silver from Spain's possessions in America. In this case we are dealing with a problem in long-run equilibrium. Compared with the fifteenth century the money supply in the sixteenth century had increased. Prices rose but not necessarily in proportion since V and T changed during the century.

The equation clarifies the concern of the debtor class and others fearing deflation in the post-Civil War period. The rapid economic development of the nation in the 1870's and the 1880's required that the given money supply accomplish an increased number of transactions. With the withdrawal of greenbacks from circulation, the expectation was that the supply of money would decline. Accordingly, debtors anticipated an increase in T and a decrease in M. Since there was no reason to expect a radical increase in V, a decline in the price level seemed inevitable. This decline in P was not so serious as anticipated. The development of checking accounts as a means of payment provided for an increase in the supply of money from an unexpected source. Nevertheless, the reason for debtors advocating the issuing of greenbacks and the monetizing of silver is apparent.

Examples covering shorter periods of time are the price increases that occurred in the United States during and following every major war. In each instance the money supply had expanded and the nation experienced inflation but differences in the patterns existed. In most cases P rose as the money supply was expanding, but in the case of World War II price controls and rationing held prices relatively stable during the years in which the money supply was increasing. A decline in V, which took the form of increased idle cash balances, and an increase in T because of wartime activity balanced the increase in M in the equation. At the termination of the war and with the end of price controls, price increases led to an anticipation of additional price increases and V expanded rapidly while T remained at a high level. Thus, we can trace the immediate explanation of the price increase to a change in V. The ultimate cause is more complicated; it involves an increase in money. Table 13–1 shows that during the war years (1942–1945) wholesale and consumer price increases were small relative to the increase in the money supply. It also reveals the sharp increase in the price indices between June and December, 1946 – a period of relative stability in the money supply.

Table 13–1

MONEY SUPPLY AND PRICE LEVELS, 1940–1947

Date	Total Demand Deposits Adjusted and Currency Outside Banks (In Billions of Dollars)	Cost of Living Index (1935–39 = 100)	Wholesale Index (1926 = 100)
June, 1940	38.7	100.5	77.5
Dec., 1940	42.3	100.7	80.0
June, 1941	45.5	104.6	87.1
Dec., 1941	48.6	110.5	93.6
June, 1942	52.8	116.4	98.6
Dec., 1942	62.9	120.4	101.0
June, 1943	71.9	124.8	103.8
Dec., 1943	79.7	124.4	103.2
June, 1944	80.8	125.4	104.3
Dec., 1944	90.4	127.0	104.7
June, 1945	94.2	129.0	106.1
Dec., 1945	102.3	129.9	107.1
June, 1946	106.0	133.3	112.9
Dec., 1946	110.0	153.3	140.9
June, 1947	107.6	157.1	147.6
Dec., 1947	111.1	159.2	152.2

Source: *Federal Reserve Bulletins.*

We refer to the exchange equation as the quantity theory of money, yet it does explain changes in the level of prices which occur while the quantity of money remains relatively unchanged. Such an instance occurred in the United States during the fighting in Korea. Prices rose although the quantity of money had not increased significantly. Velocity had increased as the public, remembering shortages of goods in the previous war, began "panic" buying. The threat or expectation of shortages of goods and consequent price increases caused V, T, and P to rise while M remained constant. Table 13-2 shows the relative stability of the money supply and the rather severe increases in the consumer and the wholesale price indices.

Table 13-2

MONEY SUPPLY ·AND PRICE LEVELS

April, 1950 – August, 1951

Date	Demand Deposits Adjusted and Currency Outside Banks (In Billions of Dollars)	Consumer Price Index (1935–39 = 100)	Wholesale Price Index (1926 = 100)
April, 1950	108.9	167.3	152.9
May	109.7	168.6	155.9
June	110.2	170.2	157.3
July	110.9	172.5	162.9
Aug.	112.9	173.4	166.4
Sept.	112.6	174.6	169.5
Oct.	113.8	175.6	169.1
Nov.	115.2	176.4	171.5
Dec.	117.7	178.8	175.3
Jan., 1951	116.2	181.5	180.0
Feb.	115.2	183.8	183.6
March	113.4	184.5	184.0
April	114.1	184.6	183.6
May	114.4	185.4	182.9
June	114.8	185.2	181.7
July	115.8	185.5	179.5
Aug.	116.7	185.5	178.0

Source: *Federal Reserve Bulletins.*

The equation of exchange in the form developed by Fisher or in one of its modifications helps us to understand the relationship of the monetary factors M and V to the level of prices and to the level of output. As a guide to policy, it helps us to predict the approximate results of possible actions.

Since Federal Reserve policy takes the form of changes in M, this fact alone justifies an examination of the theory. At this point, we may note that despite criticism of the equation of exchange the Federal Reserve System continues to collect and to publish statistics regarding the quantity of money and the rate of deposit turnover.

VARIATIONS OF THE EQUATION OF EXCHANGE

We have noted the limitation of the significance of the equation of exchange because the definitions of P and T are so broad and include so much that they are meaningless. Although this limit is more serious in the cases of P and T, we may make a similar criticism of the terms M and V. One variation of the equation simply breaks the money supply into two components: currency in circulation, M; and demand deposits, M'. The terms V and V' represent the velocity of M and M', respectively. The equation then becomes $MV + M'V' = PT$. If this form is superior, it is because we benefit by analyzing the determinants of M and M' and V and V' separately. Shifts from M' to M and *vice versa* may explain the changes in the price level or the volume of transactions. For example, withdrawals of cash from bank deposits increase M at the expense of M' and apparently leave the total money supply unchanged. This change is important. The shift from M' to M may impair the reserve position of commercial banks and thus may induce further reduction in M'. If this occurs and there is no counteraction by the Federal Reserve authorities, the result is a downward pressure on the price level and the volume of trade. The crises which the nation experienced under the National Banking System began in this fashion, and the hoarding of currency which took place in anticipation of a shortage of M aggravated the conditions by reducing V.

The Current Output Form of the Equation of Exchange

In this important variation of the equation of exchange, the term O, which represents transactions involving only currently produced goods and services, replaces T with its broad definition. This eliminates transactions involving transfer and intermediate payments. Nor do speculative booms in the securities and the real estate markets affect the values in the equation. The equation becomes $MV_0 = P_0O$ where:

O = the number of units of goods and services produced during the period and sold for money.

P_0 = the average price per unit sold during the period.

M = the money supply.

V_o = the average number of times each unit of M exchanges for current output during the period.

Like the original equation, $MV_0 = P_0O$ expresses a truism. Payments for current output are equal to receipts for current output. The O in this expression is smaller than T since it omits transactions not related to current output. Accordingly, P_0O is considerably smaller than PT. The former expression is, in fact, gross national income, while PT includes gross national income plus receipts from the sale of assets such as securities. If P_0O is smaller than PT, MV_0 must be smaller than MV. Since the term M represents the supply of money in both equations, V_0 must be smaller than V. The term V_0 represents the turnover of the money supply in creating income. For this reason we refer to it as income velocity.

The equation is useful because it brings national income into the picture and helps us to understand the relationship between the monetary factors, M, V_0, and P_0, and the level of output. As a policy guide it enables us to concentrate on output rather than on transactions and on the price level of goods and services being produced. Furthermore, it introduces us to national income analysis and permits us to apply the great mass of national income statistics to the equation. Since persons responsible for monetary policy concern themselves with the level of production and the price of this output rather than with the total number of transactions, the output-income velocity equation has advantages. For example, if unemployment exists, a policy to raise output is necessary. A policy which simply raises T may result in increased transactions instead of output. Let us note, however, that the ratio of T to O will change only if the number of transfer and intermediate payments changes relative to output. Consequently, the original transactions equation or the current output variation is equally useful in the absence of speculative booms in the real estate or the securities markets.

SUMMARY

The statement of relationships which we call the quantity theory of money developed in response to a desire to explain changes in the value of money. In the early stages of monetary development, the value of money and the value of the commodity which was serving as a medium of exchange were inseparable. The value of this commodity varied as its supply changed relative to the demand for it. Since the quantity of money and the supply of the commodity were identical originally, the commodity theory of money was, in effect, a quantity theory. The modern quantity theory developed when the supply of money had begun to vary independently of the supply of its commodity base.

In America the most common expression of the relationship of the quantity of money to the price level is the equation of exchange, $MV = PT$. This equation indicates the relationship of four factors: M, the quantity of money; V, the velocity or rate of turnover of money; T, the volume of trade or number of transactions; and P, the price level. The equation leads to a better understanding of the relationship of price changes to changes in the monetary system. Since the monetary authorities who are responsible for decisions control M and a stable price level (P) is a goal, the equation serves as a guide to policy. Its reliability as a guide to policy depends upon the extent to which changes in V and T cancel each other or upon the validity of the assumption that these factors are constant. An examination of the determinants of V and T leads us to conclude that they are reasonably stable if not constant from a long-run point of view. In the short run, however, V and T are not stable nor may we assume that the changes in these two factors will cancel each other. Hence, the equation is a valuable guide to policy decisions concerned with long-run goals but is of limited use when we are dealing with short-run changes in the price level.

Opponents of the equation challenge its applicability because it does not deal directly with the problem of unemployment and because of the broad definition of T. Replacing P and T with current output and the price level of that output, economists developed a modified version of the equation to overcome this criticism. Despite the criticism of this quantity approach, actions by the monetary authorities still take the form of changes in the quantity of money.

QUESTIONS

1. Why is the statement $MV = PT$ significant despite the fact that it is a truism?
2. To what extent can the factors in the equation of exchange be influenced by the monetary authorities?
3. Since velocity refers to the rate at which the monetary units are being spent, does this factor fluctuate with the level of transactions? Discuss.
4. Other things remaining the same, how would an increase in population affect the several factors in the equation of exchange?
5. Should the "quantity theory of money" be called the "velocity theory of money"? Discuss.

SUGGESTED READINGS

American Economic Association. *Readings in Monetary Theory.* New York: McGraw-Hill Book Company, Inc., Blakiston Division, 1951.

Dean, Edwin (ed.). *The Controversy Over the Quantity Theory of Money.* Boston: D. C. Heath and Company, 1965.

Fisher, Irving. *The Purchasing Power of Money.* New York: The Macmillan Company, 1911.

Hume, David. "Of Money," *Essays, Moral, Political and Literary.* Vol. III, *The Philosophical Works of David Hume.* 4 vols. Edinburgh, 1826.

14

THE QUANTITY
THEORY OF THE VALUE OF MONEY:
The Cash Balance Approach

The cash balance approach to the analysis of price level changes is the result of studies by a number of Cambridge University economists. The equation, frequently called the Cambridge equation, serves as the basis for this approach. This version of the quantity theory, formulated by Professor A. C. Pigou,[1] became very popular in England and on the European Continent at the time that Fisher's transactions equation was gaining wide acceptance in the United States. Both equations relate the quantity of money to the price level, and each version includes factors other than the quantity of money. Monetary students may use either equation in analyzing problems and in all likelihood will reach the same conclusions. Basically, therefore, the equations are the same. We shall see that they are interchangeable in a formal sense.

Despite its apparent identity with the Fisher equation, the Cambridge version is worthy of examination; it enables us to look at monetary relations from a different point of view and provides us with additional insight into these relationships. Advocates of the Cambridge equation believe that its use leads to a better understanding of monetary problems because it emphasizes reasons for holding money. A study of the desire to hold cash serves as an introduction to the liquidity preference theory, which we shall examine in Chapter 17. Too, the cash balance approach lends itself to a supply and demand type of analysis with which students already are familiar.

[1]A. C. Pigou, "The Value of Money," *The Quarterly Journal of Economics*, 32 (1917–1918), 38–65. Reprinted in American Economic Association, *Readings in Monetary Theory* (Philadelphia: The Blakiston Company, 1951), pp. 162–183. Also reprinted in Edwin Dean (ed.), *The Controversy Over the Quantity Theory of Money* (Boston: D. C. Heath and Company, 1965), pp. 28–48.

The transactions approach, which we have just discussed, emphasizes the use of money as a medium of exchange. Since we use money for exchange purposes, it represents a means of payment to one group and receipts to another; and the truism, payments equal receipts, serves as a basis for the analysis of monetary relations. The cash balance approach emphasizes the use of money as a store of value. Once again, a truism serves as the basis for analysis. The truism states that the nation's stock of money is equal to the cash balance of all the persons and the nonbanking institutions in the nation. The validity of the statement is obvious. Every dollar must be the property of someone and must be a part of his cash balance. When an individual reduces his cash balance by spending money, another person or institution gains what the spender loses. If we were to total the cash balances of all individuals, business firms, nonprofit institutions, and the government, the total would be equal to the money supply.

A brief digression is in order so that we may see how a system for the analysis of monetary relationships develops from a simple and obvious truism. We shall draw upon our knowledge of Professor Fisher's equation of exchange and shall use it as an illustration. Merely stating the truism, total payments equal total receipts, gains for us little or nothing. By expressing total payments and total receipts respectively in terms of the stock of money multiplied by the velocity of money and the transactions multiplied by the average price, we gain a better understanding of monetary relationships. With this change, the truism becomes $MV = PT$ and is the basis for fruitful analysis. A similar circumstance exists with regard to the statement, "the money supply is equal to the total cash balances of the community." The statement is of no use as an analytical tool until we divide one or both of the terms into components.

The Cambridge equation treats the money supply as a unit but breaks the cash balance into components. We must perform this division carefully. To consider the community's cash balance in terms of the size of demand deposits and currency held by individuals, business firms, nonprofit institutions, and units of government leads to barren results. The Cambridge equation defines the cash balance in terms of ability to accomplish anticipated transactions for a certain period of time at a certain price level.[2] It bases the definition on the assumption that persons holding cash are not interested in money *per se* but rather in the power it confers upon them to finance future expenditures. To develop the equation, let us examine the position

[2]The formula presented in this text is a modification of the original Cambridge equation and it resembles Fisher's approach. Professor Pigou defined the cash balance in terms of the control over resources rather than ability to accomplish anticipated transactions.

of an individual who spends an average of $6,000 per year and currently is holding $500. If asked the size of his cash balance, he may answer that it is equal to $500. Or, he may say that he normally spends $6,000 per year and that his cash balance is large enough to cover his expenditures for one twelfth of a year. For this individual, the truism now becomes $500 = 1/12 × $6,000. Now let us ask the same question of every individual and every institution holding money. When we tally the replies, the cash balance expressed as dollars must equal the nation's money supply. Accordingly, we place the stock of money on the left side of the equation. On the right side of the equation, the product of the total annual expenditures of the nation and the fraction of the year during which the money on hand supports these expenditures expresses the cash balance for the nation. For example, given a money supply of $150 billion and annual expenditures of $3,000 billion, the truism becomes $150 billion = 1/20 × $3,000 billion.

If total expenditures are the result of 600 billion transactions at an average price of $5, we may express the cash balance as the product of three factors. The factors are: the number of transactions, T; the price level or average price of each transaction, P; and K, the time period covered, or more precisely the fraction of annual expenditures held in the form of money. The truism, money supply equals cash balances, now becomes the Cambridge or cash balance equation

$$M = KPT$$

Examination of the several terms and their interrelationship leads to insights not suggested by the axiom: the nation's money supply is equal to the aggregate cash balance of the public.

Since the three factors, M, T, and P, appear to be the same as those found in the transactions equation, K must be the reciprocal of V or equal to $\frac{1}{V}$. Monetary theorists generally accept this point of view, but they have noted minor differences in the concepts of the terms. The T in Fisher's equation represents transactions in a given period; in the cash balance approach T represents transactions involving services, goods, and other assets which the public anticipates buying in a given period. The latter T, therefore, represents resources which the public can purchase with the money it holds as a cash balance. Hence, the relative importance of certain items may differ in the two equations. The cash balance approach stresses those types of purchases which require cash to take advantage of bargains. The P's in the two equations differ slightly since they refer to the respective concepts of T, but it is unlikely that the two price levels will vary significantly. In using the equations, one may deem the differences in these two terms to be too small for consideration.

The term M represents the money supply in both equations. We noted the arbitrary nature of the definition, which restricts the money supply to currency and demand deposits, in an earlier chapter. When we considered the Fisher equation, we accepted this definition because the equation emphasizes the role of money as a medium of exchange. The cash balance equation, however, regards money as property or a store of value, which represents control over resources to its owner. Acceptance of this concept makes it more difficult to justify a definition of money which excludes savings deposits and similar liquid assets. A knowledge of the cash balance equation and the questions it raises, therefore, helps the student to understand the current controversy regarding the role of financial intermediaries found in Chapter 21.

Inasmuch as these differences in the concepts are so minute that we can disregard them, we must consider the Fisher and the Cambridge equations the same in a formal sense. The terms are interchangeable. Since K is the reciprocal of V, the same determinants control its value. Having examined these determinants in the preceding chapter, we need not cover them again in detail. It is sufficient to note that K tends to decline as credit and financial institutions develop. An increase in the regularity and the certainty of payments also causes K to decline. Finally, K may be expected to fluctuate with changes in the public's expectations concerning the level of prices, employment, and other business conditions.

At the time of the formulation of the Fisher and the Cambridge equations, the differences in their approaches were more apparent than at present. Originally, persons using the Fisher equation tended to emphasize the consequences of a change in the money supply, whereas the Cambridge school stressed changes in the public's desire to hold money. More recently, users of the Fisher equation have been stressing fluctuations in velocity so that the two approaches are analogous. The two equations still differ, however, with respect to the type of thinking stimulated and the questions suggested. The cash balance approach emphasizes the reasons why people hold a portion of their wealth in cash and the consequences of a change in decisions. The application of the cash balance equation to hypothetical examples illustrates the point.

APPLICATION OF THE CAMBRIDGE EQUATION

Consider first a change in the size of the cash balance the public desires to hold. We refer again to the person with a $500 cash balance whom we used in our previous illustration. He decides to double his cash balance. He is likely to try to implement this decision by holding $1,000 instead of $500, and he may succeed in this attempt if someone else is willing to release cash. However, this individual is of interest to us only if his decision represents similar decisions by the rest of the public. It is obvious that every individual cannot increase the amount of money he holds if the money supply remains constant. Yet the attempt to hold more money will lead to adjustments in the price level and in the volume of trade which will allow the individuals to control resources for two months instead of one month. Thus, the cash balance of everyone increases although the total amount of money everyone is holding remains constant. It is the adjustments in the price level and the volume of trade which make possible this change which is of interest to us.

For example, the individual in our illustration, in addition to the rest of the public of which he is typical, will reduce spending relative to income in an attempt to double his cash balance. This reduced spending will lead to some combination of a decline in the price level and in the volume of trade so that K will double. The cash balance equation which for the individual has been $500 = \frac{1}{12} \times \$6 \times 1,000$ will become either $500 = \frac{1}{6} \times \$3 \times 1,000$, or $500 = \frac{1}{6} \times \$6 \times 500$. The first alternative will occur if transactions remain constant while the price level falls. The second alternative occurs if the price level remains stable while a change in transactions accounts for the adjustment. Cases in between these two extremes, such as $500 = \frac{1}{6} \times \$4 \times 750$ are possible and even likely. In any case the cash balance increases but the other factors also change in the process.

The result will be the same if we use the equation of exchange and assume a decrease in velocity. People, however, think in terms of changing their cash balances rather than in terms of increasing or decreasing the velocity of money. Consequently, the cash balance approach directs our thinking to the motives which cause persons to increase their cash balances or their reluctance to spend. If a feeling of insecurity motivates the increase in the cash balance, the cash balance approach points out the relationship of uncertainty to changes in the price level and the level of output. In the preceding illustration, uncertainty regarding employment and business conditions may cause the individual to decide to increase his cash balance. Since the individual is typical of many others, the fear of unemployment and poor business conditions causes him, and others who share his fear, to act in such a way as to create these unpleasant conditions. This approach, drawing attention to the reasons why people wish to change the portion of wealth held in the form of money, provides an easy transition to the income and expenditure type of monetary theory.

The Cambridge equation also serves as a guide to policy. When we use the equation for this purpose, it is customary to treat P as the dependent variable and to observe the effects of changes in the other factors. For example, we may anticipate inflation if M and T remain constant while K declines as persons attempt to decrease their cash balances. The monetary authorities may decrease M to counteract this pressure.

GRAPHIC PRESENTATION

Employing the familiar analysis of the supply and demand curve, we may present the concept of the cash balance equation graphically to illustrate other uses for this approach. Figure 14–1 measures the quantity of money along the horizontal axis and the value of money along the vertical axis. Despite its awkwardness, using $\frac{1}{P}$, the value of money, instead of P, the price level, enables us to show D, the demand for money, as a curve sloping downward and to the right.

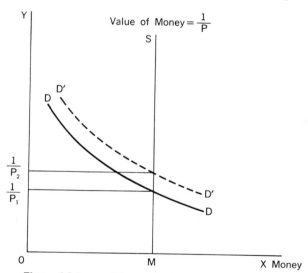

Figure 14-1.   Change in the Demand for Money

The line DD is the demand curve for money. It slopes downward and to the right for the same reason as the demand curve for items of tangible wealth. As an item becomes cheaper, other things remaining constant, the quantity people decide to hold increases. In the case of money, this means that the quantity which the public decides to hold as a cash balance increases as the value of money declines, or one may say that as the price level rises the amount of cash the public wishes to hold increases.

The line SM represents the supply of money. It is vertical since we assume that the price level does not influence the stock of money in existence. Given the public attitude with respect to holding cash, indicated by the curve DD, and the supply of money, shown by the line SM, the value of money must equal $\frac{1}{P_1}$. Only at this level will the supply of money satisfy the demand for money. If the public's demand for a cash balance increases, the demand curve will shift in the direction of D'D'. The equilibrium level for the value of money becomes $\frac{1}{P_2}$, assuming that there is a constant money supply.

Figure 14–2 shows the effect of a change in the supply of money. If the stock of money increases from OM_1 to OM_2 with no change in the demand curve, the value of money must fall to $\frac{1}{P_2}$. Thus, money, like a commodity or service, decreases in value if its supply is increasing while all the other factors remain constant.

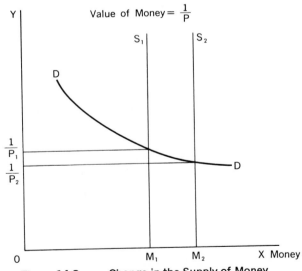

Figure 14-2.   Change in the Supply of Money

It was noted in the examination of the determinants of V and T that it is unrealistic to assume that these factors will remain constant while the stock of money is changing. Since the same conditions affect K and T, we expect a more complicated situation than that which Figure 14–2 presents. It is possible that the public's attitude toward liquidity will change with an increase in the money supply. The public may decide to increase its cash balance so that it will have control over purchases for three instead of two weeks. If this occurs, the increase in the demand for money will absorb some or all of the newly created money. In Figure 14–2 a shift of the line DD to the right will represent this increase in demand for money. A change in T may accompany a change in the money supply. If M increases at a time when unused equipment and idle workers are available, output and, therefore, transactions may increase. This increase causes the demand for money to shift to the right and counteracts some or all of the pressure for price increases. If the increase in the money supply occurs at a time of full employment, however, output cannot increase and it is unlikely that T will increase. A drop in the value of money is almost a certainty under these conditions. If this increase in the price level occurs during a period of full employment and causes the public to expect inflation, K is likely to decline. In Figure 14–2 a shift of the curve DD to the left will represent this decline in K. In this case the decline in K re-enforces the decline in the value of money.

Additional complications are possible. It is not at all certain that the assumption that the stock of money will remain constant while the demand for money is shifting is correct. If the public's attitude changes in favor of higher cash balances, individuals are likely to reduce their debts to the commercial banks. This process leads to smaller demand deposits and to a shift of the supply curve to the left. In Figure 14–1, therefore, it is possible that M will shift to the left while DD is moving to the right. If this occurs, it aggravates the increase in the value of money.

The recognition that the several factors bear complicated relationships to each other and that a change in the value of one factor may accompany an increase or a decrease in the others diminishes the usefulness of the equation as a guide to policy. As we noted in the case of the Fisher equation, an accurate prediction of the result of a change in the quantity of money is impossible, especially in the short-run period.

It is possible to analyze the effect of changes in the public's ownership of savings deposits, United States savings bonds, and other near-money through the cash balance equation. An increase in this category will not affect the supply curve if we adhere to a definition of money which includes only currency and demand deposits. However, the ownership of increased quantities of liquid assets is likely to affect the public's attitude regarding the proper size of its cash balance. If this occurs, we may expect the demand for money to decrease and the demand curve to shift to the left. Hence, a decrease in the value of money may accompany an increase in near-money. It is possible, however, that an increase in T representing increased output generated by the more rapid spending of the money supply will offset the decrease in K.

EVALUATION OF THE CASH BALANCE APPROACH

In general, the criticisms of the exchange equation approach apply to the cash balance type of analysis. The terms T and P apply to the same broad definition of transactions and prices. This criticism led to a modified version of the exchange equation which applied only to the current output and the price level of that output. A similar modification of the cash balance equation is possible. We have seen that Fisher's equation is valuable as a tool of analysis; it is of limited use as a guide to policy unless we assume that certain factors are constant. The same limits apply to the cash balance approach. We have seen that this assumption is not valid. If the stock of money changes, it is likely to affect either K or T or both of them. Consequently, the demand curve shifts with the supply curve and the net change in the value of money depends upon assumptions regarding the direction and the extent of the shifts. Likewise, it is inaccurate to assume that the demand for money will change without affecting the supply. In our monetary system, we may expect a change in demand to affect the amount of deposits being created by the banking system.

One criticism applies to the cash balance approach alone. The concept of the cash balance is awkward. People do not think of their cash balances in terms of an ability to conduct normal purchasing activities over a certain period of time. We are familiar with a monetary economy and think of a cash balance in terms of monetary units. We are more likely to make decisions concerning the rate of spending on the basis of increases or decreases in the number of monetary units we hold rather than on the value of the purchasing power of each unit. As the value of money changes, each individual may change his attitude regarding what constitutes an appropriate cash balance, but this mental adjustment takes place gradually. In the short run, moderate changes in the value of money have little effect.

There are several deficiencies in both approaches of the quantity theory. The equations emphasize the role of money as a medium of exchange rather than as a store of value. The cash balance approach stresses the retention of money to make purchases of goods and services in the future. It downgrades, if it does not ignore, the possibility of holding money to purchase securities. Accordingly, the theory does not connect the quantity of money and the interest rate to the level of output and employment. A second deficiency follows: the theory does not provide an adequate explanation of the determinants of the level of output and employment. This defect is not serious so long as we assume that full employment is the normal condition. Therefore, the acceptance of the theory was widespread in the 1920's, and the theory reacquired some popularity after World War II. However, it appears inadequate in comparison with later monetary theories which do offer an explanation of less than full employment.

Despite their limitations these approaches do make a valuable contribution to our knowledge of monetary economics and set the stage for Keynes' liquidity preference theory. If we confine our interest to movements over a long period of time, these approaches provide an approximate indication of monetary forces affecting the price level.

SUMMARY

The cash balance approach to the quantity theory of money developed as an alternative to the velocity transactions approach. The cash balance equation is a truism which states that the stock of money is equal to the cash balance the public holds. We express the cash balance in terms of its ability to accomplish an anticipated number of transactions for a certain period of time at a certain level of prices. Hence, the cash balance becomes the product of three factors: the number of transactions per year, the price level, and the fraction of a year covered, or $M = PKT$.

The cash balance equation is interchangeable with the Fisher equation in a formal sense. However, the cash balance approach leads to an emphasis on the motives for holding wealth in the form of cash. The criticisms, noted in Chapter 13, of the quantity theory apply to the cash balance equation. Despite these criticisms and its limited use as a guide to policy, the cash balance equation provides us with additional insight into the relationship between monetary factors, the price level, and the level of economic activity.

QUESTIONS

1. What are the economic conditions which cause the public to demand a larger cash balance?
2. If an individual wishes to increase the size of his cash balance is he likely to be satisfied if K increases; that is, if the absolute level of his cash holdings remains constant while the price level falls? Discuss.

3. How may the expectation of inflation become the cause of inflation? Use the cash balance equation as the basis for your explanation.
4. What would be the effect of a condition of increasing unemployment on the value of the several factors in the cash balance equation? Discuss.

SUGGESTED READINGS

See the Readings listed under Chapter 13.

15
NATIONAL INCOME ACCOUNTING

The quantity approach dominated monetary thinking for the two decades prior to the depression which began in 1929. In the years which followed, the need for a better theoretical framework relating money to other economic activity became apparent. A changed attitude concerning the economic problems confronting the United States and other nations was largely responsible for the recognition of this need. Long-run stability of the price level continued to be a desirable objective, but policies designed to achieve this end and only this end were not acceptable. Many believed that other problems, such as unemployment and the low level of output which occurred during the periods of transition to new long-run equilibrium positions, were important. Closely related to this feeling was the increased intolerance of less than full employment. A suspicion that unemployment might be the usual state of affairs began to challenge the belief of earlier generations that full employment was the normal condition. There was also the belief that full employment, if it was the normal condition, would not occur for a long time.

There was a need for a theory that would explain the level of output, employment, and prices; one that would contribute to an explanation of fluctuations in these levels. It was this desire to explain prolonged periods of unemployment and business fluctuations as well as variations in prices and output which motivated the development of the income and expenditure approach to monetary theory during the 1930's. Many economists contributed to this development. Among these contributors, John Maynard Keynes was a leader. His book, *The General Theory of Employment, Interest, and Money*, published in 1936, receives credit for the first presentation of the complete theory. Honoring his name, we refer to it as the Keynesian theory. We also refer to it as macroeconomic theory since it deals with aggregate phenomena rather than with the actions of individuals. After its presentation, the theory immediately became the basis for policy recommendations designed to overcome the depression, and persons sometimes call it "depression economics" for this reason. This name is unfair, however, for the theory is applicable to conditions of overfull employment and inflation as well as unemployment and depression.

The income and expenditure approach de-emphasizes the quantity of money and analyzes both the flow of funds to recipients of income and the expenditure of this income to buy goods and services. It raises a question regarding the sufficiency of aggregate expenditures to purchase the goods and the services produced at full employment levels. In introducing the income and expenditure approach, this chapter presents an overall view of the circular flow of wealth. It surveys the system of national income accounting and examines the several components of this system. Succeeding chapters will analyze the determinants of these components and therefore of national income.

FLOW OF INCOME AND EXPENDITURE

Figure 15–1 shows the flow of income and expenditure of a simple economy. In the interest of brevity, it labels all owners of productive agents as households even though government and business firms own some of the factors of production. It applies the same oversimplification to the group called productive units. We shall drop this simplified approach when we divide aggregate income and aggregate expenditures into their several components. At the present time the oversimplification is justifiable since it allows us to concentrate on the circular flow of real wealth and of money in opposite directions and to avoid the diversion of following complicated diagrams.

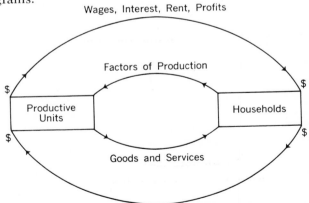

Figure 15-1.   Flow of Wealth

The inner path represents the essential economic activity. Owners of the factors of production supply them to the productive units who use them to create goods and services. These goods and services then return to the persons who furnished the labor, capital, and land. Classical economists concentrated on this inner path. They felt, quite properly, that the production of goods and services and their transfer to and use by consumers were the significant economic events. They recognized that money moved in the outer path while these essential processes occurred, but the classical economists did not believe that the monetary system affected the flow in the inner path unless the monetary system was out of order. The quotation from J. S. Mill, cited in Chapter 1, in which he referred to the insignificance of money summarizes this belief. Modern economists take the position that conditions relating to the monetary system affect the level of output. That is, they believe that the flow of money in the outer path affects the flow of goods and services in the inner path. Therefore, we shall concentrate on the outer path.

Owners of the productive factors receive remuneration which they regard as wages, rent, or other forms of income. To the productive units, however, these same payments represent the cost of producing goods and services. The recipients of income may save this money or they may spend it to purchase goods and services. It is our purpose to examine the circular flow of funds to see if the aggregate expenditures for goods and services are sufficient at the current level of prices to purchase all the products produced. If aggregate expenditures are too small to accomplish this, sales do not cover the costs of production and some combination of deflation and unemployment must result. If aggregate expenditures are too large, a combination of inflation and increased employment results.

ACCOUNTING CONCEPTS

As a first step we shall examine the concept of national income accounting and the conventional terminology. The national income accounts have important applications in several areas. They serve as an indicator of the aggregate performance of the economic system and as a means for recognizing and measuring fluctuations as well as the long-term rate of growth. These accounts allow for an admittedly imperfect comparison of the accomplishments of one nation with the economic performance of other nations. In addition, national income accounts are the basis for forecasts and policy planning, and they provide a framework for theoretical analysis and for the testing of hypotheses.

Gross National Product

Gross national product is the market value of all the final goods and services produced within a nation during a given period of time, usually one year. Although our ultimate concern is the tangible and the intangible output of the nation, it is obviously impractical to attempt to add together such dissimilar items as tons of steel, bushels of wheat, medical services, *et cetera*. For this reason and because money is a common denominator for all these products, we adopt the market value concept.

It is not within the scope of this text to consider in detail the problems of estimating GNP. Suffice to say that we must count once and only once the market value of every item produced. Interfirm transactions cause problems. Steel companies buy iron ore and coal and, in turn, sell steel to metal fabricators. If we add the market value of the finished products of the metal fabricators, the steel, the coal, and the iron companies in estimating GNP, it is obvious that we are including the value of the more basic products more than once. The proper interpretation of the adjective "final" in the definition of GNP enables us to avoid this error. The word "final" tells us that GNP does not include the value of these intermediate products. There are other approaches to the problem of estimating the value of a nation's output. The United States Department of Commerce, which computes GNP, avoids the danger of counting intermediate output more than once by using the value added by each industry rather than the value of the final product.

As a result of using market value data, the level of prices as well as the volume of output affects the size of the GNP. This is not satisfactory if GNP is to indicate changes in the level of output over time. For this reason the Department of Commerce computes the GNP in terms of constant dollars as well as current dollars. Table 15–1 shows GNP in current and in constant dollars for selected years since 1929. Figure 12–3 presents data graphically for the intervening years.

In future chapters we shall have occasion to refer to the level of GNP in discussing the nation's monetary problems and policies. GNP data portray growth as well as fluctuations in the economy. If Figure 12–3 had presented quarterly instead of annual data, the fluctuations in the level of output would be more pronounced. GNP ignores the depletion of capital goods in its estimate of the total output for a given year. Long-run economic planning, of course, must consider this depletion. Nevertheless, GNP data are useful for war-time planning and for other short-run emergencies where deferred capital replacement is possible.

Net National Product

Upon occasion economists refer to two other measurements. As the term gross implies and as we noted previously, GNP refers to the

Table 15–1

GROSS NATIONAL PRODUCT IN CURRENT AND
IN CONSTANT (1954) DOLLARS

Selected years
(In billions)

Year	GNP Current Dollars	GNP Constant 1954 Dollars
1929	104.4	181.8
1932	58.5	130.1
1933	56.0	126.6
1937	90.8	183.5
1938	85.2	175.1
1940	100.6	205.8
1945	213.6	314.0
1946	210.7	282.5
1950	284.6	318.1
1955	397.5	392.7
1957	442.8	408.6
1958	444.5	401.3
1960	502.6	439.9
1961	518.7	447.9
1962	556.2	476.4
1963	583.9	492.6
1964	622.6	516.0

Source: United States Department of Commerce, *Survey of Current Business.*

Table 15–2

NET NATIONAL PRODUCT, 1962–1964

(In billions of dollars)

Item	1962	1963	1964
Gross national product	556.2	583.9	622.6
Capital consumption allowances	48.7	50.8	53.4
Net National Product	507.5	533.1	569.2

Source: United States Department of Commerce estimates.

size of the nation's output before making allowance for capital consumption. For this reason GNP is an inaccurate estimate of a nation's ability to produce goods and services for a prolonged period. The Department of Commerce has developed net national product estimates to correct this fault. The net national product, NNP, is equal to GNP minus a capital consumption allowance. Table 15–2 shows the NNP for 1962, 1963, and 1964.

From a conceptual point of view, NNP should be a very important measurement in the analysis of economic growth as well as in the study of business cycles. Unfortunately, the estimates of capital consumption are not accurate. Whereas the estimates of the market value of all the goods and the services produced used in finding GNP are objective, at least in concept, those of capital consumption allowances tend to be arbitrary. Basing these estimates on the depreciation charges of producers disqualifies them for national income accounting purposes, for the producers design the charges to comply with tax laws and to keep the monetary value of their firms' accounts intact. The case of equipment which becomes obsolete provides us with an example of the arbitrary nature of capital consumption allowances. The accounts show a depreciation allowance which is large enough to reduce the money value of the equipment to zero even though the equipment is in good condition and is contributing to the productive process. Infrequent use of NNP data is the result. The concept is useful but the method employed in estimating the value seriously diminishes its utility.

For our purposes in this chapter, we have little use for the concept of NNP regardless of the reliability of the data. We are interested in the aggregate demand for the goods and services produced in the nation. GNP rather than NNP measures this demand. It is of no immediate concern to us if the goods purchased replace worn-out equipment or represent a net addition to capital.

National Income

At one time the national income concept was the basis for a large portion of the analyses of the nation's economic activity, but GNP has replaced it. National income refers to the money paid to the owners of the factors of production for the service of those factors. It consists of wages, rent, interest, and profits paid to those persons who supply labor, land, capital, and business enterprise to the productive process. National income differs from GNP because the latter includes sources of income which are not payments to the factors of production. We refer to these additional sources or payments for which the payers do not receive a current service as transfer payments. When considering national income, these transfer payments include pensions, indirect taxes, and the profits of government enterprises. With this concept in mind, we may note that we may compute national income by using one of two methods. We may start with GNP and deduct items that do not represent payments for the use of a factor of production, or we may total the several items which do represent payments for the use of a productive agent. Table 15–3 shows both methods applied to 1963 and 1964 data. The reader may infer the relationship of GNP, NNP, and national income to each other from the data presented in this table in addition to using these estimates as the basis for computing national income.

Table 15–3

NATIONAL INCOME, 1963–1964

(In billions of dollars)

Method A

	1963	1964
Gross national product	583.9	622.6
Less: Capital consumption allowances	50.8	53.4
Indirect business tax and nontax liabilities	55.9	59.4
Business transfer payments	2.4	2.5
Statistical discrepancy	−2.7	−1.7
Plus: Subsidies less current surplus of government enterprises	1.0	.9
Equals: National income	478.5	509.8

Method B

	1963	1964
Compensation of employees	340.3	361.7
Proprietors' income	50.6	52.0
Rental income of persons	12.3	12.4
Corporate profits and inventory valuation adjustment	50.8	57.0
Net interest	24.4	26.8
National income	478.5	509.8

NOTE: Components may not add to totals because of rounding.
Source: United States Department of Commerce estimates.

ANALYSIS OF GNP

Although several measurements are available to us in the system of national accounting, we shall use GNP as the basis for analysis. We may view GNP, the market value of the nation's output, in two ways. The total expenditures for the purchase of goods and services is one approach. In this way we are viewing GNP as gross national expenditure. Since money spent must become the property of someone in the economic system, we may also view GNP as total receipts or in terms of gross national income. Hence, as in the preceding chapter, we have an identity, gross national expenditure equals gross national income as the basis for our analysis. The procedure followed is similar to the one used for the quantity theories. The statement which is true but appears to be meaningless becomes very valuable as an analytical tool when we break both sides of the identity into components.

Table 15–4

EXPENDITURE COMPONENTS OF GROSS NATIONAL PRODUCT
for selected years
(In billions of dollars)

Year	Consumption (C)	Gross Private Domestic Investment (I)	Net Exports (E)	Government Expenditures (G)	GNP
1929	79.0	16.2	.8	8.5	104.4
1932	49.3	.9	.2	8.1	58.5
1933	46.4	1.4	.2	8.0	56.0
1937	67.3	11.7	.1	11.7	90.8
1938	64.6	6.7	1.1	12.8	85.2
1940	71.9	13.2	1.5	14.1	100.6
1945	121.7	10.4	−1.4	82.9	213.6
1946	147.1	28.1	4.9	30.5	210.7
1950	195.0	50.0	.6	39.0	284.6
1955	256.9	63.8	1.1	75.6	397.5
1957	285.2	66.1	4.9	86.5	442.8
1958	293.2	56.6	1.2	93.5	444.5
1960	328.2	71.8	3.0	99.6	502.6
1961	337.3	68.8	4.6	108.0	518.7
1962	356.8	79.1	4.0	116.3	556.2
1963	375.0	82.0	4.4	122.6	583.9
1964	399.3	87.7	7.0	128.6	622.6

NOTE: Components may not add to totals because of rounding.
Source: United States Department of Commerce estimates.

Gross National Expenditures $C + G + I_g + X_n$

GNP viewed as expenditures for the national output comprises four categories: (1) personal consumption expenditure, (2) gross private domestic investment, (3) net foreign investment, or net exports, and (4) government purchases of goods and services. The assignment of a specific expenditure item to one of the categories must be arbitrary in some cases. For example, an automobile purchased for pleasure only is a consumption expenditure item. If used for business purposes only, it is an investment expenditure. However, if the individual uses it to commute to his place of employment, it fits into either category. We shall avoid a discussion of the precise dividing line between consumption and investment and between the other categories by stating that we must include every expenditure once and only once.

Table 15–4 shows the value of each component for selected years.

Personal consumption expenditures. As the name implies, this component consists of expenditures by consumers for goods and services. It includes money spent to purchase tangibles, such as automobiles and clothing, and intangibles, such as medical and other services. The Department of Commerce divides this component into the subcategories: durable goods, nondurable goods, and services. Table 15–5 shows the relative value of each subcategory for 1963 and 1964.

Gross private domestic investment. This component includes all expenditures by individuals and business firms for capital goods. As might be inferred from the adjective gross, this category includes

Table 15–5

PERSONAL CONSUMPTION EXPENDITURES, 1963–1964

(In billions of dollars)

Item	*1963*	*1964*
Durable goods	52.1	57.0
Nondurable goods	167.5	177.3
Services	155.3	165.1
Personal consumption expenditures	375.0	399.3

NOTE: Components may not add to totals because of rounding.
Source: United States Department of Commerce estimates.

expenditures for the maintenance and the replacement of capital goods as well as the acquisition of new capital items. Major subdivisions in this component are: expenditures for residential and other buildings; expenditures for producers' durable goods, such as machinery and other equipment; and changes in business inventory. The first two subdivisions obviously represent the selling price, or market value, of a portion of the nation's output. The third element, change in business inventories, is a balancing term. Depending upon whether businesses are depleting or are increasing their inventories, the value of the national output may exceed or may be less than total sales. We can make an adjustment by including a figure which represents the value of the change in business inventory. In effect, we are treating the depletion of inventory as negative investment, or disinvestment, and an increase in inventory as an expenditure for capital goods.

Changes in business inventories may be the result of decisions to invest, or they may be inadvertent if actual sales vary from forecasts on which entrepreneurs based production schedules. Inventory changes which are the result of deliberate plans reflect the tenor of business confidence. If the changes are involuntary, they may be significant because of their effect on future decisions.

Table 15–6 shows the level of gross private domestic investment for recent years and illustrates the size of the fluctuations in this component.

Table 15–6

GROSS PRIVATE DOMESTIC INVESTMENT, 1962–1964

(In billions of dollars)

Item	1962	1963	1964
New construction	44.2	46.6	48.9
Producers' durable equipment	29.0	31.0	35.1
Change in business inventories	5.9	4.4	3.7
Gross private domestic investment	79.1	82.0	87.7

Source: United States Department of Commerce estimates.

Net foreign investment or net exports. The term net foreign investment can be misleading. This component, the only one expressed in net rather than in gross figures, requires more explanation than the others. To understand the reason for the inclusion of this component, we must remember that we are estimating the market value of the nation's output by totaling the expenditures made for the purchase of goods and services. Yet, we make some expenditures for the purchase of imported consumption and investment goods and services. Accordingly, imports cause gross expenditures to overstate the market value of the nation's production of goods and services. By a similar reasoning process, we see that exports represent national output which domestic consumption and investment expenditure data do not include. Consequently, exports cause gross expenditures to understate the market value of the national output. In summary, GNP expenditure data include expenditures on imports and exclude exports. Since we want to measure the value of total output including exports, we must add net exports to estimated domestic expenditures. If exports are equal to imports, no adjustment is necessary. However, if exports exceed imports we must add the surplus, called net exports or net foreign investment, to gross expenditures. For an import surplus the adjustment is negative. Table 15–7 shows that exports and imports did not balance in recent years.

Table 15–7

NET EXPORTS OF GOODS AND SERVICES
OR NET FOREIGN INVESTMENT

1962 – 1964
(In billions of dollars)

Item	1962	1963	1964
Exports	29.2	30.7	35.2
Imports	25.2	26.3	28.2
Net exports of goods and services	4.0	4.4	7.0

Source: United States Department of Commerce estimates.

Government expenditures for goods and services. This component consists of the expenditures of the several levels of government for goods and services. In the United States, government spends many billions of dollars to purchase weapons, fuel, building materials, and other tangible products. This represents a portion of the national output just as consumer and business expenditures do. In addition there are government payrolls. These represent expenditures for the services performed by government employees and are, therefore, a portion of the nation's output. Table 15–8 on page 254 shows government expenditures for goods and services for 1962 to 1964.

Gross national expenditures—conclusion. Adding together the several components of gross national expenditures, we obtain GNP.

Table 15-8

GOVERNMENT PURCHASES OF GOODS AND SERVICES

1962-1964

(In billions of dollars)

Item	1962	1963	1964
Federal	62.9	64.7	65.5
National defense	53.6	55.2	55.4
Other	10.2	10.3	11.2
Less: Government sales	.9	.8	1.1
State and local	53.5	57.9	63.0
Government purchases of goods and services	116.3	122.6	128.5

NOTE: Components may not add to totals because of rounding.
Source: United States Department of Commerce estimates.

Table 15-4 shows the relative importance of each component. For ease in theoretical analysis, it is customary to express gross national expenditures algebraically, using letters to represent the several components. We usually merge gross private domestic investment (I) and net foreign investment (E) in order to simplify the statement. Then,

$$GNP = C+I+G$$

where: C = Private consumption

I = Total investment; that is, gross private domestic investment plus net foreign investment

G = Government purchases of goods and services

An examination of the data in Table 15-4 serves as an introduction to material presented in later chapters. Net foreign investment does not account for a large segment of GNP in any of the years. This explains the lack of emphasis on this item in monetary theory and in debates over policy in the United States. For nations whose economy depends on foreign trade to a greater extent than the United States, net foreign investment may be an important item. Consumer expenditures are the largest component and although changes occur these expenditures are relatively stable. Government purchases of goods and services fluctuate for reasons that are easy to understand. War and periods of international tension cause large increases. This component is important when considering stabilization policy since its size is subject to discretionary control. Gross private domestic investment expenditures show the greatest fluctuation. This is particularly noticeable in the 1929-1933 period, but it is present to a lesser degree in later recessions. After noting this high degree of instability, the emphasis which national income theory places on the determination of investment is understandable.

GNP as Gross National Income

We noted that gross national expenditures must equal gross national income for any given period of time. We noted also that this statement is useless as a basis for the analysis of GNP until we separate each side of the identity into its several components. Since we have separated the expenditures into components, we must treat gross national income in the same fashion. There are several methods which we may use to divide income into subcomponents. Listing the various classes of industry in the economy and noting the income for each sector is one approach. Thus we obtain gross national income by adding the income of the agricultural, manufacturing, financial, commercial, and other sectors. Or we may classify income on a functional basis. In this case we add wages and salaries paid to labor to the rental income of landlords, the interest income of the owners of capital, and the profits of business enterprise to obtain GNP. Both of these methods, in addition to other possible suggestions, yield important information for certain purposes; but they are of little help in solving our immediate problem. We wish to examine the circular flow of money as it becomes income and as income becomes expenditure. Therefore, we wish to divide gross national income into components which provide logical partners for analysis with the consumption, investment, and government components of gross national expenditure.

We accomplish this by dividing the economy into three sectors: personal, business, and government. We note the income accruing to each sector and, more important, the income which that sector retains and has at its disposal. When using this method, the components of gross national income are: disposable personal income, disposable business income, and disposable government income. The practical problems of estimating the value of each of these components are not our concern. It is sufficient to note that private, business, and government sectors include all income elements of the economy once and only once. Each sector experiences an inflow of money which we may call gross income. After transfer payments, net disposable income for each sector remains.

Disposable government income. The disposable government income for any given period is the money available to the several levels of government after receipt of all taxes and other income and disbursement of all transfer payments. Total government revenue consists of taxes plus fees and other nontax receipts. Since taxes are the largest single item, we refer to total government revenue as gross taxes. From gross taxes the government makes payments for which it currently does not receive services. These are: (1) an item the Department of Commerce officially labels transfer payments, which includes social security benefits, pensions, and relief payments; (2) subsidies of various sorts; and (3) interest on the public debt. These payments, of course, are receipts to individuals or to businesses and become part of business or personal income. Gross taxes minus transfer payments, interest, and subsidies paid leave disposable government income, also called net taxes and represented by T_n in algebraic formulas. Table 15–9 shows the value of net taxes for 1962–1964 and the method of computation.

Table 15–9

DISPOSABLE GOVERNMENT INCOME, 1962–1964

(In billions of dollars)

Item	1962	1963	1964
Personal tax and nontax receipts	57.9	61.6	59.5
Corporate profits tax accruals	23.2	24.6	25.6
Indirect business tax and nontax accruals	52.8	55.9	59.4
Contributions for social security	23.9	26.9	28.7
Equals: Gross government receipts	157.8	168.9	173.3
Less: Transfer payments	32.3	34.3	35.7
Subsidies less current surplus of government enterprises	1.6	1.0	.9
Net interest paid	8.0	8.6	9.2
Equals: Disposable government income	115.9	125.1	127.5

NOTE: Components may not add to totals because of rounding.
Source: United States Department of Commerce estimates.

The government disposes of its income by purchasing goods and services. If these purchases are equal to net taxes ($G = T_n$), the government is maintaining the circular flow of funds at a constant level. If T_n exceeds G the government is operating at a surplus, which we regard as saving. This means that a portion of the income which the government receives does not re-enter the circular flow of funds as expenditures. Government surpluses, therefore, tend to reduce GNP. A similar process of reasoning shows us that a government deficit tends to increase GNP. The reader should note that this surplus or deficit is not necessarily the same as that indicated by the administrative budget which the President submits to the Congress each year. It is different because the surplus or deficit which is the result of a comparison of G and T_n reflects the activities of all levels of government and makes adjustments for transfer payments.

Disposable personal income. Disposable personal income is the income available to individuals, or households, after taxes and other transfer payments. Since this income is available for saving or spending at the discretion of the individual, we label it personal disposable income. Table 15–10a shows the items which contribute to gross personal income and the necessary deductions which enable us to arrive at disposable personal income. The two items deducted from gross personal income become, of course, a portion of the tax and nontax item in the disposable government income statement. We may compute disposable personal income by the method shown in Table 15–10b. An examination of the alternate method further illustrates the relationship of personal disposable income to GNP.

Table 15–10a

DISPOSABLE PERSONAL INCOME, 1962–1964

(In billions of dollars)

Item	1962	1963	1964
Wages and salaries	297.1	312.1	331.6
Other labor income	12.3	13.1	14.1
Proprietors' income	49.8	50.6	52.0
Rental income	12.2	12.3	12.4
Dividends	16.5	18.0	19.8
Personal interest income	30.0	32.9	36.0
Transfer payments	34.7	36.7	38.2
Less: Personal contributions for social insurance	10.3	11.8	12.7
Equals: Total personal income	442.4	464.1	491.4
Less: Personal tax and nontax payments	57.9	61.6	59.5
Equals: Disposable personal income	384.6	402.5	431.8
Less: Personal consumption expenditures	356.8	375.0	399.3
Equals: Personal saving	27.8	27.5	32.5

NOTE: Components may not add to totals because of rounding.
Source: United States Department of Commerce estimates.

Table 15–10b

DISPOSABLE PERSONAL INCOME, 1962–1964

(In billions of dollars)

Item	1962	1963	1964
Gross national product	556.2	583.9	622.6
Less: Capital consumption allowances	48.7	50.8	53.4
Indirect business tax and non-			
tax liability	52.8	55.9	59.4
Business transfer payments	2.4	2.4	2.5
Statistical discrepancy	−1.8	−2.7	−1.7
Plus: Subsidies less current surplus			
of government enterprises	1.6	1.0	.9
Equals: National income	455.6	478.5	509.8
Less: Corporate profits and inven-			
tory valuation adjustment	48.4	50.8	57.0
Contributions for social in-			
surance	23.9	26.9	28.7
Plus: Government transfer payments	32.3	34.3	35.7
Net interest paid by government	8.0	8.6	9.2
Dividends	16.5	18.0	19.8
Business transfer payments	2.4	2.4	2.5
Equals: Personal income	442.4	464.1	491.4
Less: Personal tax and nontax payments	57.9	61.6	59.5
Equals: Disposable personal income	384.6	402.5	431.8
Less: Personal consumption expenditures	356.8	375.0	399.3
Equals: Personal saving	27.8	27.5	32.5

NOTE: Components may not add to totals because of rounding.
Source: United States Department of Commerce estimates.

Individuals and households dispose of this income by spending it for consumer goods and services or by saving it. The portion spent for consumer goods and services obviously returns to the circular flow as an expenditure. It is, in fact, the consumption component of gross national expenditures, or C, which we discussed previously. The portion not spent is personal saving and we use the symbol S_p to represent it. Disposable personal income, therefore, is equal to $C + S_p$.

Disposable business income. The disposable business income concept is similar to those used for the government and the personal sectors. Disposable business income consists of funds available to corporations after they have paid taxes and dividends to government and individuals, respectively. Table 15–11 shows the several elements involved in the computation of disposable business income S_b and the value of each item for 1962 to 1964.

Table 15–11

DISPOSABLE BUSINESS INCOME, 1962–1964

(In billions of dollars)

Item	1962	1963	1964
Corporate profits and inventory valuation adjustment	48.4	50.8	57.0
Capital consumption allowances	48.7	50.8	53.4
Equals: Gross money available	97.1	101.6	110.4
Less: Dividends paid	16.5	18.0	19.8
Corporate profits tax liability	23.2	24.6	25.6
Equals: Disposable business income	57.4	59.0	65.0

Source: United States Department of Commerce estimates.

The gross amount available to corporations is equal to profit plus capital consumption allowances. Since the latter item represents money at the disposal of corporations, we add it to net income in order to counteract its exclusion from corporate net profit. Subtracting direct taxes—that is, taxes levied on corporation profits—and dividends from this gross figure, we arrive at business disposal income. It may be simpler to think of disposable business income as undivided corporate profits after taxes plus capital consumption allowances. The symbol S_b, business saving, represents disposable business income in the algebraic formulas.

GROSS NATIONAL INCOME EQUALS GROSS NATIONAL EXPENDITURE

Gross national product has been examined in terms of gross national expenditure and gross national income. As expenditure it has been divided into four components: consumption expenditures, gross private domestic investment expenditures, government purchases of goods and services, and net exports or net foreign investment. Algebraically, this is expressed as $GNP = C + I + G + E$, or as $GNP = C + I + G$ if the I and E terms are combined.

As gross national income, the components of GNP are: disposable personal income, disposable business income, and disposable government income. These components, in turn, become income for consumption, personal saving, business saving, and net taxes. Using algebraic symbols, GNP as income becomes $C + S_p + S_b + T_n$. When we merge the two saving items, we have GNP $= C + S + T_n$. Since gross national expenditure must equal gross national income, $C + S + T_n = C + I + G$. For 1964 the respective values in billions of dollars are: $(C)399.3 + (S)97.5 + (T_n)127.5 = (C)399.3 + (I)94.7 + (G)$ 128.6. The Department of Commerce tables, which are the source of these data, include an item labeled statistical discrepancy which is equal to $\$-1.7$ billion for 1964. We should add this item to the income side. Any remaining inequality is the result of the rounding of numbers. Table 15–12 shows the size of gross national income components for the same years selected for gross national expenditure components in Table 15–4. A comparison of the two tables shows the years in which a government deficit or surplus counterbalanced an inequality between S and I.

We must emphasize that the dollar amounts do not prove or disprove the equality of the left and right hand terms of the identity. The expression is an identity whose terms must be equal at all times by definition. Therefore, any inequality in the dollar figures indicates imperfections in the gathering and the processing of the statistical data.

Gross national expenditure is equal to gross national income at all times but certain conditions arise in the process of maintaining this equality. It is these conditions we wish to examine, and it is for this reason that we have classified gross expenditure and gross income into their several components. The terms on either side of the equal sign form logical pairs for purposes of study. The two consumption terms are identical, of course, and after canceling them we have $S + T_n = I + G$. In studying this expression, we must remember that we are interested in tracing the circular flow of money as gross expenditure becomes gross income and returns to the circular flow as new gross expenditure.

Savings and net taxes, if considered alone, represent withdrawals from the circular flow. Investment and government purchases, in turn, represent additions to the circular flow. The two terms T_n and G represent the government sector of the economy and form a logical pair for analysis. Although we know that the government frequently operates with a deficit and occasionally with a surplus, we shall assume that G is equal to T_n until we reach the section on fiscal policy. This assumption simplifies the discussion of S and I, the remaining logical pair of terms. If G is equal to T_n, S must equal I. In the chapters that follow we shall examine the conditions resulting

Table 15–12

GROSS NATIONAL PRODUCT AS DISPOSABLE PERSONAL, BUSINESS, AND GOVERNMENT INCOME

Selected years (In billions of dollars)

Year	(1) Disposable Personal Income (2) + (3)	(2) Personal Consumption Expenditures, C	(3) Personal Saving S_p	(4) Disposable Business Income S_b	(5) Disposable Government Income T_n^a	(6) Statistical Discrepancy	(7) Gross National Product (2) + (3) + (4) + (5) + (6)
1929	83.1	79.0	4.2	11.5	9.5	.3	104.4
1932	48.7	49.3	-.6	2.7	6.4	.8	58.5
1933	45.7	46.4	-.6	2.6	6.7	.9	56.0
1937	71.0	67.3	3.7	7.8	12.3	-.2	90.8
1938	65.7	64.6	1.1	7.8	11.2	.5	85.2
1940	76.1	71.9	4.2	10.4	13.3	.8	100.6
1945	150.4	121.7	28.7	15.6	43.1	4.5	213.6
1946	160.6	147.1	13.5	13.1	34.8	2.1	210.7
1950	207.7	195.0	12.6	27.7	50.0	-.7	284.6
1955	274.4	256.9	17.5	42.1	80.0	1.0	397.5
1957	308.8	285.2	23.6	45.6	88.9	-.6	442.8
1958	317.9	293.2	24.7	44.8	83.3	-1.5	444.5
1960	349.9	328.2	21.7	50.7	105.1	-3.0	502.6
1961	364.7	337.3	27.3	51.2	105.4	-2.6	518.7
1962	384.6	356.8	27.8	57.4	115.9	-1.8	556.2
1963	402.5	375.0	27.5	59.0	125.1	-2.7	583.9
1964	431.8	399.3	32.5	65.0	127.5	-1.7	622.6

^{a}T_n is equal to the net tax receipts published in the *Report* plus "foreign net transfers by government."
NOTE: Components may not add to totals because of rounding.
SOURCE: Department of Commerce estimates printed in the *Economic Report of the President*, January, 1965. Also printed in the *Federal Reserve Bulletins*.

from the achievement of this equality and the significance of these conditions with respect to the level of prices, output, and employment.

SUMMARY

The market value of all the goods and services produced within a nation in a given period of time is the gross national product. We express and measure GNP in terms of total expenditures for goods and services. Dividing these expenditures into components, we have: consumption, gross private domestic investment, net foreign investment, and government purchases of goods and services. Expressed algebraically this becomes: $GNP = C + I + G$. We may also express and measure GNP in terms of the income accruing to the several sectors of the economy. Viewed as income, GNP is equal to disposable personal income plus disposable business income and disposable government income. Algebraically this becomes: $GNP = C + S + T_n$. Hence, we have an identity, $C + S + T_n = C + I + G$. Consequently, $S + T_n$ must equal $I + G$ at all times. In succeeding chapters we shall examine the determinants of the various terms in this identity and shall note the employment and price level conditions created in order to achieve equality of income and expenditure.

QUESTIONS

1. What is the difference between GNP and total expenditures, MV, in the equation of exchange?
2. How does the concept of GNP differ from that of national income? How useful is the latter concept?
3. In estimating GNP we make use of gross data for private domestic investment and net data for exports. Why do we use gross figures in one case and net figures in the other?
4. What are transfer payments? Estimate the level of transfer payments for a given year using current sources or the tables in this chapter.
5. We may regard GNP as gross national expenditures or as gross national income. What are the components of each concept?

SUGGESTED READINGS

Ackley, Gardner. *Macroeconomic Theory.* New York: The Macmillan Company, 1961.

Greenhut, Melvin L., and Jackson, Frank H. *Intermediate Income and Growth Theory.* Englewood Cliffs, N. J.: Prentice-Hall, Inc., 1961. Chapters 10 and 11.

Hansen, Alvin H. *Business Cycles and National Income.* Expanded ed. New York: W. W. Norton & Company, Inc., 1964. Chapters 6, 7, and 8.

Keynes, John Maynard. *The General Theory of Employment, Interest and Money.* New York: Harcourt, Brace and Company, 1936.

McKenna, Joseph P. *Aggregate Economic Analysis.* Rev. ed. New York: Holt, Rinehart and Winston, Inc., 1965.

16

CONSUMPTION, SAVING, AND INVESTMENT

We have seen that GNP is equal to aggregate expenditures for consumption, investment, and government goods and services as well as being equal to the disposable income of business, government, and persons. We discussed the logic behind the statement that aggregate expenditure equals aggregate disposable income, but we did not consider the employment, price level, and output conditions created in order to achieve this equality. In this chapter we shall see that gross national expenditure equals gross national income because of adjustments in the level of GNP and, therefore, in the level of prices, employment, and output. As a first step we shall consider the determinants of the magnitude of the several components of GNP.

We can classify the several components of aggregate expenditure and aggregate disposable income according to the sector of the economy they represent. Consumption, C, and private saving, S, are components of the private sector while government purchases of goods and services, G, and net taxes, T_n, are government components. To eliminate complications we shall assume in this chapter that G is equal to T_n and that their values are constant. This enables us to consider the private components without the complications which G and T_n create. This simplification does not detract from the insight we gain concerning the theory of income determination. In discussing consumption, saving, and investment, we must bear in mind that as long as we assume G and T_n to be equal and constant in value S must equal I. At this point our interest lies in the determinants of C, S, and I, and we wish particularly to compare the determinants of S with those of I in an effort to learn the conditions which cause them to be equal.

THE CONSUMPTION FUNCTION

Consideration of many factors and influences is necessary when we attempt to answer the question: What determines the level of consumption? One factor, the level of income, is dominant. There is

264

general agreement that consumption expenditures vary as income varies. Table 16–1 illustrates this relationship in a general fashion. Reality is present only in one respect. A rise in consumption expenditures accompanies a rise in income, but the rate of increase is slower. We should note that this type of analysis assumes a constant price level. Consequently, the several values of income represent different levels of output of goods and services. It follows that the figures in the consumption and saving columns reflect the volume of goods and services consumed or withheld from consumption. We shall continue to make this assumption as we analyze investment and the other components of GNP.

Table 16–1

INCOME, CONSUMPTION EXPENDITURES,
AND SAVING

Income	Consumption	Saving
0	20	−20
40	50	−10
80	80	−
120	110	10
160	140	20
200	170	30
240	200	40
280	230	50

In Table 16–1 consumption expenditures are in excess of income for the very low levels of income. Therefore, saving, which is the difference between income and consumption, must be negative. The available factual evidence seems to substantiate this assumption concerning the consumption function. Income reaches equality with consumption at the level of eighty, and as income continues to rise the slower rate of increase for consumption allows income to exceed consumption, thereby generating positive saving. Furthermore, the absolute difference between income and consumption is increasing as income rises. Figure 16–1 illustrates this principle in graphic form.

The values for income, represented by the symbol Y, are measured along the horizontal axis and the values for C along the vertical axis. By using the data from Table 16–1, the line C, representing consumption expenditures for given levels of Y, is plotted. The line drawn at a 45° angle to both the axes is called the reference line. Because of the equidistance of every point on this line from the horizontal and the vertical axes, a condition in which C is equal to Y for all levels of income is represented. By use of the reference line, the extent by which Y is exceeded by or is less than consumption at

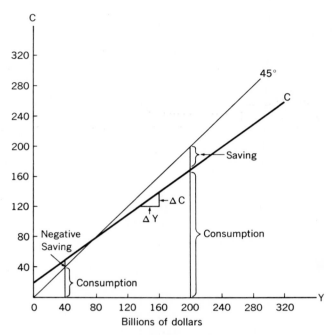

Figure 16-1.   The Consumption Function

various income levels is seen quickly. Since consumption plus saving is equal to income, gross saving for various levels of income is represented by the vertical distance between the reference and the C lines.

For many purposes, it is convenient to express algebraically the relationship of consumption to investment. We can say that consumption is a function of income. In the specific case illustrated in the preceding table and graph, the equation expressing the relationship is $C = 20 + \frac{3}{4}Y$. This tells us nothing that we cannot infer from the table or the graph, but it shows us very quickly that for every $4 change in income there is a $3 change in consumption. Whether we express the relationship of consumption to income numerically by table, diagrammatically by graph, or by an equation, certain characteristics are observable. Noting these characteristics, we also become familiar with conventional terminology.

The average propensity to consume, APC, is a very simple concept. APC is equal to C divided by Y. Since we assume that Y rises more rapidly than C, the average propensity to consume declines as Y increases. The marginal propensity to consume, MPC, is the change in C which accompanies a change of one unit in Y. In Figure

16–1 *MPC* is equal to $\Delta C \div \Delta Y$ (the change in consumption divided by the change in income) or it is equal to the coefficient of $Y(\frac{3}{4})$ in the algebraic expression. In our example the relationship of C to Y is linear; hence *MPC* is constant with respect to the level of income. We have adopted this linear relationship because of its simplicity rather than because of its realism, but there is evidence which suggests that the *MPC* is approximately the same for different income levels. If we assume that the *MPC* changes as income changes, the nonlinear C function fits into the theory of income determination without difficulty as long as the *MPC* is less than one. However, this assumption that the *MPC* is less than one is extremely important. The explanation of the method by which income reaches an equilibrium position rests on the assumption that changes in C accompany changes in Y and that these changes are in the same direction but smaller in magnitude. We turn, therefore, to an examination of the validity of this assumption.

There are several reasons for the belief that the *MPC* is less than one. First, it is consistent with our knowledge of human nature. Most people feel that they will save a larger portion of their incomes if their incomes increase. This may not be a convincing reason by itself, but other human characteristics support the conclusion. While we may admit that human wants are insatiable, we must recognize also that not all wants have the same priority. The necessities and the comforts of life have top priority and involve expenditures on consumption goods. As our income rises, we satisfy those wants which have lower priorities. These include the desire for the security and the convenience gained from the possession of financial assets. Hence, saving begins at a higher level of income. Second, budget studies of the Bureau of Labor Statistics indicate that consumption expenditures measured as a fraction of income are smaller for the higher as opposed to the lower income groups. These studies also show that families whose incomes have increased have a lower average propensity to consume after the increase.

When considered alone no one of these pieces of evidence proves conclusively that C increases less rapidly than Y. After examining all the evidence, however, we can be reasonably certain that the *MPC* is less than unity, especially for the range of income levels which is a realistic expectation. There is another reason for believing that C increases less rapidly than Y. In the theory we are about to examine, it is the consumption function and its companion, the saving function, which bring income and the price level into an equilibrium position. If our theory of income determination is correct and the *MPC* were one or greater than one, GNP would be much less stable than it is.

Determinants of the Consumption Function

The consumption function indicates that consumption expenditures vary with changes in income. However, we must not regard the consumption function as a device which predicts the level of C for the various levels of Y which may be applicable in the future. The consumption function shows the level of C for various levels of Y if all other conditions remain unchanged. With the passage of time these other conditions change and the consumption function changes also. We shall examine the conditions which affect the shape of the consumption function. By making this examination, we shall learn why the consumption function changes; thus, we shall understand better one cause of economic instability. At the same time we shall increase our knowledge of the determinants of consumption expenditures.

A consumer's expectations concerning future income, employment, and the level of prices influence his decision regarding the portion of disposable income he spends for consumption goods and the portion he saves. If an individual expects his income to rise in the future, his consumption expenditures from current income are likely to be higher than will be the case if he anticipates no change, or if he expects a decline in income. For the nation, individuals with bright expectations balance, in part, those persons who anticipate a fall in income, but evidence indicates that group expectations rise and fall. A close relationship exists between expectations concerning future employment and income expectations but they are not quite identical. The effect on the consumption function is likely to be the same, however. Persons anticipating a period of unemployment are likely to spend less and to save more from a given income than they will if they are expecting steady employment. In addition, expectations regarding the future level of prices affects the consumption function. Anticipation of rising prices is likely to cause consumers to increase the portion of a given income spent for consumption purposes.

Past experience influences the present pattern of consumption. Persons whose incomes have recently risen to a certain level probably spend less on consumption than do persons whose income has declined to this same level. When dealing with the consumption expenditures of an entire nation, these individual income changes cancel each other for some periods. There are many occasions, however, when there is a change in income distribution. Past consumption experience is also an important factor. Households may hold a sizable inventory of durable goods or these items may be scarce. The relative scarcity of these goods will influence consumption expenditures.

Another factor affecting the consumption function is the size and the composition of the population. For any given aggregate disposable personal income, the portion spent for consumption purposes is likely to be large if the population consists of relatively few adults and many children. Also, for a given level of personal disposable income, consumption will be higher if this income is shared by a large as opposed to a small population.

Several additional factors are worthy of our attention. The pattern of income distribution in a society influences the consumption function. The amount of assets, especially liquid assets, the public holds has an effect on the portion of income it spends for consumption goods and services. During our examination of the cash balance approach to monetary theory, we discovered that velocity is greater when the public owns sizable amounts of liquid assets. Now we are expressing the same concept in terms of the income and expenditure approach. We may apply the same reasoning process to debt. If the volume of debt owed by consumers is large, the portion of income spent for consumption is likely to be small. Now what about the attitude toward thrift? A society which teaches the individual to regard thrift as a virtue should expect consumption expenditures at the various levels of income to be low. This is an attitude which can change, of course, but it is unlikely to change rapidly.

We can draw conclusions from the examination of the determinants of the consumption function. While we have stated that at any given moment the consumption function indicates the size of consumption expenditures for varying levels of income, we have seen that conditions affecting the consumption function are subject to change. Some of the determinants, such as the size and the composition of the population, are not likely to change rapidly so that we consider them to be stable. Others, such as expectations regarding future incomes and the price level, can change suddenly. We must conclude, therefore, that the consumption function can change. If a change occurs, we can show it by a new C line which differs in terms of position, shape, and slope from the one we presented in Figure 16-1.

An unstable consumption function creates difficulties for those persons responsible for stabilization of the economy. It is imperative that we bear this in mind when we study the section on stabilization policy. However, the concept of a changing consumption function does not interfere with our development of the theory of income determination so long as the MPC is less than unity.

THE SAVINGS FUNCTION

We defined saving as the difference between private disposable income and consumption expenditures. Therefore, the development of a consumption function automatically produces a savings function. Since $Y = C + S$ and we have adopted the hypothetical consumption function, $C = 20 + \frac{3}{4}Y$, the savings function must be $S = \frac{1}{4}Y - 20$. Figure 16–2 presents this savings function along with the consumption function from Figure 16–1.

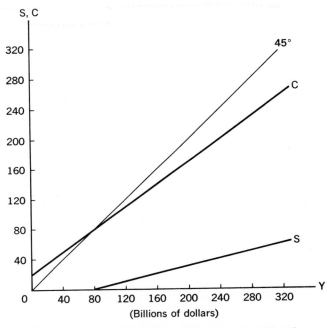

Figure 16-2.   The Saving and Consumption Functions

Considering the relationship of consumption and saving to income and remembering the conclusion reached regarding the average propensity to consume, we see that the average propensity to save must increase as income rises. For the same reason, the marginal propensity to save, *MPS*, must be less than one but more than zero.

Gross private saving equals personal saving plus business saving. Acknowledging that conditions which cause consumption to increase occasion decreases in saving, or *vice versa*, we can apply the comments made and the conclusions drawn regarding the determinants of the consumption function to the personal saving component. However, one possible determinant of private saving, the interest rate, warrants comment. This comment is necessary because the interest rate is a determinant of the level of investment and investment is equal to saving. Consequently, we must ask if the converse is also true; that is, the interest rate is a determinant of saving. The evidence indicates that it is not.

We should note that the decision to save or to consume is a choice between present and future consumption. In our society, numerous factors influence the division of income into saving and consumption. Families desire the security and convenience afforded to them by the ownership of liquid assets. Certain heavy expenditures, such as the education of children and the purchase of housing and other durable assets, can be foreseen. Or there may be a desire to accumulate a fund which will provide an income at retirement. Also, our society regards thrift as a virtue so that saving becomes an end in itself rather than a means to an end. A large volume of saving is institutional in nature and the saver regards it as an expense. Premiums on life insurance policies are an important example of institutional saving.

A change in the rate of interest is unlikely to influence the level of saving in the face of these other incentives. In fact, if a person is saving in order to accumulate a specific sum of money for some future date, a higher interest rate allows him to accumulate this sum with smaller amounts of current saving. Consequently, a high interest rate may discourage saving in some cases. After considering the many reasons for personal saving, the conclusion that the interest rate is not important seems correct.

Business saving, or disposable business income, comprises capital consumption allowances and undivided profits. Capital consumption allowances depend upon the stock of capital previously accumulated and the depreciation policies of industry. In the United States, the stock of capital is large and the depreciation policies are conservative so that this component of saving is sizable. It is also relatively stable because its determination is the result of capital accumulations of past years and of policies which change slowly. The size of undivided profits depends upon corporate profits and the dividend policy. American corporations tend to declare regular dividends so that undivided profits are a residual item. Accordingly, the size of this component of saving fluctuates with corporate profits.

After an examination of the determinants of saving, we can state that both personal and business savings are a function of income. This statement agrees with our conclusions regarding consumption.

INVESTMENT

Since investment is a component of gross national expenditure, we shall analyze it in terms of demand for goods and services. Investment is equal to saving; therefore, we are particularly interested in the determinants of the level of investment for we wish to know if the same factors determine both the decision to invest and the decision to save. We have noted the types of investment goods and services which the public demands. They are residential construction, other construction, producers' durable equipment, and the change in business inventory. In this section it is our purpose to examine the determinants of the level of investment expenditures. In approaching this question we assume that people act in a rational manner when making investment decisions. They weigh the benefits which they expect will accrue to them against the cost of each investment project. The public spends money for investment purposes in all cases where anticipated benefits outweigh costs.

Interest Cost

We define the cost of an investment project as the interest on the amount expended. Interest cost may be explicit in the form of money payments to creditors or the buyer of an investment may pay cash, in which case the interest cost takes the form of a lost opportunity to receive interest income.

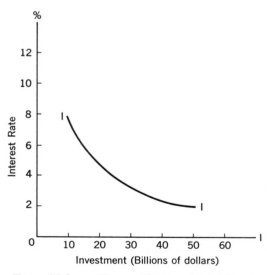

Figure 16-3.   **Demand for Investment Goods**

Since a demand for investment goods and a cost element defined in terms of an interest rate exist, we may assume as a first approach that the demand for investment goods follows the pattern which Figure 16–3 on page 272 indicates.

Figure 16–3 measures the interest rate vertically and the investment expenditures horizontally. The principles of demand come from value theory. The II curve slopes downward and to the right because we assume that as the price (interest cost) decreases the amount purchased (investment expenditures) increases. It is, of course, unrealistic to speak of an interest rate since actually there is a structure of rates depending on risk, the amount borrowed, and other conditions. In analyzing the demand for investment, however, our assumption that there is a single, average rate of interest will not affect the validity of our conclusions.

THE MARGINAL EFFICIENCY OF CAPITAL

It is not sufficient for us to assume that the demand curve for investment goods and services slopes downward and to the right because other demand curves have this characteristic also. Instead, we must examine the determinants of the shape and the position of the curve. The examination takes the form of an inquiry into the expected benefits to be derived from investment expenditures. We must emphasize that we are considering the anticipated rather than the recorded benefits, or yield, from investments. The need to focus our attention on expectation is obvious if we remember that we are discussing the determinants of decisions to make investment expenditures.

The nature of the benefits expected varies with the type of investment. For owner-occupied residential construction, anticipated benefits take the form of comfortable living and status in the community. Obviously, we cannot express these benefits in precise dollar terms or as a per cent of the cost of the investment in comparing them with the rate of interest. Nevertheless, it is reasonable to assume that, other things being equal, expenditures for residential construction vary inversely with the rate of interest. Factual data which are available substantiate this belief.

Most investment expenditures involve a business decision, and the firm expects the investment to increase its net revenue. Net revenue, for our purposes, is the increase in revenue attributable to investment after deducting all costs pertaining to the investment except the interest cost. There is a possible exception in the case of changes in business inventory. These changes are not always the result of decisions by the investor. However, inventory changes account for only a small portion of total investment, and some of these changes are the result of conscious planning since an increase in inventory can create additional net revenue. For certain kinds of investment, the anticipated increases in net revenue take the form of rental income. Or the investment may lead to increased output or a decreased cost of production. In any case we can express the expected increase in net revenue as the yield on investment stated in percentage terms. In discussions of monetary theory, it is customary to refer to this anticipated yield as the marginal efficiency of capital, or *MEC*.

Using the *MEC* concept, we can explain the downward slope of the investment demand curve as it moves to the right. At any given moment business leaders throughout the nation have many opportunities to make investment expenditures. After examining the investment opportunities, these leaders may conclude that projects costing $3 billion will yield an expected annual return of 15 per cent or better. An additional $1 billion in projects will yield 14 per cent; $1 billion more, 13 per cent; and so forth. If we systematize this information, we arrive at the schedule of the marginal efficiency of capital, *MEC*. Table 16-2 summarizes it.

Table 16-2 shows that $3 billion worth of investment projects is available which will yield an anticipated annual return of 15 per cent

Table 16-2

SCHEDULE OF THE
MARGINAL EFFICIENCY OF CAPITAL

MEC (%)	Investment (In billions of dollars)
15	3
14	4
13	5
12	7
11	9
10	11
9	13
8	15
7	17
6	20
5	26
4	35
3	48
2	70

or better; $4 billion worth, an anticipated 14 per cent or better; and so forth. Figure 16–4 presents this information in diagrammatic form. It corresponds to the demand curve presented in Figure 16–3 and confirms the assumption on which we based that figure. Here we call it the *MEC* curve.

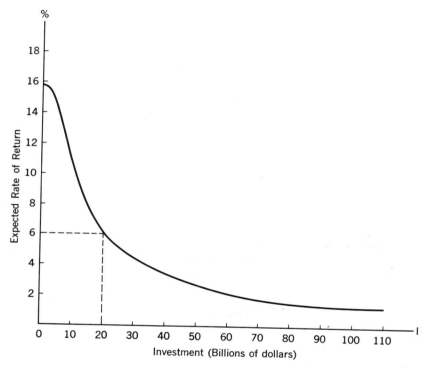

Figure 16-4.   The Marginal Efficiency of Capital

The vertical axis measures both the interest rate and the *MEC*; the horizontal axis measures the amount of investment expenditures. Since a comparison of the interest rate and the expected annual rate of return is the basis for investment decisions, an interest rate of 6 per cent will lead to $20 billion in investment expenditures for the case illustrated in Figure 16–4.

The *MEC* curve, or function, must slope downward and to the right because the investment expenditures are a cumulative measurement. Obviously, there are more investment opportunities with expected yields of 5 per cent *and higher* than of 6 per cent and higher. While the *MEC* curve always slopes downward and to the right, there is room for variation with respect to the degree of the slope, the location, and the exact shape of the curve. A number of factors, some of which are subject to rapid change, determine these characteristics.

The size of the stock of capital goods which has accumulated in previous periods is an important factor. If capital facilities are plentiful so that there is sufficient capacity to satisfy the demand for output, high-yield investment opportunities are relatively scarce. If there is excess capacity, very few investment opportunities with an anticipated high yield will be available. By contrast the number of investment projects promising a high yield will be large if the existing stock of capital goods is small relative to the demand for output. If this were the only factor under consideration, mature nations, those with large stocks of capital goods, would have a very low level of investment expenditure. At times emphasis on this factor has caused economists to overlook other factors and has led to predictions of economic stagnation. Historic evidence does not support the stagnation thesis; therefore, other influences on the *MEC* must exist.

The composition of the stock of capital goods is important. Relative modernity of the existing capital goods affects the opportunities for high-yield investments. If most of the existing equipment is obsolete, obviously there is more opportunity to find high-yield investment projects than if capital equipment is modern and efficient. Closely related to this factor is the inventiveness and the resourcefulness of the nation. Resourceful and inventive persons cause the rate of innovation to be high so that a large portion of the existing capital goods rapidly becomes obsolete. Expectations regarding the demand for consumer goods affect the *MEC* by influencing the attitude of business leaders regarding the needed volume of capital goods. The current and the anticipated levels of wages affect decisions to replace labor with capital and, therefore, the *MEC*.

A final factor is the attitude of business leaders regarding future business conditions. This attitude, called business psychology by Keynes, alludes to the degree of optimism or pessimism displayed by businessmen. It affects all of the factors discussed previously. If an optimistic outlook prevails, business leaders anticipate relatively high annual returns from the investment projects which they regard with suspicion at other times. Although time may not justify these great expectations, this does not concern us at this point. We are considering the determinants of investment decisions, and businessmen must base them on expectations. When an optimistic attitude prevails, expectations are high. With a psychology of pessimism, expectations regarding the same investment projects are low. Much of the literature on investment expenditures stresses the role of business psychology. It is a factor which changes rapidly and it has an important effect on the level of income. Of necessity, the changes in business psychology have their origins in imperfect knowledge, and there is a suspicion that changed attitudes are irrational at least to some degree.

These factors determine the location of the MEC curve and its shape including the degree of slope. The location and the slope of the curve are important since they reflect the responsiveness of investment expenditure to changes in the interest rate. This is apparent to anyone who is familiar with the concept of elasticity of demand curves. If the slope of the MEC curve is steep, investment expenditures change very little in response to a drop in the interest rate. Monetary policy, designed to increase gross national product, is likely to have little effect in this case. While considerable discussion has taken place and some disagreement concerning the responsiveness of investment to interest rate changes is evident, we can say that the degree of responsiveness differs depending upon the industry. Construction and investment in the utilities seem most responsive. The industries in which salesmanship is important are relatively unaffected by the interest rate. Factual evidence does not lend itself to evaluation easily, for it is valid only to the extent that all factors other than the interest rate remain unchanged. Existing evidence suggests that shifts of the *MEC* curve are a more important reason for changes in the level of investment than changes in the interest rate and the corresponding movement along the *MEC* curve.

EQUALITY OF SAVING AND INVESTMENT

We have examined the determinants of investment decisions and have found that they are not the same as the determinants of saving. Saving is a function of income; the interest rate and the MEC influence the decision to invest. Furthermore, the general public makes saving decisions; but business leaders, a smaller group, are responsible for most of the investment decisions. Therefore, there is no reason to assume that saving and investment decisions are identical. This is a conclusion that apparently contradicts the statement that saving must equal investment.

The apparent contradiction disappears if one reads the statements carefully. Saving *decisions* and investment *decisions*, also called planned saving and planned investment, need not be equal; but *actual* saving must equal *actual* investment. We may explore this apparent contradiction more thoroughly by using the *ex ante* and *ex post* concepts which the Swedish school developed.[1] We refer to planned saving and planned investment as saving *ex ante* and in-

---

[1]Credit for this development belongs to the Swedish economists Bertel Ohlin, Gunnar Myrdahl, and Erik Lindahl.

vestment *ex ante*, respectively. Expectations regarding income, prices, and similar factors determine the level of saving *ex ante* while expectations regarding the rate of return on capital and the interest rate determine investment *ex ante*. Since their determinants are different, it is very unlikely that saving *ex ante* will equal investment *ex ante*. Actual saving and actual investment bear the names saving *ex post* and investment *ex post* and are equal to each other by definition. Saving *ex post* is the portion of output withheld from consumption; we define investment *ex post* in the same terms.[2] Therefore, they must be equal. Note that the saving and investment data presented in the tables in Chapter 15 are *ex post* measurements.

We see the adjustment mechanism that causes S *ex post* = I *ex post* if we assume that S *ex ante* > I *ex ante*. The latter expression indicates that the public intends to save more than it plans to spend for investment goods. By referring to the concept of the circular flow of income and expenditure, we see that we are removing more dollars from the circular flow by saving than we are adding by investment expenditures. Therefore, income declines but as income declines saving also declines. Income and saving continue to decline until the actual saving, or S *ex post*, is equal to I *ex post*. At that point, of course, income reaches an equilibrium level. In summary, we can say that if the public plans to save more than it plans to invest, income will decline until the relative poverty of the population will cause actual saving to be equal to investment. The reverse is also true. If S *ex ante* < I *ex ante*, income will rise until S *ex post* and I *ex post* are equal. The change in income takes the form of some combination of changes in the price level and the level of employment and output. These changes are the basis for our earlier statement that we would examine the employment, output, and price level changes created by the fact that saving is equal to investment.

Saving *ex ante* and investment *ex ante* are unrelated but saving *ex post* and investment *ex post* are both related to income. Therefore, adjustments in the level of income bring the two into equality. The equilibrium level of income is the level at which saving equals investment. There is no reason to assume that this is a static level, however. We must expect changes in the determinants of saving and investment and each change will produce a new equilibrium level of income.

INCOME DETERMINATION—FIRST APPROXIMATION

We are now in a position to draw certain conclusions concerning the theory of income determination. We continue to assume that G is

[2]The simplifying assumption at the beginning of this chapter eliminates G and T_n from our consideration.

equal to T_n and is a constant. By making this unrealistic assumption, we eliminate the government sector. This allows us to use a simple formula for income determination and does not affect the validity of our conclusions regarding theory. If we prefer, we may think of G and T_n as constants added to I and S, respectively.

We have seen that consumption is a function of income but that the level of income does not affect investment directly. Instead, the rate of interest and the marginal efficiency of capital determine I. Since this is a first approximation of income determination, we shall postpone questions regarding the factors controlling the interest rate. For our example we shall assume that the interest rate and the MEC schedule are such that their interaction leads to a level of investment equal to 40. We shall retain the consumption function previously cited. We may present the foregoing information as follows:

(1) $Y = C + I$

(2) $C = 20 + \frac{3}{4}Y$

(3) $I = 40$

By substitution we find that $Y = 240$. C therefore is equal to 200. Saving, in turn, must equal 40, the difference between Y and C. Or we can use the saving function, in which case we determine the equilibrium level of income from the following statements:

(1) $S = I$

(2) $S = \frac{1}{4}Y - 20$

(3) $I = 40$

In either method, $Y = 240$ and saving equals investment.

A comment concerning this approach is in order. We shall use the saving function as our example. We begin with three statements: number one expresses the relationship of saving to investment; number two, the relationship of saving to income; and number three tells us that investment is constant at the level of 40. No one of these statements is of great use if considered alone. If all the statements are true and if we consider all three at the same time, we find that Y and S must equal 240 and 40, respectively. It follows that 240 is the equilibrium level of income. We have determined this equilibrium level by solving simultaneous equations, a technique which we can apply to sets of relationships involving more variables than we used in this example.

Figures 16–5[3] and 16–6[3] present the same set of relationships in diagrammatic form. Figure 16–5b shows consumption as a function of income. This is identical to Figure 16–1. Figure 16–5a shows that, given the interest rate and the marginal efficiency of capital, the level of investment is constant despite changes in the income level. In Figure 16–5c we have added investment so that the $C + I$ curve indicates the size of expenditures for varying levels of income. $C + I$

[3]Ignore the dotted lines at this time.

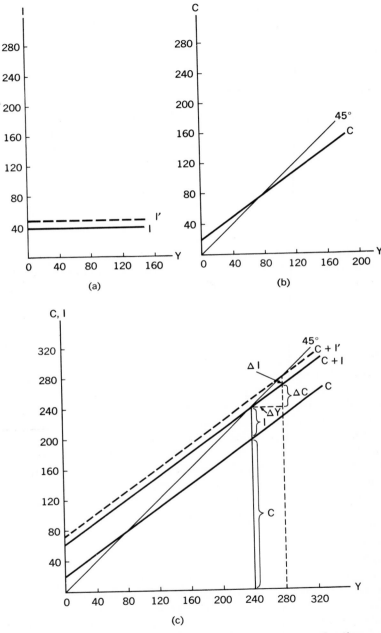

Figure 16-5.   Income Determination—First Approximation

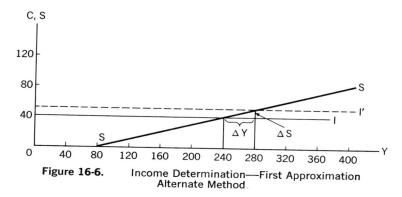

Figure 16-6.   Income Determination—First Approximation
Alternate Method.

must, of course, equal Y; but this is possible only if $Y = 240$, the point where income composed of $C + I$ is equal to income indicated by the 45° reference line.

In Figure 16–6 we approach the problem of income determination by way of the saving function. Once again investment is constant with respect to Y. Saving is a function of Y as the line SS indicates. Saving must equal investment and this occurs only if income is equal to 240.

In our simple example of income determination, saving equalled investment. We expected this result since we defined the components of GNP so that S is equal to I as long as G and T_n are equal. At this point we have not specifically identified the device which brings S and I into equality. However, we have suggested the solution by showing that investment influences the level of income which, in turn, affects the level of saving and consumption. Accordingly, it is worthwhile examining the effect of investment changes on income, consumption, and saving. As you will see in the process of this examination, we shall do more than isolate the device which causes S to equal I.

THE MULTIPLIER

The multiplier refers to the change in Y which is the result of a change in I. We call this the multiplier effect because a change of $1 in the level of investment expenditure causes a change of more than $1 in income. This result is implicit in the consumption function but it deserves additional study. Since I is a component of Y, we know that an increase in I will cause Y to change. The consumption function tells us that this change in Y will cause C to change. This change in C will cause Y to change again and the process goes on indefinite-

Table 16-3

INCREASE IN INCOME INDUCED BY AN INCREASE
OF $1.00 IN INVESTMENT

	Time Periods							
	I	II	III	IV	V	VI	. . . .	∞
Investment	1.00	1.00	1.00	1.00	1.00	1.00		1.00
		.75	.75	.75	.75	.75		.75
			.56	.56	.56	.56		.56
				.42	.42	.42		.42
Increase in Consumption					.32	.32		.32
						.24		.24
								. . . .
								. . . .
Increase in Income	1.00	1.75	2.31	2.73	3.05	3.29		4.00

ly. We now ask what is the limit to this change in income? The numerical example in Table 16-3 suggests the answer.

For this example we have included a time element in our theoretical framework so that the process by which Y adjusts to a change in I takes place over a series of time periods. We start from an equilibrium position and assume that the level of investment expenditures has increased by $1. Throughout all the adjustment periods, I maintains this higher level. The increase in I raises Y by $1 in the first period. For succeeding periods we compute the increments to income by applying the consumption function.

Accepting the consumption function presented in the preceding pages, we find that three fourths of the dollar added to income in period I returns to the income stream as a consumption expenditure in period II and we add it to the investment dollar for that period. By period III, the increment to income will consist of the incremental dollar of investment for period III plus consumption expenditures of 75 cents from the $1 increase in Y in period II, plus three fourths of the 75 cents, or 56 cents, increase in C caused by the $1 in period I. An examination of the increased income for the several time periods shows the series $1, $1.75, $2.31, $2.73, $3.05, and so on, which approaches $4.00 as a limit although we need an infinite number of periods to reach this limit. The multiplier, therefore, is 4; that is, a change of $1 in investment expenditure causes a $4 change in income.

We can explain the limit to the increase in income and consequently to the size of the multiplier in terms of the saving function. In the particular saving function used as an example in this chapter, the marginal propensity to save is equal to .25. Therefore, the saving process removes one fourth from the income stream before the next time period. We call this leakage. We could develop a table corresponding to Table 16–3 showing the increments to saving because of an increase in investment. The saving series will be 0, .25, .44, .58, .68 and will approach a limit of $1. At that limit the leakage from income because of saving will just equal the addition to the income stream attributable to the added investment. The income level, therefore, will be stable and saving will equal investment. This example illustrates the way in which saving and investment reach equality as the income level reaches a state of equilibrium. The dotted lines in Figures 16–5 and 16–6 present this principle in diagrammatic form. An increase in investment from I to I' leads to increased consumption and saving and a higher level of income.

Since investment and saving are always equal, a change in saving, called ΔS, must accompany an equivalent change in investment. Or, ΔS must equal ΔI. Saving, however, is a function of income; therefore, a change in income must occur if saving is to change. The size of the change in income depends upon the precise relationship of incremental income to incremental saving. We have discussed this relationship and have called it the *marginal propensity to save*. Thus, since we assume the MPS to be .25, S will change by $1 for every $4 change in Y. In terms of a formula $\Delta I = \Delta Y \cdot MPS$, or $\Delta Y = \dfrac{\Delta I}{MPS}$. The multiplier becomes $\dfrac{1}{MPS}$. Because of the relationship of saving to consumption, the multiplier can also appear as $\dfrac{1}{1\text{-}MPC}$.

We have presented the multiplier as part of a demonstration of the way in which the income level changes in order to keep saving equal to investment. This relationship of investment expenditures to the level of income also serves as a guide to policy. If planners wish to change the level of GNP, they may try to do so by changing the level of investment. If they know the approximate size of the multiplier, they also know the change in I necessary to achieve a desired level of income.

A NOTE ON THE ACCELERATOR

One last relationship between the components of GNP needs attention. This is the effect on investment of a change in the level of consumption expenditures. While we noted the reverse effect in the explanation of the multiplier, we said nothing specific concerning the change in I induced by a change in C. There is an implicit assumption that the level of consumption expenditures has no direct effect on investment in the statement that the interest rate and the MEC determine the level of I. For this reason we held investment constant in previous illustrations as income changed. We shall modify that assumption at this point. This modification may take the form of an admission that a change in C can influence the MEC and so, indirectly, affect investment. Or, we may approach the topic more directly.

Persons acquire capital goods in order to produce consumption goods. While it is true that some capital goods have the function of producing other capital goods, the ultimate purpose of capital goods is the production of consumer goods. Consequently, we have reason to question the assumption that investment demand is constant despite changes in the level of income and, therefore, of consumption. Is it not reasonable to suppose that an increase in consumption necessitates additional capital equipment? The answer to the question must be, yes, unless there is an excess of productive capacity at the time the increase in consumption occurs. In the illustration which follows, we have divided the total demand for capital goods into two components: (1) replacement of worn out equipment, and (2) demand representing a net addition to stock. In Table 16–4 we use a time period analysis to show the effect on investment demand of an increase in consumption given the following assumptions.

1. Capital equipment is being used to capacity.
2. One unit of capital goods is needed for every 1,000 units of consumer goods produced.
3. Worn out capital units must be replaced every ten time periods. The present units are of such an age that one unit must be replaced each period.

If a nation is not using its capital equipment to capacity when an increase in the demand for consumption goods occurs, there is no need for a rise in the demand for capital goods. In our example, however, we assume that the nation is fully utilizing its capital equipment. Consequently, a change in the level of consumption causes a disproportionate but temporary change in the level of investment expenditures. In this instance a 10 per cent permanent

Table 16–4

THE ACCELERATOR

Time Period	Capital Goods Start of Period (Units)	Demand for Consumption Goods (Units)	Demand for Replacement of Capital Goods (Units)	Demand for Net Addition to Capital Goods (Units)	Total Demand for Capital Goods (Units)
I	10	10,000	1	0	1
II	10	10,000	1	0	1
III	10	11,000	1	1	2
IV	11	11,000	1	0	1
V	11	11,000	1	0	1

increase in consumption causes a temporary 100 per cent increase in investment. We can see why the acceleration concept affords us an explanation for some of the tendency of our economy to fluctuate. In fact, in maintaining the assumption concerning replacement, we create a "built in" fluctuation scheduled for periods 12 and 13. The rigid assumptions for the table, of course, are not realistic. Both the replacement schedule and the ratio of capital goods to consumption goods are flexible. Nevertheless, the accelerator concept is useful as a means of explaining some of the economy's instability.

Now that we have noted the possibility that a change in consumption may lead to a change in investment, we shall return to the previous conclusion that the level of investment expenditure is not related directly to the level of income. This conclusion allows us to develop a simpler theory of income determination in the succeeding chapters, and it is not truly in conflict with the accelerator principle. We can shift the *MEC* curve to allow for the changes in investment demand which are the result of changes in consumption expenditures.

A NOTE ON THE STRUCTURE OF INTEREST RATES

The concept of a single rate of interest is very useful for analytical purposes but it is unrealistic. Instead of an interest rate there are a great number of rates at any given moment. These several interest rates exist in the market for a number of reasons. First, there are regional differences. The rates are higher in certain sections of the country because of the relative scarcity of loanable funds. These differences do not interfere with the development of an analytical system which contains an interest rate since we can use the rate in the average region, or we can confine our analysis to a single region.

We find the second reason for different interest rates in the difference between the theoretical concept of interest and the interest cost in the money market. In discussing monetary theory, it is customary to describe interest as the price paid for the use of money. We may call this the pure interest rate. The interest rate charged in the market, however, includes the cost of other services. There is the possible loss of principal. It follows that the interest rate must include a payment for risk bearing. The degree of risk varies with the credit worthiness of the borrower and interest rates vary accordingly. Also, the lender must add the cost of administrative services, such as credit analysis and collection activities, to the pure interest rate. These costs, expressed in percentage terms, depend upon the size and the type of the loan. Large, single-payment loans involve less administrative cost than do small, installment-type loans. The several interest rates in the market reflect these differences in overhead costs.

In addition securities differ in terms of tax liability. The Federal Government excludes interest paid on state and local government securities from its definition of taxable income. Interest on securities of the United States Government, in turn, is exempt from state income taxes. Buyers of these securities receive a benefit, the privilege of tax-free income. Lower interest rates on tax exempt securities reflect this valuable privilege. The value of the privilege, and hence the size of the reduction in interest rates, depends upon the tax structure of the several governments involved and the income bracket of the marginal buyer.

In the preceding discussion, we saw that the rate of interest charged in the market is the price paid for the use of money to which we must add charges for the assumption of risk and the payment of overhead. Where applicable the tax-exempt privilege leads to a rate reduction. Since the risk, the overhead, and the tax-exempt privilege factors vary for different types of securities, there are a series of interest rates instead of a single rate. The several rates have a relationship, however, since lenders and to some extent borrowers can shift from one segment of the market to another if the difference in rates makes such action profitable.

There is an additional reason for a series of rates instead of a single interest rate in the market—the difference in maturity. Examination of this difference raises an interesting question concerning the concept of a pure rate of interest and adds to our understanding of the role of the interest rate. The effect of the maturity date on the interest rate in comparing the yields[4] of securities which are alike in all other respects is apparent. Table 16–5 presents the interest yields of United States securities of varying maturity dates or terms. Since the risk, overhead cost, and tax factors are the same, the difference in maturity must cause the difference in yields.

Table 16–5

INTEREST YIELD ON UNITED STATES SECURITIES OF VARYING MATURITIES
1963 – 1965

Security	December 1963	June 1964	December 1964	June 1965
3 – month bills	3.52	3.48	3.84	3.80
6 – month bills	3.66	3.56	3.94	3.86
9 – 12 month issues	3.69	3.70	3.96	3.89
3 – 5 year issues	4.04	4.03	4.07	4.09
Bonds (long-term)	4.14	4.13	4.14	4.14

Source: *Federal Reserve Bulletins.*

United States Government securities are risk-free. The interest is subject to the federal income tax, and transactions in these securities are usually in such large amounts that the overhead cost is small. Therefore, the yield on United States Government securities is a near approximation to the pure rate of interest. There is a tendency to regard interest on United States securities as *the* rate of interest. In Table 16–5, however, there are several rates of interest or, more accurately, interest yield. Which of these rates is *the* rate of interest? Curiosity arises also regarding the reason for different yields on securities of varying lengths.

We can understand the reason for the spread by considering the problem faced by a buyer who must choose between three-month bills and ten-year bonds. For this example we shall assume that the interest yields are the same for securities of long and of short maturity at the date of purchase. Conditions in the money market change, however, and the buyer must expect changes in interest yields. If our prospective buyer purchases bills and market conditions change so that interest yields are lower at the end of two months, this bill owner

---

[4]In the literature on monetary theory, the terms interest rate and interest yield are sometimes interchangeable. Technically, they are different. The interest rate refers to the return based on the face value of the security. Thus, for a $1,000 bond with a 4 per cent coupon rate, the interest rate is 4 per cent. Interest yield refers to the return based on the market value of the security. Hence, if this same bond sells for $980, the interest yield is something in excess of 4 per cent.

faces a reduction in income in one month, at which time he must reinvest his funds. On the other hand this change in money market conditions does not affect significantly the market value of his asset because of its short maturity. A rise in the interest yield reverses the results. Uncertainty regarding future interest yields, therefore, leads to uncertainty concerning the income from short-term securities, but it does not affect their capital value.

If the prospect purchases bonds maturing in ten years, he is certain of the income for that period of time. However, a rise in interest yields will cause the market value of his asset to decline. The reverse is true if interest yields decline. Hence, the owner of a ten-year bond can be certain concerning the level of his income but faces uncertainty regarding the future capital value of his asset.

To the prospective buyer the choice between securities with short and long maturities depends upon his expectations regarding the future level of interest yields. There is also the likelihood that certain individuals and institutions are more reluctant to accept the risk of capital loss than that of income loss, or *vice versa*. For the reasons we have described, the attractiveness of short-term as opposed to long-term securities increases if investors expect interest yields to rise. The reverse occurs if prospective lenders anticipate a decline. The market demand for securities with short and long maturities reflects this difference in attractiveness.

These same expectations influence the borrowers who wish to sell bonds and bills. They constitute the supply side of the market. The expectation of a rise in interest yield, which is interest cost to the borrower, increases the attractiveness of bond sales as a method of financing while the expectation of a decline has the opposite effect. In the example used in Table 16–5, the bond seller is the United States Government; but we can extend the illustration to include the market for private securities. These same expectations along with other factors, such as the desire to finance durable assets with long-term securities, influence private borrowers.

In the case of no expected change in interest yields, it seems logical to conclude that yields on long- and short- term securities will be identical. However, this overlooks other factors which influence the yields. Evidence indicates that bond yields tend to be higher than bill yields. Yet, the spread between the two varies as expectations change. An expected rise in the interest rate causes bonds to be relatively less attractive to buyers but more desirable to borrowers. The tendency for lenders to shift their demand to the bill market while borrowers increase the supply of bonds causes the interest rate on bonds to rise and that on bills to fall. Thus, an expectation of a rise in the interest rate increases the spread between the rates. By the same reasoning, an expectation of a decline in interest rates causes the spread to decrease.

The expectation of a change in the interest rate accounts for the several interest rates for securities of different maturities. This fact is of some significance for it emphasizes the important role of expectations in monetary affairs. The question of which one of these rates is *the* interest rate remains unanswered. For purposes of analysis of the determination of the income level, it need not be answered. Seeing the term interest rate in monetary theory, we think of the average of these rates. Our inability to express the concept of the interest rate as a precise, realistic number does not affect the final conclusion.

SUMMARY

We have examined the factors which determine the levels of consumption, saving, and investment and their effects on the level of income. Consumption is a function of income. The level of consumption expenditures varies with the level of income but at a slower rate. The exact relationship depends upon a number of conditions including expectations regarding income and prices, income distribution, and holdings of liquid assets. Saving is the difference between income and consumption and is a function of income. The level of investment expenditures depends upon the interest rate and the schedule of the marginal efficiency of capital. Inasmuch as different factors influence saving and investment decisions, it is likely that planned saving and planned investment will not be equal. In that case income changes so that actual saving and actual investment are equal. Since the determinants of consumption, saving, and investment are subject to change, adjustments in income are frequent. The equilibrium level of income is the income level at which saving is equal to investment.

The multiplier refers to the change in income which a change in investment expenditures creates. The net change in income is greater than the increment to investment because the initial change in the level of income leads to changes in consumption expenditures. The accelerator is a term which refers to the change in investment expenditures induced by a change in consumption.

It is customary to speak of the rate of interest when discussing monetary theory, but actually there is a structure of rates not a single rate. Interest rates vary because of differences in risk, overhead costs, and tax liability. Differences in the maturity of securities is an additional reason for a structure of rates instead of a single rate. A relationship between the various rates exists because borrowers and lenders can shift from one segment of the money market to another if the spread in the rates makes it worthwhile.

QUESTIONS

1. Does the consumption function provide for a realistic explanation of the determinants of the level of consumption expenditures? Why is it a useful concept?
2. How are the consumption and the saving functions related?
3. Expectations are the basis of the marginal efficiency of capital concept. To what extent does the immediate past influence the shape and position of the MEC curve?
4. If we accept the set of functional relationships presented in this chapter, is it possible for investment *ex post* to differ from investment *ex ante*? Can saving *ex post* differ from saving *ex ante*? Explain your answers.
5. How is the multiplier related to the consumption function?
6. Does the accelerator principle contradict earlier statements concerning the MEC and the determination of the level of investment?

SUGGESTED READINGS

Greenhut, Melvin L., and Jackson, Frank H. *Intermediate Income and Growth Theory.* Englewood Cliffs, N. J.: Prentice-Hall, Inc., 1961. Chapters 5–7.

Hansen, Alvin H. *Business Cycles and National Income.* Expanded ed. New York: W. W. Norton & Company, Inc., 1964. Chapters 9–10.

Also, see the Readings listed at the end of Chapter 15.

17

INCOME DETERMINATION
The Role of Money

Up to this point we have examined the factors determining the level of income, but we have not developed a monetary theory. We have noted that there is a circular flow of money as income and as expenditure, but we have not considered specifically the role money plays in the determination of the level of income. In this chapter we shall see that money has an influence on the level of income through the interest rate. In the preceding chapters we noted that the interest rate was one of the determinants of the level of investment, but we avoided a more thorough discussion of the interest rate by assuming that it was a "given" quantity. It is now time to ask the questions: What determines the rate of interest and what are the consequences of this process? In developing an answer to these two questions, we shall develop a theory of income determination as well.

The interest rate has had a place in the concept of the economic system since the period of the classical economists. However, the role assigned to it has varied. Classical economists believed that full employment was the normal condition of the economy, and their theory of the interest rate was consistent with that belief. Since the full employment assumption is a major point of difference between the classical and the modern approach to the income and the interest rate theories, some comments concerning the basis of this assumption are necessary.

SAY'S LAW

Classical economists did not believe that a nation could produce a general oversupply of goods and services; that is, goods and services which producers could not sell. Expressed in more modern terminology they did not believe that aggregate supply could be greater than aggregate demand. The statement, "supply creates its own demand," called Say's law,[1] summarizes this belief. The classical economists based this conclusion on what they considered a characteristic of human nature. They felt that human wants were insatiable, and that man worked and produced because he desired goods and services. If each individual produced the types of commodities he desired and consumed, demand obviously would be equal to supply. In a society of specialists an individual produced a specific type of good or service in excess of his wants but only because he intended to trade it for other things which he desired. In this case, aggregate demand would be equal to aggregate supply because every action which increased the supply of one good increased the demand for other goods. Hence, general oversupply and unemployment were impossible. The classical economists believed that money was useful to an individual only if he spent it to secure goods or services. It followed that the existence of goods produced by persons whose motivation was a desire to acquire money did not alter the basic principle These economists felt that money performed useful services as a medium of exchange and a standard of value. It enabled persons to do easily what they would otherwise have accomplished with difficulty; thus it contributed to economic progress. To these theorists, however, money did not affect the level of aggregate demand.

In their view the unemployment and apparent excess of supply over demand which occurred occasionally was a maladjustment of production. People were producing too large a quantity of certain goods and were unable to sell them. The people produced these goods only because they wanted some other article, so that aggregate demand still equaled aggregate supply. A scarcity of item Y balanced the oversupply of item X. Consequently, unemployment and the low level of income were abnormal and temporary. Unemployment would disappear as the factors of production shifted from the unprofitable production of the type of goods in oversupply to the profitable production of the scarce commodities. Full employment remained the normal or long-run equilibrium condition of the economy.

Since the factors of production were fully employed in the equilibrium position of the economy, the nation's capacity to produce determined the level of real income. A change in the equilibrium position of the level of income was possible in monetary terms only through changes in the price level. This reasoning and the resulting conclusions explain the emphasis on the price level and the relative unconcern for employment and the level of output in the early monetary theories.

[1]Jean-Baptiste Say, A Treatise on Political Economy (Philadelphia: Grigg and Elliot, 1832), Ch. XV.

THE CLASSICAL THEORY OF THE INTEREST RATE

There was a place for saving and investment in the classical theory. It recognized the process of saving as a decision to enjoy goods in the future instead of the present. Applying modern terminology, we can say that it regarded saving as leakage from the income stream which reduced aggregate demand. However, an increase in demand from persons who borrowed and spent the savings of others balanced this reduction. In the terms of the preceding chapter, saving equals investment and aggregate demand remains unchanged.

The interest rate was the device which kept saving equal to investment. To demonstrate this we start from a position of equilibrium and assume that saving increases and tends to become larger than investment. Idle cash balances accumulate in the hands of savers who cannot find a borrower at the current rate of interest. Competition among the savers who wish to receive interest income forces the interest rate down. As the interest rate drops, borrowing and consequently spending increase until saving and investment are equal. Hence, the interest rate is the device which channels all saving into a demand for goods and services. The basis of this reasoning is an implicit assumption that all savers desire to receive an interest income from their savings rather than to allow them to accumulate as an idle cash balance. To the classical economists this seemed reasonable. Notice that it is not necessary to assume that a desire to earn interest motivates the saving process. The theory is valid even if we assume that the level of saving is independent of the interest rate. However, we must hold to the assumption that people who have saved prefer to lend the accumulated funds to others and to earn interest rather than to hold idle cash balances. In the next section of this chapter, we shall challenge this assumption.

We can present the classical theory of the interest rate in a simple supply and demand diagram. In Figure 17-1 the SS line represents saving, or the supply of funds available for lending. The line II represents the demand for borrowed funds which we call investment. We interpret this supply and demand diagram in the usual fashion. The equilibrium position shows an interest rate of 6 per cent and a quantity of saving and investment of 25. The interaction of the supply and demand function has determined the interest rate and the quantity saved, borrowed, and spent.

The solid line SS indicates that saving is responsive to changes in the interest rate. We have noted that this sensitivity is not necessary in order to achieve equilibrium. The broken line S'S' represents a saving function which is constant with respect to the level of the interest rate. The system attains equilibrium as long as investment varies inversely with the interest rate.

The classical theory of the interest rate probably presented an oversimplified picture of the economic system as it existed even when the theory was new. Certainly the conclusions reached by this chain of reasoning are invalid in a modern society. Nevertheless, it does make some contribution to our understanding of the economic system. It shows that the interest rate has an effect on the level of investment and, therefore, on the allocation of goods between consumption and capital accumulation. Hence, the interest rate plays a significant role in determining economic growth if not the level of current income. However, the defects in the theory are impressive. Even if the conclusion that full employment is the normal condition were correct, the emphasis on long-run equilibrium conditions and lack of concern for conditions in the short run, or the period of adjustment, would be unsatisfactory for a modern society. To understand this criticism we must remember that theories are valuable because, among other things, they serve as the basis for policy decisions. The classical theory of the interest rate served as a guide only for long-range policy decisions. Lord Keynes in the statement "In the long run we'll all be dead" expressed the inadequacy of such a theory. We acknowledged in the opening sentences of Chapter 15 this increased concern which Keynes expressed for the problems of the transition, or short-run, period.

A more basic criticism applies to the conclusion that full employment is the normal condition. For this conclusion to be valid, we must assume that all savings are available for lending and, in fact, are loaned to persons who spend the money. Since this assumption is the basis for disagreement between the classical and the modern

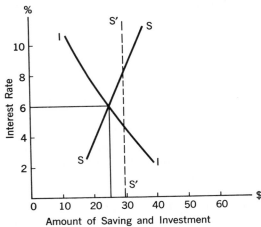

Figure 17-1.   Classical Interest Rate

theory of the interest rate and the determination of the level of income, it deserves further examination even at the risk of some repetition.

The classical theorists' concept of human nature is the basis for the assumption that all savings become borrowed funds. Since they considered human wants to be insatiable, they believed that a person who saved money and deferred consumption would lend his savings to others so that he would receive an interest income. Future consumption then would be higher and would compensate the saver for deferring consumption. It seemed unreasonable to suppose that people would hold idle money when borrowers were willing to pay interest for its use. Modern theorists agree that human wants are insatiable; they do not restrict these wants to a desire for tangible goods and such obvious intangibles as education, medical services, legal services, and so forth. People also want the security, the convenience, and the opportunities for profit that a cash balance affords them. In brief, people want liquidity as well as necessities, material conveniences, and services. If we accept this more modern concept of human nature, it is reasonable to assume that people may wish to save without lending.

LOANABLE FUNDS THEORY OF THE INTEREST RATE

We can regard the loanable funds theory as an intermediate step between the classical point of view and the modern approach to interest theory. This theory treats the interest rate as a price which the supply of and demand for loanable funds determines. In the treatment of interest rate theory as an analysis of supply and demand, it is similar to the classical theory; however it recognizes that there is no force compelling persons to lend their savings to others. Many savers lend their savings to borrowers and receive interest; others prefer to hold their savings as idle cash balances and to enjoy the benefits of a liquid position. Therefore, the supply of loanable funds is not identical to the supply of saving. The supply side of the market consists of current savings plus funds released from the accumulation of past savings. We must consider the latter portion because a person who has held past saving as idle cash may reverse his decision. We call this process of releasing to the loan market funds previously saved and held idle dishoarding. It follows that the two components of supply are current saving and dishoarding. For the purposes of this analysis, dishoarding includes any net increase in the stock of money.

In Figures 17–2a and 17–2b, the lines S and DH show the size of these components at varying interest levels. The S curve, which

represents saving, possesses very little elasticity. This reflects conclusions reached in the preceding chapter that the decision to save is
independent of the interest rate. By contrast, *DH*, the dishoarding
curve, is elastic with respect to the interest rate. The reason for this
should be clear. We have noted that certain benefits accrue to persons who are in a liquid position. The lost opportunity to receive
interest is the price one must pay if one is to receive these benefits.
Since it is a generally accepted fact that for any good or service the
amount purchased decreases as the price rises, we can assume that
the willingness to hold idle funds decreases as the interest rate rises.
Therefore, *DH* is elastic with respect to interest.[2]

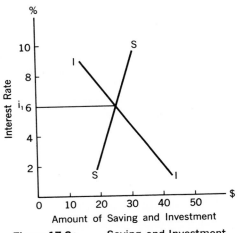

Figure 17-2a.   **Saving and Investment**

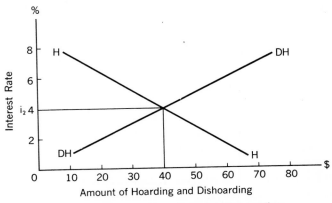

Figure 17-2b.   **Hoarding and Dishoarding**

[2]The "speculative motive" section of this chapter presents a more thorough discussion.

The demand side of the market also has two components. Persons borrow money in order to use it for investment expenditures. The I curve in Figure 17–2a represents this component. The investment section of the preceding chapter described the determinants of its shape and location. The second component consists of the demand for funds to increase idle cash balances. The H line in Figure 17–2b represents this component, called the demand for hoarding. It includes any net decrease in the stock of money. It is elastic and varies inversely with the interest rate for the reasons suggested by the discussion on dishoarding. As the cost of holding idle funds falls, the amount "hoarded" increases.

Examining the components in separate pairs, we see that i_1 is the rate of interest at which saving equals investment. We see also that i_2 is the rate at which dishoarding equals hoarding. That is, if the interest rate is equal to i_2 there is no tendency to change the size of idle cash balances. In our example i_1 is not equal to i_2. The consequences of this inequality are evident when we examine Figure 17–3 which treats the loanable funds market as a unit.

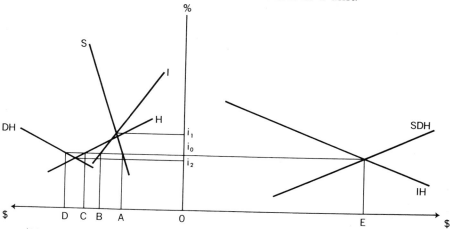

(Note: the direction of the X axis is reversed in the left portion of the diagram.)

Figure 17-3. Loanable Funds Interest Rate Theory

In Figure 17–3, we have added S and DH horizontally to produce the supply curve for the market labeled SDH. It represents the total funds supplied to the market at varying rates of interest. The components I and H added horizontally produce the line IH which is the demand curve. The point of intersection of these two lines determines the market rate of interest, called i_0. At this point current saving plus dishoarding is equal to investment plus hoarding and the market appears to be in an equilibrium position. The appearance of equilibrium becomes suspect, however, upon careful consideration of the several components of supply and demand and the recall of principles covered in the previous chapter. At i_0, the market rate of interest, saving is equal to OA and investment is equal to OB. Investment, therefore, exceeds saving by AB. Hoarding is equal to OC while dishoarding equals OD. Net dishoarding equals CD and AB equals CD.

We are not concerned at this point with the inequality of hoarding and dishoarding, but we saw in the previous chapter that either saving must equal investment or the level of income must change. Therefore, if we apply the principles of income determination to this illustration, income will rise because investment exceeds saving. As income rises the amount saved will increase and the S and the SDH curves will shift to the right. In the equilibrium position, saving will equal investment and hoarding will equal dishoarding. However, we cannot determine directly the level of income nor the interest rate at which this will occur from the diagram.

Nevertheless, the loanable funds theory demonstrates that the interest rate is not a device which brings saving and investment into equality. The theory improves upon the classical approach by recognizing that current saving and the supply of funds to the loan market are not identical. It directs our attention to the influence of the interest rate on the decision to hold savings as an idle cash balance or to lend them to others; thus it prepares us for the concept used in the liquidity preference theory. From this theory we may infer that saving, investment, and the interest rate have a relationship to the level of income; but a direct connection is missing. We must look to a later theory for this connection.

THE LIQUIDITY PREFERENCE APPROACH TO INTEREST RATE THEORY

In the liquidity preference approach, interest rate theory is a part of the theory of income determination. The preceding chapters covered the concepts involved in this theory with the exception of the process of interest rate determination. We turn to that process before examining the relation of the interest rate to the income theory.

This theory of the interest rate consists of a supply and demand type analysis as was the case in the preceding theories. The composition of the supply side and the demand side of the market is different from the two preceding theories, however, for two reasons. Earlier theories implied a time period. The supply side consisted of a flow of funds to the loan market and the demand side absorbed these funds during an unspecified period of time. The saving and the investment that took place during the period, therefore, influenced supply and demand. In the liquidity preference approach, we consider the supply and the demand sides of the market as they exist at a certain point in time. We may think of this picture as a snapshot showing the results of forces and influences as of a given instant. Hence, the rate of saving and the rate of investment are not part of the supply and the demand.

The second difference involves the concept of the function of the interest rate. We noted previously that we regard saving as a function of income and that its volume is independent of the interest rate. However, persons who have accumulated wealth through saving have a decision to make. They may hold idle cash balances or they may hold other, less liquid, assets. Since people prefer liquidity they must have an inducement if they are to hold less liquid forms of wealth. The interest rate provides this inducement. Thus, the term liquidity preference suggests that people prefer liquidity; the interest rate is the price paid to those who give up their liquid position. Supply and demand analysis now becomes a study of the supply of and the demand for liquidity.

For this analysis we separate the demand for liquidity into two components which, in turn, represent three different motives for holding cash. Since we discussed two of these motives in the chapters on the quantity approach to monetary theory, we need only summarize at this point.

Transactions Motive

The transactions motive for holding cash arises because the flow of payments and receipts does not coincide for either households or business firms. Households must hold some cash to cover the expenses of living from payday to payday. Business firms must hold some cash for the same reason. Bills come due and there are payrolls to meet during the intervals between the receipts of revenue. Demand for cash based on the transactions motive is independent of the level of the interest rate. However, it does vary with the income level.

Precautionary Motive

The precautionary motive refers to the desire to hold cash as a protection against an unforeseen decline in receipts or increase in expenses. It is different from the transactions motive because of this element of uncertainty. The amount of cash held for precautionary reasons depends in part on the level of income. It also depends on the degree of uncertainty which exists in the minds of the public. The degree of uncertainty is more pronounced in periods of crises and great change. Finally, it depends upon the level of the interest rate, for this is the price required if one is to feel secure despite these uncertainties.

Because the amount of cash held for precautionary reasons depends in part upon the level of income, we can combine a portion of this demand with the transactions demand. This gives us the portion of total demand for cash which is a function of income. This portion is the L_1 demand for money. Figure 17–4 shows the relationship of L_1 to income. The relationship drawn here is a linear one. It assumes that the cash held for this purpose is a constant proportion of income. As is true of some other diagrams, we assume the relationship to be linear because of the need for simplicity. If we use nonlinear relationships, the principles developed are the same.

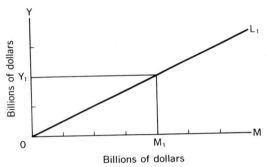

Figure 17-4. L_1 Demand for Liquid Balances

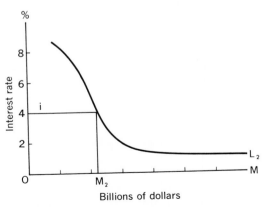

Figure 17-5. L_2 Demand for Liquid Balances

Speculative Motive

The second component of the demand for liquid balances is L_2. It consists of the demand for precautionary motives not included in L_1 plus the demand based upon speculative motives. The speculative motive is a term which refers to the desire to hold cash because this ownership creates opportunities to take advantage of price and interest rate changes. The advantage of holding cash as opposed to other assets becomes clear if we compare the position of a person possessing cash with that of a person holding bonds. The bondholder faces the danger of a loss if the interest rate on long-term obligations rises causing the present value of bonds to decline. By contrast the person holding money can buy bonds at the new, low price. In brief, uncertainty concerning future prices including the long-term interest rate motivates people to hold money instead of a "useful" or interest-yielding asset.

The amount of cash which people desire to hold for speculative reasons varies inversely with the interest rate. A rise in the rate increases the reward for assuming the risks of uncertainty; therefore, demands for cash balances decline. There is a psychological factor as well. The public adopts an attitude regarding the normal or correct rate of interest. If the rate is low, it is assumed that the probability of a rise is greater than the likelihood of a decline. Hence, people tend to desire to hold cash and to wait for a rise in the interest rate. Conversely, a high rate leads to the belief that future rates will be lower and that cash should be exchanged for securities at the present time.

Figure 17–5 shows the relationship of the L_2 demand for cash to the interest rate. As drawn in this figure, the L_2 relationship is not linear. Instead, the curve becomes horizontal as the interest rate approaches 1½ per cent. This feature of the L_2 curve reflects a belief that there is a floor under the interest rate. The risk and the administrative cost involved in the acquisition and the retention of nonliquid assets cause all such assets to be unattractive if the rate of return is below this floor. There is also the speculative motive. At very low rates of interest, the only change possible is an upward movement. Therefore, we may argue that idle balances will absorb an infinite amount of cash. We shall note the significance of this nonlinear relationship and the assumed floor under the interest rate in a later section of this chapter. As L_2 appears in Figure 17–5, there is a ceiling on the interest rate at approximately 10 per cent. At this rate the public will hold no cash—an impossible condition. However, this hypothetical upper limit, unlike the lower limit, has not played a role in economic decision-making theory.

Figures 17–6a to 17–6c show the demand for liquidity. Figures a and b present the L_1 and L_2 functions, respectively. For Figure c, we assume an income level of *OY*. At that level the quantity of cash people wish to hold for L_1 reasons is OM_1. The quantity OM_1 added to the L_2 demand produces the curve $L_1 + L_2$. We must note, therefore, that Figure 17–6c represents the demand for money for a given level of income, *OY*. If income changes, the curve will shift. We should remember also that other factors which give the curve $L_1 + L_2$ its specific shape and location are subject to change.

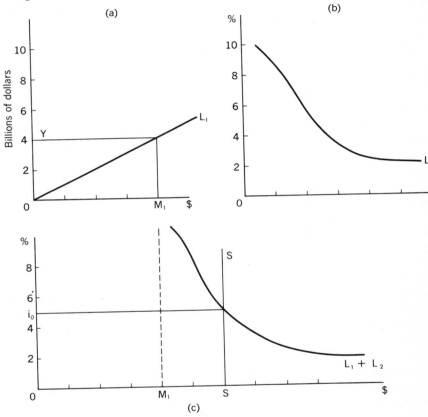

Figure 17-6.   Liquidity Preference Interest Rate Theory

Supply of Liquidity

The supply of liquidity is a simple concept. It is the stock of money in existence and is constant, therefore, at any given moment in time. *SS* represents the supply in Figure 17–6c. Given the demand curve $L_1 + L_2$ and the supply curve *SS*, the interest rate must be i_0, the point of intersection. We have noted that all money must be the possession of someone. The equilibrium level of interest is the rate at which the public is willing to hold neither more nor less than the quantity of money in existence.

The liquidity preference theory of the interest rate has some features which can be confusing. We began our discussion by stating that a person who owns assets can choose to hold his wealth as an idle cash balance or he may choose to surrender liquidity in order to earn interest. We concluded by stating that someone must own all the cash in existence. Therefore, the public must hold an idle cash balance. Do these statements contradict each other? Has the "choice" disappeared so that we cannot say the public prefers liquidity but rather that it has liquidity forced upon it? A reader who is familiar with supply and demand analysis and especially with those cases involving a fixed supply can answer the question quickly. Both statements are true. The public considered as a unit must hold the money which is in existence, but each individual member of the public body has a choice. If an individual feels that he holds too large a cash balance for the given interest rate, he can purchase securities. If this individual is typical of the majority—that is, the public wishes to decrease its cash balance—competition in the securities market will force the interest rate down to the point where the demand for cash is just equal to the supply of money.

THE INTEREST RATE
AND INCOME DETERMINATION

With the exception of the government factors, which we shall consider in the next chapter, we have now considered all the determinants of the level of income. All that remains is to assemble these factors and relationships into a system. The series of figures, 17–7a to 17–7e, presents a simple approach to the assembly problem. Certain factors and relationships are "given." That is, conditions outside the system determine their values. These are: (1) the stock of money, (2) the L_1 relationship, (3) the L_2 relationship, (4) the marginal efficiency of capital, and (5) the saving and consumption functions. All of these factors and relationships are familiar to us.

In Figure 17–7a, we assume a tentative level of income Y_0. The L_1 function then indicates the amount of cash absorbed because of L_1 motives. Figure 17–7b adds the L_2 function and the "given" supply of money, SS, to the system to determine the interest rate i_0. Figure 17–7c applies this interest rate to the MEC relationship and determines the size of investment expenditures. In Figure 17–7d we compare this "determined" level of investment with the savings function and we see that an income equal to OY is necessary for

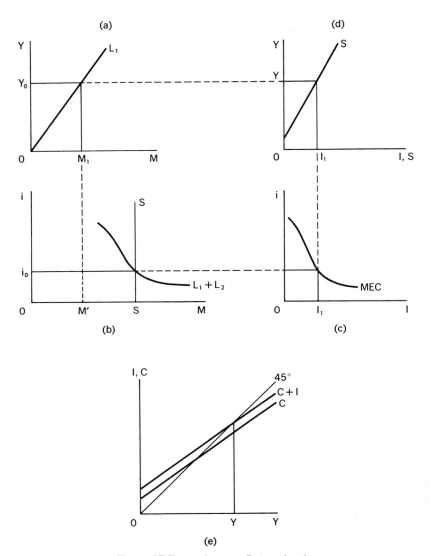

Figure 17-7. Income Determination

savings to equal investment. Or we may use the consumption function, as in Figure 17–7e. The income level, therefore, appears to be
OY. But this level may not be the same as the Y_0 level which we
assumed in order to determine M_1 in Figure 17–7a. We have shown
how the demand for liquidity influences the level of income, but we
have ignored the effect of the level of income so determined on the

demand for liquidity. If OY is larger than Y_0, the amount of cash absorbed for L_1 motives will be larger than the diagrams indicate. This will raise the interest rate and will cause changes in each figure including the level of income in 17–7d. The system will be in equilibrium when the level of income in 17–7d (or 17–7e) is equal to that in 17–7a. At that point there is no tendency to change unless one of the "given" factors changes. If we are to illustrate the determination of the equilibrium level of income as demonstrated in Figures 17–7a to d, many diagrams may be necessary before the trial and error process yields the correct answer.

A somewhat more complicated diagram solves this problem. For this we turn to Figure 17–8, which contains the same diagrams as those in Figures 17–7a to d with some shifts in position. Quadrant I

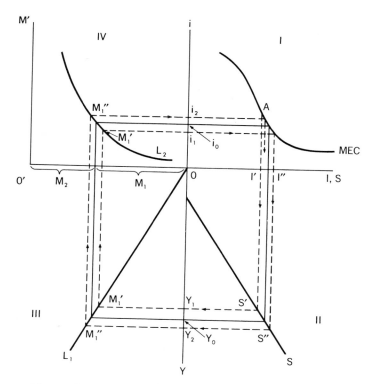

This method of illustrating the theory of money, interest, income, and investment was developed in Ira O. Scott, Jr., "An Exposition of the Keynesian System," *Review of Economic Studies*, 19 (1951), 12-18.

Figure 17-8. Income Determination, Alternate Method

is the *MEC* relationship. Quadrant II is the savings function drawn with income measured in a downward direction. Quadrant III is the L_1 relationship also with income measured in a downward direction. Quadrant IV is the L_2 relationship with the origin shifted to O'. In this diagram $O'O$ is equal to the stock of money in existence. Therefore, it is the supply of liquidity which the public must hold for L_1 and L_2 motives. The quantity held for L_1 motives is M_1, measured from O to the left. We measure from O' to the right the quantity held for L_2 motives, called M_2. $M_1 + M_2$ must equal $O'O$, the stock of money.

If we start with an income level of Y_0 and follow the solid line, we find the level of M_1 from quadrant III. Moving to quadrant IV and remembering that $M_1 + M_2 = O'O$, we find M_2 and the rate of interest i_0. Moving to quadrant I and the *MEC* curve, we determine the level of investment at the i_0 rate of interest. Quadrant II, in turn, shows us that income must be equal to Y_0 for saving to be equal to investment. This is the income level we used at the beginning of our example. It is the equilibrium level.

We see the value of the diagram when we start from a position that is not one of equilibrium. For this purpose we begin in quadrant I, point A on the *MEC* curve, and follow the broken line in a clockwise direction. We note that this line traces a cobweb pattern. It indicates income levels of Y_1, Y_2, and so forth, and approaches the equilibrium level of Y_0 as a limit. We may interpret this cobweb pattern in terms of the economic conditions it represents. Point A on the *MEC* curve in quadrant I indicates an investment expenditure level of I'. Moving into quadrant II and applying the saving function, we see that this level of investment leads to the income level Y_1. Using the L_1 function in quadrant III, we note that the public absorbs cash equal to M_1' because of the transactions motive at this income level. In quadrant IV, the L_2 function shows us that an interest rate of i_1 is necessary to induce the public to hold the remainder of the money supply as a speculative cash balance. Returning to quadrant I, we see that this interest rate causes investment to increase to I''. If we continued this quadrant-by-quadrant description, we would note that income, investment, saving, and the interest rate fluctuate but the system approaches equilibrium.

The factors and the relationships given in Figure 17–8 are the same as those in Figures 17–7a to d; namely, (1) the stock of money, (2) the L_1 relationship, (3) the L_2 relationship, (4) the marginal efficiency of capital, and (5) the saving function. From these we determine the following values: (1) the level of income, (2) the level of investment expenditures, (3) the interest rate, (4) the cash balance held for L_1 motives, and (5) the cash balance held for L_2 motives. In addition, we know the level of consumption and saving when we determine income and investment.

SIGNIFICANCE OF THE LIQUIDITY PREFERENCE THEORY AND THE THEORY OF INCOME DETERMINATION

We have presented income determination as an exercise in geometry, but we must not regard the theory as a formula for the computation of the statistical value of the level of income, the size of investment expenditure, and the other dependent variables. We believe the relationships, such as the quantity of money to the L_1 and the L_2 demand for money and the MEC, to be correct in principle; but we do not know the precise nature of the functions. For example, we believe that, other things remaining unchanged, an increase in the volume of investment expenditures will accompany a decline in the interest rate; we do not claim to know the precise size of this increase. In other words we believe the MEC curve slopes downward and to the right, but we do not know the precise degree of this slope. The same condition of imperfect knowledge applies to the L_1, the L_2, and the saving function. Hence, we cannot use the formulas as computing or forecasting devices.

The theory, however, does serve a very useful purpose. It helps us to understand the reasons for a particular income level and explains changes in that level. As we noted previously this theory, like most theories, developed in response to a problem. Earlier theories contained assumptions that led to the logical conclusion that income was normally at a full employment level. Lengthy periods of unemployment and depressed business conditions created doubts concerning the validity of such a theory. A new explanation that would provide for the possibility of something other than full employment as a normal condition was needed.

The theory of income determination, of which the liquidity preference theory of the interest rate is a part, furnishes this explanation. The significant feature of this theory is the concept of the interest rate as a price paid to induce people to surrender liquidity. The interest rate influences the level of investment expenditures and so income, but the equilibrium level of income thus determined need not be one of full employment. Instead, one may claim that full employment is a coincidence. On occasion critics have charged that the advocates of this theory claim that it proves that unemployment is the normal condition. This is not correct. Nothing in the theory suggests that the equilibrium level of income is one of underemployment, full employment, or overfull employment. Any one of these conditions is possible. The reader may check this conclusion by reviewing the theory and asking the question: What factor causes the equilibrium level of income to be one of full employment, under-employment, or overfull employment? No such factor or influence is present. Hence, we must conclude that various degrees of employ-ment are possible. It is true that we can demonstrate underemploy-ment equilibrium by making certain assumptions pertaining to the quantity of money in existence, the shape of the MEC curve, and the shape of the liquidity preference curve. Such demonstrations, how-ever, depend upon these special assumptions. Recognition that the economy is not constantly moving toward full employment represents a major change in our understanding of the economic system as compared to previous concepts. We shall see that attitudes toward policy reflect this change. Monetary theory like other economic thinking is problem- and policy-oriented.

Changes in the Level of Income

A second problem, short-run fluctuations in the level of income, served as an additional motivation to develop a better theory of in-come determination. The contribution which the theory makes to our understanding of the causes of changes in the level of income be-comes apparent if we consider the possibility for change in each determinant and the consequences of such a change.

A change in any one of the five given factors destroys the equilib-rium of the system. Adjustments occur in the other variables until the system reaches a new equilibrium position. Thus, if a shift in the L_1 curve occurs, the amount of cash held for L_1 motives changes. The system is no longer in equilibrium. The shift of the L_1 curve causes changes in the cash held for L_2 reasons, the rate of interest, the size of investment expenditures, and the level of income. These several changes, or adjustments, re-establish equilibrium conditions in the system.

Figure 17–8 is useful as a means of determining the effect of the several possible changes. If the positions of the L_1, the L_2, the MEC, and the S curves as well as the stock of money change one by one, the result in terms of a new equilibrium level of income is apparent. Since shifts in these "given" factors have important effects, some comments on the reasons for change are in order.

The demand for liquidity (L_1 and L_2). In the chapters on the quantity approach to economic theory, we examined the reasons for changes in velocity and the cash balance—V and K in the two theo-ries. The same conditions govern the demand for L_1 and L_2 type balances. The L_1 relationship of demand for cash balances to income can change but the adjustment is likely to be gradual. Since the nonsynchronization of receipts and payments is the basis for the L_1 relationship, this factor will change only as payment customs and institutions change. It follows that shifts in the L_1 relationship are significant only when long-run problems are under consideration. The L_2 component of demand for cash is subject to sudden shifts, however. The L_2 relationship depends in large part on expectations as to the future rate of interest. Attitudes may change causing the public to regard a given interest rate as abnormally high or low. Such a change causes the L_2 curve and hence the $L_1 + L_2$ curve to shift. If the shift is to the right—that is, the public demands larger cash balances—the interest rate will rise. The level of investment expenditures and, therefore, of income will fall. There is an exception. If the supply of money intersects the $L_1 + L_2$ curve in the horizontal position, a shift in the curve need not affect the interest rate. Figure $17-9$ illustrates this point. With a stock of money equal to OM_2, a shift in liquidity preference from L_2 to L_2' does not affect the interest rate.

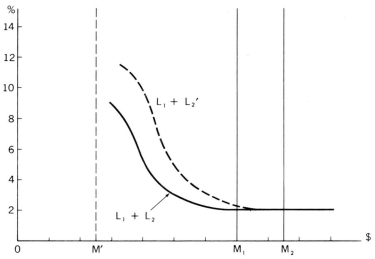

Figure 17-9. Changes in the Stock of Money and in the L_2 Function

Shift of the MEC. The preceding chapter treated the marginal efficiency of capital at some length. The *MEC* curve is subject to sudden and sizable shifts because it depends upon expectations. A change toward optimism shifts the curve to the right and causes investment expenditures and income to rise. The reader may investigate the effect of a shift in the *MEC* by drawing a new curve in quadrant I of Figure $17-8$.

A change in the saving function. The saving function appears to be relatively stable. However, it depends upon the public's attitude toward thrift and this attitude can change. Such changes generally will be gradual but sudden shifts may occur. In most instances it is possible to trace short-run changes to specific causes, such as the fear of a shortage of consumer goods following the outbreak of war. Regardless of the reason, an increase in the thrift habit allows saving to equal investment at a lower level of income. We can illustrate the effect of increased thrift by moving the saving curve upward in quadrant II.

Changes in the stock of money. Finally, there is the stock of money. The values of this determinant can change. However, since the Treasury Department and the Federal Reserve authorities control this factor, we regard it as a policy implement for influencing the level of income. If the quantity of money increases, the point of intersection with the $L_1 + L_2$ curve changes. The interest rate declines; investment expenditures and income rise. We can demonstrate the effect of an increase in the money supply by shifting to the left the line $O'M'$ in quadrant IV of Figure 17–8. The L_2 line also moves to the left and leads to a new equilibrium position with a higher level of income. There is an exception to this principle. If the original stock of money intersects the horizontal portion of the $L_1 + L_2$ curve, an increase in the money supply will not affect the interest rate. To demonstrate this exception, we return to Figure 17–9. An increase in the stock of money from OM_1 to OM_2 does not affect the interest rate (for this purpose we use the solid $L_1 + L_2$ curve). Consequently, this change will not influence the level of income and employment. This point is of incidental interest in the study of abstract monetary theory, but it is important in a discussion of monetary policy. If the economy is operating in the horizontal area of the liquidity preference function, the monetary authorities have little opportunity to affect the level of income.

SUMMARY

Interest rate theory concerns the forces which determine the level of the interest rate and the consequences of the rate of interest upon economic activity. The classical school of economists regarded interest as a price paid for the use of saving. Supply and demand forces which consisted of saving and investment, respectively, determined the rate. The rate of interest was the device which brought savings and investment into equality. It influenced the allocation of resources between consumption and investment and, therefore, had an effect on economic growth. This concept of the interest rate permitted the classical economists to regard full employment as the normal condition of the economic system.

The loanable funds theory, like the classical theory, regarded interest as a price determined by the forces of supply and demand. However, it recognized the advantages of holding idle cash balances. Consequently, total demand consisted of a demand for funds for investment purposes plus a demand for funds to increase cash balances, called hoarding. Total supply in turn consisted of saving plus funds released from cash balances previously accumulated, called dishoarding. The intersection of the supply and the demand curves determined the level of the interest rate. This rate cleared the loanable funds market but did not require that saving equal investment. Therefore, the theory provided for a change in the level of income.

The liquidity preference theory uses many ideas developed in the classical and the loanable funds approaches. It analyzes supply and demand. This theory treats the interest rate as a price paid to the person who surrenders liquidity. Accordingly, it examines the supply of and the demand for liquidity or cash balances. The level of income and the psychological preference for liquidity determine the demand, while the supply of liquidity is equal to the stock of money in existence. The rate of interest determined by these forces is one determinant of the level of investment expenditures and therefore of the level of income. In brief, the level of income affects the rate of interest and the rate of interest affects the level of income. The system is in equilibrium when income is at such a level that the demand for liquidity is just equal to the stock of money. There is no guarantee that this equilibrium level of income will be a condition of full employment. This denial of full employment as the normal, or long-run equilibrium, condition is the most significant contribution of the liquidity preference approach.

This chapter has presented several interest rate theories in the form of a historical development. This may suggest that we should regard the older theories as errors leading to the present great truth. Obviously, such an attitude is in error. Inadequacies existed in the older theories and we have noted them. We have suggested that the liquidity preference theory offers the best explanation of the determination and the role of the interest rate at this time. Like its predecessors, it contains imperfections and theorists have improved it in the years since its first presentation.

QUESTIONS

1. In what way was the classical theory of the interest rate related to income determination?
2. Can the loanable funds theory of the interest rate be used to explain a prolonged period of general unemployment? Discuss.
3. What are the common features of the liquidity preference theory of the interest rate and the quantity theory of money?
4. What are the probable consequences if saving *ex ante* exceeds investment *ex ante*?
5. How is the interest rate related to the level of GNP in the liquidity preference approach?

SUGGESTED READINGS

Dillard, Dudley. *The Economics of John Maynard Keynes.* New York: Prentice-Hall, Inc., 1948.

Hansen, Alvin H. *Business Cycles and National Income.* Expanded ed. New York: W. W. Norton & Company, Inc., 1964. Chapter 11.

Keiser, Norman F. *Macroeconomics, Fiscal Policy, and Economic Growth.* New York: John Wiley & Sons, Inc., 1964. Chapters 5–7.

Also, see the Readings listed at the end of Chapter 15.

18

THEORY OF INCOME DETERMINATION:
Concluded

THE GOVERNMENT SECTOR

To this point, we have ignored the role of the government sector of the economy in the determination of the level of output, employment, and income. We shall now remedy that omission. Almost every government activity affects the level of income. Such functions as maintenance of law and order, public education, conduct of international affairs, and antitrust activities have some effect on the marginal efficiency of capital, the consumption function, and the public attitude toward liquidity. Accordingly, these actions influence the level of income, but it is difficult if not impossible to determine their precise effect. The host of forces which shape the MEC, the consumption function, and the L_1 and the L_2 relationships includes these government activities. They do not specifically concern us in this chapter, for here our concern is the government's financial operations which have a direct influence on national income. These financial activities are: government purchases of goods and services, tax and nontax receipts, and government transfer payments; that is, G and T_n, which we defined in Chapter 15.

Reasons for Treating the Government
Sector Separately

The addition of factors representing government financial activities does not alter the logic of the theory of income determination which we developed in the preceding chapters. Government purchase of goods and services, G, is an addition to the circular flow while net taxes, T_n, is a leakage. To this extent they are like I and S, respectively. Consequently, we could include government financial activities in our theory by changing the definitions of I and S to include G and T_n. The level of saving and investment would be higher; or, if we thought in terms of the diagrams representing these

313

functions, the I and S curves would shift their positions. The equilibrium level of income would continue to be that level at which newly defined saving and investment would be equal to each other. This result should be obvious because of the conclusions reached in a previous chapter that $G + I = S + T_n$.

If G and T_n were constant in value, this simple approach to their roles in income theory might be acceptable. However, both G and T_n are subject to change. Hence, including them in I and S, respectively, compels us to ignore some comprehensible changes in the levels of investment and saving and causes us to forfeit an opportunity to increase our understanding of the reasons for fluctuations in the level of income. Consequently, we treat G and T_n separately. We analyze the causes for changes in these factors and the effect of those changes on income just as we examined the reasons for and the effect of changes in the saving function and the *MEC*.

There is another reason why we wish to consider G and T_n separately. In the previous chapter we noted that only one of the determinants of the level of income, the money supply, was subject to discretionary control. Independent forces, such as the liquidity preference and the marginal propensity to save, control the others. Hence, if we ignore G and T_n, the Government and the other public authorities appear to have only limited power to change the level of income if it is unsatisfactory. However, both G and T_n are important factors in determining the level of income and they are subject to discretionary control. Obviously, we must examine the effect of changes in G and T_n on the level of income. However, we shall not treat fiscal policy directly until a later chapter even though one of the motives for this study is the desire to understand the effects of government actions designed to influence the economy. At this point we shall concentrate on fiscal analysis.

Government Purchases of Goods and Services

Government purchases of goods and services, the factor G, is similar to I in that both are components of gross national expenditure. A different set of determinants establishes the level of G, however. The interest rate and the marginal efficiency of capital do not affect G, nor is there any determinant or group of determinants that exhibits a recognizable functional relationship to G. The level of G depends upon political decisions of the Congress, state legislatures, and local governing bodies. International political conditions, the size of the school-age population, and in general the attitude of the public regarding the services government should provide influence these decisions. While there are many such determinants of the level of G, we are unable to show that the level of income is a direct determinant. There is some evidence that the Federal Government deliberately raises its purchases of goods and services when income declines but that state and local governments tend to follow the opposite policy. Therefore, it is customary to consider the level of G as constant relative to the level of income for purposes of theoretical analysis. In this respect G is similar to I and the role of government purchases in the determination of the level of income is the same as

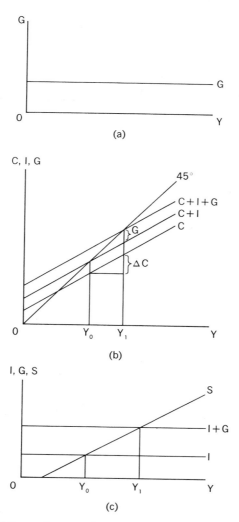

Figure 18-1.   Income Determination Including G but Excluding T_n

that for investment.

The effect of government purchases on the level of income can be illustrated by adding the G factor to the diagrams which have been presented. G is shown as constant with respect to Y in Figure 18–1a. In Figure 18–1b G has been added to the income determination diagram of Figure 17–7e. In Figure 18–1c the saving function has been used to determine the equilibrium level of income.

Note that these diagrams illustrate the effect of the addition of G to our analysis but they ignore T_n. Consequently, they illustrate a system that is not complete; they are useful nevertheless. In Figures 18–1b and 18–1c, we see that the addition of G to the previous income determination diagram causes income to rise from Y_0 to Y_1. Furthermore, this increase in income is greater than G, the amount of expenditures added directly. Government purchases, therefore, have the same effect as investment expenditures. Income rises by the amount of the government purchases, but this rise in income leads to increased consumption expenditures. This is particularly evident in Figure 18–1b where $OY_1 - OY_0 = G + \Delta C$.

The effect of government purchases of goods and services can be illustrated by means of algebraic formulas. If the factor G is assigned a value of 20 and is added to the formulas presented in Chapter 16, we have

$$Y = C + I + G$$
$$C = 20 + \tfrac{3}{4}Y$$
$$I = 40$$
$$G = 20$$
$$Y = 320$$
$$C = 260$$

If we compare this income level to that determined by the equation in Chapter 16, we note that the addition of a G factor of 20 has caused income to rise by 80. Consumption expenditures have risen by 60 to account for the difference.[1] The result indicates that the multiplier principle applies to government purchases in the same manner as it does to investment expenditures. The formula is $\Delta Y = \Delta G \div MPS$. We conclude by stating that the determinants of the level of G and the level of I are different but the effects on the level of income are the same.

T_n—Net Taxes

Net taxes like saving is a component of gross national income. The determinants of the level of net taxes are different, however. In

---

[1] If we apply the data from this illustration to the saving function in Chapter 16, $S = \tfrac{1}{4}Y - 20$, we find that $S = 60$. This is correct since we have ignored T_n. Therefore, in our illustration saving must equal $I + G$.

order to examine the determinants, we shall first separate net taxes into its two subcomponents: (1) tax and nontax receipts, which we call gross taxes, and (2) net transfer payments.

The level of gross taxes depends upon the structure of tax rates and the tax base to which these rates apply. This structure is the result of acts of the Congress, the state legislatures, and the local governing bodies. Given the present tax structure in the United States, we can expect the level of gross taxes to vary with the level of income. The personal income and the corporate profits taxes levied by .the Federal Government obviously are sensitive to income changes. In those states which levy personal income and corporate profits taxes, the same result occurs. Sales and excise taxes levied by the several levels of government vary with the level of consumption expenditures and, therefore, with income. Some receipts, such as property taxes and certain nontax forms of revenue, are relatively constant with respect to income; but the overall result is an increase in gross taxes as income increases and a decrease as income declines. An exact statement of the degree of sensitivity of gross taxes to income requires an extensive study of the tax structure including the provisions for deductions and exemptions. This is beyond the scope of this text but it is apparent that the change in gross taxes induced by a change in income is sizable. Furthermore, the rate of change in the level of gross taxes is greater than the rate of change in income because of the graduated rate structure of the personal income tax and the tendency for corporate profits and therefore corporate taxes to change more rapidly than income.

Transfer payments consist of interest on the public debt, pensions, unemployment compensation, and various types of welfare payments. Interest payments vary with the interest rate and the size of the debt. Since there is not a direct tie to the level of income, we treat this subcomponent as a constant factor. The level of pension payments depends upon the age distribution of the population and the eligibility requirements. For our purposes we may consider pension payments to be constant with respect to income. Unemployment compensation and welfare payments, however, vary inversely with income. The change in this type of transfer payment is most obvious if a change in the level of employment accompanies the change in income.

Since some types of transfer payments are constant while others vary inversely with respect to income, we must conclude that there is an overall tendency for transfer payments to vary inversely with income. The degree of this variation depends upon the relative size of the several types of transfer payments. For example, the sensitivity of transfer payments to income changes is high if unemployment compensation payments are large relative to interest payments and low if the reverse is true. In addition the cause of a change in income influences this sensitivity. If there is a short-run cyclical fluctuation in income, it will affect the level of unemployment and thus of unemployment compensation payments to a greater degree than if the income change is the result of long-run growth accompanying a population increase.

Gross taxes minus *transfer payments* equal T_n. Since gross taxes vary directly and transfer payments inversely with income, we must conclude that T_n varies directly with income. Although we know the direction, we cannot determine the degree of change in the level of net taxes induced by a given change in income without extensive study which is beyond the scope of this text.

We cannot illustrate the effect of net taxes on income in the straightforward manner that we applied in examining government purchases. The diagrams which we have employed up to this point do not provide directly for the T_n function. However, T_n affects the level of private — that is, personal and business — disposable income and, therefore, the saving and consumption functions. Hence, we trace the effect of net taxes on income by considering its effect on consumption and saving.

If net taxes were constant with respect to income, we would illustrate the effect by shifting the C and the S functions downward a fixed amount for all levels of income. Figure 18–2 illustrates this hypothetical condition. The solid lines represent consumption and saving in the absence of net taxes; the dotted lines show the effect after net taxes. Since $C + S + T_n = Y$, the vertical difference between C and C' plus that between S and S' must equal T_n.

However, we have seen that T_n is not constant with respect to

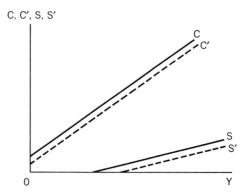

Figure 18-2.   The Consumption and the Saving Functions
Adjusted for a Constant Level of Net Taxes

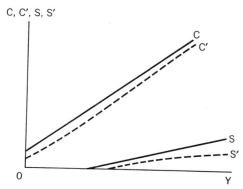

Figure 18-3.   The Consumption and the Saving Functions
Not Constant with Respect to the Income Level

income. Certainly the absolute value of T_n increases as Y increases. Accordingly, the lines representing consumption and saving before and after the consideration of net taxes cannot be parallel. The C and the S functions still would be linear if net taxes were a constant proportion of income; but we have seen that the ratio of net taxes to income increases as income rises. For this reason the consumption function, or the saving function, or both must be nonlinear. If we are to determine the shape of these functions with more accuracy, we must consider separately the several subcomponents of net taxes. Given the United States tax structure, a change in the level of gross taxes affects those individuals and business firms with a high marginal propensity to save. A change in transfer payments, particularly those in the welfare category, affects groups that have a high marginal propensity to consume. Therefore, depending on the nature of the change, a given change in the level of T_n may produce different results in C and S. Figure 18–3 illustrates a plausible effect of T_n on the consumption and the saving functions. The solid lines again represent conditions before and the dotted lines the conditions after consideration of the effects of net taxes. As presented in this diagram, the effect is greater on consumption at low levels of income and on saving at higher levels. In this diagram, we have assumed that at low income levels taxes come from funds otherwise available for consumption expenditures. At higher income levels taxes reduce saving. There are, of course, many other possible and plausible relationships.

Effect of the Government Sector
on the Level of Income

Figures 18–4a and 18–4b illustrate the effect of including both government purchases and net taxes in the theory of income deter-

mination covered in Chapters 16 and 17. In Figure 18–4a the intersection of the 45° reference line and the line $C + I$ represents the
equilibrium level of income, OY_0, under the assumed conditions of
the previous chapters; that is, no government sector. When we
include the government sector, the consumption function shifts from
C to C' because of net taxes. To the new consumption line, C', we
add investment and government expenditures. Thus, the line
$C' + I + G$ represents gross national expenditure, taking both G and

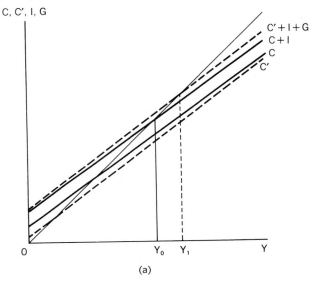

(a)

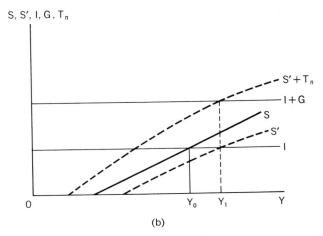

(b)

Figure 18-4.   Income Determination with the Government
                        Sector Included

T_n into consideration. This level of income OY_1 is greater than OY_0, the previous level.

In Figure 18–4b the saving function serves as a means of determining the equilibrium level of income. Once again the solid lines S and I represent saving and investment in the absence of government activity. S' represents saving after net taxes, and $S' + T_n$ represents saving plus net taxes. The $I + G$ line represents investment plus government purchases. In the absence of government activity, income is equal to OY_0. When we include the government sector, saving plus net taxes must equal investment expenditures plus government purchases at the equilibrium level of income. Consequently, income must equal OY_1.

From the preceding discussion it is apparent that the effects of G and T_n on Y tend to cancel each other. Under certain conditions, the effects may be equal in magnitude and so reduce the net effect of the government sector to zero. This is unlikely, however, and there are sound reasons for constructing Figures 18–4a and 18–4b so that the addition of the government sector leads to a net increase in the level of income. First, we must remember that the level of government purchases and net taxes need not be equal and are, in fact, unlikely to be equal. Second, the effects of the two components on income may not be equal even if the level of G is equal to that of T_n. Referring to the multiplier principle once again, we see the reason for these unequal effects.

We have noted that the multiplier principle applies to government purchases. Thus, a change in the level of G leads to an even greater change in the level of Y with the ratio of ΔG to ΔY dependent upon the marginal propensity to consume. We might expect that a reduction in T_n would lead to the same result as an increase in G. However, more careful consideration shows that the result is similar but not identical. We shall use the time-period type of analysis which was the basis for Table 16–3 to illustrate the point. Referring to Table 16–3, we note that if G increases by \$1 the entire amount is spent for goods and services in the first period. In subsequent periods saving reduces this amount to 75, 56, 42 cents, and so forth given a marginal propensity to consume of 3/4.

In the case of a decrease in T_n of \$1, there are several possible results. We shall consider two of these possibilities. If T_n declines by \$1 because of a reduction in taxes, private disposable income rises by this amount. However, with a MPC of 3/4 only 75 cents of this dollar is spent on consumption goods in the first period. In the second, third, and subsequent periods, the figures become 56, 42, 32 cents, and so forth. In this case, therefore, the multiplier is smaller for T_n than for G. For the second example we shall assume that T_n

declines by \$1 because of an increase in unemployment compensation. Since this extra dollar goes to unemployed persons, we may assume that their MPC is above the nationwide average of 75 cents. If these people have been unemployed for some time, their MPC may be equal to 1, in which case the multipliers of G and T_n are the same. The multiplier for T_n may be smaller than that for G, but it cannot be larger so long as we assume that the government has a MPC of 1. These two examples do not exhaust the reasons why the multiplier for G may be different from that for T_n, but they are sufficient for our purpose. We shall have occasion to refer to this principle again when we consider a tax cut and government spending as alternative implements of fiscal policy.

These illustrations direct our attention to the need for caution in the use of the multiplier concept. We have noted previously that the marginal propensity to consume is a theoretical concept, and that it is difficult if not impossible to measure it. Even if we accept the assumption that the MPC on a nationwide basis is ¾, however, we see that the multipliers for G and the two cases of T_n vary. The multipliers for G and T_n are the result of different but plausible assumptions regarding the MPC of groups within the nation.

MONETARY THEORY—CONCLUDING COMMENTS

We have considered the quantity approach and the income and expenditure approach to monetary theory. These two approaches seem and in fact are quite different. Nevertheless, they have many common features which we must not overlook because of their unique terminology.

Common Features of the Two Approaches

The income and expenditure approach explains the determinants of the level of money income. It recognizes that the level of money income reflects some combination of the level of output, the level of employment, and the level of prices. In the quantity approach the price level is of prime concern, but this approach does not neglect the other two factors entirely. The factor T, transactions, reflects the level of employment and output along with other influences. Both approaches recognize that the public prefers a liquid position and treat that preference as a determinant of the system. In this area the terms are different but the approaches are so similar that the literature on the determinants of V and K is very helpful in explaining the L_1 and the L_2 functions. Finally, the stock of money is a determinant in both approaches, notwithstanding that changes in M

become meaningless in the income expenditure approach if the economy is operating in the horizontal position of the L_2 curve. The two approaches have enough in common to supplement each other in serving as alternative methods of analysis.

Differences in Emphasis and Scope

Although many similarities exist there are important differences. We have noted these differences previously and need only summarize them here. The quantity approach emphasizes long-run problems and long-run equilibrium conditions. It concentrates on the price level as the important problem and on the quantity of money as the chief determinant of that level. The income and expenditure approach, by contrast, emphasizes conditions and problems in the short run. It recognizes the level of employment and output as an economic problem which is equal to, if not more important than, the price level. Finally, it downgrades the importance of the stock of money as a determinant of the level of employment, output, and prices. It treats the stock of money as one of the determinants along with the marginal efficiency of capital, the consumption function, the liquidity preference function, government purchases of goods and services, and net taxes.

The income and expenditure approach is more comprehensive than the quantity approach with regard to the determinants of the system and the questions it attempts to answer. This is probably the result of different concepts concerning the problems which exist. The income and expenditure approach directly or indirectly includes all the factors of the quantity approach. In addition, it directs our attention to a study of such items as the saving function, the consumption function, the determinants of the level of investment, and the role of government financial operations in determining the level of output, employment, and prices. Consequently, the income and expenditure approach provides for a much more thorough study of the level of economic activity.

Consequences of the Two Theories

We find the main significance of the two approaches in the different attitudes toward social and political problems exhibited by their respective adherents. It would be naive to claim that the acceptance of one approach leads to certain attitudes since the causal relation may flow in the opposite direction; nevertheless, there is a connection between the respective theories and certain attitudes. The variance in attitudes is the result of the disagreement in emphasis of the two schools of thought and the different problems which they recognize.

We return to the fact that the quantity theories developed in a period when many economists still subscribed to the earlier belief that a condition of less than full employment was a temporary problem which would correct itself in the long run. It is true that many prominent quantity theorists regarded unemployment as a serious problem. Irving Fisher was one of these, and he worked very hard to promote reform measures designed to overcome instability in both the price level and the volume of employment. However, the quantity theories did not provide a basis for the refutation of the belief that general unemployment was impossible. For this reason, reform measures were likely to emphasize the elimination of fluctuations in the level of economic activity and to ignore the danger of long-run unemployment.

Furthermore, most of the quantity theorists felt that the danger of inflation was greater than that of deflation. Consequently, their recommendations featured methods for restraining inflation by preventing too rapid an increase in the stock of money. In general, acceptance of the quantity theories was consistent with attitudes which opposed intervention in the economic system by the government or its agencies with the exception of restrictions on the supply of money. It also led to the nonrevolutionary conclusion that improvements in technical areas, such as check clearing or in other phases of the payments process, increased velocity. One must note, however, that there are many exceptions to the general principle that quantity theorists advocated nonintervention. We referred to Irving Fisher's reform proposals in the preceding paragraph. Professor A. C. Pigou is another notable exception; he was a socialist as well as a quantity theorist.

Occasionally there was concern over the quantity of liquid assets, particularly in international trade; in general the quantity theories appealed to persons who felt that the economic system would operate best if left alone. These persons regarded the government's role as one of controlling the money supply for which service they preferred some automatic device such as the gold standard. In summary, the quantity approach is compatible with the conservative attitude which regards government intervention in the economic system as harmful.

By contrast, persons accepting the income and expenditure approach recognize the possibility of underemployment as well as overemployment and inflation. When this approach was in the process of development, the emphasis was on underemployment. There was also some reason to believe that changes in the stock of money would be an ineffective policy for reasons noted in the section on the L_2 function. If these conditions of "economic stagnation" are present and if we accept the income and expenditure theory, government intervention is the only alternative to chronic underemployment and low output. Even in the absence of stagnation conditions, government action is a valid policy weapon. For this reason, the term "Keynesian" became and remains a synonym not only for the income and expenditure approach but for government intervention in the economic system. Since this intervention usually takes the form of government spending, "Keynesian" and high government expenditures also have become synonymous in political debate.

The two approaches lead to different attitudes regarding saving, consumption, and investment. A quantity theorist who considers full employment as the normal condition must regard consumption as an alternative to investment. The factors of production devoted to the output of consumer goods are not available for investment purposes. Saving, by reducing consumption, permits investment and economic growth. The Keynesian follower concerns himself with investment and saving not only as they affect economic development but as factors influencing the level of employment. If the economy is operating at full employment, the nation continues to face the choice between consumption or investment. However, they are not competitors for scarce resources if the system is operating at less than full employment. In the latter case an increase in both consumption and investment is possible. In fact, an increase in one component is likely to stimulate an increase in the other. Furthermore, the process of saving ceases to be a virtue and becomes a social vice if persons practice it to excess. This statement is not precise since saving is not harmful in itself. The desire for liquidity is the culprit. Nevertheless, the reputation of saving as a virtue does suffer as a result of acceptance of the income and expenditure approach.

The income and expenditure approach leads to a changed attitude with regard to the government budget by revealing the relationship of government finance to economic activity. Logically, this attitude should apply to all units of government, but it is customary to concentrate on the federal level. Other things remaining the same, a surplus as opposed to a balanced government budget causes income to decline while a deficit budget leads to a rise in income. This statement is an oversimplification for we have seen that we must consider also the types of taxes, transfer payments, and expenditures in assessing the effect of the government sector on the level of income. Furthermore, the statement "other things remaining the same" is an important qualification. Nevertheless, development of the income and expenditure approach encouraged economists to adopt a different view of government finances. Previously the distribution of the tax burden and efficiency in government were the subjects studied by persons interested in public finance. With the acceptance of the income and expenditure approach, it became necessary to consider the effect on the level of GNP as well as these other issues. The explanation of the reluctance of the more conservative elements of our society to accept the Keynesian analysis lies in part in the conclusions regarding government finance to which it leads. When we accept the Keynesian analysis, we cannot consider a balanced budget desirable at all times. Because of this analysis, a government deficit becomes intellectually and morally respectable.

SUMMARY

Government purchases of goods and services and net taxes are the components of the government sector of the economy. A study of the determinants of these two factors and their effect upon the level of income adds to our understanding of the principles of income determination. In addition, the components of the government sector are the only factors subject to discretionary control and thus become important in a study of stabilization policy.

The determinants of the level of G are different from those influencing I, but these two components are similar in many respects. In this study we have assumed that both G and I are constant with respect to changes in the level of Y. The level of G, like that of I, is a determinant of the level of Y. A change in G leads to a change in Y. The induced change in Y is in the same direction as the change in G but is greater in magnitude. Thus, there is a multiplier effect accompanying a change in G just as there is for I.

Like saving, T_n is a leakage from the income stream. The net taxes component varies inversely with income and is also a determinant of income; income varies inversely with the level of net taxes if all the other factors remain constant. The degree to which changes in T_n influence the level of Y depends upon the cause of the change in T_n. If T_n changes because gross taxes change, the result is likely to be different from that caused by a change in transfer payments.

The basic principles of the two approaches to monetary theory are not in conflict. They differ, however, in terminology, in the emphasis accorded certain problems and policies, and in the attitudes which their respective adherents tend to adopt. The quantity approach emphasizes fluctuations in the price level as a major problem and suggests that control of the money supply is the appropriate policy to correct this problem. The income and expenditure approach does not ignore the problem of changes in the price level; it places more emphasis on the level of income and output. Furthermore, it regards government intervention as an appropriate device for stabilizing the economy. The two approaches also lead to different attitudes regarding the role of saving, investment, and consumption in the economic system. Finally, the two approaches lend themselves to different interpretations regarding a government budget surplus or deficit.

QUESTIONS

1. What are the significant differences between private investment and government purchases when we regard them as components of GNP? In what ways are the two components alike?
2. Is it correct to state that the level of income determines the level of net taxes? How do the determinants of net taxes differ from those which affect saving?
3. Are the differences between the income and expenditure and the quantity approaches merely one of emphasis or are there substantive differences? Discuss.
4. Is there a logical explanation for the reluctance of conservative opinion to accept the principles of the theory of income determination? Discuss.

SUGGESTED READINGS

Hansen, Alvin H. *Business Cycles and National Income.* Expanded ed. New York: W. W. Norton & Company, Inc., 1964. Chapter 12.

Keiser, Norman F. *Macroeconomics, Fiscal Policy, and Economic Growth.* New York: John Wiley & Sons, Inc., 1964. Chapters 12–13.

Lekachman, Robert (ed.). *Keynes and the Classics.* Boston: D. C. Heath and Company, 1964.

V

FINANCIAL INSTITUTIONS

19

FINANCIAL INSTITUTIONS: Role and Type

In our study of the monetary system, we have considered only three institutions—the commercial banks, the central bank or Federal Reserve banks, and the United States Treasury. There is a reason for this concentration. These three institutions provide the nation with a circulating media, thereby performing a valuable and highly specialized service. Yet, other financial institutions serve the community. These include among others: mutual savings banks, savings and loan associations, small loan companies, investment banks, and insurance companies. None of these institutions is able to create circulating media, however. It is obvious that none of these institutions can issue currency. Several of them contain the word bank in their titles; but, unlike commercial banks, they do not hold deposits which are subject to transfer by check. Consequently, they cannot create any of the deposit component of the money supply. Because of this inability to create money, it is customary to refer to them as "other" financial institutions and to treat them separately from the commercial banking system when discussing monetary economics.

In a later section we shall have occasion to review the school of thought which challenges the belief that commercial banks are different from other financial institutions. In this chapter, however, we treat these institutions as agencies which are unable to create money. We shall examine their role in the economic system and the services they perform, and we shall consider the organizational structure of the more important types. Of necessity this examination will be brief. Students should consult the suggested readings at the end of this chapter if they wish more detailed information.

NEED FOR FINANCIAL INSTITUTIONS

The need for financial institutions arises because many individuals receive income in excess of their consumption expenditures. There would be a need for agencies similar to financial institutions even in a nonmonetary economy. In an economy without a monetary system, self-sufficient family units might store that portion of their

331

output which was in excess of their consumption. They might use it for further production; i.e., investment, or they might lend their "savings" to neighbors who were consuming more than they were producing or who wished to use it for productive purposes. Borrowers and lenders could deal directly in transferring these savings; however intermediaries serving as brokers would be very useful if the market were large. In a previous chapter we saw that the use of money enlarged the market for the transfer of goods and services. Consequently, we should expect that the need for intermediaries would be even greater in a monetary economy.

In a monetary economy, saving takes the form of money income which is in excess of consumption expenditures for some individuals. The economist also regards the retained earnings and the capital consumption allowances of business as saving. In the aggregate these savings are quite large in the United States, as Table 19–1 indicates. The volume and the disposition of saving have an effect on the economy. We have seen that saving constitutes a leakage from the income stream. Accordingly, investment spending or a government deficit is necessary if the nation is to maintain a high level of income. An individual or a corporate saver may spend his savings for investment type goods and services. Many savers, however, will find direct investment inconvenient. Fortunately, there are large numbers of individuals who wish to spend in excess of their income. Consequently, the system escapes a net leakage from the income stream if the savers transfer their excess income to others who spend it. This latter group, which we may call spenders, consists of business firms, consumers, and government.

Table 19–1 shows the volume of saving in the United States in recent years and the disposition of that saving. This table underestimates the volume of personal saving as defined for the purposes of the discussion in this chapter. In the table personal saving is a net figure which ignores the fact that some individuals transfer their savings to others who spend the funds for consumption purposes. It does, however, allow us to appreciate the magnitude of the transfer of funds operation. If the system works perfectly, the transfer of funds from savers to the group we shall call spenders accomplishes two major purposes: It prevents a net leakage from the income stream and provides for the optimum allocation of resources. We noted previously the need to prevent a net leakage because of saving, but the optimum allocation of resources concept requires additional explanation. The ability to transfer savings to borrowers influences the allocation of resources. In the absence of this opportunity, an income earner would have to consume his income as he received it or spend his savings for investment goods and services.

Table 19–1

SOURCES AND USES OF GROSS SAVING

1957–1964
(In billions of dollars)

Year	Saving					Investment		
	Personal Saving	Gross Business Saving	Total Saving	Less Statistical Discrepancy	Adjustment for Govt. Deficit (−) Surplus (+)	Total Investment	Gross Private Domestic Investment	Net Foreign Investment
1957	23.6	45.6	69.2	.6	+ 1.0	69.6	66.1	3.5
1958	24.7	44.6	69.5	1.5	−11.4	56.6	56.6	− .1
1959	23.6	51.3	74.9	3.0	− 1.5	70.4	72.7	−2.3
1960	21.7	50.7	72.3	3.0	+ 3.9	73.2	71.8	1.4
1961	27.3	51.2	78.5	2.6	− 4.2	71.8	68.8	3.0
1962	27.8	57.5	85.3	1.8	− 1.9	81.5	79.1	2.4
1963	27.5	59.1	86.7	2.7	+ .9	84.8	82.0	2.8
1964	32.6	65.0	97.6	2.1	− 2.9	92.6	87.7	5.0

NOTE: Components may not add to totals because of rounding.
Source: United States Department of Commerce, published in the Economic Report of the President (Washington: Government Printing Office, 1965), p. 212.

Such a system may be desirable for some individuals but it is unsatisfactory to the majority. First, the consumption pattern over time will be unsatisfactory for many persons. Second, output will be low if each owner of capital has to combine this factor with his own labor. Furthermore, the size of the capital units will be small.

By contrast, if savers transfer funds to consumers both lender and borrower can achieve an optimum consumption pattern with respect to time. If the saver transfers funds to investors, large capital units and a high degree of specialization are possible. This transfer permits persons with managerial ability and no capital to have access to this factor of production. Because of the opportunity for interest yield, the portion of income allocated to saving and investment will be large and will lead to economic growth and a higher welfare level in the future. Thus, we see that the ability to transfer funds from savers to spenders influences the allocation of income. The pattern of consumption changes along with the allocation of resources between current consumption and investment, which represents future consumption. Since individuals have freedom of choice, we must conclude that they transfer savings only if the resulting reallocation of resources leads to an improved consumption pattern or a more desirable division of resources between consumption and investment.

GENERAL FUNCTIONS
OF FINANCIAL INSTITUTIONS

On the basis of the preceding discussion, we may conclude that the perfect operation of a system for transfer of funds from savers to users leads to an optimum allocation of resources and a high, sustained level of output. Financial institutions have as their general function the facilitation of this transfer of funds. Assistance in transferring funds is necessary because (1) the volume of saving is large, and (2) a highly developed and complex society creates certain barriers to the transfer of funds by individuals. In Chapter 16 we saw that the volume of saving is large in a high income society which regards thrift as a virtue. We also saw that institutionalized saving, which the saver may regard as an expense, adds to the volume. A reminder may be in order that the economist classifies debt repayment and capital consumption allowances as saving since these funds must find an investment outlet.

Barriers to the transfer of savings to spenders exist because of the size of the country and the complexity of our social system. We define "barrier" as a hindrance to the transfer of funds from one individual to another. For purposes of discussion, we shall divide the barriers to this transfer into three classes: (1) risk, (2) inconvenience and cost of transfer, and (3) desire to avoid illiquidity.

The risk element is an obvious barrier. Any prudent individual is reluctant to transfer funds to another person, or he may refuse to transfer funds because of skepticism regarding repayment. The inconvenience and the cost of the transfer operation are apparent also. The prospective lender must spend time and effort in order to find an appropriate borrower. In addition there are legal and other administrative costs connected with the transfer process. We have discussed the desire for liquidity in previous chapters. A prospective lender is reluctant to transfer his idle funds to another person because he feels that he may desire repayment before he has the legal right to demand it. Financial institutions serve the community by helping individuals overcome these barriers.

SPECIFIC FUNCTIONS OF FINANCIAL INSTITUTIONS

It is customary for savers to use one of two legal forms in transferring funds—a loan or an ownership claim. The various debt instruments which we considered in Chapter 5 constitute the evidence of a loan. Shares of stock in a corporation are the most common type of ownership claims. While the two forms are quite different legally, they have common features with respect to the problem under examination. Both forms accomplish the transfer of savings to someone who will spend them. In both cases there are the elements of risk, inconvenience and cost, and illiquidity.

Investigation and Credit Analysis

An individual who transfers his savings to others can minimize the risk element by careful investigation and credit analysis of the recipient. Such a study involves the collection of information regarding the past record of the enterprise, the market in which it operates, its present financial position, and other conditions which affect its ability to repay the debt or to earn profits. The collection and evaluation of this information requires specialized skills and the expenditure of time. Since it is impractical for an individual saver to accomplish this task, financial institutions perform a specific service by doing it for him. Some agencies, such as investment consultants, specialize in this particular service; all financial institutions carry out this function as part of their normal operation.

A hypothetical example illustrates the need for and the value of this service. An individual with $1,000 in savings is considering a loan to someone who will use the funds to buy real estate. In an effort to minimize risk, the saver can investigate the credit worthiness of the borrower and can evaluate the likelihood of repayment. This is difficult and inconvenient even if the prospective borrower is a neighbor whose financial operations are simple. It is next to impossible if the prospective debtor is a giant corporation. Furthermore, it is necessary for other savers to repeat the investigation if the debtor wishes to borrow a large amount. An institution, such as a savings bank, collects the funds of many depositors. Since it operates on a large scale, it can employ specialists and it can serve many savers with a single investigation. To summarize, a financial institution achieves the advantages of large-scale operations. This allows it to specialize and thus to provide a better quality of service at a lower cost. In the process it allows the saver to specialize in an area other than investigation and credit analysis.

The investigative and analytical functions of financial institutions serve the community in another way. These institutions conduct many investigations; hence, they acquire information concerning the relative merits of many enterprises. By disseminating this information they allow the saver to choose the user who offers the best combination of yield, safety, and liquidity. The enterprise he chooses receives funds and thus acquires the use of resources. In a market-oriented economic system, this choice should lead to the optimum allocation of resources.

Matching the Supply and the Demand for Funds

Financial institutions perform what is essentially a brokerage function: they bring the savers and the users of funds together. This function is, in part, a by-product of the service they perform when gathering and disseminating information. They also approach the task directly. These institutions provide conveniently located offices through which savers may transfer funds to users. Certain types of institutions accomplish this function by purchasing securities in large quantities. They hold these securities and sell them in smaller lots. Regardless of the method used, financial institutions perform the specialized task of matching the supply of savings to the demand for funds. In the process they also enable one large user to borrow from many small savers with a minimum of overhead cost.

Diversification and Insurance Against Risk

We have already noted one method of minimizing risk — careful investigation and credit analysis. Another well-known approach to the problem of risk is diversification. A saver seeking an outlet for his funds knows that some debtors will fail to repay their loans. He may even know the approximate ratio of delinquent debtors to total debtors, but he does not know which individuals will fail to meet their obligations. If a saver lends his funds to many borrowers in several industries, he is reasonably certain that not all of them will become bankrupt. By diversifying his lendings he accepts the certainty of a small loss but he avoids the danger of a heavy loss.

In the absence of financial institutions, diversification is not practical except for very wealthy persons. Financial institutions provide this diversification. In our previous example the saver who contemplated lending funds to the buyer of real estate faced the risk of losing everything. He can avoid this risk of heavy loss by depositing his savings in a mutual savings bank. The savings bank lends his savings and the savings of many others to large numbers of borrowers. Failure of any single borrower to repay affects all savers slightly but no one suffers a severe loss.

Provision for Liquidity

We have noted that the desire for liquidity increases the reluctance of savers to transfer money to spenders. The individual saver feels that he may need money prior to the maturity of the debt instrument which he receives for his savings. Or if he buys stock, he may fail to find a purchaser when he wishes to liquidate his holdings.

Financial institutions increase the liquidity of financial assets. They accomplish this through their brokerage function which provides an organized market where the investor can find a buyer for his debt or ownership claim. Furthermore, certain types of institutions are constantly accepting savings from individuals who receive claims against the institution's assets in return. If a client of such an institution wishes to liquidate his claim, the institution can pay to him funds it is receiving currently. A third method is available because of specialized financial institutions whose function it is to buy debt or ownership claims if they feel the price is abnormally low and to sell if the price is abnormally high. These institutions, known as speculators, create a market for financial assets. An individual cannot be sure that he can sell his claim to them at a price of his own choosing, but their presence increases his chances of receiving good value for his security. Through these combined operations, financial institutions increase the liquidity of financial assets.

TYPES OF FINANCIAL INSTITUTIONS

All financial institutions are specialists in the area of the transfer of funds. Some institutions specialize to a greater degree and perform only one of the specific functions. However, most of the institutions perform more than one specific service although they may emphasize one more than another. In the discussion which follows, we shall note the manner in which a number of institutions accomplish these functions. The survey will be incomplete. We shall postpone the study of government financial institutions until the next chapter and shall include only a selected group of the private agencies. Before considering these institutions, we should note that commercial banks perform many of the same functions. In our study of the commercial banking system, we concentrated on its role as the creator of the circulating media. However, commercial banks provide specific services in competition with the other financial institutions. In some areas—for example, the collection and investment of savings—commercial banks and other institutions are in direct and often spirited competition.

Mutual Savings Banks

A mutual savings bank, as the name suggests, is a co-operative type organization. Control, however, rests with a board of trustees which is self-perpetuating and not with the bank's clients. There is no provision in federal law for the granting of a charter to a mutual savings bank and only eighteen states provide for such institutions. Nevertheless, these banks play an important role in certain areas, particularly in New York and New England. Mutual savings banks have existed in the United States since the early nineteenth century. The founders of the system were not profit-motivated. They wished to provide an income-earning, safe depository for the savings of persons of low and modest income. By so doing they hoped to benefit the individual savers and to encourage a higher rate of saving. When saving increased, the accompanying reallocation of resources from consumption to investment led to economic growth and higher standards of living.

A modern mutual savings bank must compete vigorously for deposits—an action that causes some critics to question the validity of its nonprofit objectives. Basically, however, the objectives remain the same although the definition of "modest income" has changed.

Mutual savings banks encourage savers to deposit funds. Since their charters recognize the original, philanthropic motive, these banks must limit the size of the individual's deposit. In return the depositor, as a member of the co-operative organization, has a claim to a share of the earnings of the institution. Hence, from a legal point of view the depositor has an ownership claim and receives dividends rather than interest. By contrast, a depositor in the savings department of a commercial bank possesses a debt claim and receives interest. To most depositors this distinction is unimportant. In each case the institution pays the depositor for the use of his money. Mutual savings banks invest the depositors' funds. They use the earnings on these investments to pay overhead expenses and to create a reserve for unforeseen losses. They return the remainder to the depositors as dividends. Mutual savings banks legally may require notification before a depositor withdraws funds but in practice they pay on demand. Consequently, these deposits are liquid assets to their owners.

Since mutual savings banks serve modest-income persons who cannot afford to lose their savings, their investment policies emphasize safety rather than high yield. Government regulations applicable to mutual savings banks reflect this emphasis on safe investments. In addition the Government provides for additional protection through

Table 19-2

ASSETS OF MUTUAL SAVINGS BANKS

1941-1964

(In billions of dollars)

As of Dec. 31	Loans		Securities			Cash Assets	Other Assets
	Mortgages	Other	U.S. Govt.	State and Local Govt.	Corporate and Other		
1941	4.8	.1	3.6	1.8		.8	.7
1945	4.2	.1	10.7	1.3		.6	.2
1956	19.6	.2	8.0	.7	3.5	.9	.4
1957	21.0	.3	7.6	.7	4.3	.9	.5
1958	23.0	.3	7.3	.7	5.0	.9	.5
1959	24.8	.4	6.9	.7	4.8	.8	.6
1960	26.7	.4	6.2	.7	5.1	.9	.6
1961	28.9	.5	6.2	.7	5.0	.9	.6
1962	32.1	.6	6.1	.5	5.2	1.0	.7
1963	36.0	.6	5.9	.4	5.1	.9	.8
1964	40.3	.7	5.8	.4	5.1	1.0	.9

Source: *Federal Reserve Bulletins.*

the Federal Deposit Insurance Corporation to which most mutual savings banks belong.

Table 19–2, showing the total assets of mutual savings banks, indicates the importance of these institutions in the financial market. We also can infer the allocation of resources by noting the composition of these assets. The desire for safety rather than proper allocation of resources has guided the banks' investment policy. Resource allocation occurs as a by-product. From the table it is rather obvious that these banks facilitate the transfer of resources from personal consumption to the improvement of real estate.

Savings and Loan Associations

Savings and loan associations have many features in common with mutual savings banks. The great majority of these institutions are co-operative organizations. Both the states and the Federal Government grant charters. Consequently, we have a dual system of regulation similar to the one prevailing in the field of commercial banking. Persons leaving funds with the association become members and have the right to vote for the directors. Like the mutual savings banks, these associations are specialists who invest the savings of persons of low and modest income. They, too, have their origin in the early nineteenth century. However, the reason for the development of these institutions is different. The organizers of the early associations wished to encourage home ownership. They faced two problems in achieving this objective: (1) moderate-income families had few opportunities to invest their savings while accumulating a down payment; and (2) having acquired a down payment, these families had difficulty in securing mortgage funds. A co-operative association solved both problems. Savers who became members contributed regularly to the savings and loan association. The association, in turn, transferred this money to mortgage loan members who had accumulated sufficient savings for the required down payment. From a legal standpoint the savers did not acquire a deposit account. Instead, they bought shares in the association and received as dividends the interest paid by the debtors.

With the passage of time, the need for funds caused savings and loan associations to solicit funds from savers who did not intend to use the money for the purchase of real estate. They also began to lend money on mortgages without regard to former membership in the association. At the present time these associations operate like a savings bank. Savers, most of whom do not know that they are buying shares rather than depositing money, leave funds with the association. The shareholders may withdraw their funds after giving reasonable notice to the association. Since the association usually waives the notification requirement, withdrawals upon demand usually are possible. Like the mutual savings banks, savings and loan associations are institutions which serve as the investor of the savings of persons of moderate income. Also like the mutual savings banks, they must emphasize safety. This emphasis on safety combined with their objective of promoting home ownership causes them to concentrate on mortgages. It follows that these associations allocate resources to home construction.

United States Government agencies guarantee many of the mortgage loans. In addition many associations are members of the Federal Savings and Loan Insurance Corporation, a government agency similar to the FDIC. The FSLIC insures accounts in member associations up to $10,000. Table 19–3 shows the growing importance of these institutions as well as the importance of real estate mortgages in their investment program.

Table 19–3

ASSETS OF SAVINGS AND LOAN ASSOCIATIONS

1941–1964

(In billions of dollars)

As of Dec. 31	Total Assets[a]	Mortgages	U.S. Govt. Securities	Cash	Other
1941	6.0	4.6	.1	.3	.8
1945	8.7	5.4	2.4	.5	.4
1956	42.9	35.7	2.8	2.1	2.2
1957	48.1	40.0	3.2	2.1	2.8
1958	55.1	45.6	3.8	2.6	3.1
1959	63.5	53.1	4.5	2.2	3.7
1960	71.5	60.1	4.6	2.7	4.1
1961	82.1	68.8	5.2	3.3	4.8
1962	93.6	78.8	5.6	3.9	5.3
1963	107.4	90.8	6.4	4.0	6.2
1964	119.2	101.2	7.0	4.0	7.0

[a]Prior to 1958, mortgages are net of mortgage-pledged shares. Asset items may not add to total assets which include gross mortgages with no deductions for mortgage-pledged shares.
Source: *Federal Reserve Bulletins.*

Life Insurance Companies

Life insurance companies are important financial intermediaries in the American system. By selling annuities and other pension plans, insurance companies encourage regular saving by individuals. They also serve as the intermediary which invests the savings of its clients. In addition the insurance companies serve as intermediaries in their role of insurers of lives. Since aggregate premiums collected each year are larger than benefit payments, the net difference represents savings of insured persons. Insurance companies invest these savings for their clients.

Most life insurance companies are mutual associations. Like mutual savings banks and savings and loan associations, they must choose safe investments even at the sacrifice of high yield. Unlike the two previous institutions, however, life insurance companies place no limit on the size of the account of an individual. Legally, there is only limited provision for withdrawals through policy loans and the cash surrender of policies. Considered only as a device for saving, life insurance is not appropriate for the person who places a high value on liquidity. The companies, in turn, are able to make long-term investments. Table 19–4 on the next page shows the relative importance of life insurance companies in the financial market. It also shows the types of investments and, therefore, indicates the allocation of resources.

The three institutions we have covered have a number of common characteristics. They all serve as intermediaries which invest the savings of low- and medium-income families. Life insurance companies do not deal exclusively with this group but they devote a large portion of their activities to it. All these institutions adjust their activities to fit the needs of the savers. The nature of their clients causes them to emphasize safety rather than high yield in their investment policies. When we examine the effect of their investment policy on the allocation of resources, we find that they serve to channel resources into the construction and real estate field. Business and government borrowers receive a relatively modest volume of funds. This investment policy has influenced the character of the nation's development and also its pattern of living. In the next chapter we shall see that government agencies encourage such a policy by regulations and by direct financial support.

Investment Companies

Some savers are willing to accept a high degree of risk in return for the chance of a sizable yield or the appreciation of capital assets. Generally, these individuals have higher incomes than the persons who use savings banks or savings and loan associations as intermediaries. These persons are willing to accept risk; nevertheless, they find it necessary to obtain information concerning investment

Table 19–4

ASSETS OF LIFE INSURANCE COMPANIES

1941–1964

(In billions of dollars)

As of Dec. 31	Total Assets	Government Securities		Business Securities		Mortgages	Real Estate	Policy Loans	Other Assets
		United States	State and Local	Foreign	Bonds	Stocks				
1941	32.7	6.8	2.0	.7	9.6	.6	6.4	1.9	2.9	1.8
1945	44.8	20.6	.7	1.2	10.1	1.0	6.6	.9	2.0	1.7
1956	96.0	7.6	2.3	1.2	38.0	3.5	33.0	2.8	3.5	4.1
1957	101.3	7.0	2.4	1.3	40.7	3.4	35.2	3.1	3.9	4.3
1958	107.6	7.2	2.7	1.4	43.0	4.1	37.1	3.4	4.2	4.6
1959	113.7	6.9	3.2	1.5	45.1	4.6	39.2	3.7	4.6	4.9
1960	119.6	6.4	3.6	1.7	46.9	5.0	41.8	3.8	5.2	5.3
1961	126.8	6.1	3.9	1.9	49.0	6.3	44.2	4.0	5.7	5.7
1962	133.3	6.2	4.0	2.3	51.3	6.3	46.9	4.1	6.2	6.0
1963	140.9	5.8	3.9	2.7	53.8	5.7	50.5	4.3	6.7	7.5
1964	149.3	5.5	3.8	3.0	55.7	6.4	55.2	4.5	7.1	8.1

Source: Institute of Life Insurance estimates published in the *Federal Reserve Bulletins*.

opportunities. Investigation of these opportunities is necessary also and some degree of diversification is desirable. Investment companies exist to supply these specialized services.

Investment companies sell shares to individuals and usually invest the funds thus obtained by purchasing stock in a variety of enterprises. There are many such companies and they differ with respect to the degree to which they emphasize gain rather than safety. The individual saver may select the company whose policy best fits his needs. In return for bearing the overhead costs, called loading, the saver receives the specialized service of investigation. He also receives the benefits of diversification.

Investment companies of the "open end" type stand ready at all times to sell or to redeem shares at book value adjusted for the load factor. This allows the individual saver to liquidate his investment whenever he chooses; however, he cannot be certain that the redemption price will be as high as the purchase price. "Closed end" companies have a fixed number of shares outstanding. A saver can acquire these shares only by purchasing them from the present owner and can liquidate his holdings only by selling.

We cannot follow our previous practice and identify with precision the industries to which these companies allocate investment funds and consequently resources. They purchase securities in a great number of enterprises and industries. Most of the clients of these companies regard their operations as an indirect means of securing a gain from the stock market. Generally, they hope for capital gain rather than dividend income. It follows that the companies tend to concentrate on the purchase of securities of "growth" industries. Beyond this we need not generalize concerning their investment patterns. The companies encourage saving and discourage "hoarding" by providing ready investment outlets. They increase the mobility of resources, and since specialists control investment decisions we assume that the resulting pattern of resource allocation improves upon the one which would prevail in their absence.

Investment Banks

The name of these institutions may be misleading. They do not conduct a banking type operation if we define banking in terms of accepting and holding deposits. They do, however, serve to channel savings into investment by performing the specific functions of investigation, underwriting, and distribution. A hypothetical example illustrates the value of these services. A manufacturing firm wishes to raise capital funds by issuing securities — either shares of stock or bonds. There are problems. The corporation desires to know the approximate amount it can raise in this fashion, and it wishes to acquire the money quickly. Also, it is impractical to hire a staff of specialists on a temporary basis to sell these securities. Turning to the other side of the market, we know that the prospective buyers of these securities must learn of their availability. Also they must solve the problem of investigation and analysis.

Investment banks solve these several problems. The company wishing to issue securities contacts one or more of these banks. The bank or banks investigate and analyze the financial soundness of the company. If the result is satisfactory, a bank underwrites the issue or several banks may form a syndicate which underwrites the issue. That is, the bank or syndicate guarantees that it will sell the securities by a certain date or will buy and hold the unsold units. Negotiation or competitive bidding sets the price of the securities and the other terms. The investment bank sells the securities thus acquired to individuals or to institutions. Since these banks have excellent reputations, the purchaser is confident that the investigation has been thorough and competent. Furthermore, because of the underwriting function, he knows that the investment bank supports its judgment with its own funds. Although we have used a private corporation as an example, state and local units of government avail themselves of these services also.

Basically, investment banks conduct a merchandizing operation. They buy new securities in wholesale lots and sell them in retail units. Like other merchandizers, investment banks must have a thorough knowledge of the product they are distributing. Also like other merchandizers, investment banks support their judgment of the product's quality by assuming the risk of holding unsold units. In the course of these operations, they channel savings into investment. Since experienced specialists guide the savings stream, we may assume that the resulting allocation of resources is close to the optimum. Table 19–5a, showing new issues, suggests the size of this operation.

This table records the flow of funds year by year. It differs in this respect from the three preceding it in this chapter which show accumulated assets on a specific date. We must not assume that investment banks handled all the securities represented by this table. Purchasers of United States securities have no need for investigative service, and other institutions may sell securities to institutionalized savers directly, as the column "privately offered" shows.

When we question the allocation of resources, Table 19–5a shows the division between the public and the private sectors. Table 19–5b gives us some indication of the allocation within the private sector.

Table 19–5a

TOTAL NEW ISSUES, 1956–1964

(In billions of dollars)

Period	Noncorporate					Total Corporate	Corporate			
	Gross Proceeds	U.S. Govt.ᵃ	U.S. Govt. Agencyᵇ	State and Local	Otherᶜ		Bonds		Stocks	
							Publicly Offered	Privately Offered	Preferred	Common
1956	22.4	5.5	.2	5.4	.3	10.9	4.2	3.8	.6	2.3
1957	30.6	9.6	.6	7.0	.6	12.9	6.1	3.8	.4	2.5
1958	34.4	12.1	2.3	7.4	1.1	11.6	6.3	3.3	.6	1.3
1959	31.1	12.3	.7	7.7	.6	9.7	3.6	3.6	.5	2.0
1960	27.5	7.9	1.7	7.2	.6	10.2	4.8	3.3	.4	1.7
1961	35.5	12.3	1.4	8.3	.3	13.1	4.7	4.7	.4	3.3
1962	30.0	8.6	1.2	8.6	.9	10.8	4.5	4.5	.4	1.3
1963	31.6	7.2	1.2	10.1	.9	12.2	4.7	6.2	.3	1.0
1964	36.6	10.7	1.2	10.5	.8	13.4	3.6	6.7	.4	2.7

ᵃIncludes guaranteed issues.
ᵇIssues not guaranteed.
ᶜForeign governments, International Bank for Reconstruction and Development, and domestic nonprofit organizations.
Source: Securities and Exchange Commission estimate, published in the *Federal Reserve Bulletins.*

Table 19–5b

MAJOR GROUPS OF CORPORATE SECURITY ISSUES,

1962–1964

(In billions of dollars)

Group	1962	1963	1964
Manufacturing	3.2	3.5	3.0
Commercial and miscellaneous	.9	.8	1.1
Transportation	.6	1.0	.9
Public utility	2.8	2.6	2.7
Communications	1.3	1.1	2.2
Real estate and financial	1.8	3.1	3.4
Totals	10.6	12.1	13.3

Source: Securities and Exchange Commission estimate, published in the *Federal Reserve Bulletin*, March, 1965, p. 465.

Securities Dealers and Securities Exchanges

We include stockbrokers and stock exchanges in our survey of financial institutions because they enable a saver to remain relatively liquid even though he exchanges money for debt or ownership claims. For our purpose we need not consider the legal and the organizational details of the system of securities dealers and exchanges existing in the United States. It is sufficient to recall that one barrier to the movement of savings funds into investment is the fear of illiquidity. The system of securities exchanges and brokers maintains conveniently located offices and a communication network for the use of prospective purchasers and sellers of debt and ownership claims. Clients learn the price and other pertinent information regarding previously issued securities, and buyers and sellers contact each other indirectly through this brokerage service. These institutions permit a saver to be confident that he can liquidate the securities he purchases at any time. Accordingly, they facilitate the transfer of funds. The information their communication network provides leads to a better allocation of resources and allows savers to choose securities with safety and yield characteristics best suited to their needs.

Commercial Paper Houses

Investment banks specialize in newly issued securities while securities brokers and exchanges deal in previously issued debt and ownership claims. Both systems emphasize services to the individuals and the firms that have funds which they are willing to invest for a relatively long period of time. In so doing they direct resources to agents who will use them to purchase capital assets which yield benefits slowly. However, individuals and corporations exist who wish to lend funds to others for short periods; there are in existence groups which wish to use funds for short periods. In response to the need for a broker, there are financial institutions which specialize in serving these groups by investigating, furnishing information, providing for diversification where desired, and creating a market for short-term securities. A very important institution in this area is the commercial bank. Also in existence and in competition with commercial banks are the commercial paper houses.

We apply the term commercial paper to promissory notes, acceptances, and similar debt instruments which businesses issue in financing trade. When we use the term in connection with commercial paper houses, we refer only to promissory notes of large denominations ($5,000 and over) issued by firms with excellent credit ratings. Commercial paper houses, making a profit on the spread between the buying and the selling rate, buy these debt instruments from the debtor firms and sell them to corporations which temporarily have excess cash. Debtor firms which acquire funds from the commercial paper market in preference to borrowing from a commercial bank do so because of lower rates or because the amount they require is in excess of the legal lending capacity of the local bank. Furthermore, they may enhance their credit rating in this fashion since the commercial paper market handles top-quality debt instruments only.

We are interested in the effect rather than the operational details of these institutions. The commercial paper houses and the commercial paper market of which they are a key component serve to allocate resources to working capital uses. They also permit corporations with temporarily idle funds to invest them profitably until needed. In recent years corporations have become increasingly aware of this opportunity and have held idle cash balances to a minimum. This practice reduces the amount of cash held for transactions and precautionary motives and perhaps for speculative motives. Described in terms of the income and expenditure approach to monetary theory, it allows the $L_1 + L_2$ curve to shift to the left. If we are to use the vocabulary of the quantity approach, we can say that V increases or that its reciprocal K decreases. Previously we observed that financial institutions contribute to a high level of output and employment. The preceding comments express this idea in more technical terms.

Factoring

We shall consider one additional institution which supplies funds for working capital purposes. As we noted in Chapter 5, manufacturers generally sell products on open-book credit. Thus they are, in fact, lending working capital to their customers. Since manufacturers are not specialists in the supply of credit, it is to their advantage to transfer this function to another institution, the factor.

Factoring firms purchase the accounts receivable of manufacturers. Under the terms of the purchase the factor usually assumes the task of collecting the debt and the risk of nonpayment. Thus, the manufacturer transfers the risk element and the credit investigation task to a specialist. The productive system becomes more efficient because each of the several units operates in the area of its specialty. Factors also have the advantage of a large-scale operation. They need to investigate a debt customer only once in serving several clients. In the process, of course, the clients of factors receive working capital. To summarize, factors furnish the specific services of risk assumption and investigation. They also increase the liquidity of a client's assets.

The main problem encountered in the use of factors is the lack of public understanding of their functions. Some industries, like textiles, traditionally have used the services of factors. In others, there is a tendency to suspect the credit worthiness of a firm which sells its accounts receivable. It follows that firms in these industries are reluctant to permit the public and their customers to know of the relationship.

Small Loan Companies

All the institutions described in the preceding pages serve to channel saving into investment. Institutions exist, however, which transfer the funds of savers to persons who spend the money for consumption purposes. The small loan departments of commercial banks are active in this field along with small loan companies, sales finance companies, and other institutions.

For many years it was unprofitable for legitimate credit institutions to advance credit in the small amounts consumers usually borrow. Usury laws placed a ceiling on interest charges which did not allow lending institutions to cover the relatively high administrative costs of small loans. As a result the consumer had to borrow from illegal operators, called loan sharks, or live without the services of credit institutions. All the states now have small loan laws which permit higher rates of interest. The small loan companies and the small loans departments of commercial banks operate under these laws. While the small loan laws permit high interest charges, they also regulate the conditions for repayment of the loans and protect the borrower in other ways.

The activities of small loan companies affect the allocation of resources. A consumer can spend in excess of his income by borrowing from a small loan company. This tends to raise the MPC and to increase the ratio of consumption to investment expenditures. Payment of the debt by installments forces the consumer to save; i.e., his income must be higher than his expenditures for consumption purposes. It follows that during repayment the MPC and the ratio of consumption to investment expenditures tend to decline. When we apply this reasoning to the concept of the aggregate economy, we conclude that the MPC rises and the allocation of resources to consumer as opposed to investment industries increases when there is an expansion of consumer debt. The reverse occurs if the volume of outstanding consumer debt is contracting.

By applying the theory of income determination to the conclusions regarding the *MPC*, we see that an expansion of consumer debt raises the level of income. Contraction, of course, has the opposite effect. The variations in income may take the form of a change in output and in employment or a change in the price level. Finally, we note that the existence of small loan institutions weakens the preference for liquidity which, in turn, affects the level of economic activity.

Sales Finance Companies

These institutions have the same effect on the economic system as small loan companies, so we need not treat them at great length. As their name suggests, sales finance companies supply credit to consumers for the purchase of consumer goods. Unlike small loan companies, they do not lend cash to the individual. However, they achieve the same end by permitting a consumer to purchase an automobile, furniture, a household appliance, or other goods on the installment plan immediately instead of saving the required amount of money in advance. In a transaction involving sales finance companies, the purchaser receives possession and use of the commodity. The sales finance company pays the seller in full and holds legal title to the goods pending repayment by the purchaser. From a legal point of view, sales finance companies differ significantly from small loan companies. They have the same effect on the allocation of resources and the level of income.

Table 19-6

INSTALLMENT CONSUMER CREDIT OUTSTANDING

1939–1964

(In billions of dollars)

As of Dec. 31	Total	Installment				Noninstallment		
		Automobile Paper	Other Consumer Goods Paper	Repairs & Modernization Loans	Personal Loans	Single Payment Loans	Charge Accounts	Service Credit
1939	7.2	1.5	1.6	.3	1.1	.8	1.4	.5
1941	9.2	2.5	1.9	.4	1.3	.8	1.6	.6
1945	5.7	.5	.8	.2	1.0	.7	1.6	.8
1956	42.3	14.4	8.6	1.9	6.8	3.3	5.0	2.4
1957	45.0	15.3	8.8	2.1	7.6	3.4	5.1	2.6
1958	45.1	14.2	9.0	2.3	8.1	3.6	5.1	2.8
1959	51.5	16.4	10.6	2.8	9.4	4.1	5.1	3.1
1960	56.0	17.7	11.5	3.1	10.5	4.5	5.3	3.4
1961	57.7	17.2	11.9	3.2	11.3	5.1	5.3	3.7
1962	63.2	19.5	12.6	3.2	12.6	5.5	5.7	4.0
1963	69.9	22.2	13.8	3.4	14.4	6.0	5.9	4.3
1964	76.8	24.5	15.3	3.5	16.1	6.5	6.3	4.6

NOTE: Components may not add to totals because of rounding.
Source: *Federal Reserve Bulletins.*

Table 19–6 shows the amount of consumer credit outstanding for selected years. From the amount outstanding we may conclude that these financial institutions play a significant role in the American economy. We may also draw inferences concerning the effect on the allocation of resources from the column headings. The column labeled "charge accounts" represents credit extended by retailers rather than by credit institutions, but this does not change the economic effect.

SUMMARY

The financial institutions with which this chapter deals do not create and extinguish money. They do facilitate the transfer of funds from savers to users in the financial markets. Their services are valuable because savers face several barriers which impede the flow of funds to the individuals and institutions that are the spenders. These barriers are risk, administrative costs of transfer, and the fear of illiquidity. Failure to transfer funds to investment type spenders, the government sector, or other consumers leads to a poor resource allocation pattern and to a decline in the level of income. Financial institutions lower these barriers by specializing in the specific functions of: (1) investigation, analysis, and the dissemination of information; (2) diversification and insurance against risk; (3) brokerage; and (4) supplying a market that provides for the liquidity of financial assets. As a result of their operations, the economic system moves closer to the optimum allocation of resources. In addition these institutions lower the frictional barriers to full employment and maximum output. In more technical terms they reduce the preference for liquidity. This shifts the $L_1 + L_2$ curve to the left and lowers the "institutional floor" of the interest rate.

QUESTIONS

1. What is the significance of the term "financial intermediaries"?
2. How do financial institutions encourage saving? Do they discourage saving?
3. Use the information acquired from earlier chapters as the basis for a discussion of the extent to which commercial banks perform the functions discussed in this chapter.
4. What is the nature of the resource allocation caused by financial institutions? Use the statistical data found in this chapter and current sources as the basis for your answer.
5. Discuss the role of financial institutions in terms of the quantity theory of money and in terms of the income and expenditure approach to monetary theory.

SUGGESTED READINGS

Cooke, Gilbert W., Prather, Charles L., Case, Frederick E., and Bellemore, Douglas H. *Financial Institutions, Their Role in the American Economy.* New York: Simmons-Boardman Publishing Corporation, 1962.

Ludtke, James B. *The American Financial System.* Boston: Allyn and Bacon, Inc., 1961. Parts 3 and 4.

Prochnow, Herbert V. (ed.). *American Financial Institutions.* New York: Prentice-Hall, Inc., 1951.

Robinson, Roland I. (ed.). *Financial Institutions.* 3d ed. Homewood, Illinois: Richard D. Irwin, Inc., 1960. Chapters 15–20.

————. *Money and Capital Markets.* New York: McGraw-Hill Book Company, 1964.

Woodworth, G. Walter. *The Money Market and Monetary Management.* New York: Harper & Row, Publishers, 1965. Chapters 6 and 7.

20

THE GOVERNMENT AND
THE CREDIT MARKET

In the preceding chapter we examined private financial institutions with only an occasional reference to government activity. Government, however, plays a significant role in the financial markets. Through our study of the commercial banking system, we have become familiar with government methods. We saw that the states influence the commercial banking system through their chartering and regulating functions. The Federal Government uses these powers also. In addition it participates in the commercial banking system more directly by sponsoring such institutions as the FDIC and the Federal Reserve banks. Government uses the same methods to influence other components of the financial system. The states confine their activities to the chartering and the regulating function. The Federal Government in addition to chartering and regulating financial institutions organizes and operates agencies which serve as debtors, creditors, and financial intermediaries.

In the United States we adhere to the principle that private enterprise operating in free markets leads to the optimum allocation of resources. While exceptions exist, in general our practice is consistent with this principle. Since government intervention in the financial markets obviously violates this principle, an explanation is in order.

Not all government participation is the result of a deliberate decision to intervene. States, municipalities, and the Federal Government participate in the financial system as debtors. This participation is sizable. In 1964 net state and local debt equaled $85.7 billion. The gross federal debt equaled $318.7 billion and the net debt totaled $267.0 billion.[1] A government becomes a user of savings and the financial system channels the funds of savers to it whenever it operates at a deficit. It becomes a saver on those occasions when

[1]The difference between gross and net federal debt represents United States securities held by Government trust funds such as the Social Security System.

354

the budget shows a surplus. A government's role as a borrower or a saver is inadvertent in the sense that a deficit or a surplus is not the result of a decision to intervene in the financial market. Nevertheless, government decisions with regard to debt management must influence the market because public debt accounts for approximately one third of all debt, both public and private.

The state and local government relationships with the financial market are similar to those of private debtors. These units do not attempt to use their debtor position to influence the financial system. The Federal Government did not incur the large national debt for the specific purpose of intervening in the economic system. Since the debt does exist, however, it uses debt management as one means of controlling the monetary system. This causes us to return to the basic question: Why does government intervene in the financial market?

Intervention is the result of a feeling that without some form of government guidance the operation of financial institutions leads to an unsatisfactory allocation of resources. Or we may express the idea in financial terms by saying there is an imperfect allocation of credit. Some misallocation of resources occurs because financial institutions cannot accomplish perfectly the specific functions of investigation, analysis, and dissemination of information. This hinders savers in their attempt to invest wisely and denies funds to some deserving creditors. Government regulations requiring the full disclosure of information by financial institutions are an attempt to correct this fault. Closely related to these regulations are those which restrict the type of assets life insurance companies, savings and loan associations, and similar institutions may acquire. A saver knowing the investment policy of these institutions feels free to leave his funds with them without making a careful study of the particular institution. Despite these regulatory activities the feeling persists that certain sectors of the economy do not receive a proper allocation of resources.

The Government may take direct action to remedy this condition. In some instances it creates agencies which lend money to these sectors. When this occurs the Government is acting as a financial intermediary inasmuch as it must borrow this money from savers. If there is a budget surplus, the Government is saving and is acting as a creditor. More often the government agency encourages private financial institutions to supply the necessary funds by guaranteeing repayment of the debt.

In political debate it is customary to discuss these practices in terms of "protecting the small saver," "helping the farmer," or "aiding the homeowner." From an economist's viewpoint, it is more precise to speak in terms of the allocation of resources. Also, the latter phrase is less likely to arouse emotional bias. We must remember, however, that the term "optimum allocation of resources" implies a value judgment with regard to both the objectives of our economic system and the methods of achieving this objective.

REGULATORY ACTIVITY
Charters

The states and the Federal Government regulate institutions to some extent in the process of issuing charters. A corporate charter permits certain types of activity, prohibits others, and on occasion requires that the institution supply specific services to the public. The charter often provides for other regulatory controls. It may require that the institution submit reports to the government and make public disclosure of its financial condition. The extent to which government regulates private institutions is not uniform; for example, insurance companies are subject to stringent restrictions regarding the types of assets they may acquire. The amount of the various assets they hold becomes public information. The government also requires that they assume certain responsibilities toward their policyholders. Savings and loan associations and mutual savings banks operate under regulations of approximately the same degree of severity. By contrast, factors and commercial paper houses are relatively free of government controls.

The motive for imposing government regulation upon private institutions is a desire to protect the savings of the policyholders and depositors. Therefore, we may regard the influence on resource allocation as predominantly a by-product. However, a desire to influence resource allocation may determine the form and the details of the regulatory process. We saw an example of this principle in our study of the National Banking Act of 1863. The Act compelled national banks to purchase and to hold United States Government bonds equal to a certain percentage of their capital. There were two objectives: the protection of noteholders and the allocation of credit resources to the Government. We find applications of this principle in the regulation of other financial institutions: government tends to consider the credit needs of agriculture, urban real estate, and other groups in preparing lists of "safe" securities.

Government does not confine its regulatory activities to issuing organizational charters. Statutes such as the "blue sky laws" protect the saver against the sale of securities issued on a fraudulent basis. There are many state laws creating commissions which regulate insurance companies and other savings institutions. Their purpose is not only to prevent fraud but also to ensure that these institutions emphasize safety when investing funds.

Securities and Exchange Commission

There is legal protection for the purchaser of securities as well as the patron of savings institutions and life insurance companies. The Securities and Exchange Act of 1934 created the Securities Exchange Commission to administer the Securities Act of 1933 and the amendments to it. It is the purpose of these Acts to ensure truth and fairness in selling newly issued securities and in trading those already in existence. The Commission does not attempt to restrict trading to high-quality issues nor does it grade securities and label them as sound, speculative, or unsound. Its function is to require the registration of securities dealers and to require also that firms issuing securities make full disclosure of their financial condition. The Acts assume that the investor can choose wisely if he is fully informed.

The results of the various government regulatory activities are not perfect. No one claims that through them we achieve *the* optimum allocation of resources. There are several reasons why we must expect imperfections in this activity. Students of financial markets agree that full information regarding investment opportunities is desirable but this is a relative term. To have full information in a literal sense, one must be able to predict the outcome of investment proposals. The present system for ensuring disclosure of information has faults. Critics claim that SEC regulations force the firm which issues securities to describe its financial condition in technical terms which only the professional investor understands. We may note other shortcomings in the regulatory procedure. Of necessity it creates an overhead cost. The cost of legal and technical assistance in complying with certain regulations discourages small issues. Regulations which require institutions to follow certain policies in acquiring assets may force the professional investment adviser, a specialist in the field, to act contrary to his good judgment.

Despite these imperfections, government regulation has a beneficent effect. It improves the allocation of resources. It also allows the saver to transfer funds to others with less fear of loss.

FEDERAL CREDIT AGENCIES

In addition to its regulatory activities, the Federal Government operates a number of agencies which function as credit institutions. We have noted the reason for discussing these institutions. Their general function is to improve the allocation of resources. More specifically, they serve to provide safe investment areas for savers and to increase the supply of credit to certain sectors of the economy. Although they represent Federal Government participation in business, these agencies have not aroused the vigorous opposition of the private financial community. This lack of opposition supports the claim that they supplement rather than compete with private institutions.

AGENCIES WHICH ENCOURAGE SAVING

The Government encourages saving through its sale of Series E and H Savings Bonds. While these instruments provide safe and liquid earning assets for savers, their primary function is to finance the Government debt. Other government institutions have the encouragement of saving and the protection of savings as their primary motives.

Postal Savings System. Among the oldest government financial institutions is the Postal Savings System. Congress authorized the System in 1910 to solve a problem. Commercial banks of that period were not the secure depositories for the funds of savers that they are today. Furthermore, other institutions which served the small saver were less numerous than they are at present and travel to the office of a savings institution was difficult. As a result many savers were unable to invest their funds. This discouraged saving. In 1910 the United States Post Office Department organized the Postal Savings System. Its many offices alleviated the problem of traveling to the inconvenient locations of depositories. A saver could open an account by depositing from $1 to $2,500. However, the System did not accept individual accounts in excess of the latter amount. Depositors received interest at the rate of 2 per cent. By paying a low rate the System avoided competition with private institutions.

For over fifty years, the Postal Savings System offered its services to the public on these terms and invested the funds of the depositors in United States securities. In periods of bank failures and low-interest rates in the private sector, the System expanded. In recent years its low-interest rate has attracted few depositors and total deposits in early 1965 were equal to only $400 million, or less than one eighth of the amount held at the end of World War II. This decline in absolute terms and relative to other financial institutions indicates that the public no longer needs the Postal Savings System. For this reason, the Federal Government has decided to eliminate the program. The System no longer accepts deposits and is in the process of returning funds to depositors.

When studying government agencies, one often hears that once created an institution expands indefinitely. The Postal Savings System, however, is an exception. Congress created the System to fill a need. When private institutions expanded and adjusted their operations to render the necessary services, the government agency withdrew from the field.

Insuring savings institutions. There are other Federal institutions which assist savers. We have noted the existence of the Federal Deposit Insurance Corporation. This institution includes mutual savings banks among its members, and it insures the savings as well as the demand deposits of commercial banks. A similar institution, the Federal Savings and Loan Insurance Corporation, guarantees the accounts of savings and loan associations up to $10,000. The operations of this institution parallel those of the FDIC. All federally chartered savings and loan associations must, and state chartered associations may, join the Corporation. Approximately sixty per cent of the associations, representing ninety per cent of all association assets, have joined. Members of the FSLIC pay an insurance premium and the insurance corporation in return settles each account of an insured association which is in default. The operation differs from that of the FDIC because of the nature of default in a savings and loan association. Since the accounts represent ownership shares rather than deposits, a greater length of time elapses between the date of the failure to pay and the formal declaration of default.

These agencies benefit savers primarily; however they assist indirectly persons who wish to borrow funds. The practice of guaranteeing accounts overcomes the public's reluctance to entrust its savings to savings institutions and thus increases the supply of money available for loans. For the most part the Federal Government assists rather than competes with private institutions. The Postal Savings System, which is terminating its service, is a competitor but the volume of deposits is small. Sales of United States savings bonds is another form of competition. In this case the volume is large but is not increasing. The commercial banking system, a private agency, serves as the chief selling agent. The two insurance corporations, of course, serve to increase the volume of saving going to private institutions.

AGENCIES SERVING BORROWERS

The Federal agencies which serve individuals and firms desiring to borrow are numerous. Also their presence in the credit market and their operations are more controversial than those agencies serving the supply side of the market. We noted previously that these agencies exist because of a feeling that reallocation of resources is desirable. More specifically, certain sectors of the economy claim that private institutions do not channel the proper volume of credit into their areas. Acting on this belief agriculture, real estate, and certain business interests have persuaded the Government to organize and to operate agencies which increase the flow of funds to their areas. Since these three groups account for most of the economic system, we must question their special interest characteristics. The explanation lies first in the degree of aid which each group receives: Federal agencies channel more funds into the agricultural and the real estate sectors than into the business sector. Second, each category contains subcategories and the aid rendered is not uniform between these subclasses. For example, residential real estate receives most of the funds going to that sector, and only special classes of business receive assistance from government credit agents.

CREDIT AGENCIES SERVING AGRICULTURE

The agriculture sector was the first group to benefit from a Federal credit agency. For many years farmers claimed that the amount of mortgage money available for the purchase of farms was inadequate. Persons on the demand side of a market usually desire an increase in supply, but we cannot dismiss the farmers' complaints this easily. They based their case on imperfections in the market system. The supply of credit was concentrated in the cities, but the farmers who wished to borrow were scattered throughout the rural areas. Consequently, contact between the two sides of the market was difficult and credit investigation was expensive. Furthermore, the farmers claimed that the bankers and other lenders were not familiar with the agricultural industry. Because of this lack of knowledge, they judged loan applications too harshly. It followed that credit was often unavailable. When farmers did secure mortgage loans, they claimed that the down payment required and the interest rate were unnecessarily high and that the maturity terms were too short.

Federal Farm Loan Banks. The Federal Government attacked this problem through the Federal Farm Loan Act of 1916, which provided for the establishment of two credit agencies: the Federal Farm Loan banks and the National Farm Loan associations. The Federal Government divided the nation into twelve districts and organized a Federal Farm Loan bank in each district. The Government subscribed the original capital and administered the banks, initially through the Treasury Department and later through the

Farm Credit Administration. These banks sell their own bonds and channel the funds to farmers seeking mortgage money.

National Farm Loan associations. National Farm Loan associations serve as the local lending agencies. These are co-operative associations formed by ten or more agriculturists who wish to borrow money. Members subscribe to stock in the association and choose its directors. The association, in turn, subscribes to stock in the district land bank. It investigates the credit applications and endorses the notes of members who wish to borrow from the land bank for the purchase of real estate and equipment.

The principle of the operation is simple. The association and the banks pool the mortgage paper signed by individual farmers. The Federal Farm Loan banks pledge these notes as collateral when issuing bonds, the proceeds of which they loan to the farmers. Although these banks are government agencies, the United States is not contingently liable for the bonds. Because of the pooling operations, the banks operate on a large enough scale to tap the major credit sources. Furthermore, the investigative features of the association plus its endorsement of the individual's note reduce the risk to the creditor. As a result credit mobility increases, terms are more favorable to the borrower, and credit is available to a wider range of individuals. The banks charge an interest rate of 6 per cent or 1 per cent more than the rate they pay on bonds they have issued, whichever is lower.

Subscriptions to stock by the association have allowed the land banks to retire the original stock purchased by the United States Treasury. Consequently, this federal credit agency is not lending government funds. It serves as an intermediary which provides investigative services, insures against risk, and transfers funds.

An emergency measure — the Federal Farm Mortgage Corporation. The Government has not confined its assistance to owners of agricultural real estate to these two institutions. In 1934 an Act of the Congress established the Federal Farm Mortgage Corporation to relieve distressed farmers whose mortgages were in default as well as the creditors who held these mortgage loans. The Federal Farm Mortgage Corporation sold its stock to the United States Treasury and sold bonds guaranteed by the Treasury to private investors. It used the funds thus acquired to purchase bonds of the Federal Land banks and to make direct loans to them. By this action it supplied funds to the farm mortgage market indirectly. It also loaned money directly to farmers on first and second mortgages. Since its purpose was the alleviation of distress rather than the making of a profit, the FFMC granted easy terms to the debtors. The Congress created this agency to deal with the problems of the depression of the 1930's. Having served its purpose, the FFMC ceased its lending operations in 1947.

This last agency operated on a different principle than the Federal Land banks and the National Farm Loan associations. In the latter two, the Government provides guidance but not a subsidy. Through co-operative associations, farmers are able to overcome technical difficulties in the credit market. The FFMC served to overcome imperfections in the credit market also. However, the Government used this agency to furnish a subsidy to farmers in an emergency. Both types of activity influence the allocation of resources but a subsidy represents the more direct method.

Other credit agencies serving farm owners. Two more government credit agencies serving farm owners deserve mention. The Farmers Home Administration lends money to farmers who are unable to borrow elsewhere on "fair and reasonable" terms. The loans are to finance improvements in farm practice and to acquire or to improve farm housing. The Administration may also insure loans made to farmers by private agencies. Thus, this government agency acts to direct resources to the improvement of farm practices and homes. Since it assumes risks and makes loans which private agencies avoid, a subsidy element is present.

The Congress created the Rural Electrification Administration in 1935. Its purpose is to direct resources into a particular investment area — the provision of electrical energy to rural sections. To accomplish this the Administration loans money to co-operative associations who construct and operate the facilities. Proceeds from the sale of electricity enable the co-operative association to service the debt. For a number of years the interest rate which the REA has charged has been less than the interest cost the Government must bear when it borrows money. Consequently, the REA is subsidizing the co-operative association and is not purely a credit agency.

Farmers have not confined their complaints about the inadequacies of private institutions to the long-term credit conditions. They claimed that private agencies did not supply sufficient intermediate-term and short-term credit, types of credit which normally finance the purchase of equipment and the raising of livestock. The shortages were particularly acute during periods of falling farm prices and during the years when commercial bank failures were numerous in rural areas. These conditions were present during the 1920's and the early 1930's. The government agencies created in response to these conditions still exist.

Federal Intermediate Credit banks. The Congress created the Intermediate Term Credit System in 1923. It provided for the establishment of a Federal Intermediate Credit bank in each of the twelve Federal Land Bank districts. As their name suggests, these banks are to make intermediate-term credit available to farmers on reasonable terms. Intermediate Credit banks do not lend directly to farmers. Instead they discount negotiable agricultural loan paper which commercial banks and other lending agencies present to them. The original capital for the banks came from the United States Treasury. In addition, the credit banks acquire private capital by selling debentures. Since 1956, these sales have been large enough to allow the Government to withdraw some of its investment.

Production Credit Corporations. Federal Intermediate Credit banks did not solve the problem of a shortage of intermediate-term and short-term credit. These banks served farmers only indirectly and could not aid farmers in areas which did not contain a solvent lending agency. This was a serious defect in the system during the period of widespread bank failures. To remedy the situation, Congress in 1933 provided for the establishment of Production Credit Corporations and their affiliated co-operative associations. The Government chartered and provided the original capital for a Production Credit Corporation in each of the federal land-bank cities. The corporations assist in the organization and the initial capitalization of Production Credit Associations. Since these associations are co-operative credit agencies, a borrower must purchase stock in the association. Members may borrow from the association which can present the debt instrument to the Intermediate Credit Bank for discount. Thus, the associations serve as local lending agencies.

Central Bank for Co-operatives. We have not exhausted the list of government credit agencies serving agriculture. The Congress created the Central Bank for Co-operatives in 1933. By extending credit it encourages co-operation among farmers in purchasing equipment, planting, harvesting, and marketing. Indirectly, therefore, Congress uses a credit agency to help farmers reduce the cost of production and it encourages a social institution, the co-operative association.

Commodity Credit Corporation. There is also the Commodity Credit Corporation. Its function is to support the prices of farm products and thus to raise farm income. As a result of its activity, the Government in effect buys surplus crops at the support price. Legally, however, farmers borrow from the Government on a nonrecourse basis with a commodity as security for the loan. When used as security, the value of the commodity is appraised at the official support price. If the borrower cannot sell the commodity at or above this price, he defaults on the loan and the Government becomes the owner of the surplus crop. The operations of the Commodity Credit Corporation cost the taxpayers more than any of the other institutions we have examined, and it is part of an agricultural policy that is quite controversial. Although it is technically a credit agency, we should evaluate the Commodity Credit Corporation in terms of the objectives of government intervention in the commodity market rather than in the credit market.

Agricultural credit agencies — an evaluation. Agriculture was the first sector of the economy to receive assistance from government credit agencies. This assistance began in 1916 and expanded during the period of rural bank failures in the 1920's. A second period of expansion occurred during the period of bank failures and economic depression of the 1930's. In our discussion we stressed imperfections in the private market as a motivating factor. Accordingly, it is the purpose of many of these institutions to increase the ease with which private institutions can transfer funds and to reduce the risk element in the lending operation. In back of this type of operation lies the assumption that private credit institutions will achieve a satisfactory allocation of resources if information concerning risk and opportunity is available and if lenders act without bias. If this assumption is correct, government credit agencies acting on this principle will not operate at a loss.

Not all the activities of government credit agencies in agriculture have as their objective improvement of the credit allocation mechanism of the private market. There is reason to believe that private enterprise operating in free markets will eliminate most of the family-size farms. Many persons feel that this result is socially undesirable. Others accept the result but feel that the Government should act to alleviate hardship by lengthening the period of transition. For the individual who adopts either of these viewpoints, government credit agencies become instruments which prevent the free operation of the market system rather than a means of perfecting this mechanism. The Government has adopted this objective to some extent; however, we must remember that it is customary to use different terms in political debate. We must expect that government credit agencies which have this type of reallocation of resources as an objective will operate at a deficit. The deficit is not necessarily a sign of inefficiency or waste but is rather a subsidy which achieves certain social and political goals.

Residential Credit Agencies

Government agencies are active in the residential credit market. Like the farmers, purchasers of residential real estate had claimed for many years prior to the 1930's that the supply of credit available for mortgage loans was inadequate. Also like the farmers, they pointed to the presence of many small borrowers and the failure of large credit centers to serve them. When credit was available, interest rates were high, maturity terms were short, and down-payment requirements were large by modern standards. There was an additional defect in the system. Most of the debt contracts were "straight" type mortgage loans; that is, the principal was repaid in one lump sum on the maturity date. These conditions existed for many years; they reached the crisis stage during the depression of the 1930's.

As an emergency measure Congress established the Home Owners Loan Corporation in 1933. This government credit agency relieved both debtor and creditor by refinancing defaulted home mortgages with long-term loans which the debtor amortized on an installment basis. It ceased making loans in 1936, by which time Congress had created two permanent institutions.

Federal Housing Administration. The National Housing Act of 1934 created the Federal Housing Administration. The purpose of the FHA is to encourage the flow of credit to the housing market and to correct the defects in the lending process. It accomplishes these ends by insuring loans extended to buyers of homes and rental apartments by savings and loan associations, banks, and other private institutions. Thus, it is not a lending agency but rather an insurance type institution. By insuring a loan it substitutes the credit reputation of the Government for that of the private borrower. In the event of default the lender may foreclose on the property and may transfer title to the FHA. In return the lender receives the unpaid principal from the FHA in notes bearing the same maturity date as the original mortgage loan. In return for this insurance service, the FHA charges a premium of one half of one per cent of the unpaid balance of all insured loans. In its thirty years of operation, it has been able to meet all demands made upon it from the proceeds of this fee. The high quality and consequent high marketability of the debt instrument encourages the flow of credit into the residential mortgage market.

The FHA corrected the defects in the market by establishing eligibility requirements. The eligibility requirements permit mortgage loans involving small down payments and long maturities. To be eligible for FHA insurance, the interest rate may not exceed the maximum figure set by the Administration. This ceiling changes infrequently in response to market conditions and government policy. Also, the loan must be of the installment type. The regulations also contain acceptable construction standards and thus influence the design of small houses.

Veterans Administration as a credit agent. The Federal Government operates another agency which influences the residential credit market. The Servicemen's Readjustment Act of 1944, commonly known as the "G. I. Bill," requires the Veterans Administration to insure loans which veterans secure from private institutions for the purchase of housing. As the title of the Act suggests, the motivation behind this action is service to veterans rather than reform of the credit market. Nevertheless, the implementation of the Act created the same effect as that produced by the FHA.

The FHA and the VA have had a profound effect on home financing. Through their activities they have attracted private capital to this field. Probably more important they have altered the terms of home financing through their eligibility requirements. During the years in which they have operated, the ratio of homeowners to tenants has increased significantly. High incomes and prosperous economic conditions, of course, contributed to this change but the federal agencies also deserve credit.

By insuring loans the Government does take the risk of substantial loss if the housing market collapses and defaults become numerous. The record, however, has been very good. The management of the FHA and the VA cannot claim all the credit for this fine record. Prosperous times and rising real estate prices played an important role in keeping the default rate low.

Federal National Mortgage Association. The insurance of loans is not the only device the Government uses to channel capital into the residential credit market. Through the operations of the Federal National Mortgage Association, it uses a more direct approach to influence the supply of credit. The Congress established this agency, popularly known as "Fanny Mae" because of its initials, in 1938. FNMA buys mortgages from private lenders who are short of capital. It also sells mortgages on the capital market if government policy calls for this action. By buying or selling it moves funds into or out of the market and thus affects interest rates and the other terms of credit. FNMA secures funds by borrowing from the United States Treasury as well as from private lenders. Table 20–2 shows how greatly "Fanny Mae" has become involved in the mortgage market.

Government Credit Agencies Serving Business

We have already noted the activities of the FDIC and the Federal Reserve banks which serve the commercial banking industry. There are a few other government credit institutions serving nonagriculture types of business directly. Indirectly, of course, agencies such as the FHA serve contractors and other businesses selling to homeowners.

The largest of these institutions, the Reconstruction Finance Corporation, is no longer in existence. The Government created the RFC in 1932 as an emergency measure. The RFC loaned government funds to private business which used the money for capital improvement. Thus, it was an early example of a government stabilization policy. With the passing of the depression, RFC modified its objectives and continued to operate until 1954. During its lifetime it made loans to private business, to other federal lending agencies, and to authorities created by state and local governments.

The Congress established the Small Business Administration in 1953. This agency lends government funds and increases the loans of private lenders to small business enterprises. It is similar in motivation to the federal institutions serving agriculture and homeowners. Through its activities the Government hopes to realize a social objective — the preservation of small business.

The last institution we shall mention has a specialized function. The Export-Import Bank, established in 1934, facilitates the foreign trade of the United States by loaning government funds and by insuring the loans of private lenders to exporters and importers. The Bank also serves as the agent for the United States in its foreign aid programs.

Government Credit Agencies — Concluded

The data which Tables 20–1 and 20–2 present allow us to judge the size of government participation in the credit field. The agencies and programs listed in these tables do not correspond precisely with the material in the text. Table 20–1 lists the dollar value of loans and guarantees administered by some agencies which we did not discuss. The credit programs which these agencies administer are the means by which the Government supports certain activities and directs resources to them. In most cases they involve a subsidy. The titles of the administering agencies suggest the specific purposes. In the last year covered by the tables, the agencies which we discussed in the text account for $4.7 billion and $22.8 billion, respectively, of the direct loans and the guarantees.

Table 20-1

OUTSTANDING DIRECT LOANS, GUARANTEES AND INSURANCE
FOR MAJOR FEDERAL CREDIT PROGRAMS
1964-1965

(In billions of dollars)

Agency or Program	1964		1965	
	Direct Loans	Guarantees and Insurance	Direct Loans	Guarantees and Insurance
Department of Agriculture:				
Commodity Credit Corporation	.8	2.5	—	1.9
Rural Electrification Administration	.3	—	.4	—
Farmers Home Administration	.5	.2	.6	.2
Department of Commerce	.2	—	.3	—
Department of Health, Education, and Welfare	.1	—	.3	—
Department of State:				
Agency for International Development	1.9	—	1.8	.2
Housing and Home Finance Agency:				
Public Housing, Urban Renewal, etc.	.8	1.3	.9	1.5
Federal National Mortgage Association	.2	—	.4	.3
Federal Housing Administration	.2	13.0	.2	13.8
Veterans Administration	.5	3.1	.5	3.2
Export-Import Bank	.8	1.3	1.2	1.9
Small Business Administration	.4	—	.5	—
Miscellaneous	.2	.1	.1	.2
Total	6.9	21.5	7.1	23.3

Source: Estimates from *The Budget of the United States Government, Fiscal Year Ending June 30, 1966* (Washington: Government Printing Office, 1965), p. 406.

In addition, agencies with mixed ownership—government and private—administer several loan programs. Generally, private ownership takes the form of a co-operative enterprise. In some cases the private segment is in the process of buying the Government's share of the enterprise. In all of these agencies, the Federal Government has certain management functions and some financial responsibility; however, the bonds which these institutions issue are not direct obligations of the Government. Table 20-2 shows that the market

Table 20-2

OUTSTANDING LOANS FOR MAJOR QUASI-PUBLIC CREDIT PROGRAMS

1963-1965

(In billions of dollars)

Agency	1963	1964	1965
Mixed ownership enterprises and trust funds:			
Farm Credit Administration:			
Banks for co-operatives	.7	.7	.8
Federal intermediate credit banks	2.0	2.3	2.5
Housing and Home Finance Agency:			
Federal National Mortgage Association (secondary market operations trust fund)	2.9	2.1	2.0
Veterans Administration:			
Life insurance fund	.5	.6	.6
Subtotal, mixed ownership and trust funds	6.1	5.7	5.9
Other quasi-public credit programs:			
Federal land banks	3.0	3.2	3.5
Federal home loan banks	2.8	3.3	4.8
Federal Reserve, Board of Governors:			
Federal Reserve banks	.1	.1	.3
Subtotal, other quasi-public credit programs	5.9	6.6	8.6
Total	12.0	12.3	14.5

Source: Estimates from *The Budget of the United States Government, Fiscal Year Ending June 30, 1966* (Washington: Government Printing Office, 1965), p. 414.

involvement of these mixed ownership enterprises and other quasi-public operations is sizable. The data in these two tables show that federal credit agencies, including the mixed ownership group, account for a significant portion of the financial market. The critics and the friends of these agencies agree that their growth has caused Washington, D. C., to challenge New York City as the financial center of the United States.

SUMMARY

It is customary to describe the American economic system as one in which private enterprise operates in free competitive markets.

Supporting this system is the belief that it leads to an optimum allocation of resources and hence to maximum output. This description is correct in general but there are exceptions. The Government intervenes in the economic system in several ways. Our concern in this chapter has been with government intervention in the credit field.

Government influences the flow of credit from savers to those persons using the funds through the regulation of private institutions. The Government may regulate private institutions by means of its chartering function and through the action of regulatory agencies such as the Securities and Exchange Commission. In political discussion we tend to refer to the objectives of these regulatory actions as protection to individual savers and investors. As economists we think of them as a means of improving the allocation of resources. Government works toward this objective by aiding in the dissemination of information, insuring against risk, and providing for liquidity.

The Federal Government intervenes in the market directly by organizing and operating credit agencies. These programs also strive to improve the allocation of resources. To accomplish this objective, they channel credit to sectors of the economy which, in the judgment of our responsible government leaders, do not receive an adequate supply from private institutions. Government agencies increase the supply of credit by lending money to private borrowers and by insuring the loans made by private lending institutions. Agriculture and residential real estate have been the chief beneficiaries of government credit agencies.

QUESTIONS

1. How can we justify the government's operation of a credit agency? Can you formulate a set of principles which would determine when and how the government should participate in financial markets?
2. Compare the data in Tables 20–1 and 20–2 with those in the tables in Chapter 19 and discuss the degree of government participation in the credit market.
3. To what extent do government credit agencies compete with private lenders? Discuss.
4. Why does the government guarantee loans advanced by private firms in preference to lending money directly to borrowers?

SUGGESTED READINGS

American Bankers Association. "Government Loan and Credit Programs," *Banking*, Vol. LVI, No. 10 (April, 1964), 141–176.

U.S. Bureau of the Budget. *The Budget of the United States Government, Fiscal Year Ending June 30, 1966.* Washington: U.S. Government Printing Office, 1965.

Woodworth, G. Walter. *The Money Market and Monetary Management.* New York: Harper & Row, Publishers, 1965. Chapter 8.

Also, see the Readings listed under Chapter 19.

21

FINANCIAL INSTITUTIONS
AND MONETARY POLICY

In the preceding chapters we treated commercial banks and other financial institutions separately. Since an earlier discussion explained the reason for this separate treatment, we need only summarize it here. Commercial banks are different because they hold demand deposits which are subject to transfer by check. This feature allows them to create the demand deposits which constitute the main component of the nation's money supply. The creation or destruction of a portion of the stock of money affects the level of prices and the level of income. It follows that the actions of commercial banks may lead to inflation or deflation and full employment or underemployment. As a consequence of this important position, commercial banks are subject to monetary policies designed to stabilize prices and income.

We treated other financial institutions, including the saving and time deposit divisions of commercial banks, as financial intermediaries. These institutions facilitate the transfer of savings to persons who spend the funds for investment or consumption purposes. This is an important function since it allows the nation to achieve a better allocation of resources. However, this function does not have the direct bearing on the price level and employment conditions that the creation of demand deposits has.

This has been the conventional approach of students of finance. In chapters 19 and 20 we did hint at opposition to this point of view. We noted that the presence of the noncommercial bank types of financial institutions influenced the public's preference for liquidity. Thus, we indicated that these other institutions had some effect on the level of spending. Now we shall examine more thoroughly the relationship of these financial institutions to the monetary system. We shall ask, are "other" financial institutions significantly different from commercial banks? In the process of considering the question, we shall augment our understanding of monetary economics.

372

FINANCIAL INSTITUTIONS
IN THE MONETARY SYSTEM

This question has given rise to considerable controversy in recent years. We shall seek an answer to the question by reviewing the arguments which the disputants have presented. The name most prominent among the opponents of the conventional point of view is John G. Gurley,[1] of the Brookings Institution. The following paragraphs rely heavily upon his arguments. Dr. Gurley and those who side with him claim that commercial banks are not different in a significant way from other financial institutions. Furthermore, they claim that other financial institutions have been growing at a more rapid rate than commercial banks. Yet, monetary theory continues to emphasize and monetary policy continues to concentrate on commercial banks, virtually ignoring the other financial institutions. If we accept the argument that commercial banks and other financial institutions are alike, this concentration on one segment is unfair. It is also likely to be ineffective.

Commercial Banks Are Different—
Summary of Arguments

There are, of course, features which commercial banks and other financial institutions have in common. They both serve as intermediaries; consequently they promote a better allocation of resources. Nevertheless, we customarily think that commercial banks are different. Since the question of difference is at the heart of the controversy, a summary of the conventional description of their different characteristics is in order even at the risk of being repetitious.

Commercial banks differ from other financial institutions because (1) they create money, (2) the creation process is one of multiple expansion of reserves, and (3) there are inflationary consequences resulting from commercial bank actions. In addition, there is the claim that the volume of commercial bank assets and liabilities is more volatile than the holdings of other financial institutions.

Commercial Banks Are Not Different—
Summary of Arguments

The group that opposes this conventional point of view disputes each of these assertions. This group admits that only commercial

---

[1]Dr. Gurley has expressed his point of view in several articles. See particularly his address before the 1959 Conference on Savings and Residential Financing printed in the *Proceedings* and reprinted in Lawrence S. Ritter (ed.), *Money and Economic Activity: Readings in Money and Banking* (2d ed.; Boston: Houghton Mifflin Company, 1961), pp. 315 –326. For a thorough explanation, see the listing of Gurley and Shaw in the suggested readings for this chapter.

banks can create money as we have generally defined the term. Our usual definition of money includes only currency and demand deposits. However, other institutions can create financial assets, such as savings deposits, which are a close substitute for money. An example elucidates the process of creating financial assets. In this illustration we make the same assumptions we used in describing the creation of demand deposits by commercial banks: we ignore overhead and interest items and we assume that the institution holds a monopoly position and that its depositors do not withdraw cash.

In this example a saver deposits $1,000 in a mutual savings bank and receives a debt claim in return. This debt claim is a financial asset from the depositor's standpoint. The bank's balance sheet shows:

Assets		*Liabilities*	
Cash	$1,000	Savings deposits	$1,000

The bank loans the $1,000 to an individual who spends the money for home improvements. Let us assume that persons working for the building contractor receive this money in wages and deposit it in the savings bank. In practice the transactions tend to be more complicated. The funds probably pass through the demand deposit accounts of commercial banks during the transfer from savings bank to homeowner, to contractor, and finally to the wage earner. However, at the conclusion of the transfer process, the savings bank's balance sheet shows:

Assets		*Liabilities*	
Cash	$1,000	Savings deposits	$2,000
Notes receivable	1,000		

We can continue this lending, spending, and depositing sequence to raise the deposit accounts to still higher levels. However, the increase of deposits from $1,000 to $2,000 is sufficient to indicate that savings banks create savings deposits just as commercial banks create demand deposits. In both cases the bank's lending operations lead to the creation of deposits. The process is more direct for commercial banks which buy assets with newly created deposits. Savings banks must act indirectly. They lend cash to the public which uses it to buy assets. The seller of the asset then redeposits the cash in the bank thus creating a new deposit. In both cases the creation of deposits to which we refer is, in fact, multiple expansion of reserves. This is more obvious for commercial banks where the legal reserve requirement places a limit upon expansion. There are no legal reserve requirements for savings banks; they do hold a cash reserve as we saw in Table 19–2. Since savings banks have sound reasons for keeping this reserve at least equal to some fraction of deposit claims, there is a limit to expansion. A large portion of this cash reserve is generally held as a demand deposit in a commercial bank. This fact further complicates the task of separating the role and influence of one type of institution from the other.

It appears that both the commercial banks and the mutual savings banks, which serve in our example as the representative for all other financial intermediaries, create deposits. However, the commercial banks can create demand deposits while the savings banks can create only savings deposits. Is this difference significant? According to our definition, demand deposits are money while savings deposits are "near-money." Both types, however, are financial assets from the point of view of the depositor. They both serve as a store of value. Savings deposits are not media of exchange, but their conversion into money is a simple matter. Are these several differences of sufficient importance for us to label them significant?

We are unlikely to resolve this issue by considering only technical and legal differences. Our study will be more fruitful if we examine the effect of the creation of these different financial assets on the economic system. Both types of institutions and the debt claims they issue facilitate the transfer of funds from savers to persons who use them. Thus, they both serve to improve the allocation of the nation's resources. The two types of institutions appear to differ with regard to their ability to create inflationary pressure. The creation of demand deposits increases the money supply and in this way creates inflationary pressure. Since the creation of other financial assets leaves the money supply unchanged, apparently there is no inflationary pressure. It follows that commercial banks differ from other financial institutions in a significant manner.

Critics of the conventional point of view question this conclusion. Using the concepts and logic of the quantity theory, they point out that excessive spending leads to inflation. Aggregate spending consists of MV. Commercial banks affect the size of M by creating or destroying demand deposits. However, the creation of other financial assets affects V. Persons are more willing to spend currency and demand deposits if they hold savings deposits, saving and loan shares, or other financial assets. Hence, financial institutions other than commercial banks have an influence on the problem of inflation through their effect on velocity. Or, we might use the income and expenditure approach to monetary theory. The creation and ownership of financial assets affects the liquidity preference function; it moves the $L_1 + L_2$ function to the left, thus lowering the interest rate and increasing the volume of investment spending.

If we accept this line of reasoning, it is obvious that the operations of both commercial banks and other financial institutions have inflationary consequences. It follows that we must question the present tendency of monetary theory and of monetary policy to concentrate on commercial banks. In the light of the preceding arguments, this policy seems inequitable and also would appear to be less effective than a policy which affects all financial institutions.

Critics of the present system have suggested an additional reason for changing our conventional pattern of thinking and our policies. They cite statistical studies which, they claim, show that other financial institutions are growing at a more rapid rate than commercial banks.[2] Consequently, policies designed to manage the monetary system concentrate on a segment which is declining in importance.

Assuming that the preceding criticisms of the commercial monetary concepts are valid, it follows logically that monetary policy should affect all financial institutions. Consequently, we should develop and apply to other financial institutions controls similar to the reserve requirements, the discount rate, and the open-market operations which the Federal Reserve System applies to commercial banks. Here is another example, incidentally, of a discussion of monetary theory which leads to policy recommendations.

Evaluation of the Arguments

The group that defends the conventional approach to monetary theory and policy denies the claim that the relative importance of commercial banks in the system is declining. The statistical evidence is such that several conclusions are possible depending on the years chosen for analysis and the way the student defines the term "relative importance." However, this specific controversy is beyond the scope of this text. The relative decline or increase in the importance of commercial banks affects the extent to which present thinking and policies may be incorrect; it does not affect the basic question of the difference between commercial banks and other financial institutions.

Both types of institutions create financial assets. Consequently, the issue revolves around the question, how is money different from other financial assets? In an early portion of this text (Chapter 2), we saw that money was the most liquid of assets. However, savings deposits and other forms of "near-money" approach it quite closely. In this respect, therefore, the difference seems slight.

With regard to inflationary influences, we know that the creation

---

[2]The chief statistical study is the work of Raymond W. Goldsmith. See the reference in the suggested bibliography at the end of this chapter. See also Ritter, *op. cit.*

of demand deposits increases M, a factor in the aggregate spending equation. In our discussion of the quantity theories, we noted that an increase in the money supply affects velocity. Furthermore, the readiness of commercial banks to lend money by creating deposits induces the public to reduce cash balances. Therefore, commercial banks influence M and V in the equation of exchange. Other institutions create financial assets which influence V but not the quantity of money. Since commercial banks affect two and other institutions influence only one factor in the monetary system, the former appear to be significantly different. However, it is unwise to leap to hasty conclusions. Both types of institutions affect the interest rate; yet it is possible that the creation of money has less of an effect than the creation of other financial assets. Furthermore, changes in the quantity of money exert an influence on the interest rate when the public uses its excess cash to acquire savings deposits and other financial assets. Thus, the operation of the two types of institutions are interrelated — a fact which further complicates the problem of appraising individually their influence on the monetary system. With respect to the recommendations that monetary policies apply to other financial institutions, we may observe that open-market operations do affect these institutions.

We cannot resolve this controversy but we can offer some ideas. We noted in earlier chapters that the creation of money affects the price level and the level of output and employment. In this chapter and the two which precede it, we see that the existence of other financial assets also affects these levels, perhaps to a lesser degree. It seems, therefore, that commercial banks are not the unique institutions that they appear to be in conventional monetary thinking. However, they seem to be less like other financial institutions than the critics of the conventional school admit. The discussion does emphasize the need to consider financial institutions in a study of monetary economics. It also shows that the process of defining money is not simply an academic exercise; differences in the definition and the concept of money lead to different policy recommendations.

FLOW OF FUNDS ANALYSIS

In the preceding two and one-half chapters, we have been considering the system by which persons with excess funds transfer them to persons who spend them for investment and consumption purposes. This transfer of funds has an important effect on the allocation of resources as well as the level of prices, employment, and output. For this reason economists wish to know as much as possible

Table 21–1

FLOW OF FUNDS, UNITED STATES, FOURTH QUARTER, 1964

Seasonally Adjusted Annual Rates
(In billions of dollars)

Types of Transactions	Private Domestic Nonfinancial Sectors						U. S. Govt.	
	Households		Business		State and Local Govts.			
	U	S	U	S	U	S	U	S
1 Nonfinancial sources and uses								
2 Capital consumption		54.3		46.7				
3 Net saving		45.7		11.0		−2.5		−6.5
4 Consumer durables	56.1							
5 Residential construction	18.5		6.5					
6 Plant and equipment	3.9		55.3					
7 Inventory change			5.5					
8 Subtotal, nonfinancial	78.4	100.1	67.3	57.7		−2.5		−6.5
9 Financial sources and uses								
10 Gold, official U. S. foreign exchange, Treasury currency							.4	− .
11 Demand deposits and currency	4.2		− .9		3.4		−1.9	
12 Time and savings accounts	23.8		3.2		3.1		.1	
13 Life insurance reserves	4.9							
14 Pension fund reserves	11.0					3.1		1.
15 Consolidated bank items								
16 U. S. Govt. securities	1.1		− 3.5		−4.5			1.
17 State and local securities	1.4				.4	5.6		
18 Corporation and foreign bonds	3.4			4.2	1.3			
19 Corporation stocks	− 1.7			− 1.5				
20 Mortgages	6.5	16.4		12.8	.4		− .4	
21 Consumer credit		6.0	1.5					
22 Other loans and credit	− .3	.4	5.5	15.9		.4	4.5	1.
23 Equity in noncorporate business	− 2.4			− 2.4				
24 Miscellaneous	.7		10.7	.4			− .3	−
25 Subtotal, financial	52.6	23.0	16.4	29.3	4.1	9.0	2.4	4
26 Statistical discrepancy	− 8.0		3.3		2.5		−4.8	
27 Total	123.0	123.0	87.0	87.0	6.6	6.6	−2.4	−2

NOTE: U = uses, S = sources. Details may not add to totals because of rounding.
SOURCE: *Federal Reserve Bulletin*, April, 1965, p. 604.

about the volume of dollars being transferred. They also wish to know what sectors of the economic system are the source, what sectors use the funds, and what type of transactions facilitate this transfer. We have seen that the transfer process is not a simple one. There are the original savers and the ultimate users in addition to the intermediaries who receive and disperse funds. Consequently, the task of collecting and interpreting data concerning this process is difficult. The tables in the preceding chapters have presented data for certain private and government credit institutions, but we have not seen the overall picture.

    The comprehensive view is obtained through the Flow of Funds Tables of the *Federal Reserve Bulletin*. This method of presenting

Table 21 – 1 (continued)

	Monetary Authorities		Commercial Banks		Nonbank Finance		Rest of World		Statistical Discrepancy		All Sectors		
	U	S	U	S	U	S	U	S	U	S	U	S	
													1
		.2	.4			.3						101.7	2
				.8		1.3		– 5.5				44.5	3
											56.1		4
				.2							25.0		5
					.2						59.4		6
											5.7		7
		.2	.2	1.2	.2	1.6		– 5.5			146.2	146.2	8
													9
	– .4						.7	1.3	.5		1.2	1.2	10
		5.4		6.3	.3		.2		6.5		11.8	11.8	11
			16.0		.3	15.9	1.4				31.9	31.9	12
						4.8					4.9	4.9	13
	.1	– 1.6	– 1.6	.1		6.9					11.0	11.0	14
	5.0			1.4	– 1.0		3.1				– 1.5	– 1.5	15
				2.9	.9						1.6	1.6	16
			.2	.4	3.5	1.9	.2	2.1			5.6	5.6	17
					3.4	2.7	– .4	.1			8.6	8.6	18
				3.9	18.6	– .2					1.3	1.3	19
				2.5	2.1						29.0	29.0	20
	.1		15.9	.3	4.2	.1	– 1.3	5.2	– 4.6		6.1	6.1	21
											24.0	24.0	22
		.9	.2	.7	3.3	3.5	2.0	1.3	– 10.00		– 2.4	– 2.4	23
											6.6	6.6	24
	4.9	4.7	25.4	23.9	35.6	35.7	6.0	10.0	– 7.6		139.8	139.8	25
				– .5	1.5		– 1.5						26
	4.9	4.9	25.1	25.1	37.3	37.3	4.5	4.5			286.0	286.0	27

financial data was developed approximately a decade ago by Professor Morris A. Copeland.[3] The statistical work is accomplished by the staff of the Board of Governors of the Federal Reserve System. A flow of funds table is designed to measure and to record the sources and uses of funds in the capital and money markets. For this purpose the economic system is divided into several decision-making sectors. The many transactions which involve the transfer of funds in the financial market also are classified. On the basis of this double classification, the dollar value of each transaction is reflected in the appropriate use and source block. The concept of the flow of funds system of accounting is best understood by reference to Table 21 – 1.

[3]See, Morris A. Copeland, A Study of Moneyflows in the United States (New York: National Bureau of Economic Research, Inc., 1952).

Table 21-1 divides the economic system into eight decision-making sectors. Note that organizational structure or functions are the basis for classification. We can use a larger or a smaller number, whichever better serves the purpose of our study. This table also classifies transactions into two major categories, nonfinancial and financial, and a number of subcategories. Determining the number of subcategories involves a compromise. If the number is too few, we may ignore some useful information; if we use too many classes, the volume of detail may overwhelm the analyst.

Each sector secures and disposes of funds through a series of transactions. The classification of sectors and transactions allows us to record the effect of each transaction in the appropriate use and source block. We shall use the household sector to illustrate the principles which govern the construction of this table. Households secure funds through two nonfinancial sources, capital consumption and net saving. The capital consumption item reflects the depreciation of durable assets while net saving is the excess of income over expenditure for consumption goods and services. These two items, which equal gross saving, total $100.1 billion for 1964. This does not exhaust the sources of funds for the sector. By examining the various financial transactions, we note that households secure $16.4 billion from mortgage loans, $6.0 billion from consumer credit transactions, and a smaller sum from other loans and credit sources. The grand total from all transactions equals $123.0 billion.

The sector uses these funds to purchase investment type goods and services — i.e., nonfinancial assets — and to acquire financial assets. In the use column we note that the purchase of consumer durables, residential construction, and plant and equipment account for $78.4 billion. Increases in currency and demand and savings deposits plus claims against life insurance companies, pension funds, government, and other institutions account for the disposition of the remainder. Where a negative figure appears in the use column, such as corporate stock, it reflects a net decrease in the holdings of that type of financial asset by the sector. It is a source of funds in terms of its effect. In the case of a few transaction categories — for example, mortgages — a figure appears in the use and the source column. This indicates that some individuals in this sector are borrowing while others are lending on mortgages. Continuing to concentrate on the consumer sector, we note that the total in the source column equals $123.0 billion. Since the sector must use these funds in some way, it follows conceptually that total sources equal total uses. Because of imperfections in the many estimates, the statistical discrepancy item is necessary to balance the accounts.

These same principles apply to the other sectors. Because of the nature of its activities, each sector displays a different pattern with regard to the importance of the several types of transactions. However, uses equal sources for each sector and for the entire system.

An examination of the data in Table 21–1 reveals valuable information for the study of the services of financial intermediaries. The total of the use and the source column for each sector is the same; however the subtotal for nonfinancial sources and nonfinancial uses need not be equal. For the household sector, nonfinancial sources, or gross saving, exceeds nonfinancial uses. Since the grand totals are equal, the sector must dispose of its surplus funds through financial transactions. The consequent surplus of financial uses over financial sources represents a transfer of funds to other sectors. In these other sectors the inequalities in the subtotal figures must be reversed. It is this transfer of funds which is of interest to us.

For each financial-type transaction, the total funds in the use blocks equal the total funds in the source blocks. This is not true for nonfinancial-type transactions. However, for financial types the reason is obvious if we look at one example, consumer credit. Some person or institution must be the creditor for every dollar of consumer debt. To the debtor, this dollar is a source; to the creditor, it represents one way of using funds.

Uses of Flow of Funds Data

The flow of funds data provide the same type of information regarding transfer of funds in the financial markets that national income accounting does for the production of goods and services. National income accounts measure the value of the several categories of currently produced goods and services. Flow of funds accounts measure the activity of the several sectors in the financial market. The data show the sectoral pattern of the supply and the absorption of funds. By comparing the data for a number of years, we may recognize changing patterns. The table also allows us to note the relative importance of the several types of transactions.

The information, therefore, is very useful to persons analyzing financial markets. There are details which the table omits but it does present a great deal of information in a form which lends itself to analysis. At this time, however, economists have not incorporated the flow of funds into the analytical process to the same extent as the national income accounts.

SUMMARY

In the preceding chapters we regarded commercial banks as ·
distinct from other financial institutions. We cited their ability to
create money and the effect of this action on the level of prices and
income. Logically, therefore, stabilization policy concentrates on this
institution. We now challenge this school of thought. Other financial
institutions create financial assets which possess varying degrees of
liquidity. Some of these financial assets are a close substitute for
money. Although other financial institutions do not create money,
they do create assets which influence the level of prices and income
through their effect on spending decisions. This effect may not be as
great as that of commercial banks; nevertheless it appears that commercial banks and other institutions are not as dissimilar as claimed
by conventional theory.

Flow of funds accounts measure the funds supplied to the financial market by the several sectors. These accounts also record the
type of transaction which produced this supply. The absorption of
funds from the market receives the same type of analysis. This information enables us to recognize the pattern of the flow of funds
through financial intermediaries and directly among the several
sectors.

QUESTIONS

1. Is there a significant difference between a savings account and a checking
   account from the viewpoint of the depositor? Can you call one of these
   items money and the other near-money?
2. Does the government have the same power to influence financial intermediaries as it has to influence commercial banks? Review Chapters 19
   and 20 in answering this question.
3. Use the flow of funds table (pages 378–79) in answering the following
   questions:
   a. The table indicates that transactions in United States Government
      securities were a source of funds to the United States Government.
      From what sectors did the Government obtain these funds?
   b. Time and savings account transactions account for a sizable flow
      of funds. Comment on the net transfers; that is, which sectors
      transfer funds to others and which sectors receive funds.
   c. The business sector has nonfinancial uses in excess of non-
      financial sources of funds. What sectors make up the difference?
4. Can you find a relationship between the flow of funds data in Table 21–1
   and the GNP data presented in Chapter 15?

SUGGESTED READINGS

Goldsmith, Raymond W. *Financial Intermediaries in the American Economy Since 1900*. Princeton: Princeton University Press, 1958.

Gurley, John G., and Shaw, Edward S. *Money in a Theory of Finance*. Washington: The Brookings Institution, 1960.

Ritter, Lawrence S. (ed.). *Money and Economic Activity: Readings in Money and Banking*. 2d ed. Boston: Houghton Mifflin Company, 1961. Chapter 12.

VI

DEVELOPMENT OF
STABILIZATION POLICY

22

STABILIZATION POLICY, 1914 – 1929

In the earlier sections of the text, we examine the factors which determine the quantity of money and the rate at which it circulates. We also consider the means by which the monetary authorities control these factors. In making these studies, we are assuming implicitly that the monetary system affects the economic well-being of the nation. In the section on monetary theory, we analyze the relationship between these monetary factors and specific indicators of economic well-being, such as the level of GNP, the degree of unemployment, the rate of economic growth, and the level of prices. In the chapters which follow, we shall note the practical application of these relationships as we review the development of policies designed to achieve economic objectives by influencing the monetary system.

The economic objectives of a society change from time to time, and differences of opinion exist regarding the relative importance of the several objectives. At the present time, however, there is widespread agreement that full employment of the factors of production, a stable price level, and a high and sustained rate of economic growth are goals of monetary policy. Or one might claim that the ultimate objective is a high standard of living in which case these goals of monetary policy become instruments for achieving that end. In an emergency, the financial support of the Government may be an important goal, but we consider this abnormal. Other objectives, such as the elimination of the deficit in the balance of payments and the provision for an adequate supply of credit and currency, may be of immediate concern; they are intermediate goals. The attainment of these objectives is important because they affect our ability to stabilize prices, to achieve economic growth, and to maintain full employment.

Our objectives in the next three chapters are similar to those noted in the earlier historical section. Monetary and fiscal policy are interesting in their own right, but we wish to do more than merely examine specific events. Studying the history and the policies of institutions, we shall enhance our understanding of the present system, and we shall gain a perspective from which to judge present policy and theory. In the course of this study, we shall see how the objectives of policy changed as the nation developed and as new problems arose. We shall also see that the policies and the theories which are the basis of those policies changed with the times.

Previous chapters traced the development of American monetary institutions and policy from the colonial period to 1914. In treating these developments, we considered government action regarding the currency and the monetary standard separately from developments in the banking system. However, in studying policy after 1914, this approach is impractical. The interrelation of bank activity and the currency system had been increasing during the earlier period. After the creation of the Federal Reserve System, the relationship became so close that we cannot study one independently of the other. In addition to money and banking, we shall examine fiscal policy, particularly in the years after 1930. We referred to fiscal policy while discussing monetary theory and we noted specific instances where government financial operations affected the monetary system. However, government did not plan these effects prior to the 1930's. In this portion of the text, we shall treat government finance more extensively and shall examine its use as a policy measure.

EARLY YEARS OF THE FEDERAL RESERVE SYSTEM
1914-1921

An Act of Congress created the Federal Reserve System in 1914. It was a reform measure designed to correct certain defects in the banking system. However, it was not a radical reform instrument; Congress did not intend that it should change the entire economic structure nor even the monetary system. Confidence in the *laissez-faire* philosophy, the gold standard, and a minimum of government intervention in the economy continued. The Federal Reserve System fitted into this framework. Consequently, its power to influence the economy was less than it is today. The prevailing philosophy also affected the goals of monetary policy. The Federal Reserve System was to prevent liquidity crises and to keep the nation on the gold standard. This contrasts strikingly with the present goals of price stability, full employment, and economic growth. Of course, the prevention of liquidity crises, as well as the preservation of the gold reserve, remains an objective.

In our previous discussion (Chapter 10), we noted that the rediscount rate was the Federal Reserve System's only discretionary weapon in its early years. The powers to change legal reserve requirements and to impose selective controls were not available.

Open-market operations were possible but the authorities did not understand their use. Nor was moral suasion an effective weapon since the System had acquired neither a large membership nor the necessary prestige. Consequently, the System had to rely upon the rediscount rate plus eligibility requirements to control the volume of credit. We need only summarize the theory behind this policy; we discussed the principle in Chapter 10 in the section describing the discount rate and the "true bills" theory. Its purpose was to supply an adequate amount of credit to productive activities. If the Reserve banks rediscounted only eligible paper, and if they defined eligibility to include only short-term debt instruments arising from agricultural, manufacturing, or commercial activities, then commercial banks would lend money only for those purposes. The volume of eligible paper would be a good indicator of the magnitude of productive activity and, therefore, of the need for credit. In general, the work of the Federal Reserve authorities would be passive. The one discretionary weapon, the rediscount rate, would allow them to exert some, but not too much, influence on the commercial banks' willingness to borrow.

There was a rather obvious defect in this chain of reasoning. A commercial bank which rediscounted paper increased its reserves. It was then free to expand credit to all classes of debtors. Good banking practice required that a bank make *some* eligible loans so that it could rediscount paper if necessary. However, one must question the claim that the type of paper presented for rediscount was typical of the type of loans the bank was making. Fortunately, or otherwise, the Federal Reserve authorities did not have the opportunity to test this theory properly. World War I started between the date of the passage of the Federal Reserve Act and the opening of the Federal Reserve banks. The war in Europe created unforeseen problems for the new banks. Later the active participation of the United States caused the System to adopt a different objective and to follow other policies.

The outbreak of war in Europe created near-crisis conditions in American money markets. This condition, which was caused by European investors liquidating securities, had nearly passed by the late autumn of 1914 when the Reserve banks opened; nevertheless a new problem developed. The large export surplus of the United States led to a heavy inflow of gold. This gold inflow increased commercial bank reserves which combined with an increased demand for goods and services to create inflationary pressures. The Federal Reserve System had no policy implements to deal with this situation: the rediscount rate and the eligibility requirements were effective only if commercial banks were deficient in reserves. Such was not the case. In the absence of an effective policy to prevent inflation, the price level rose by approximately 40 per cent.

Financing World War I

When the United States entered the war, its financial policies followed a pattern with which we should now be familiar. Wartime conditions called for the reallocation of resources from private to public uses. The Government imposed some direct controls to assist in the reallocation process but for the most part the nation relied upon the price system. Use of the price system required heavy financial outlays by the Government and difficulties arose. There was a tendency to underestimate the total cost of the war. This error did not create but it did aggravate the financial problem. Also, the nation could not avoid expanding the money supply in the process of financing the war.

The nation's leaders recognized the danger of financing the war by methods which increased the stock of money. They sought to avoid the danger, first, by taxation; and, second, by borrowing from individuals and institutions other than commercial banks. In either instance, the Government acquired money already in existence and a decline in private spending balanced the increase in government expenditures. Unfortunately, the Treasury Department was unable to raise sufficient funds by these two methods. The war years cost the Federal Government approximately $33 billion, an enormous sum in that period. Taxes during those years equaled $10 billion. Consequently, the public debt, which had been $1.2 billion at the end of 1916, rose to $25.5 billion by the end of 1919. The Treasury campaigned vigorously to sell bonds representing this $23 billion debt increase to the public but it was only partially successful. Of necessity, it sold securities to the commercial banks. It also encouraged commercial banks to lend to individuals who would use the proceeds to buy government bonds. Both of these latter methods involved an increase in deposit currency. Also, both of these methods relied upon the co-operation of the Federal Reserve banks to create member bank reserves.

The Treasury believed these methods created less inflationary pressure than direct sales of bonds to the Reserve banks. Monetary authorities felt that individuals would save in order to eliminate their debt to commercial banks; the commercial banks, in turn, would be anxious to extinguish their debt to the Reserve banks.

The Congress had not created the Federal Reserve System as an instrument to finance the Government, but the System's usefulness in this field quickly became apparent. The Federal Reserve System issued Federal Reserve notes to meet the increased demand for currency. Member banks were permitted to borrow from the Reserve banks by pledging Government securities as collateral. This process increased the reserves of commercial banks and enabled them to buy more United States securities and to extend loans to private borrowers who used the loan proceeds for productive purposes and to buy government securities. The discount rate was low enough to make this profitable.

At the beginning of the war, the commercial banks held excess reserves. These reserves plus those borrowed from the Reserve banks permitted commercial banks to expand deposits from $22.3 billion on June 30, 1916, to $32 billion on June 30, 1919. During the same period, currency outside banks increased from $1.9 to $3.6 billion. Velocity appears to have been relatively stable and, since output was close to the maximum in 1916, prices rose in response to the increased money supply. By mid-1919 wholesale prices were 25 per cent above the 1917 level and almost double the 1914 level.

In many respects the effect of World War I finance was the same as that of the Civil War and even the American Revolution. The money supply increased, inflation occurred, and the rise in prices served to reallocate resources by reducing consumption. However, there were differences. The inflation was less severe and the financial administration was much more efficient; there were no financial crises nor did the nation leave the gold standard. Ironically, the Federal Reserve System received praise for this. Its first worthwhile service to the nation was the facilitation of inflationary practices.

Other consequences of the war effort are worthy of note. The nation realized that the Federal Reserve System was an important force in the economic system. There was also a change in philosophy. The *laissez-faire* attitude had been appropriate in peacetime when the goals of the economy were varied and when there were different opinions regarding what these goals should be. With the advent of war, the nation could agree upon a clearly defined goal. The public accepted the Federal Reserve System as a quasi-government agency which worked toward that goal. Naturally, this attitude weakened the independent central bank concept, which the Congress had been careful to write into the law. Also, reliance upon automatic controls and the true bills doctrine disappeared.

It is unfair to criticize the Federal Reserve System for its wartime policies despite the fact that the effect was inflationary. The managers of the System acted in accordance with public opinion. One may criticize public policy for not defraying a larger portion of the cost of the war through taxation; but the Reserve authorities, faced with the decision not to tax heavily, had little choice. They had two objectives which were mutually exclusive: restraint of credit expansion and the consequent inflation, or support of the national war effort. They selected the goal with the higher priority.

Postwar Adjustments

Postwar conditions called for more difficult decisions. By the end of 1919, the Treasury was operating with a surplus and was confining its borrowing to refunding operations. At the same time prices were rising as industry readjusted to peacetime operations. The Federal Reserve authorities wanted to raise the discount rate to restrain the credit expansion which was feeding inflation. This policy met with opposition from the Treasury, which felt that higher interest rates would interfere with its refunding operations. Treasury officials also claimed that the resulting decline in the price of outstanding securities would work a hardship on persons who purchased bonds during the war. Inflated prices eventually led to an outflow of gold, and the Reserve System then raised the discount rate. Treasury opposition, however, had delayed this action until late in 1919, by which time the inflationary boom had spent its force.

Beginning in the spring of 1920, prices and output declined, unemployment rose, and the nation experienced a brief but severe depression. The imposition of a high discount rate did not cause this depression, but the Reserve System's refusal to reverse its tight-money policy added to its severity. Modern writers have criticized the System for this action, but it was merely following the traditional procedure of a central bank. The Federal Reserve System did not have a mandate to stabilize employment, prices, and production. However, it was to maintain a sound currency and to prevent credit crises. Faced with a gold outflow, it raised the discount rate. In accordance with the theory of the gold standard, the authorities expected that the higher rates in the nation's money market would discourage the use of credit for holding large inventories. This would depress prices and would halt the gold outflow. Also, the high money-market rates would attract gold from abroad. Orthodox economic thinking held that depressed business conditions would disappear without government or Reserve bank interference. In this case, the economy did recover quickly—a fact which may have been unfortunate. It prevented a careful study of Federal Reserve policy including the time factor. Bad timing in making policy changes had caused the System to practice monetary ease during periods of inflation and restraint during deflation.

PROSPEROUS YEARS, 1922–1929

During the depression of 1920–1921, the Federal Reserve System played the passive role that was traditional for central banks. It protected the gold position of the United States and did not reverse its policy of credit restriction until 1922, when its gold reserve position improved. This approach to economic problems changed in the following decade. Beginning in 1922, the System had its first opportunity to develop under "normal" conditions and it changed rather drastically. There was little structural or legal change; it did redefine its objectives and alter its policies.

The decade of the 1920's, or more precisely 1922–1929, was a prosperous period which in retrospect seems even more prosperous because of the severe depression which followed. Incomes were high and output was high and rising. The level of investment was high and the rate of technological advance was rapid. The period was, in general, stable as well as prosperous. The price level remained steady and the rate of unemployment did not exceed 5 per cent of the labor force.

Monetary conditions were quite different from those existing when Congress passed the Federal Reserve Act. The war had increased the public debt which had become an important factor in the money market. Although the United States remained on the gold standard, the other major commercial nations had abandoned it. These nations were now trying to re-establish this monetary standard. Furthermore, the United States, in addition to becoming a creditor nation, had become the dominant financial power in the world.

In this environment the old policy in which the volume of eligible paper and the condition of the gold reserve automatically determined the amount of credit to be created or extinguished was inappropriate. The Reserve authorities developed new policies and new objectives. They accepted some responsibility for stabilizing prices and business conditions, although they recognized their inability to accomplish this with the powers they possessed. During the period, the System also attempted unsuccessfully to restrain security speculation or, more precisely, the use of bank credit for speculation. In addition, it accepted some responsibility for assisting other nations in re-establishing the gold standard.

Open-Market Operations

The System used its power to alter the discount rate and a new policy implement, open-market operations, to achieve these goals. The Federal Reserve banks had always possessed the power to purchase commercial paper and government securities. Therefore, effective open-market operations were possible when the System's managers learned how to use them. Prior to 1922, the Reserve banks had purchased assets but not for purposes of monetary management.

In 1922, the Reserve banks purchased securities because they needed earning assets. The increase in commercial bank reserves and the decline in the market rate of interest which followed served to inform the authorities of the effect of open-market operations. Coincidentally, the existence of the public debt and the development of a market in government securities increased the opportunity for open-market operations. The Reserve banks adopted open-market operations as an implement of monetary policy and formed a committee to co-ordinate the actions of the twelve Reserve banks in 1923. However, the committee did not acquire statutory recognition until 1935.

Adoption of open-market operations as an implement of policy marked the acceptance of discretionary control over the monetary system. The abandonment of automatic devices was not complete, however. Eligibility requirements lingered on as did the reliance on the gold standard; nevertheless the increased emphasis on open-market operations represented a change in the monetary philosophy of the System. It recognized that the important factor was the quantity of credit outstanding rather than the type of debt instrument serving as the credit base.

During the years 1923–1927, the Reserve System applied its policies successfully. To offset excessive activity in the domestic economy, it first sold securities on the open market. This eliminated excess reserves and caused member banks to borrow from the Reserve banks. The Reserve banks raised the discount rate to apply the proper degree of restraint. In times of credit stringency, the System reversed the procedure. The Federal Reserve System restrained credit by this method in 1923 and again in 1925–1926. It eased credit when mild recessions occured in 1924 and 1927.

At the same time that the System was exerting countercyclical pressure on the domestic economy, it was assisting other nations in re-establishing the gold standard. In the post World War I era, England and the nations on the European Continent faced a situation similar to the one the United States had faced after the Civil War. Inflation was more severe in these countries than it was in the United States. Consequently, a hasty re-establishment of the gold standard would have led to a gold flow from these countries to the United States. By the middle of the 1920's these countries had recovered sufficiently to attempt a return to the gold standard. The Federal Reserve System aided the effort by keeping interest rates low in the United States. These rates, which were lower than those abroad, removed the incentive to change foreign currency into gold and to send the gold to the United States for investment purposes.

Fortunately, the need for a policy of monetary ease to aid other nations in stabilizing their monetary systems occurred during a period when this policy was appropriate for the domestic economy. The existence of two objectives implies the possibility of a need for two contradictory policies. In the case just cited, the Reserve System admitted that credit ease in 1927 may have been excessive from the point of view of the domestic economy but was necessary on the international level.

Bank Failures

In contrast to the decade which followed, the 1920's seem prosperous. However, not all sectors of the economy present a picture of stable prosperity. Agriculture did not recover from the depression of 1920–1921. It remained depressed during the decade, and one may question its recovery as of the present time. During the decade commercial bank failures continued at a high rate. Table 22–1 on page 396 shows that in the nine-year period, 1921–1929 inclusive, over 5,700 banks failed. This is one bank failure for every 5.3 banks in existence at the beginning of the period.

The monetary reform measure which created the Federal Reserve System did not deal with the problem of bank insolvency. The national banking system and the Federal Reserve System could find some consolation in the fact that the failure rate was highest among nonmember banks, although it was not low among national and state member banks. Bank failures were most prevalent among the small, country banks. This fact, plus other evidence, suggests that larger banks with branch offices might have solved the problem. The nation did little or nothing to find and to eliminate the cause of bank failures during the 1920's. The situation was to become worse in the 1930's before it became better.

The Securities Market

The bull market in securities which developed during the decade presented the monetary authorities with a major problem. Stock prices rose steadily in the first half of the decade and by 1926 Standard and Poor's Corporation index of stock prices was double the 1921 level. In the following year, the rate of increase accelerated and prices continued to rise until they reached a peak in 1929. The early rise did not cause concern because corporate profits rose at approximately the same rate. A rise in stock prices which parallels a rise in profits merely represents an adjustment of the economy to changing conditions. The security market reflects the increased efficiency and productivity of industry and attracts funds to the most profitable and,

Table 22–1

COMMERCIAL BANK SUSPENSIONS
1921–1929

| Year | Number | | | | | Deposits (in millions of dollars) | | | Estimated Loss to Depositors |
| | Total | Member Banks | | Nonmember Banks | | Total | Member Banks | Nonmember Banks | |
		National	State	State	Private				
1921	505	52	19	390	44	172.2	38.1	134.1	60
1922	366	49	13	281	23	91.2	27.2	63.9	38
1923	646	90	32	501	23	149.6	46.8	102.8	62
1924	775	122	38	578	37	210.2	78.5	131.6	79
1925	618	118	28	433	39	167.6	65.5	102.1	61
1926	976	123	35	766	52	260.3	67.5	192.9	83
1927	669	91	31	514	33	199.3	63.5	135.8	61
1928	498	57	16	406	19	142.4	46.7	95.6	44
1929	659	64	17	547	31	230.6	58.1	172.6	77
	5,712	766	229	4,416	301	1,623.4	491.9	1,131.4	565

Source: Board of Governors, Federal Reserve System, *Banking and Monetary Statistics* (Washington, 1943), p. 283.

we assume, the most productive areas. Conventional economic theory also explains and suggests approval of a rise in stock prices in excess of a recorded increase in profits if it is consistent with reasonable profit expectations. Beginning in 1927, the increase in stock prices did not fit this description. Instead, it had a speculative base.

There are many definitions of speculation. However, for our purposes we define a speculative stock purchase as one in which the purchaser buys in anticipation of reselling at a higher price and gives little or no consideration to profit and dividend expectations. The term has become opprobrious; nevertheless a moderate amount of speculation is socially desirable. We have seen that the presence of speculators in the market guarantees that there is a demand for securities and thus increases the liquidity of financial assets. However, excessive speculation is harmful for two reasons. First, experience indicates that a collapse of prices follows a speculative rise and inflicts hardship upon those unfortunate individuals who purchased at the top of the market. Second, the speculative boom diverts credit resources and human talent from productive areas. It is difficult at all times to draw a line between moderate and excessive speculation; it is virtually impossible to do so while a boom is in progress. In retrospect, there is general agreement that speculation became excessive in 1927 and grew progressively worse during the next two years.

In the 1920's, the Federal Reserve authorities did not feel that they were responsible for curbing speculation in the securities market. However, they had a definite mandate to prevent the use of bank credit for speculative purposes. The System became concerned with the volume of bank credit which entered the securities market in 1927. Table 22–2 shows the cause of this concern. The index of common stock prices and the loans to brokers both increased by about 100 per cent in the period 1927–1929. The greater portion of the increase in loans to brokers did not come directly from banks. However, there was reason to believe that much of it originated with commercial banks. In any event, it represented a diversion from productive uses as defined by the Federal Reserve System. The data for the post-1929 period show that there was a sound basis for the belief that the boom would end in a crash. They also reveal the near total removal of credit from the securities market by 1932.

What could the Reserve System have done to prevent the use of bank credit for the purchase of securities? One possibility was the adoption of a tight-money policy, but this approach contained a serious defect. A tight-money policy restricts the total volume of credit in the economy. The high rates on brokers' loans would have attracted the available funds to the securities market so that the chief impact would have fallen upon the commercial and industrial sec-

Table 22-2

INDEX OF STOCK PRICES AND VOLUME
OF LOANS TO BROKERS
Selected dates, 1921-1932
(Loans, in millions of dollars)

Date[a] (Sept.)	Stock Price Index (1935-1939 = 100)	Loans Total	N.Y. City Banks	Outside	Others
1921	56.2	990	370	255	365
1922	77.0	1,820	855	445	520
1923	69.3	1,520	600	420	500
1924	78.6	1,970	1,070	440	460
1925	97.8	2,930	1,060	950	920
1926	110.1	3,220	960	1,000	1,260
1927	134.8	3,910	1,170	1,060	1,680
1928	165.4	5,510	880	1,020	3,610
1929	237.8	8,529	1,095	79	6,640
1930	157.1	3,670	1,715	760	1,195
1931	86.3	1,220	840	90	290
1932	61.5	510	390	25	95

[a]The stock price index is the average for the month. Loan data are for the end of the month, except for 1928 and 1929 which are reports of October 3 and 4, respectively. Source: Board of Governors, Federal Reserve System, *Banking and Monetary Statistics* (Washington, 1943), pp. 480-481.

tors. With the exception of the securities markets, there was no evidence of excessive activity or inflationary pressure in the economy. Wholesale and retail prices were stable, wage rates were not rising, and labor did not appear to be in short supply. In fact, after August of 1929, industrial production declined and unemployment rose. This incident illustrates a type of problem which the monetary authorities frequently must face. They have objectives that call for contradictory policy measures: in this case, monetary restraint because of security speculation and monetary ease because of conditions in the rest of the economy.

At this stage in the development of monetary policy, the Federal Reserve System could do little to solve the problem. The discount rate and open-market policy are quantitative implements which affect the entire economy. Selective controls were not available. Consequently, the Board of Governors tried moral suasion. It informed member banks that they should not make loans secured by stock while they were in debt to the Federal Reserve banks. This attempt at direct action had little effect, possibly because it did not have the enthusiastic support of all of the Reserve banks. In addition the System sold securities on the open market and raised the discount rate. That is, it chose the objective which it felt had the higher priority. The tight-money policies apparently did little to restrain security speculation but they did aggravate the downward movement of the economy which began in the summer of 1929.

End of the Decade

The collapse of the stock market was the most spectacular and probably the most publicized event of the decade. Table 22–2 shows the extent of the price decline, most of which occurred after and not during 1929. The break in the securities market contributed to the severity of the depression of the 1930's, but we cannot list it as *the* cause. We noted previously that employment and industrial production had begun to decline several months before the crash.

Although the collapse of the market created many problems, it solved an immediate one for the Federal Reserve System. The end of the bull market eliminated the dilemma which the System was facing. Accordingly, the Reserve banks lowered the discount rate and bought securities on the open market. These measures moved the System in the right direction; unfortunately this did not halt the decline. In the judgment of many critics, monetary policy was "too little and too late."

FISCAL POLICY

By modern standards, there was no fiscal policy during the years we have just discussed. Government did not consciously use its power to tax, to spend, and to borrow as a device to stabilize the economy. Nevertheless, the several levels of government taxed, spent, borrowed, and repaid. Of course, these actions affected the level of economic stability. We have noted the extent to which the financial operations of the Federal Government affected the decisions of monetary authorities during World War I. Government spending and deficit financing were major contributors to the strength of the inflationary pressure.

During the 1920's, the Federal Government operated with a surplus budget and reduced the national debt from $23.7 billion in 1920 to a low point of $16.5 billion in 1929. The Federal Government, therefore, "saved" at the rate of $.9 billion per year. Accordingly, one might conclude that government finance exerted a defla-

Table 22–3

NET PUBLIC DEBT, 1920–1929

(In billions of dollars)

Year	Total	Federal	State and Local
1920	29.6	23.7	5.9
1921	29.6	23.1	6.5
1922	30.5	22.8	7.7
1923	30.0	21.8	8.2
1924	30.0	21.0	9.0
1925	30.3	20.3	10.0
1926	29.9	19.2	10.7
1927	29.7	18.2	11.5
1928	29.8	17.5	12.3
1929	29.7	16.5	13.2

Source: United States Department of Commerce, *Historical Statistics of the United States* (Washington, 1958), p. 664.

tionary pressure during the decade. This is incorrect for it overlooks the other levels of government. During these years state and local government expenditures exceeded revenue and by coincidence their deficits just equaled the Federal surplus. Consequently, government fiscal operations were neither deflationary nor inflationary if one considers only gross revenue and expenditures and ignores the methods of taxation and the type of expenditures. Table 22–3 shows the pertinent information regarding public debt.

LESSONS FROM THE PERIOD

We shall divide the first fifteen years of the development of the Federal Reserve System into two periods: World War I and the postwar years (1914–1921) and the years of stable prosperity (1922–1929). During the first period, the Federal Reserve System proved that a central bank could render very valuable service by assisting the Treasury in financing a war. From these years, we also learn that a central bank loses its independent status in times of major crisis and becomes an instrument of the Treasury. In the immediate postwar years, we should note the reluctance of the Treasury to release the Federal Reserve System from its obligation to support the Government bond market. We shall observe this same reluctance a quarter of a century later.

In the years 1922–1929, the nation quickly learned that the eligible paper requirements and other automatic devices which relied upon the structure of a central bank's operations were unsatisfactory. Discretionary controls and reliance on human judgment were unavoidable. It also learned that the effect of monetary policy was limited. Some of the limits were self-imposed because we were reluctant to assign power to a centralized agency. Other limits were unavoidable. An example of such a limit was the Reserve System's inability to restrain and to ease credit simultaneously in different sectors of the economy.

SUMMARY

Congress created the Federal Reserve System in order to secure an adequate, but not excessive, supply of credit. The Reserve banks were designed to accommodate, not control, the money market. The System relied upon eligibility requirements and the gold reserve position to determine the proper amount of credit. The rediscount rate was the only discretionary implement available to the Federal Reserve authorities.

World War I eliminated the possibility of a true test of this approach to monetary policy. After the United States entered the war, Treasury finance determined monetary policy. The Federal Reserve System enabled the Treasury to finance the war at a low interest rate and to avoid financial crisis. In the process it added to the inflationary pressure. Since monetary policy continued to support government security prices until the end of 1919, it did not restrain credit until the postwar inflationary boom had spent its force.

During the 1920's the System accepted new responsibilities. Also it abandoned its policy of reliance on eligible paper as an automatic device to control credit. With the development of open-market operations in 1922, it became an active participant in the credit market. The stock market boom culminating in the crash of 1929 revealed a weakness in the System's implements of control. The Reserve System wished to restrain the use of credit for speculation and to maintain relatively easy credit conditions for the rest of the economy. This it was unable to do.

Prior to the 1930's the nation did not regard fiscal policy as a legitimate device to stabilize economic conditions. Nevertheless, government financial operations had an effect on the level of economic activity.

QUESTIONS

1. How did the monetary policies in World War I differ from those followed in the American Revolution and in the Civil War? Did the different policies achieve the same results?
2. What were the objectives of monetary policy in the 1920's? Describe the policies designed to achieve each of these objectives.
3. Why did the 1927–1929 boom in the securities market present a special problem for the Federal Reserve System?
4. Discuss the reasons for the development of open-market operations by the Federal Reserve System.

SUGGESTED READINGS

Barger, Harold. *The Management of Money.* Chicago: Rand McNally & Company, 1964. Chapters 1–4.

Chandler, Lester V. *Benjamin Strong, Central Banker.* Washington, D. C.: The Brookings Institution, 1958.

Friedman, Milton, and Schwartz, Anna Jacobson. *A Monetary History of the United States 1867–1960.* Princeton: Princeton University Press, 1963. Chapters 5 and 6.

Studenski, Paul, and Krooss, Herman E. *Financial History of the United States.* 2d ed. New York: McGraw-Hill Book Company, Inc., 1963. Chapters 23–26.

Trescott, Paul B. *Financing American Enterprise.* New York: Harper & Row, Publishers, 1963. Chapter 9.

23

STABILIZATION POLICY, 1929–1940

The economic decline which began in 1929 continued with few pauses until early 1933. The accompanying tables show the extent of the decline in terms of gross national product, physical output, rate of unemployment, and price level. These tables show that recovery was slow and that it was incomplete at the beginning of World War II. The data suggest but do not describe the hardships suffered by the unemployed, the bankrupt, and the others sustaining a loss of income. Nor do they show the high rate of bank failures or the crisis in international finance — events which were the result of as well as a contributing cause of the depression. In the period under discussion, the rate of bank failures in the United States reached the crisis stage, international trade declined drastically, and conditions approaching chaos developed in the field of international finance.

Economic historians have difficulty explaining the reason for the length and severity of the depression. There was a variety of causes which, perhaps by coincidence, occurred in such an order as to produce a powerful cumulative effect. We are familiar with the cumulative process by which a decline in either investment or consumption expenditures leads to a further decline in income. In the 1930's, events such as bank failures and developments in the area of international trade added to the downward pressure. The nation had not developed adequate monetary and fiscal policies to correct business depressions nor was it philosophically ready to use them had they been available.

It is not our purpose to analyze the causes of the downturn in business nor the slow recovery. However, Table 23–2, which describes the decade in terms of modern income analysis, deserves examination. Note particularly that gross private domestic investment had almost disappeared in 1932 and had not recovered by the end of the decade. Consumption expenditures were much more stable and government purchases of goods and services declined very little during the downswing. The theory of income determination, which we discussed in earlier chapters, developed during the

Table 23–1

ECONOMIC INDICATORS

1929–1940

Year	GNP (in billions of dollars)	Index of Industrial Production (1935–1939 = 100)[a]	Per Cent of Labor Force Unemployed[b]	Wholesale Price Index (1926 = 100)[c]	Consumer Price Index (1939 = 100)[c]
1929	104.4	110	3.2	95.3	119.2
1930	91.1	91	8.7	86.4	115.1
1931	76.3	75	15.9	73.0	103.5
1932	58.5	58	23.6	64.8	92.5
1933	56.0	69	24.9	65.9	88.9
1934	65.0	75	21.7	74.9	94.1
1935	72.5	87	20.1	80.0	97.4
1936	82.7	103	16.9	80.8	99.5
1937	90.8	113	14.3	86.3	103.8
1938	85.2	89	19.0	78.6	101.1
1939	91.1	109	17.2	77.1	99.8
1940	100.6	125	14.6	78.6	100.6

[a]Board of Governors, Federal Reserve System, Index of Industrial production.
[b]United States Department of Labor estimates. Published in the *Economic Report of the President*.
[c]Bureau of Labor Statistics.
Source: National Industrial Conference Board, *The Economic Almanac, 1953–1954* (New York: Thomas Y. Crowell Company, 1953), pp. 85, 90, and 370.

Table 23–2

COMPONENTS OF GNP

1929–1940

(In billions of dollars)

Year	GNP	Personal Consumption Expenditures	Gross Private Domestic Investment	Net Exports of Goods and Services	Government Purchases of Goods and Services
1929	104.4	79.0	16.2	.8	8.5
1930	91.1	71.0	10.3	.7	9.2
1931	76.3	61.3	5.5	.2	9.2
1932	58.5	49.3	.9	.2	8.1
1933	56.0	46.4	1.4	.2	8.0
1934	65.0	51.9	2.9	.4	9.8
1935	72.5	56.3	6.3	−.1	10.0
1936	82.7	62.6	8.4	−.1	11.8
1937	90.8	67.3	11.7	.1	11.7
1938	85.2	64.6	6.7	1.1	12.8
1939	91.1	67.6	9.3	.9	13.3
1940	100.6	71.9	13.2	1.5	14.1

Source: United States Department of Commerce estimates. *Economic Report of the President* (Washington: Government Printing Office, 1965), p. 189.

period. Examination of Table 23–2 shows the reason for the emphasis this theory puts on determinants of the level of investment.

In this chapter we shall consider the problems, objectives of policy, and effectiveness of policy in terms of the theories we studied previously. In earlier chapters we stressed the importance of theory as a guide to policy. We shall retain that attitude.

DECLINE, 1929–1932

The National Bureau of Economic Research, which is the authority on dates of business cycles in the United States, places the beginning of the decline in August, 1929. The upswing began in March, 1933. Many events occurred during this period to make the depression more severe and to complicate the problem which confronted persons making policy decisions. Two of these complicating factors deserve study before we consider monetary and other policies of those years.

Bank Failures

The rate of bank failures, which had been high during the prosperous 1920's, increased during the depression. The primary cause was the existence of an excessive number of banks in relation to the volume of bank business. As a consequence, many of the banks were small and the weaker ones failed. As incomes of individuals and firms in debt to the banks declined, the number of bank failures rose. A vicious circle developed. The high rate of bank failures destroyed public confidence in the surviving banks and caused the withdrawal of deposits. This forced banks to restrict loans to business firms and contributed to the bankruptcy rate which led to more bank failures. By 1933 conditions reached the crisis stage. Many state governors declared bank holidays: a device which closed banks in the state and allowed them legally to suspend payments. As a result many of the banks which were still solvent were not open by the time President Roosevelt took office on March 4, 1933. Table 23–3 shows the record for this period.

Table 23–3

COMMERCIAL BANK SUSPENSIONS

1930–1933

		Number			
		Member Banks		Nonmember Banks	
Year	Total	National	State	State	Private
1930	1,350	161	27	1,104	58
1931	2,293	409	107	1,697	80
1932	1,453	276	55	1,085	37
1933	4,000	1,101	174	2,616	109
	9,096	1,947	363	6,502	284

Deposits (in millions of dollars)

Year	Total	Member Banks	Nonmember Banks	Estimated Loss to Depositors
1930	837.1	372.8	464.3	237.0
1931	1,690.4	733.2	957.2	391.0
1932	706.3	269.4	436.9	168.0
1933	3,596.7	2,393.9	1,202.8	540.0
	6,830.5	3,769.3	3,061.2	1,336.0

Source: Board of Governors, Federal Reserve System, *Banking and Monetary Statistics* (Washington, 1943), p. 283.

The Federal Reserve System was unable to correct this condition. It had no regulatory control over nonmember banks, nor could it prevent the issuance of a state charter to an institution in an area it considered "overbanked." Nevertheless, the rate of bank failures influenced the Reserve System's policy and to some extent nullified its effect.

The International Gold Standard

Most countries that had abandoned the gold standard during World War I had re-established it by 1929, and international trade and finance was operating on the gold standard by the beginning of 1930. By the end of 1930 several countries had again abandoned the gold standard. During 1931 and early 1932, the collapse of the international gold standard became complete as most of the world suspended payments in gold. The United States and France were two of the few exceptions.

An important cause of the breakdown was the worldwide depression. International lending virtually came to an end; moreover low prices and low incomes made it difficult for debtor nations to pay their debts, many of which were short-term or demand obligations. Under these conditions trouble spread rapidly. The immediate cause of panic was the failure of the largest bank in Austria. This failure stimulated withdrawals from banks in other countries and led to more failures. Many of the withdrawals were in gold, particularly those involving an international transaction. Gold withdrawals forced nations to suspend payment in gold. This impaired confidence, led to more withdrawals, and forced more nations to suspend payment in gold.

The United States did not leave the gold standard until 1933. Nevertheless, it felt the effect of the collapse of the international standard. Withdrawals from United States banks increased and contributed to the rate of bank failures. In addition, the rate of exchange of United States dollars for foreign currency shifted and discouraged exports. There was a psychological impact: as long as we regarded the maintenance of the gold standard as a desirable goal, the danger of a loss of gold affected our domestic policies.

Monetary Policy during the Decline— the Federal Reserve System

The stock market crash of 1929 removed the dilemma facing the Federal Reserve System, which followed an easy-money policy for the next two years. The System lowered the rediscount rate several times. The result was a drop from a high of 6 per cent to 1½ per cent by 1931. The Reserve banks also purchased securities on the open market and increased the volume of commercial paper they purchased from banks.

Let us consider these measures in terms of the quantity theory and the equation of exchange, $MV = PT$. We know that the objective was an increase in the price level and in the volume of trade. Quite logically the Reserve System encouraged an increase in the stock of money. In terms of the theory of income determination, which was to develop later in the decade, the System was attempting to increase investment expenditures and income by lowering the interest rate.

It is more difficult to justify the policy which began about September, 1931. The abandonment of the gold standard by England in that month led to withdrawals of gold from United States banks in September and succeeding months. These withdrawals caused commercial bank reserves to decline and forced the commercial banks to borrow from the Reserve banks. The Federal Reserve System could have balanced the effect of gold withdrawals with open-market purchases of securities. The System did not adopt this policy. Instead, the Reserve banks raised the rediscount rate. Consequently, the Federal Reserve System adopted a tight-money policy in the middle of a severe business depression.

By modern standards such a policy is hard to comprehend. At the time, however, maintenance of the gold standard remained an objective of monetary policy and fear of further withdrawals might have influenced the decision to tighten credit. The continuation of a tight-money policy in the face of worsening business conditions was the result of a structural defect in the Federal Reserve Act. In accordance with the true bills doctrine, the Federal Reserve Act required that Reserve banks have collateral for all outstanding Federal Reserve notes. Only gold and eligible paper discounted by commercial banks were acceptable as collateral. Because of the low level of business activity, eligible commercial paper was scarce. Accordingly, the Reserve banks had to use gold as collateral well beyond the 40 per cent minimum required by law. This placed the Reserve System in an odd position. It held gold reserves well in excess of the minimum legal ratio. Nevertheless, it could not use its excess gold reserves to expand credit. Open-market buying would have reduced the volume of member bank rediscounting and would have intensified the shortage of eligible paper. The Federal Reserve banks did not have sufficient gold reserves to allow them both to expand credit *and* to back Federal Reserve notes in excess of the 40 per cent minimum.

Congress solved the problem with the Glass-Steagall Act in February, 1932. This Act permitted the use of government securities as collateral for Federal Reserve notes. Hence, it effectively "re-leased" some of the gold held by the Reserve banks. In addition, the Act authorized advances to member banks on their promissory notes secured by any assets acceptable to the Federal Reserve banks. This allowed banks to discount their own notes in addition to rediscount-ing eligible paper. With the passage of the Act, the System began to purchase securities on the open market and lowered the discount rate. It continued this easy-money policy for the remainder of the period.

Monetary Policy during the Decline— Other Than the Federal Reserve System

During the decline several Government actions affected the monetary system. One reaction of the Administration to the decline was the denial of its existence. More precisely, the President and other national leaders frequently predicted an immediate and rapid recovery. We can analyze this form of moral suasion with the aid of the theory of income determination. Its purpose is to create optimis-tic expectations and thus to shift the MEC curve to the right. This action suggests that persons in responsible positions understood and applied certain policies in advance of the development of a formal theory explaining cause and effect.

In January, 1932, the passage of an act creating the Reconstruc-tion Finance Corporation provided more tangible assistance. The RFC loaned approximately $1\frac{1}{2}$ billion to commercial banks and others during 1932. The loans to banks reduced the rate of bank failures but did not prevent the eventual collapse of the banking system. Loans to nonbanks prevented some bankruptcies and fi-nanced some investment expenditures.

Fiscal Policy during the Decline

In Chapter 18 we noted the effect of changes in the level of net taxes and government expenditures on the level of income. This analysis suggests that an appropriate policy to halt an economic decline and to restore prosperity should include tax reduction and an increase in government spending. Neither the leaders of the nation nor the general public accepted this doctrine in the early 1930's. The Administration's first objective was to balance the budget. Its leaders believed that this evidence of fiscal integrity on the part of the Gov-ernment would restore business confidence and thus would consti-tute the first step toward recovery. To a modern observer, the causal relation between a business leader's confidence in the fiscal integrity of the Government and his willingness to expand his own business is not clear. At the time, however, this was the orthodox approach to fiscal policy. Accordingly, the Administration attempted to cut government expenditures and to raise taxes. In pursuit of this goal, the Congress provided for the largest peacetime tax increase in our history in the Revenue Act of 1932.

Despite these efforts, expenditures exceeded revenue for the years under discussion. The public debt data presented in Table 23–4 indicate the extent of deficit financing. The table shows that government followed an expansionary fiscal policy in practice despite efforts to do otherwise. A drastic decline in tax revenue as incomes declined was the main reason for the failure to balance the budget. In addition the President and Congress recognized the need for increased expenditures on certain programs. Examples are: public works, the RFC, and public welfare by the end of the period.

Table 23–4

NET PUBLIC DEBT, 1929–1933

(In billions of dollars)

Year	Total	Federal	State and Local
1929	29.7	16.5	13.2
1930	30.6	16.5	14.1
1931	34.0	18.5	15.5
1932	37.9	21.3	16.6
1933	41.0	24.3	16.7

Source: United States Department of Commerce. *Economic Report of the President* (Washington: Government Printing Office, 1965), p. 254.

Policy Effects

One can criticize the policy of the Federal Reserve System during the decline as being "too little and too late." On one occasion, of course, the System chose the wrong policy. The events of the period revealed defects in the structure of the Federal Reserve System and led to corrective legislation. The events of the period also destroyed any remaining tendency to base monetary policy on automatic controls. Finally, the reputation of the Federal Reserve System as an effective stabilizing device suffered. During the rest of the decade, its role was relatively unimportant.

Other actions, such as the creation of the RFC, had a positive effect but, like Federal Reserve actions, were "too little and too late." Fiscal policy in practice was slightly expansionary despite attempts to raise taxes and to reduce government spending.

RECOVERY, 1933–1940

These years, the era of the "New Deal," include two periods of recovery and one of recession. The Roosevelt Administration's program for recovery contained relief measures, reform legislation, monetary policy, and fiscal policy. During the first period of recovery, 1933–1937, emergency relief measures and changes in the monetary system were the chief instruments of policy. In the recovery following the recession of 1937–1938, fiscal policy became important. Also important during the period were changes in attitudes regarding government participation in the economy. We shall review the events prior to our evaluation of the policies of the recovery program.

Monetary Policy—Federal Reserve System, 1933–1940

Monetary policy using the implements of the Federal Reserve System did not play a significant role in the recovery. The discount rate was low at the beginning of the period. It declined further to 1½ per cent and remained at approximately the same level for the remainder of the decade. In 1933 the Reserve banks held approximately $2½ billion in United States securities as a result of earlier purchases on the open market. The figure changed only slightly during the years under review. This indicates an absence of net sales or purchases.

There was a reason for this passive role. From 1934 until the end of the decade, the commercial banks held reserves far in excess of their legal requirements. Because of this condition, a low discount rate was rather meaningless; commercial banks had little or no need to borrow from the Reserve banks. Open-market buying was also futile; it would only increase the volume of excess reserves. The commercial banks, holding more than adequate reserves, needed loan applicants; the Federal Reserve banks could not satisfy this need. The volume of loans by commercial banks remained constant during the period. Deposits increased, however, because the banks purchased United States securities with some of their excess reserves. This experience is the basis for the belief that monetary policy can control the economy in only one direction: a tight-money policy, if vigorously applied, will halt expansion and will even force contraction; however, easy-money policies cannot force expansion or stop contraction. These policies ensure that a supply of credit is available. They cannot ensure that the public will borrow and will spend the proceeds.

Legislation affecting the Federal Reserve System deserves mention. The legislative changes did not affect the immediate recovery program, but they gave the Board of Governors power to avoid trouble in the future. The Securities and Exchange Act of 1934 gave the Board of Governors the power to require a minimum margin when purchasing securities on credit. During the decade the Reserve authorities expressed concern over the excess reserves held by commercial banks. Open-market selling to reduce reserves did not seem wise pending full recovery. To solve the problem, Congress granted to the Board of Governors the power to vary reserve requirements. Also, the Federal Open Market Committee, which had been operating for over ten years, gained statutory recognition in 1935.

Other Monetary Policies

Monetary policy of the United States did not have to rely on the weapons available to the Federal Reserve System. If we think of monetary policy in the broad sense of any government action which affects the level of private spending, there were several courses of action available. During the recovery period, the Administration consistently tried to raise the level of commodity prices, acting on the premise that this would stimulate business activity. Some of the measures adopted, such as the National Recovery Administration (NRA), dealt with the structure of production and distribution methods. Other actions belong in the fiscal policy category, but many had their effect on the economy through the monetary system. We turn to these policies.

Reopening the banks. The most pressing monetary problem facing the new Administration in 1933 was the need to restore the commercial banking system to normal operations. As noted in a previous section, many banks had failed by March, many more were in danger of failing, and many of the surviving banks had closed in response to the bank holidays declared by state governors. President Roosevelt approached this problem by proclaiming a nationwide bank holiday which closed all banks. A bank could reopen only after an examination indicated that it was sound. This action was designed to combat the panic psychology of the public. From this point forward, the public could be confident that the banks which reopened would remain solvent. The banking system also received the support of the RFC and could secure emergency loans from the Reserve banks. A temporary deposit insurance system began operations in 1933. The FDIC replaced the temporary system in 1935.

The reform of the banking system was one of the more successful New Deal programs. During the period 1934-1940, bank failures declined to an average of 45 per year. Thus, the nation at long last had developed a banking system in which the public could deposit funds without fear. New Deal policies cannot claim all the credit since thousands of the weaker banks had been eliminated prior to the inception of these measures. Nevertheless, the changes in the system made a major contribution.

The gold policy. The gold policy was consistent with other attempts by the New Deal to stimulate the economy by raising commodity prices. The United States abolished the gold coin standard as soon as President Roosevelt took office in 1933. The Government suspended payments in gold, ordered private financial institutions to do the same, and required the public to turn all gold coins and certificates into the Treasury. The Treasury used its power as the major purchaser in the gold market to raise the price of gold from $20.67 to $35 per ounce. Or we could say that the dollar was devalued in terms of gold. The Government stabilized the price of gold at the higher level in 1934 and established the modified gold bullion standard which is still in effect.

Devaluation of the dollar in terms of gold did not automatically cause a general devaluation; that is, a rise in commodity prices. However, the suspension of gold payments removed some of the pressure from commercial banks. The elimination of the gold coin standard combined with the higher price for gold made possible an easy-money policy. Finally, devaluation of the dollar in terms of foreign currency discouraged imports and encouraged exports.

Raising the price of gold had the immediate effect of increasing the value of the stock of gold held by the Treasury. It also stimulated domestic gold production and the melting of scrap gold. Furthermore, the policy of the United States was responsible, at least in part, for the increase in foreign gold production. Because of a combination of conditions—the export surplus of the United States, political uncertainty, and fear of war abroad—the newly produced gold and much of the existing gold stock in foreign countries accumulated in the United States. As a result of this gold inflow, United States reserves far exceeded the amount needed as a basis for the monetary system. Table 23-5 shows the effect of all these events on the United States stock of gold.

Silver again. The monetary policy of the recovery period included the purchase of silver. Conditions in the 1930's were similar to those prevailing in the late nineteenth century when the silver policy had been a major issue. Again, silver prices were low, the silver industry was unprofitable, and the general economy was depressed. Silver advocates argued that the purchase of silver for monetary use would not only aid the silver industry but would raise the price level and would lead to economic recovery.

Table 23–5

GOLD STOCK OF THE UNITED STATES
1933–1940

(In billions of dollars)

Year As of December 31	Gold Stock[a]
1933	4.0
1934	8.2
1935	10.1
1936	11.3
1937	12.8
1938	14.5
1939	17.6
1940	22.0

[a]Gold valued at $20.67 per ounce for 1933; thereafter at $35 per ounce.
Source: Board of Governors of the Federal Reserve System, *Banking and Monetary Statistics* (Washington, 1943), p. 536.

There were some proposals for the unlimited purchase of silver, but the Administration selected a more moderate program. The Treasury bought limited quantities of silver. The purchase price varied but was above the market rate and favored domestic over foreign producers. By paying for the metal with silver certificates, the Treasury could claim that the policy cost the taxpayers nothing. The goal was a stock of silver, valued at $1.29 per ounce for this purpose, that would be equal in value to one fourth the monetary base of the United States. However, the rapid increase of the gold stock in this period caused the goal to recede despite heavy silver purchases.

The Treasury did not purchase as much silver nor pay as high a price as the silver interests desired. Nevertheless, the policy aided the silver mining industry at home and abroad. Otherwise, there were no positive results. The monetary system absorbed the silver certificates, but this had little or no effect on the commodity price level. The nation could have achieved the same increase in the money supply by issuing Federal Reserve notes or United States notes. Furthermore, the purchase of silver continued after World War

II and added to the inflationary pressure of that period. Officially, the Treasury did not withdraw its offer to buy silver until 1963.

The stock of money. These measures exhausted neither the proposals nor the legislative enactments designed to increase the supply of money. The Thomas amendment to the Agricultural Adjustment Act of 1933 authorized the President to issue up to $3 billion in greenbacks, to restore bimetallism, and to devalue the dollar further.[1] The President did not use any of these discretionary powers. Nevertheless, the money supply increased rapidly during these years in response to gold and silver purchases and actions of the banking system. Table 23–6 shows the increase in currency and deposits. The price level rose during these years but at a slower rate (see Table 23–1).

Table 23–6

UNITED STATES STOCK OF MONEY
1933–1940

(In billions of dollars)

Date (June 30)	Total Demand Deposits Adjusted and Currency Outside Banks	Demand Deposits Adjusted	Currency Outside Banks
1933	19.2	14.4	4.8
1934	21.4	16.7	4.7
1935	25.2	20.4	4.8
1936	29.0	23.8	5.2
1937	30.7	25.2	5.5
1938	29.7	24.3	5.4
1939	33.4	27.4	6.0
1940	38.7	32.0	6.7

Source: Board of Governors of the Federal Reserve System, *Banking and Monetary Statistics* (Washington, 1943), pp. 34–35.

An increase in spending was necessary if commodity prices and the level of output were to rise. A rise in the quantity of money, M, a more rapid rate of turnover, V, or some combination of the two, MV, could accomplish this objective. We have examined the policies

[1]Senator Thomas of Oklahoma achieved fame as a persistent advocate of measures to increase the money supply. He succeeded in attaching his famous "inflation" amendment as a rider to the Agricultural Adjustment Act which the President signed in May, 1933.

designed to increase the money supply. We turn next to Government credit agencies which encouraged a higher rate of turnover.

Government credit agencies. Creation of government credit agencies was an important feature of the New Deal era. The practice did not start at this time for the previous Administration had created the Reconstruction Finance Corporation. Also, we noted that similar institutions existed to serve agriculture as early as 1916. However, the Roosevelt Administration used them as a policy weapon more vigorously than its predecessors.

Congress authorized many of these institutions as emergency measures. They were to halt the panic and to break the vicious circle of bankruptcy. Accordingly, temporary agencies, such as the Home Owners Loan Corporation, bought mortgages to prevent foreclosures and made loans for investment projects that would not have been profitable at the market rate of interest. Others, such as the Federal Deposit Insurance Corporation and the Federal Housing Administration, were permanent. These institutions served to facilitate the movement and the spending of funds by correcting structural defects in the financial markets. We became familiar with many of these institutions in Chapter 20.

Regulation of financial institutions. Many of the government regulatory activities which we discussed in Chapter 20 had their origin in this period. Regulatory acts of government affected the recovery program by restoring public confidence in the financial system. The New Deal created one important agency, the Securities Exchange Commission, for a specific regulatory function. However, many other new federal credit agencies, such as the FDIC, developed into important regulatory bodies. In addition, the Federal Reserve System and other existing institutions gained new powers to regulate the financial market.

Fiscal Policy

The Roosevelt Administration inherited a favorable condition for the use of fiscal policy. Government spending had been relatively stable while GNP declined. Accordingly, the relative importance of the government sector and the influence of government financial activity in the economy had increased. However, the Roosevelt Administration did not accept the doctrine of active fiscal policy immediately upon taking office.

President Roosevelt campaigned for election on a platform pledging economy in government and a balanced budget. Upon taking office the Administration immediately increased the level of expenditures for unemployment relief and other welfare programs. Also, the numerous emergency credit agencies we have mentioned disbursed government funds. Furthermore, the Federal Government increased expenditures on public works and, through a system of grants, encouraged states and municipalities to increase public spending. The Administration justified these expenditures, however, on the premise that government spending was necessary to provide vital services. It was not a device to increase the level of GNP. The President apologized for the deficit and promised to balance the budget when the emergency passed. The best evidence of nonacceptance of the fiscal policy doctrine is the passage in 1933 and 1934 of bills increasing the rate of taxation. Since the burden fell on corporations and the high-income group, these taxes served to redistribute the wealth. This redistribution increased the marginal propensity to consume, but the chief motive for passage of the bills was a desire to increase revenue and decrease the deficit.

In 1937, we have another example of a tax increase in the midst of a depression. Again, the Administration attempted to balance the budget through a combination of higher taxes and reduced spending. Tables 23–1 and 23–2 show the results. GNP promptly declined and unemployment increased. Of course, factors other than fiscal policy contributed to this decline. Nevertheless, the incident apparently convinced the Administration of the relationship between government finance and the level of economic activity. After the recession of 1937–1938, government leaders accepted the idea that an active fiscal policy was an appropriate part of the recovery program. Budget deficits did not call forth an apology but rather an assertion that the policy contributed to employment. Table 23–7 shows the result of deficit financing in terms of an increase in the public debt. This table suggests that the New Deal applied an expansionary fiscal policy during the entire recovery period. What it does not show is the change in attitude. Prior to 1937, fiscal policy measures were a by-product of other Government actions. After that date the policy was deliberate.

The Government's fiscal policy led to partial but not full recovery. One explanation for this incomplete recovery is the Government's failure to be consistent in the period prior to 1937. We have already noted that tax increases cancelled part of the effect of increased expenditures during this period. In later years after administrative leaders better understood fiscal policy, they were unable or unwilling to increase sufficiently the magnitude of government spending to achieve full recovery. If the Government had attempted to do so, public distrust of deficit financing, particularly by the busi-

Table 23–7

NET PUBLIC DEBT, 1934–1940

(In billions of dollars)

Year	Total	Federal	State and Local
1934	46.3	30.4	15.9
1935	50.5	34.4	16.0
1936	53.9	37.7	16.2
1937	55.3	39.2	16.1
1938	56.5	40.5	16.0
1939	58.9	42.6	16.3
1940	61.3	44.8	16.5

Source: United States Department of Commerce. *Economic Report of the President* (Washington: Government Printing Office, 1965), p. 254.

ness community, might have led to a loss of confidence and might have nullified the effect of extremely heavy government spending. When the Government did spend heavily during World War II, recovery became complete, which suggests that a similar volume of expenditure might have produced the same results in the 1930's.

SUMMARY

In the years 1929–1933, the monetary policies of the Federal Reserve System failed to stop the decline into a depression. There was some confusion concerning the objectives. Also, the Reserve System was unable to intervene effectively because it operated within a framework designed to prevent excessive intervention in the private sector of the economy. Not until the ties to the "true bills" doctrine and the traditional gold standard had been broken could it operate freely.

In the period 1933–1940, the Administration used monetary and fiscal policy freely. Still the economy did not recover fully, although there were a number of successes. Government action overcame the bank panic, and the reform measures were generally successful in preventing future trouble. However, they did little to promote immediate recovery.

The effect of monetary policy was particularly disappointing. Throughout the recovery years, interest rates were low and the banks held excess reserves. Despite easy-money policies, the depression continued. One might conclude that monetary policy is of little use as a stabilizing device but this is hardly accurate. By the time the authorities applied an easy-money policy with consistency, the depression was so severe that stronger measures were needed. The experience emphasizes the lesson that monetary policy must be used promptly if it is to be effective.

Fiscal policy was at first accidental. Relief payments and other emergency measures caused the Government deficit to increase. Prior to 1937, the Government attempted to balance the budget by raising taxes. After the recession of 1937–1938, it followed a more consistent fiscal policy. Despite all these measures, recovery was not complete.

QUESTIONS

1. What were the causes for the high rate of bank failures during the years 1930–1933? Were bank failures the cause or the result of the business depression?
2. Use the data in Table 23–2 as the basis for a discussion of the relationship of the several components of GNP. Does the table serve as a good example of the multiplier?
3. Outline the monetary policies which the New Deal used in an effort to raise the level of prices. How effective were these policies?
4. How does fiscal policy differ from monetary policy?
5. Why was monetary policy ineffective in the period 1929–1933?

SUGGESTED READINGS

Barger, Harold. *The Management of Money*. Chicago: Rand McNally & Company, 1964. Chapter 5.

Friedman, Milton, and Schwartz, Anna Jacobson. *A Monetary History of the United States 1867–1960*. Princeton: Princeton University Press, 1963. Chapters 7–9.

Studenski, Paul, and Krooss, Herman E. *Financial History of the United States*. 2d ed. New York: McGraw Hill Book Company, Inc., 1963. Chapters 27–29.

Trescott, Paul B. *Financing American Enterprise*. New York: Harper & Row, Publishers, 1963. Chapter 9.

24

STABILIZATION POLICY SINCE 1940

Many changes in the monetary system and in monetary policy occurred during World War II and the decade which followed. Unlike the changes in the 1930's, these were not the result of Congressional acts altering the system. Rather, they were the result of changes in the application of existing monetary powers to new conditions. World War II began in Europe in September, 1939. From the summer of 1940 forward, defense and later war finance replaced the economic recovery program as the dominant influence on monetary and fiscal policy. In this chapter, we shall examine the methods of financing World War II and shall analyze the monetary results of this program. We shall consider the effect of these conditions on monetary policy and shall trace the development of that policy after the war.

FINANCING WORLD WAR II

World War II was extremely expensive. Government expenditures averaged $63 billion per year during the period 1942 to 1945. This is in striking contrast to the average of $7.6 billion during the last five years of the 1930's—a period in which government spending had been at record peacetime levels. Consequently, the nation had difficulty comprehending the vast quantities of money which the war would require and there was the usual tendency to underestimate the cost. Nevertheless, the nation realized that the war would be costly.

With the experience of World War I in mind, the country recognized the desirability of financing a war in a noninflationary manner. The Congress increased tax rates and imposed new levies. These higher rates and new levies combined with rising incomes to produce record government revenues which, nevertheless, paid for no more than one-half the cost of the war. This represented an improvement over previous experiences, but the Treasury still had to borrow $210 billion. Hence, fiscal policy, motivated by the need to finance the war and not by the desire to stabilize the economy, was the dominant factor in the economy during these years. Table 24–1 shows the dollar volume of Treasury receipts and expenditures. For this table we use the consolidated cash statement of the Treasury since the cash inflow and outflow which it records reflect the influence of government finance on GNP more accurately than the administrative budget. The latter includes as government expenses transfers to trust funds, such as social security accounts and other items, which are not expenditures. After 1940 the difference between the administrative budget and the consolidated cash statement is large enough to be significant.

Table 24–1

CONSOLIDATED CASH STATEMENT OF THE
UNITED STATES TREASURY, 1941–1946

(In billions of dollars)

Fiscal Year	Receipts	Payments	Cash Surplus (+) or Deficit (−)
1941	9.2	14.0	−4.8
1942	15.1	34.5	−19.4
1943	25.1	78.9	−53.8
1944	47.8	94.0	−46.1
1945	50.2	95.2	−45.0
1946	43.5	61.7	−18.2

Source: *The Budget of the United States Government, Fiscal Year Ending June 30, 1966* (Washington, 1965), p. 491.

The Treasury had two objectives in financing the deficit. It wished to borrow at low rates of interest and to avoid methods which would expand the money supply. Unfortunately, these objectives required policy measures which conflicted with each other under the conditions prevailing during the war. To avoid monetary expansion, the Treasury borrowed the savings of the private sector of the economy. It conducted a vigorous campaign to sell savings bonds, also known as Series E bonds, to individuals. These nonmarketable bonds were (and still are) redeemable on demand for the purchase price plus accrued interest. The nonmarketable redemption-on-demand feature avoided the problem which had occurred after World War I when the decline in bond prices had led to hardship and to bitterness on the part of bondholders unfamiliar with the practices of financial markets. However, these bonds were liquid assets and, as a result of this feature, a potential source of inflationary pressure. The Treasury absorbed additional private saving by selling conventional type bonds to individuals, financial intermediaries, and corporations with excess cash. Table 24–2 shows the amounts held by the several classes of savers at the beginning and at the end of the war. Unfortunately, the increase in the holdings of these groups was insufficient to finance the deficit.

Table 24–2

UNITED STATES GOVERNMENT SECURITIES HELD
BY THE PUBLIC EXCLUDING COMMERCIAL BANKS
1941, 1945

(In billions of dollars)

End of Year	Total	Mutual Savings Banks	Insurance Companies	Other Corporations
1941	31.1	3.7	8.2	4.0
1945	136.6	10.7	24.0	22.2

End of Year	State and Local Governments	Individuals		Foreign and Miscellaneous
		Savings Bonds[a]	Other Securities	
1941	.7	5.4	8.2	.9
1945	6.5	42.9	21.2	9.0

[a]Some of the difference between 1941 and 1945 represents accrued interest and not net sales of savings bonds. Source: *Federal Reserve Bulletins.*

Of necessity the Treasury had to resort to bank credit. Unlike World War I, it did not encourage individuals to borrow from banks in order to buy government bonds; it sold securities directly to the commercial banks. At the beginning of the period, the banks held excess reserves but these were not sufficient to support the war-induced expansion of credit. However, the Reserve banks purchased any securities which the market could not absorb. The purchases increased commercial bank reserves, and these institutions responded by buying more government securities.

At the beginning of the war the Federal Reserve authorities agreed to co-operate with the Treasury to maintain the structure of low interest rates then prevailing. They achieved this by a simple policy: the Reserve banks agreed to buy or to sell at a fixed price all government securities offered to them. The "fixed price" was set to produce the desired structure of interest rates. This was the policy popularly known as "pegging" the price of government securities. It is important to note that the Federal Reserve System did more than simply maintain a low average rate of interest. It maintained the pre-war structure of interest rates on United States securities. These rates ranged from a low of ⅜ of 1 per cent on 90-day bills to a high of 2½ per cent on securities of the longest maturity. Thus, the "pegging" operation carried the structure of interest rates, which was the result of market conditions and monetary policy in the depression, into the inflationary period of the war and postwar years. Since the Government was issuing securities in excess of the ability of the private sector of the market to absorb them, the Reserve banks purchased the excess. The Reserve System's agreement to buy all securities offered to Reserve banks caused long- and short-term issues to be equally liquid. As a result the private sector purchased the high yield, long-term issues and the Reserve banks absorbed a large portion of the 90-day bills. The Treasury, incidentally, borrowed money throughout the war at an average interest cost of approximately 2 per cent.

In effect the Reserve System was using open-market operations to maintain market rates of interest favorable to the Treasury. As a consequence, it lost its ability to use this and other policy implements to achieve other objectives, particularly to curb inflation. In supporting the Treasury's low interest rate policy, the banking system including the Reserve banks became a device for expanding the money supply. Table 24–3a shows the results in terms of demand deposits and currency. In Table 24–3b we see that the

Table 24–3a

UNITED STATES STOCK OF MONEY
1941, 1945

(In billions of dollars)

At End of Year	Total Demand Deposits Adjusted and Currency Outside Banks	Demand Deposits Adjusted	Currency Outside Banks
1941	48.6	39.0	9.6
1945	102.3	75.9	26.5

Table 24–3b

SELECTED ASSETS AND LIABILITIES OF COMMERCIAL BANKS[a]
1941, 1945

(In billions of dollars)

At end of Year	Cash and Due from Banks	Private Loans and Investments	U. S. Securities	Demand Deposits Adjusted	Time Deposits
1941	26.6	28.9	21.8	39.0	15.9
1945	34.8	33.4	90.6	75.9	30.1

[a]Demand deposits adjusted *exclude* United States Treasury deposits. Consequently the increase in assets is larger than the increase in liabilities indicated by this table.

Table 24–3c

SELECTED ASSETS AND LIABILITIES
TWELVE FEDERAL RESERVE BANKS
1941, 1945
(In billions of dollars)

At end of Year	Gold Certificates	Discounts	"Other" Federal Reserve Credit	U. S. Securities
1941	22.7	[a]	.1	2.3
1945	20.1	.2	.6	24.3

At end of Year	Federal Reserve Notes	Deposits, Member Banks	Deposits, U. S. Treasury	Deposits, "Other"
1941	8.2	12.5	.8	1.6
1945	24.6	15.9	1.0	1.8

[a]Less than $50 million. Source: *Federal Reserve Bulletins.*

purchase of United States securities and not the extension of credit to private borrowers was the main reason for the increase in deposits. It also shows the increase in time deposits, a liquid asset. Table 24–3c shows that an increase in government securities in the asset column was the basis for the Reserve banks' increase in Federal

Reserve notes outstanding and member bank deposit liabilities. Together the three tables support the statement that the government deficit led to an increase in the money supply.

Effect of War Finance Policies

Wartime conditions led to inflation but the rise in the price level was not in proportion to the increase in the stock of money. In Table 24–4 we see that the consumer price level rose approximately 20 per cent while the stock of money increased over 100 per cent. Also, Table 24–4 permits us to note one reason for this relatively moderate inflation. At the beginning of the period, the nation was not utilizing all of its productive capacity. Consequently, the nation was

Table 24–4

ECONOMIC INDICATORS, 1941–1945

(Stock of Money and GNP in billions of dollars)

Year	Stock of Money[a]	GNP Current Dollars	GNP in Dollars of Constant Value (1939)
1941	48.6	125.8	115.5
1942	62.9	159.1	129.7
1943	79.6	192.5	145.7
1944	90.4	211.4	156.9
1945	102.3	213.6	153.4

Year	Consumer Price Index (1939 = 100)	Wholesale Price Index (1926 = 100)	Per Cent of Labor Force Unemployed
1941	105.8	87.3	9.9
1942	117.1	98.8	4.7
1943	123.8	103.1	1.9
1944	125.4	104.0	1.2
1945	127.4	105.8	1.9

[a]Currency outside banks and demand deposits adjusted as of end of year. Source: Stock of Money, United States Department of Commerce; *Historical Statistics of the United States* (Washington: 1958); others, *Economic Report of the President* (Washington: Government Printing Office, 1964).

able to increase production in response to the rise in expenditures. The "per cent of labor force unemployed" and "GNP in constant dollars" columns, respectively, reflect the full utilization of resources and increased output.

During this period, velocity declined. This decline was the result in part of the public's willingness to hold larger cash balances. Also, the Federal Reserve System used its power to apply selective controls. This limited the use of credit for the purchase of consumer goods and real estate. The Government used direct controls to place ceilings on the price of many commodities, to regulate wages, and to allocate certain scarce resources. These measures suppressed much of the inflationary pressure during the war. The private sector of the economy used its high income to retire debt, to build large cash balances, and to acquire liquid assets such as United States savings bonds, time deposits, and shares in savings and loan associations.

World War II is another example of financing government expenditures by printing money. We observed this process first in the American Revolution and again in the Civil War. The development of commercial banks and the Federal Reserve System tends to conceal the process. Nevertheless, "currency outside banks" increased by $17 billion. A much larger increase occurred in "demand deposits adjusted." Of course, the expansion of demand deposits has the same effect as the printing of Continentals or Greenbacks.

THE POSTWAR PERIOD, 1946–1953

World War II furnishes an additional example of measures to further war objectives receiving a higher priority than anti-inflation policies. However, a study of the years immediately following the war is probably of greater value to us if we wish to enhance our understanding of current monetary problems and policies.

Conditions at the End of the War

At the end of the war, several conditions combined to create intense inflationary pressure. These conditions had existed during the war but direct controls had kept them in check. As the war progressed the private sector of the economy accumulated a large cash balance. Also, it expanded its holdings of liquid assets, such as United States savings bonds and time deposits. Since private incomes remained high at the end of the war, the private sector was in an excellent position to spend money. A desire to spend money existed because of a backlog of demand for consumer and investment goods. Throughout the depression years, consumers and businesses deferred the purchase of some durable consumer goods and industrial equipment. This deferment continued during the war when such goods were unavailable.

While the war continued, this combination of high incomes plus the need for goods did not produce its full effect on the price level because of direct controls. There was general agreement on a clearly defined objective for the economic system — namely, winning the war. Consequently, the direct control of prices and resource allocation by the Government was reasonably successful. With the end of the war, there was no longer general agreement on what the economy should produce nor who should receive the output. Public resistance to the system of direct controls increased. The controls disappeared by the end of 1946. This return to a market-oriented economy released the inflationary pressures and the price level rose as Table 24 – 5 indicates.

Table 24 – 5

PRICE LEVEL CHANGES

1945 – 1951

Year	Wholesale Price Index (1947 – 1949 = 100)	Consumer Price Index (1947 – 1949 = 100)
1945	68.8	76.9
1946	78.7	83.4
1947	96.4	95.5
1948	104.4	102.8
1949	99.2	101.8
1950	103.1	102.8
1951	114.8	111.0

Source: Bureau of Labor Statistics, *Historical Statistics of the United States* (Washington, 1958).

Fiscal Policy, 1946 – 1950

During the closing months of World War II, a number of economists had predicted massive unemployment in postwar years. The passage of time proved that their forecasts were grossly inaccurate. There was a slight decline in GNP in 1946 as industry adjusted to the production of peacetime commodities but this decline was temporary. Unemployment did not exceed 4 per cent of the labor force during the immediate postwar years. Nevertheless, the forecasts of unemployment influenced public opinion, which was not receptive to measures to control inflation. Contributing to this attitude was the recent experience of the 1930's. After a decade of depression, there was a tendency to regard severe unemployment as the normal peacetime condition. This public attitude plus other difficulties prevented the adoption of effective fiscal policy measures.

By 1947 the Federal Government had reduced cash expenditures to $36.9 billion, roughly one third of the wartime level. The new role of the United States as leader of the free world combined with troubled conditions abroad prevented further declines. Nevertheless, beginning in 1947, the cash statement of the Treasury showed a surplus. This surplus would have been larger if the Congress had not reduced tax rates in 1948. This example of a tax cut in the middle of a period of inflation is evidence that the public did not fully accept the idea that the nation should use fiscal policy to stabilize the economy. It also suggests a lack of confidence in the theory of income determination which is the basis for this policy.

During this period the income and expenditure pattern of state and local government was similar to the private sector. Like individuals and business firms, these governmental units had deferred replacements and new construction during the war. However, the deficit of state and local units did not equal the cash surplus of the Federal Government. Consequently, the fiscal policies of government, including all units, was slightly deflationary.

Shortly after the end of the war, Congress passed the Employment Act of 1946. Through this Act the Federal Government formally recognized the need to use its fiscal powers in the interest of economic stability. Framers of the Act showed more concern for the danger of unemployment than inflation; consequently the Act did little to influence the Government's policies immediately. In later years the provisions for a Council of Economic Advisers and annual reports to the Congress have increased the Government's interest in economic stability.

Monetary Policy, 1946–1950

Facing a substantial rise in the level of prices, a central bank which desires to control inflation normally initiates a tight-money policy. Accordingly, we should expect the Federal Reserve System to use some combination of higher discount rates, open-market selling, and increased reserve requirements to apply downward pressure to the monetary system through commercial bank reserves. However, the Reserve System was unable to use these measures because of its commitment to support the debt management policy of the Treasury. The situation was similar to the one prevailing at the end of World War I. In both wars, the Federal Reserve System became an instrument of Treasury finance; in both cases, it had difficulty regaining an independent status.

The Treasury Department's motives in opposing tight money were obvious. Since much of the Government debt was short-term (90-day bills), the Treasury was refunding a portion of the debt constantly. Accordingly, a rise in the market rate of interest would have raised the cost of debt service immediately. Another portion of the debt consisted of securities with longer maturities. A rise in the market rate of interest would have caused these issues to decline in value since prospective buyers could purchase new securities with higher coupon rates. Many individuals and institutions purchased these securities while the Federal Reserve System was supporting their price. The Treasury and persons who shared its point of view claimed that the nation would be breaking faith with these buyers if the System permitted bond prices to decline. Furthermore, the opponents of tight money cited the poor record of monetary policy in the depression. They claimed that monetary policy was ineffective as a stabilizing device. Hence, the only result of tight money would be a rise in the cost of debt management and increased profits for banks and other lending agencies. Accordingly, the Reserve System continued to "peg" the price of government bonds.

These years illustrate the difficulties a central bank faces when it uses its powers to support the Treasury's debt management policy. As long as the Federal Reserve System "pegged" the price of government securities, it had no power to curtail the expansion of bank credit. It could not use three implements of policy effectively. Raising the discount rate would have been meaningless since the commercial banks held $90 billion in government securities. Any bank needing additional reserves could have sold government securities and thus could have avoided borrowing. Since the Reserve System "pegged" the price, the bank had no fear of a capital loss when it sold securities. It was certain of a buyer which might in fact be a Reserve bank. Open-market operations supported the price of government securities. Hence, the Reserve System could not sell on the open market to reduce bank reserves since this would have depressed security prices. Reserve requirements were near the legal maximum so there was little to gain by raising them. All that remained was moral suasion and selective controls.

The Board of Governors used selective controls to restrict the flow of credit to the stock market and, until 1947, to consumer purchases. The System raised the discount rate with little effect for

reasons noted previously. The System also raised reserve requirements to their legal ceiling but this caused banks to sell government
securities and did not force them to borrow from Reserve banks nor
to curtail credit.

Until 1947 the Reserve System maintained the wartime pattern
of interest yields on government securities. In that year the Treasury
agreed to higher rates for short-term securities, but it did not allow
the yield on long-term securities to rise above 2½ per cent. This
monetary policy permitted postwar inflation to run its course with
little interference. In early 1949 the nation began to experience a
mild recession. This event temporarily solved the Reserve System's
problem of objectives requiring opposite policies. The Federal
Reserve System moved in the direction of monetary ease: a policy
which served both to halt the recession and to facilitate Treasury
debt management. Consequently, the growing disagreement between
the Treasury Department and the Federal Reserve authorities disappeared temporarily.

The Fighting in Korea— the Accord of 1951

Recovery from the recession was well underway by June of 1950
when fighting broke out in Korea. Inflationary pressures developed
immediately. Government expenditures did not rise appreciably
until late in the year; however consumer and business buying
increased immediately in anticipation of shortages and price rises.
The stock of money increased from $111 billion in December, 1949, to
$117 billion by December 31, 1950. Commercial banks were able to
expand credit because they could sell government securities to
secure reserves. Thus, monetary policy failed to restrain credit
expansion and effectively curb inflation. Of necessity the Reserve
System imposed selective controls on consumer credit, and the
Government applied direct controls to prices. Furthermore, velocity
increased as the public used its high cash balances to finance its
purchasing activity. The public also converted liquid assets, like
savings deposits, into money for its spending program. Table 24–6
shows the increase in the price level from June, 1950, to June, 1951.

The presence of inflationary pressures led to a renewal of the
controversy which had been developing between the Treasury
Department and the Federal Reserve System. The Treasury faced
the task of financing the fighting in Korea. The record indicates that
the Government pursued a sound fiscal policy. Cash payments to the
public rose from $43.1 billion in fiscal year 1950 to $76.8 billion in
fiscal year 1953. However, an increase in the rate of taxation com-

bined with a rise in the income level increased the Government's cash receipts by a larger amount. As a result the cash statement of the Government showed a $2 billion surplus during the years of the Korean fighting even though there was a deficit in the administrative budget. Consequently, the Federal Government's fiscal policy did not add to the inflationary pressure.

Table 24–6

PRICE LEVEL CHANGES

June, 1950 – June, 1951

Date	Consumer Prices (1947 – 1949 = 100)	Wholesale Prices (1947 – 1949 = 100)
June, 1950	101.8	100.2
July, 1950	102.9	103.0
Aug., 1950	103.7	105.2
Sept., 1950	104.5	107.1
Oct., 1950	105.0	107.7
Nov., 1950	105.5	109.3
Dec., 1950	107.0	112.1
Jan., 1951	108.6	115.0
Feb., 1951	110.0	116.5
Mar., 1951	110.4	116.5
April, 1951	110.4	116.3
May, 1951	110.9	115.9
June, 1951	110.8	115.1

Source: United States Department of Commerce and the Bureau of Labor Statistics. Published in *Survey of Current Business.*

Of course, it was difficult to foresee this course of events in 1950 and the Treasury was anxious to maintain low interest rates. The Federal Reserve System continued to support the price of government securities during 1950 but it was becoming increasingly restive. Despite the opposition of the Federal Reserve System, the Treasury continued to issue securities bearing low interest rates. Early in 1951 the Treasury announced that the existing pattern of low interest rates would continue. Furthermore, it claimed that the Federal Reserve System would support this policy. When the Reserve authorities denied this claim, the controversy came to the public's attention. The result was the famous "Accord" of March, 1951. In the Accord the Treasury and the Reserve authorities agreed that the Reserve System should renounce any rigid commitment to support bond prices at par, although it would use its powers to maintain "orderly conditions" in the government securities market. The Reserve authorities also agreed to hold discount rates at their current level of 1¾ per cent for another year. The Treasury, in turn, agreed to consider the views of the Reserve officials in its debt management policy and to issue bonds with higher coupon rates.

Development of Policy After the Accord

The immediate result of the Accord was the abandonment of the Reserve System's program supporting the prices of government securities. This change was overdue. A reasonable defense of the program was possible in the early postwar years when the public debt accounted for a larger portion of the total debt than it did by 1950. Also, the owners of long-term government securities in the early postwar years were persons who had purchased them during the war with the implicit understanding that securities prices would be "pegged" for several years. By 1951 these reasons for "pegging" were no longer valid.

A more significant result of the Accord was the reaffirmation of the principle that a central bank should be independent of Treasury control. After the Accord the Reserve System was free to adopt policies to stabilize the level of prices and to achieve other economic goals. The System did not renounce all assistance to the Treasury; however objectives of debt management no longer received top priority. Instead, support of Treasury objectives became one of several goals of the Reserve System's monetary policy.

Prior to the Accord pressures in the financial markets tended to force interest rates upward. Honoring the terms of the Accord, the Reserve System prevented a sharp increase in the rates on government securities; however it did allow a gradual increase. Interest rates in the private sector moved upward at the same time. The Reserve banks, maintaining an "orderly" market, continued to buy large quantities of government securities during the first half of 1951. After that date purchases declined.

By the end of the fighting in Korea in July, 1953, the money supply had increased by $14.4 billion. The Reserve banks had acquired an additional $6.7 billion in government securities; however most of this increase occurred before the end of 1951. The purchase of these securities expanded commercial bank reserves and permitted the expansion of demand deposits; nevertheless the free reserves of commercial banks declined because of credit expansion. Consequently, banks began to use the Reserve System's discount facilities and the discount rate regained some of its status as an implement of policy. Also, the composition of commercial bank assets had been changing in the years following World War II. Banks had reduced their holdings of United States securities and had acquired private loans and investments. Consequently, the banks and their clients were more sensitive to changes in the interest rate by 1953 than they had been in the late 1940's.

PROBLEMS AND POLICIES, 1953–1961

Monetary policy had not been an effective stabilizing device during the severe business depression of the 1930's. During World War II and the postwar period, the commitment to support the Treasury's debt management program blocked the use of policies to counter inflation. After the Accord and the end of the fighting in Korea, the Federal Reserve System had its first opportunity in twenty years to test the effectiveness of monetary policy under "normal" conditions. The Eisenhower Administration affirmed its intention to use fiscal policy to stabilize the economy if necessary; however it seemed to prefer the use of monetary policy. Also, the general attitude of the leaders of the Administration suggested that they would be less opposed to high interest rates than their predecessors. Consequently, there was greater opportunity for monetary policy.

The period which followed was a prosperous one as Table 24–7 indicates. Personal incomes and corporate profits were high. The consumer price index moved upward slowly from 93.2 in 1953 to 104.2 in 1961—a phenomenon that became known as "creeping inflation." However, some of this apparent inflation was the result of imperfections in the construction of index numbers. More disturbing was the rate of unemployment which fluctuated between a low of 2.9 per cent and a high of 6.8 per cent of the labor force. The combination of "creeping" inflation and persistent unemployment was a challenge to officials responsible for stabilization policy. Measures which corrected one problem tended to aggravate the other.

New theories developed in response to these twin problems. The "cost-push" theory of inflation de-emphasized the importance of monetary factors as a cause of inflation. Advocates of the "cost-push" thesis rejected the traditional theory that excessive demand relative to supply was the cause of inflation. They claimed that monopolistic elements in the economy forced prices upward by withholding goods and services from the market. The theory provided a plausible explanation for the existence of chronic unemployment and a slow but persistent upward movement of prices. Also if the "cost-push" thesis is correct, credit restraint will not prevent price increases but it will increase the rate of unemployment. A related theory regarded mod-

Table 24-7

ECONOMIC INDICATORS, 1953–1961

(GNP and Gold Stock in billions of dollars)

Year	GNP	GNP in Dollars of Constant Value (1954)	Consumer Price Index (1957–1959 = 100)	Wholesale Price Index (1957–1959 = 100)	Unemployment as a Per Cent of the Labor Force	Gold Stock[a]
1953	365.4	369.0	93.2	92.7	2.9	22.1
1954	363.1	363.1	93.6	92.9	5.6	21.8
1955	397.5	392.7	93.3	93.2	4.4	21.8
1956	419.2	400.9	94.7	96.2	4.2	22.1
1957	442.8	408.6	98.0	99.0	4.3	22.9
1958	444.5	401.3	100.7	100.4	6.8	20.6
1959	482.7	428.6	101.5	100.6	5.5	19.5
1960	502.6	439.9	103.1	100.7	5.6	17.8
1961	518.7	447.9	104.2	100.3	6.7	16.9

[a]Value as of the end of the year.
Source: *Economic Report of the President* (Washington: Government Printing Office, 1965).

erate inflation as necessary in order to stimulate economic growth and to prevent excessive unemployment. Advocates of this theory rationalized that a moderate degree of inflation — for example, a price rise of 1½ or 2 per cent per year — would not inflict undue hardship on debtors and the fixed-income group.

Fiscal Policy, 1953–1961

Although the Eisenhower Administration promised to use fiscal policy to counteract economic recession if necessary, it was committed philosophically to a reduction in government expenditures and to a curtailment of the role of the Government in the economy. The Administration lowered tax rates to the pre-1950 levels and attempted a substantial reduction in Federal Government expenditures. There was a temporary contraction in government spending between 1953 and 1955. After the latter date the costs of government rose in response to demands of the cold war and the need for social services. During these years state and local government expenditures doubled so that the increase in expenditures for all levels of government was sizable. Receipts did not equal expenditures for the Federal Government or the state and local units. Consequently, fiscal policy had an expansionary effect during the period. Table 24–8 on page 436 presents statistical data to support the statement. The table also serves to introduce a new concept in government accounting. Government receipts and expenditures in the national income accounts differ from T_n and G because of transfer payments. For certain purposes, Table 24–8 is a better indicator of the extent of government influence than the tables in Chapter 15.

New Problems

During the second half of the period, new problems developed. The attempts to reduce government spending led to controversy. This text has stressed the effect of government spending on the aggregate demand for products and hence on the level of GNP. Opponents of the reduction in government spending did not confine their criticism to this issue. They also cited the allocation of resources between the private and the public sector of the economy. Reduced expenditures by government caused the ratio of private to public goods to increase. The critics claimed that this led to an improper balance and to a neglect of vital social services. The choice between private and public goods and services obviously involves a value judgment, and we shall not attempt to explore the entire question. However, we must realize that the decision affects the Government's ability to use fiscal policy as a stabilizing device.

The balance of payments deficit. The United States had experienced a deficit in its balance of payments for every year between 1950 and 1961 with the exception of 1957. The deficit caused little concern prior to 1958 since it had not led to a major outflow of gold. In that year the United States lost over $2 billion in gold reserves and the outflow of gold became a problem. We shall examine this problem in some detail in Chapter 25. At this point we need only note that a tight monetary policy, which is the orthodox reaction to a gold outflow, was of questionable wisdom because of the persistent problem of unemployment.

Table 24–8

GOVERNMENT RECEIPTS AND EXPENDITURES IN
NATIONAL INCOME ACCOUNTS

1953–1961

(In billions of dollars)

Year	Federal Government		State and Local Government		Surplus (+) or Deficit (−) All Units
	Receipts	Expenditures	Receipts	Expenditures	
1953	70.3	77.7	27.4	27.1	−7.1
1954	63.8	69.6	29.1	30.1	−6.7
1955	72.8	68.9	31.7	32.7	+2.9
1956	77.5	71.8	35.2	35.7	+5.2
1957	81.7	79.7	38.8	39.6	+1.0
1958	78.5	87.9	42.0	44.1	−11.4
1959	90.3	91.4	46.6	47.0	−1.5
1960	96.6	93.1	50.4	50.0	+3.9
1961	98.3	102.6	54.5	54.4	−4.2

NOTE: Federal grants-in-aid to state and local governments are reflected in Federal expenditures and state and local receipts and expenditures. This duplication does not affect the net surplus or deficit.
Source: *Economic Report of the President* (Washington: Government Printing Office, 1965), p. 262.

The rate of economic growth. The rate of economic growth in the United States arose as a controversial issue shortly after the gold outflow problem became serious. It is impossible to measure the rate of economic growth with complete objectivity. Nevertheless, we may agree that GNP measured in dollars of constant value is the best single indicator of growth. Depending on the choice of initial and terminal years, however, the annual rate of growth varies. Obviously, the selection of an ideal rate, against which we measure the record of growth, involves a value judgment. The technical details concerning the controversy over the measurement of economic growth are beyond the scope of this text. We shall simply note the arguments of the group which alleged that the United States was growing too slowly.

Unemployment. The high level of unemployment during the years 1954–1960 was the basis for the criticism. The rate of unemployment averaged 5.2 per cent of the labor force during these years. At the same time unused capacity for production existed in the nation's industrial plants. The critics claimed that these unused resources represented capacity for growth. Furthermore, they alleged that the causes of this waste were a restrictive monetary policy and a fiscal policy whose objective was a balanced budget rather than full utilization of resources. If we accept this criticism as valid, we should note that the obvious solutions to the problem are a less restrictive monetary policy, increased government expenditures, and a reduction in taxes. These policies are the opposite of those we should recommend as a solution to the problems of the gold outflow and "creeping" inflation.

With this background we can understand that the Federal Reserve authorities did not face *a* problem nor could they devise *a* policy to achieve a single objective. There were several problems and several desirable objectives which might require contradictory policies. These objectives were:

1. Co-operation with the Treasury in the latter's debt management program. The Accord permitted flexibility in this program but the System was to maintain an orderly market.
2. Promotion of a high and sustained rate of economic growth.
3. Maintenance of a condition of full employment.
4. Maintenance of a stable level of prices. This objective and the two preceding ones became formal responsibilities as a result of the Employment Act of 1946.
5. Maintenance of the value of the United States dollar in international trade. This objective involved the maintenance of the monetary gold reserve.

These objectives continue to be the guide for policy in the 1960's.

Monetary Policy, 1953–1961

The Reserve System followed the logical, or textbook, pattern for central bank policy during these years. In general terms its actions were countercyclical: easy money during an economic recession and tighter credit conditions during prosperity. Open-market operations became the chief policy implement. The System employed open-market sales and purchases to counteract seasonal fluctuations in the credit market and changes resulting from variations in the "float" and the gold outflow. It sold securities in early 1953 and purchased them in the recession which began later in the year. It made purchases again during the recessions of 1957–1958 and 1960. During the recovery period of 1955, it sold securities. In other prosperous periods it restrained the expansion of credit by holding a constant volume of securities in the face of increased demands for credit—a policy of "leaning against the wind."

The discount rate became an effective weapon once more as declining reserve ratios forced member banks to borrow from the Reserve banks. The Reserve System raised discount rates in the prosperous periods of 1953, 1956, 1957, and 1959. It lowered the rates in the recession periods of 1954, 1958, and 1960. The overall movement was upward as rates rose from a range of 1¾ to 2 per cent in 1953 to 3 per cent in 1961.

Use of reserve requirements as a monetary weapon was de-emphasized. Of necessity, reserve requirements had been employed when the use of open-market operations had been rendered ineffective by the support of the government security market. During the period 1953–1961 reserve requirements were reduced in 1953, 1954, 1958, and 1960, all years of recession. They were not raised in the prosperous years. As a result the reserve requirements receded from their legal ceiling and the Reserve System acquired the ability to use them in the future.

At the same time, the Board of Governors reduced the number of selective controls. Like the use of reserve requirements, selective controls had been necessary expedients when open-market operations were impractical. The System discontinued controls over consumer and real estate credit in 1952. It continued to impose margin requirements on the purchase of securities since it regarded this segment of the credit market as a special area.

Early in the period the Reserve System modified its debt management objective from "maintaining an orderly market" to "preventing disorderly conditions" in the government securities market. Neither of these phrases has a precise meaning but in practice the Reserve System acquired greater freedom for permitting fluctuations in the price of securities in the latter case. Also early in the period, the System announced its intention of confining open-market operations to transactions in short-term securities, mostly 90-day bills. Reserve officials claimed that this "bills only" policy would permit a more rapid development of a broad, private market in long-term government securities. Also the open-market operations would have less immediate effect on the owners of government securities. Interventions in the bill market would influence the interest rate but this would not cause large capital gains or losses because of the short maturity of the issues involved. Of course, Reserve policies caused easy or tight conditions in the credit market and thus indirectly influenced the price of long-term securities.

As a result of monetary policy and of conditions beyond the control of the monetary authorities, the interest rate rose during these years. The stock of money increased from $124.3 billion in June, 1953, to $142.1 billion in June, 1961, or 12½ per cent, while GNP increased by 42 per cent. Hence, the cash balance of individuals and firms declined relative to income. However, the volume of time deposits and other "near-money" increased from $144.9 billion to $230.6 billion during this period. We may interpret this as evidence that a rise in the interest rate induces people to part with a portion of their L_2 balances or, in terms of the quantity theory, that a rise in V permits PT to increase more rapidly than M.

Critics of monetary policy in this decade concentrated on the errors in the timing of policy changes. They claimed that there was undue delay in imposing restraint, particularly in 1955, and delay in easing credit in 1957. In each case there was reason for honest difference of opinion regarding the signs of an impending upsurge or downturn in the economy. In addition, there was some criticism of the priorities which the Reserve System assigned to its several objectives. We have noted previously the conflicts which may arise in attempting to attain several objectives. The relative importance of these objectives is, of course, a matter of a subjective opinion.

POLICY SINCE 1961

The Administration of President Kennedy, who took office in January, 1961, proposed to use monetary and fiscal policy to achieve several objectives. They were:

1. Increase the rate of economic growth.
2. Move toward full employment.
3. Halt the outflow of gold.[1]
4. Prevent an increase in the price level.

The gold outflow problem was serious and required immediate action. We noted previously that unemployment averaged 5.2 per cent of the labor force from 1953 to 1961. By December, 1960, 6.8 per cent of the labor force was unemployed. Therefore, the unem-

[1]See Chapter 25 for a more detailed discussion of the gold outflow problem and United States policy.

ployment rate was definitely a problem. The rate of economic growth had been an issue in the election campaign and President Kennedy had promised to take measures to stimulate growth. The wholesale price index had been stable since 1958 and the consumer price index had risen approximately 1 per cent per year during this period. The record, therefore, did not indicate that inflation was a serious problem. Nevertheless, there was concern over the price level because it had risen throughout two decades, and both the public and the government leaders feared further increases.

Designing policies to achieve all these objectives was not an easy task. In a general sense, an easy-money policy would tend to increase the rate of economic growth and would move the nation toward full employment. However, this same policy would tend to increase the outflow of gold and also would lead to a rise in prices. Conversely, tight credit conditions would tend to halt the gold outflow and to prevent inflation at the cost of retarding economic growth and increasing the rate of unemployment. Fiscal policies that promoted economic expansion would tend to have the same effects as an easy-money policy.

Monetary Policy Since 1961

There had been exceptions to the "bills only" policy prior to 1961. The Federal Reserve System now discontinued this approach to open-market operations. A change was necessary since the Reserve System planned to alter the structure of interest rates in the financial market. Its objective was a relatively high rate of interest on short-term debt. This would discourage the transfer of idle funds to other countries and thus would reduce the tendency for gold to leave the United States. These high rates also would act as a restraint on the expansion of bank credit. At the same time the monetary authorities planned to maintain relatively low rates of interest in the long-term credit market. Since it is customary to finance industrial expansion with long-term credit, the maintenance of a low interest rate in this area should stimulate investment. If successful, economic growth and a movement toward full employment would accompany the expansion in investment.

The open-market operations of the Reserve System can influence the interest rate differential between securities of different maturities by buying one type and by selling another. There are limits to the Reserve System's influence, however, since some lenders and some borrowers are free to shift from one sector of the market to another as the short-term rates approach those of long-term securities. The policy to achieve this goal became commonly known as "operation nudge." Table 24–9 shows that the attempt to change the structure of interest rates achieved a degree of success. The Reserve banks increased the volume of United States securities they held from $27.4 billion in January, 1961, to $37.4 billion in March, 1965. This permitted an expansion of the money supply (seasonally adjusted) from $141.1 billion to $158.1 billion for the same period. Since this increase did not exceed the rate of economic growth, the larger stock of money did not constitute an inflationary threat.

Table 24–9

STRUCTURE OF INTEREST RATES

1961–1965

(Per cent per annum)

Period	Private Securities		3-Month Bills Market Yield	Bonds Maturing or Callable in 10 Years or More
	Prime Bankers' Acceptances 90 Days	Corporate Bonds Aaa		
Jan., 1961	2.86	4.32	2.24	3.89
July, 1961	2.75	4.41	2.24	3.90
Jan., 1962	3.00	4.42	2.72	4.08
July, 1962	3.07	4.34	2.92	4.02
Jan., 1963	3.07	4.21	2.91	3.88
July, 1963	3.41	4.26	3.18	4.01
Jan., 1964	3.70	4.37	3.52	4.15
July, 1964	3.75	4.40	3.46	4.13
Jan., 1965	4.00	4.43	3.81	4.14

Source: *Federal Reserve Bulletins.*

One other monetary occurrence is of interest. As noted in Chapter 2 the market price of silver rose to the point ($1.29 per ounce) where it equaled the monetary value of standard silver dollars and silver certificates. The high price of silver plus an Act of Congress in 1963 have enabled the Treasury to begin selling its stock of reserve silver and to replace the silver certificates in circulation with Federal Reserve notes. Thus, conditions in the commodity market have solved the traditional silver problem of the United States monetary system. A new silver problem, a shortage of coins, has replaced it and has caused the nation to change the composition of some of its coins.

Fiscal Policy Since 1961

There was reason to believe that gold movements were less sensitive to fiscal than to monetary policy since the former had less effect on interest rates. Consequently, fiscal policy was to be the means of expanding economic activity. The cash expenditures of the Federal Government increased from $99.5 billion in fiscal year 1961 to $121.4 billion in 1965. In terms of the national income theory, this represents a rise in G and in transfer payments to the public; however the purpose was not primarily an increase in the aggregate demand. Rather, it was to provide for expanded public services and to redress the imbalance, which the Administration claimed existed, between public and private goods and services.

Tax reduction was to be the chief weapon of fiscal policy. For several years, a number of economists had claimed that the progressive rate structure of the Federal tax system retarded economic expansion. They argued that the tax structure designed for a lower level of national income was not appropriate for conditions in the 1960's. As the nation's income increased, the progressive rates of the tax system reduced disposable private and business income so rapidly

Table 24–10

ECONOMIC INDICATORS, 1961–1964

(GNP and Gold Stock in billions of dollars)

Year	GNP	GNP Constant (1954) Dollars	Consumer Price Index (1957–1959 = 100)
1961	518.7	447.9	104.2
1962	556.2	476.4	105.4
1963	583.9	492.6	106.7
1964	622.6	516.0	108.1

Year	Wholesale Price Index (1957–1959 = 100)	Unemployment as a Per Cent of the Labor Force	Gold Stock
1961	100.3	6.7	16.9
1962	100.6	5.6	16.1
1963	100.3	5.7	15.6
1964	100.5	5.2	15.5

Source: *Economic Report of the President* (Washington: Government Printing Office, 1965), and *Federal Reserve Bulletin*, February, 1965, p. 318.

that economic growth was retarded. Increased government expenditures might appear to balance the reduction in private spending but taxes would again remove a sizable portion of the incremental income. Consequently, in 1963 the Administration proposed a reduction in tax rates to stimulate economic activity. The reduction in taxes became effective in 1964. In the vocabulary of national income theory, a tax cut represents an attempt to raise GNP by reducing the size of T_n. This policy is in marked contrast to earlier approaches which emphasized an increase in G. Adoption of the tax cut in spite of the existence of a sizable Treasury deficit suggests acceptance of the principles of fiscal policy by the public and the Congress.

The Administration also claimed that the tax cut, by stimulating economic activity, would relieve the monetary authorities of this responsibility. Thus, monetary policy could concentrate on other objectives; namely, retarding the outflow of gold and restraining inflationary pressures.

Table 24–10 shows the results of these policies and, of course, of influences outside the control of fiscal and monetary authorities. Policies to achieve full employment appear to have been partially successful, and the reason for this imperfect result is worthy of note. During the period, it became apparent that "structural" conditions were responsible for much of the unemployment. That is, the skill level and other qualifications of the unemployed did not match the job vacancies which existed. Monetary and fiscal policies alone could not overcome this structural defect. The Federal Government is sponsoring a program of education and training to correct it.

LESSONS FROM THE PERIOD AND REMAINING PROBLEMS

Our experience in World War II shows that the Federal Reserve System can serve as an "engine of inflation." In the United States it has served in this capacity only during periods of war but the potential exists at all times. There is a temptation to finance large government expenditures by creating bank credit rather than by taxing the public. Underdeveloped nations, wishing to spend a sizable portion of their income for economic development, frequently succumb to this temptation. If the central bank creates money to finance development projects, the nation may achieve the necessary reallocation of resources. Whether or not the resulting inflation is too high a price to pay for the development project is a matter for individual nations to decide. A knowledge of monetary principles and of the consequences of monetary expansion enhances our ability to evaluate these policies.

For many years Americans regarded an independent central banking system as a defense against the use of bank credit as a substitute for taxation. However, our wartime experiences show us that a central banking system that is independent in structure quickly becomes the servant of the Treasury in an emergency. The postwar record indicates that it is not easy for the central bank to regain its freedom. We may conclude that will power and not a structural device is necessary to prevent inflation. A knowledge of the workings of the monetary system helps the public develop this will power.

Monetary history since 1951 should eliminate any tendency to regard monetary policy as an application of a simple theory which involves practicing tight money during inflationary periods and easing credit during recessions. We noted the presence of multiple problems calling for contradictory policies. At first the problems were chronic unemployment and creeping inflation. Later we added unsatisfactory economic growth and an outflow of gold. We cannot claim that the solution to these problems has been entirely satisfactory.

Others questions await an answer. Critics of monetary policy have questioned its applicability to modern economic problems. In particular, they claim that considerable time elapses between the use of policy measures and their effect on the economy. Consequently, the conditions when the policy takes effect may be the opposite of those existing when the Federal Reserve officials make their decision. A tight-money policy adopted during an inflationary period might become effective during the following recession. We cannot avoid this problem by substituting fiscal for monetary policy since the time lag for government action is even greater. Improved forecasting techniques and prompt reaction to indicated changes will reduce, if not eliminate, this defect.

Some problems of the period serve to remind us that there are limits to the ability of fiscal and monetary policies to achieve stable economic conditions. To the extent that inflationary pressures are "cost-push" and unemployment is structural in type, other measures are necessary.

SUMMARY

In World War II monetary policy served to support the Treasury's debt policy. With the assistance of the Federal Reserve System, the Treasury was able to finance the war at very low interest rates. By supporting the Treasury's debt management program, the Reserve System surrendered its power to control inflation effectively.

High tax rates eliminated some inflationary pressure and direct controls suppressed some of the pressure which did exist. Nevertheless, the price level rose substantially.

After the war the Reserve System continued to support the debt management program until the Accord of 1951. As a result it was unable to control inflation. After the Accord the Reserve System applied restrictions to credit in periods of economic upsurge and practiced easy money during recessions. However, the need to try to achieve several goals rather than a single objective made difficult the selection of an appropriate monetary policy. Quite recently the System has attempted to curb the outflow of gold by promoting high interest rates on short-term securities. Concurrently, it has attempted to maintain relatively low interest rates on long-term credit instruments in order to encourage investment and economic growth. The Government has used fiscal policy in support of the effort to stimulate economic expansion and full employment.

QUESTIONS

1. How did monetary policy during World War II create inflationary pressures? How does this method of government finance differ from taxation?
2. Why did the Federal Reserve System continue to "peg" the price of bonds after World War II?
3. Explain the reason for inflation during the early months of the fighting in Korea in terms of the monetary theories you have studied.
4. Is it possible to separate completely fiscal from monetary policy in the post-World War II years? Explain your answer.
5. What are the current problems confronting the monetary authorities? What policies are appropriate, given current economic conditions?

SUGGESTED READINGS

Ahearn, Daniel S. *Federal Reserve Policy Reappraised, 1951–1959.* New York: Columbia University Press, 1963.

Barger, Harold. *The Management of Money.* Chicago: Rand McNally & Company, 1964. Chapters 6–8.

Friedman, Milton, and Schwartz, Anna Jacobson. *A Monetary History of the United States 1867–1960.* Princeton: Princeton University Press, 1963. Chapters 10–13.

Gaines, Tilford C. *Techniques of Treasury Debt Management.* New York: The Free Press of Glencoe, 1962. Chapters II and III.

Studenski, Paul, and Krooss, Herman E. *Financial History of the United States.* 2d ed. New York: McGraw-Hill Book Company, Inc., 1963. Chapters 30–33.

Trescott, Paul B. *Financing American Enterprise.* New York: Harper & Row, Publishers, 1963. Chapters 10 and 11.

VII

THE INTERNATIONAL
MONETARY SYSTEM

25

INTERNATIONAL FINANCE

Certain basic principles apply to an international as well as a domestic monetary system. In both cases the use of money permits greater specialization and higher productivity. Goods and services are the ultimate payment for other goods and services; however money serves as a medium of exchange in the payment process. Also, money, serving as a store of value, permits a credit system and in this way provides for a better allocation of resources on both the domestic and the international level. The use of money causes the several parts of an economic system to be interdependent. A national monetary system serves to transmit the effects of economic activities in one sector of the nation to another sector; an international monetary system performs the same service between countries.

There are, however, important differences arising from the influence of many sovereign political units within the international system. The most obvious special characteristic of the international monetary system is the existence of many different currencies. This gives rise to some problems and also provides opportunities for policy measures such as exchange controls. Furthermore, the presence of many sovereign nations within the system leads to different attitudes regarding the interdependence which accompanies the use of money. Few people object to interdependence within a nation; interdependence between nations frequently meets with opposition. Consequently, a nation may adopt monetary policies to reduce its close economic relations with other countries. Incidentally, the existence of many sovereign units, plus a spirit of nationalism, has created a wealth of statistical data concerning international finance. Similar data are not available on the domestic level.

MECHANICS OF INTERNATIONAL PAYMENTS

Payment across national boundaries normally involves at least two currencies.[1] For a simple illustration, we shall assume that only

[1]The term currency has a broader definition when used in connection with international transactions than it does on the domestic level. Foreign currency, also known as foreign exchange, refers to all monetary units of other countries.

two countries engage in international transactions and that the respective governments do not interfere in the payments process. Under these conditions, Americans who are importing British goods wish to pay for them in United States dollars since this is the only kind of money they possess. The British exporters wish to receive payment in British pounds, the currency which they must use to meet their payrolls and to pay other expenses. Thus, a problem arises which would be insoluble except for the existence of a group of British importers and American exporters who have the opposite problem. The several groups overcome their difficulties if the American importers pay dollars to the American exporters and the British importers pay pounds to the British exporters. In the process, each nation is paying for its imports with its exports. Of course, this solution is possible only if exporters and importers know of the existence of their counterparts. However, specialists exist to perform this brokerage service.

Foreign Exchange Market

Items other than imports and exports of tangible commodities enter foreign trade and call for monetary payments. Tourist expenditures, investment in foreign countries, and purchase of intangible services cause individuals to acquire foreign money. Therefore, we must be more realistic and enlarge our group of American importers to include all persons who wish to exchange dollars for British pounds. Likewise, the term British importer is to include all persons desiring to exchange pounds for United States dollars. Thus, we have the two sides of a market. In this market there are specialists, dealers in foreign exchange, who act as middlemen serving exporters and importers in a variety of ways.

Middlemen   Most large banks in financial centers, like New York City and Chicago, are dealers in foreign exchange. In addition, the market contains brokers who serve these banks. A bank dealing in foreign exchange may operate a branch office in important foreign commercial centers. More likely, it will maintain deposits in foreign correspondent banks which, in turn, will have deposits in the American bank. An example illustrates the services rendered to importers and exporters by this network of branch and correspondent bank relationships. An American importer of British sports cars must find some means of paying the English manufacturer. He solves the problem by paying dollars to a New York bank and receiving in exchange a draft drawn on the bank's branch office or on its correspondent bank in London. This draft, or bill of exchange, enables him to pay for the sports cars with British pounds. However, pounds are not always necessary when Americans are paying for British imports. The exporter is usually willing to accept a note payable in dollars since he knows that he can sell it for pounds to a British bank which wishes to increase its dollar deposits in a United States bank. In the preceding example, we implicitly assume the existence of a British importer who pays pounds in exchange for a draft payable in dollars. In reality, there are many exporters and many importers in both countries. There is also a complex network of communications, called the foreign exchange market, through which dealers transfer funds from one country to another.

Dealers in foreign exchange use a variety of credit instruments when transferring funds. We need only consider two, however, in examining the significant principles. A sight draft, or sight bill of exchange (see Chapter 5), can be transmitted in the form of a cablegram. It is payable upon demand, or presentation, and the rate of exchange of one currency for another which it represents is known as the "spot price." Transfers of funds may take the form of time drafts which usually become acceptances (see Chapter 5). Interest plus the risk of a change in the rate of exchange between the purchase date of a time draft and the payment date account for a difference in price between sight and time drafts. Frequently this difference between the rates is quite small. For example, in June, 1965, the "spot" and "90-day" rates for the British pound were $2.7945 and $2.7808, respectively. After allowing for interest for 90 days, these rates are essentially the same. This reflects the business community's confidence that the exchange rate will not change significantly in the ninety-day period.

Forward exchange. Dealers in foreign exchange perform an additional service by permitting merchants and manufacturers to "hedge" and thus to minimize the danger of a loss because of a change in the rate of exchange. Let us assume that the British manufacturer in our previous example has contracted to deliver sports cars and to receive payment in dollars in ninety days. He faces the possibility of a loss since the rate of exchange may fluctuate adversely. Of course, there is also the prospect of a gain if the fluctuation is favorable. In the absence of specialists dealing in foreign exchange for future delivery (forward exchange), the manufacturer would have to spend time and energy studying foreign exchange conditions and forecasting fluctuations. The existence of a forward exchange market allows the manufacturer to transfer the risk of loss (and the prospect of gain) to specialists in this field. Inasmuch as this exporter knows that he will be exchanging dollars for pounds ninety days after signing the sales agreement, he may hedge by contracting to buy dollars from a foreign exchange dealer in ninety days. The rate for ninety-day dollars is usually close to and varies with the spot rate.

Therefore, a change in the rate of exchange will lead to a loss in one transaction and a gain in the other. Thus, hedging, by transferring the risk of fluctuation in foreign exchange rates to a specialist in that area, permits the manufacturer to concentrate on his specialty.

It is obvious that the foreign exchange market will operate successfully only if there is a balance between the two sides. In our illustration involving only two countries, the demands of persons seeking to change United States dollars into British pounds must equal the supply of British pounds available for exchange into United States dollars. We shall examine the consequences of a failure to balance in-payments with out-payments in a later section.

Multilateral Payments

We may now drop our unrealistic assumption that only two nations exist; however the presence of many nations and many currencies does not change the basic principle. Each nation continues to pay for its imports with its exports. In a multilateral system, payments between any pair of nations need not and probably will not balance. Payments from England to the United States may exceed payments from the United States to England. In that case the United States payments to other countries must exceed receipts from them. Payments to England from these nations will exceed their receipts from that country. For any given nation, payments to all other nations must equal receipts although balancing items (see page 456) may be necessary.

If the use of money is to lead to the optimum degree of specialization, nations should not attempt to balance receipts and payments bilaterally. We understand and apply this principle within the boundaries of a single country. For example, we do not attempt to balance receipts and payments of money between New York and New Jersey. In order to maximize output, each state must specialize in the production of those goods and services in which it is most proficient. It sells these products throughout the nation, and it purchases products from other specialist states without attempting a bistate balance of receipts and payments. The same principle applies to international trade and payments if maximum output is the objective. However, in international transactions, political considerations often lead to other economic objectives. As a result, we cannot apply the principle of free multilateral payments between nations to the same extent that we can within a nation.

A system of multilateral payments leads to complications in the foreign exchange market. It is customary to refer to *the* rate of foreign exchange but in reality there are a series of rates: a rate for British pounds, French francs, and so forth. For ease in trading the structure of rates should be consistent. For example, if $2.79 = £1 and $.20405 = fr. 1, £1 should equal fr. 13.67. The presence of specialists guarantees this consistency if the market is free. If the above rate of pounds for francs changes so that £1 = fr. 15, the specialist, noting this, will simultaneously buy French francs with British pounds, United States dollars with French francs, and British pounds with United States dollars. These transactions, called *arbitrage*, will exert pressure on the supply of and demand for the several currencies which will restore consistency to the cross rates. In fact the quick reaction of arbitragers will prevent inconsistencies except for small differences explained by the overhead costs of transactions.

THE INTERNATIONAL BALANCE OF PAYMENTS

From the point of view of the United States, which we shall use as our example, one side of the foreign exchange market consists of individuals, firms, banks, and government agencies desiring to exchange United States dollars for a foreign currency. We call this group the demand side of the market, or the group which wishes to buy foreign exchange. Although foreign currency is money, we shall treat it like a commodity for purposes of this analysis. The other side of the market consists of the group which wishes to trade foreign currency for United States dollars. This is the supply side of the market, or the "sellers" of foreign exchange. In the balance-of-payments analysis, we arrange all the transactions giving rise to a demand for or a supply of foreign exchange in a logical pattern. It is customary to use the terms credit and debit rather than supply and demand. Credits, or the "plus" symbol transactions, provide the United States with claims against foreign resources. They represent the supply of foreign exchange. Debits, or the "minus" symbol transactions, provide others with claims against the United States. They represent the demand for foreign exchange. In Table 25–1 the left column contains a list of the types of transactions which create credits in the United States balance of payments. The right column presents the logical partners which create debits.

CREDIT

Types of Transactions

We shall comment on the nature of some of these types of transactions before we look at the monetary value of the United States balance of payments. Exports of merchandise from the United States cause the buyers to exchange foreign currency for United States dollars. Therefore, they are a credit item. Obviously, imports of merchandise are a debit item. Military sales and purchases, items 1B and 2B, by the United States have the same effect as exports and

Table 25-1

UNITED STATES BALANCE OF PAYMENTS COMPONENTS

Credits (+), Receipts, or Supply of Foreign Currency	*Debits (−), Payments, or Demand for Foreign Currency*

1. Exports from the U. S.
  A. Merchandise exports
  B. Military sales
  C. Income received from foreign investment (private and government)
  D. Sale of services
	2. Imports into the U. S.
	  A. Merchandise imports
	  B. Military purchases
	  C. Income paid to foreigners who own investments in the U.S.
	  D. Purchase of services

3. Remittances and pensions from abroad to persons living in the U. S.	4. Remittances and pensions from the U. S. to persons living abroad

5. Government grants and loans to the U. S.
  A. Grants by other nations to the U. S. Government
  B. Long-term loans by other nations to the U. S. Government
  C. Increase in short-term claims others hold against the U. S.
  D. Loan repayments by others
  E. Increase in miscellaneous U.S. nonliquid liabilities
	6. Government grants and loans by the U. S.
	  A. Grants by the U. S. Government to other countries
	  B. Long-term loans by the U. S. Government to other nations
	  C. Increase in short-term claims the U. S. holds against others
	  D. Loan repayments by U. S.
	  E. Increase in miscellaneous U. S. nonliquid claims

7. Private capital flows to the U. S. (excluding liquid assets)
  A. Foreign direct investments in the U. S.
  B. Other long-term foreign capital investments in the U. S.
  C. Foreign short-term capital investments in the U. S.
	8. Private capital flows from the U. S. (excluding liquid assets)
	  A. Direct investments abroad by persons in the U. S.
	  B. Other long-term capital investments abroad
	  C. Short-term capital investments abroad by persons in the U. S.

9. Errors and unrecorded
   transactions

10. Errors and unrecorded
    transactions

11. Balancing transactions
    A. Advance debt repayment
       to the U. S. and ad-
       vance payment for
       military sales
    B. Sales of special
       Government securities
    C. Increase in liquid as-
       sets (e.g., time de-
       posits) held by for-
       eigners in the U. S.
    D. Transfer of U. S. mone-
       tary reserves to other
       nations
       (1) Gold exports
       (2) Decline in IMF[a]
           balance and
           holdings of con-
           vertible currencies

12. Balancing transactions
    A. Advance repayment by
       the U. S. and advance
       payment for military
       purchases
    B. Purchases of special
       foreign securities
    C. Increase in liquid
       assets held by Ameri-
       cans in foreign coun-
       tries
    D. Transfer of foreign
       monetary reserves to
       the U. S.
       (1) Gold imports
       (2) Increase in IMF
           balance and hol-
           dings of conver-
           tible currencies

[a]International Monetary Fund.

imports of merchandise on the balance of payments. Unlike items 1A and 2A, however, there need be no physical transfer of goods from one nation to another. For example, item 2B, military purchases, represents dollars which the United States must exchange for foreign currency to defray the cost of maintaining military bases in foreign countries. Items 1C, 2C, 1D, and 2D have this same characteristic: they represent exports and imports but goods need not be sent from or to this country. Item 1C represents interest and dividends which Americans receive from investments they hold abroad. Expenditures of foreign tourists in the United States, sales of insurance to foreigners, brokerage fees which foreigners pay to the United States, and the sale of other intangibles contribute to item 1D. The reader may infer the composition of items 2C and 2D from these comments.

The titles for categories 3 and 4 explain the nature of the transactions. Categories 5 and 6 are similar to categories 3 and 4 except that in the latter cases we are dealing with grants between governments rather than between private citizens. The grants and the long-term loans to allied and underdeveloped nations appear in items 6A and 6B. Item 6C represents short-term loans which the United States Government extends to others. Item 6D is self-explanatory. The reader can infer the characteristics of items 5A to 5D. It is also likely that the reader has some knowledge of which of these matching pairs yield a net credit and which a net debit balance for the United States without consulting Table 25–2.

Items 8A to 8C represent investment by the private sector of the United States economy in other countries. If an American purchases stock in a foreign corporation or lends money to a foreign firm, he must exchange dollars for foreign currency. Consequently, it is a debit item. The same principle applies to American corporations which spend money to build plants abroad. Eventually these investments will yield interest or dividends which we shall find in item 1C, but the immediate effect is a debit. For obvious reasons investments by foreigners in the United States, category 7, are a credit item.

The Department of Commerce includes categories 9 and 10, which are really one classification, in the balance of payments because it realizes that the measurement of the other items is not perfect. Inasmuch as the United States places no legal restrictions on the transfer of funds, many transactions are unrecorded. In other transactions, the estimate of the dollar value is inaccurate. Since there are no tariffs levied against exports, there is no reason to appraise them carefully. This does not imply that the appraisal of imports that are subject to tariff charges is perfect. The value which the United States Customs Service assigns for tariff purposes frequently exceeds the market value of the commodities. Therefore, categories 9 and 10 usually yield a net debit.

The debits and credits for the United States are unlikely to be equal for any given year if we consider only the first ten categories of transactions. Consequently, there are classes 11 and 12, which are balancing items. If the United States' debits exceed its credits for categories 1 to 10, it may persuade the other nations to advance the date of debt repayment or of other payments (item 11A). Or it may induce foreign banks and other foreign creditors to accept securities (item 11B). Both of these transactions imply direct government intervention in the market. Without direct government action, foreign creditors may decide to accept liquid assets, such as time deposits (item 11C), rather than demand immediate payment in their own currency. Items 11B and 11C are balancing items from an accountant's point of view, although they represent a formal debt on which the United States must pay interest. For this reason, the distinction between these balancing transactions and short-term capital investment (item 7C) is somewhat arbitrary. Finally, the United States may satisfy claims against it by a payment of international money (item 11D), which consists of gold and foreign currency which is convertible into gold.

It follows as a matter of simple logic that if the United States had a surplus of credits in the first ten categories of transactions it would balance its accounts by advance repayment of its foreign debts, purchase of foreign securities, an increase in its foreign liquid asset holdings, and receipt of international currency (items 12A to 12D). Table 25–2 shows the dollar volume of the various types of transactions for the United States for the years 1963 and 1964. It illustrates the principles we have just considered.

Equilibrium in the Balance of Payments

In Table 25–2 we note that the value of United States exports exceeds the value of imports despite deficits in the two subcategories, military sales and purchase of services. For the remaining categories, it is customary to record net figures only. Consequently, we combine categories 3 and 4, 5 and 6, and so forth. In each of the category pairings there is a net debit. Also, there is a negative overall balance for categories 1 to 10. The United States settles this net debit by using balancing transactions (category 11). We could have treated the outflow of gold as a metallic export, but it is acceptable as money throughout the world and thus merits listing as a separate subcategory.

From an accountant's point of view, the United States balance of payments "balances." In very simple terms we may say that the United States buys goods and services, purchases investments in foreign countries, and makes gifts. It pays for these expenditures by selling goods and services, collecting the income from its foreign investments, and borrowing. Settlement of the remaining deficit takes the form of payments of international currency; that is, gold.

The title "balance of payments" suggests that the right and left columns must be equal. On a worldwide basis a credit item to one nation obviously is a debit item to another. Hence, debits equal credits for the entire system. For a single nation every purchase (a debit item) involves a payment in international currency, receipt of a grant, or an increase in its debt obligations held by other nations (all credit items). The debit and credit accounts must balance; however this may involve the inclusion of balancing items. In a general sense, these are temporary expedients necessary to achieve a balance. Their presence, therefore, denotes a disequilibrium in the balance of payments; that is, current accounts or "normal" transactions do not balance. Or we may say that the debits and credits of the autonomous factors are not equal at all times. This lack of equilibrium induces changes in the balancing items (categories 11 and 12). The United States is in this position for the years to which Table 25–2 applies.

Table 25–2

UNITED STATES BALANCE OF PAYMENTS
1963–1964

(In billions of dollars)

Transaction	1963	1964
1. Export of goods and services		
A. Merchandise	22.0	25.2
B. Military sales	.7	.8
C. Income from investments	4.5	5.2
D. Sale of services	4.9	5.4
Total exports	32.1	36.6
2. Imports of goods and services		
A. Merchandise	− 17.0	− 18.6
B. Military purchases	− 2.9	− 2.8
C. Payments on investments of foreigners	− 1.2	− 1.3
D. Purchase of services	− 5.2	− 5.6
Total imports	− 26.3	− 28.3
3, 4. Remittances and pensions, net	− .8	− .8
Balance on exports, imports, and remittances	5.0	7.4
5, 6. Government grants and loans		
A. Government grants, net	− 1.9	− 1.9
B. Government long-term loans, net	− 2.2	− 2.4
C. Change in government short-term claims, net	− .4	a
D. Government loan repayment, net	.7	.6
E. Miscellaneous U. S. Government nonliquid liabilities	a	.2
7, 8. Private capital flows, net (excluding foreign liquid assets)		
A. Direct investments, net	− 1.9	− 2.3
B. Other long-term capital, net	− 1.4	− 1.8
C. Short-term capital, net	− .8	− 2.0
9, 10. Errors and unrecorded transactions	− .3	− .9
Balance on current accounts	− 3.3	− 3.1

11, 12. Balancing transactions
    A. Advance debt repayment, advance

payment of military sales	.7	.3
B. Sales of special government		
securities	.6	.3
C. Change in liquid assets	1.6	2.2
D. Change in U. S. monetary reserves		
(1) Gold export (+), import (−)	.5	.1
(2) IMF and convertible currencies	− .1	.1
Total balancing items	3.3	3.1

Note: Details may not add to totals because of rounding.
ᵃLess than $.1 billion.
Source: Department of Commerce data published in the *Survey of Current Business,*
March, 1965, and the *Federal Reserve Bulletin,* April, 1965.

Therefore, it is proper to say that the United States has a deficit in its balance of payments even though the balancing items bring the accounts into equality. This deficit, or disequilibrium, presents a nation with a serious problem because the nation cannot use the balancing item indefinitely; the gold supply is not inexhaustible, nor will other nations accept claims against the future without limit.

Use of the Balance of Payments

The balance of payments presents data in a convenient form for the analysis of receipts and payments, and it plays approximately the same role in the discussion of international trade and finance that GNP plays in national income discussions. The government learns of the international position of the nation through balance-of-payments data. Thus it serves as a guide to the formulation of monetary and fiscal policy. Furthermore, the balance of payments presents a classified list of the transactions affecting the supply and demand sides of the foreign exchange market. An examination of these classified accounts allows the government to make decisions regarding specific political and foreign trade policies. Also, these transactions influence foreign exchange rates. We shall refer to the balance of payments in our study of the determination of these rates.

Determinants of the Balance of Payments

The credit and debit totals of the balance of payments vary with changes in the size of each of the several categories that are its components. The volume of these categories is dependent upon a number of factors, some of which are subject to sudden change. We shall consider these factors and their effect on the balance of payments in a fashion similar to our study of the determinants of the components of GNP.

Some determinants are outside the economic system. Political conditions, such as the fear of war and revolution, affect the "export" of services to tourists. Political factors also affect the volume of other exports and imports, particularly such items as military sales and purchases and government grants and loans. Other determinants are economic in nature. Because of our knowledge of the consumption function, we know that a rise in consumption accompanies a rise in income. If we assume that some of this consumption increment will consist of imported goods or goods using imported raw materials and that other things will remain unchanged, it follows that a rise in GNP will cause an increase in a nation's imports and *vice versa*. Figure 25–1 illustrates this relationship. As income moves from Y_0 to Y_1, imports rise from M_0 to M_1. Of course, a rise in the GNP of the rest of the world causes exports to rise. The reverse is true for a decrease in the GNP of the rest of the world. When we are considering the problem of equilibrium in the balance of payments, the change in domestic incomes relative to the rest of the world, and not the absolute increase or decrease, is the important determinant.

The domestic price level relative to prices abroad obviously has an effect on exports and imports. Accordingly, a nation with a deficit in its balance of payments may move toward correction of the problem by lowering its prices relative to the rest of the world, thus making its goods more attractive to foreign purchasers (It follows that inflation within a nation tends to create a deficit in the balance of payments, while deflation has the opposite effect.) A nation may lower its prices relative to those of other countries by holding prices constant while the competitors' prices rise. Or it may even allow a price rise if the rise is less severe than that which other nations are

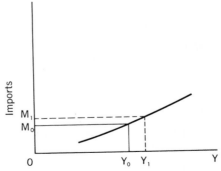

Figure 25-1.   Imports as a Function of Income

experiencing. Note that the relative level of prices rather than the absolute level is the determining factor.

Improvements in methods of production and technological — *relative* advances influence the balance of payments. By improving its methods of production and thus lowering prices, a nation may increase its exports and decrease its imports. Also, it may accomplish this result through technological progress which creates new and improved products. Conversely, such action by competing nations lowers exports and raises imports. Again the position relative to other countries, and not the absolute level of technology, is the determinant.

Changes in consumer taste influence the debit and credit totals of the balance of payments. Popular acceptance of a nation's products may change. This change may be the result of new products entering the market. In that case there is a close relationship to technological improvement. An example is the replacement of natural fibers with synthetics in many clothing items. Or there may be a change of taste without the introduction of a new product. The relatively recent popularity in the United States of imported automobiles shows this.

Conditions in the financial market influence the balance of payments. A nation in which the chances for profit from business investments appear excellent will attract capital from abroad. This involves changing foreign currency into domestic monetary units (item 7B) and adds to the credit total. Conversely, a nation in which the profit prospects are poor witnesses an outflow of capital. The interest rate affects the flow of short-term capital in the same manner. High interest rates encourage an inflow of funds while low rates stimulate an outward movement. Again, the important factor is the rate of profit or the interest rate relative to those prevailing in competing nations.

All these determinants are subject to change. It is customary for some of them to vary rapidly; others move slowly, if at all. It follows that a nation which has achieved equilibrium in the balance of payments has no guarantee that this condition will continue. Also, we may note that some of these determinants, such as the interest rate, are subject to control by the monetary authorities. Therefore, we may regard some of them as instruments of policy as well as determinants of the credits and the debits in the balance of payments.

Rate of Exchange a Determinant of the Balance of Payments

We have omitted a very important determinant, the rate of exchange. The rate at which foreign currency exchanges for domestic units affects the relative price levels of any two countries under consideration. The effect becomes clear if we use a hypothetical example which includes a shift in the rate of exchange. Let us assume that one British pound exchanges for four United States dollars and that both nations manufacture a product which we shall call commodity X. Its price is £1 in England and $4 in the United States. Hence, there is no incentive to export or to import the product. Now the rate of exchange changes so that £1 is equal to $2.80. This reduces the price of commodity X manufactured in England to a buyer holding United States dollars. He can purchase the item in England for $2.80 and, since it still costs $4 to produce and market the American product, United States imports from England increase. Conversely, the price of the American commodity X rises from £1 to £1.43 to a prospective buyer holding British pounds. If we apply this principle to other goods and services, we see that American imports from England tend to rise and exports tend to decline. This change in the rates of exchange affects United States exports to other nations. In terms of prices the devaluation of the pound places British products in a favorable competitive position in world markets and American exports suffer.

This is not the complete story, however. We now drop the simple example of commodity X. We assume instead that many products which the United States normally imports from England have a relatively inelastic demand: the number of units purchased rises at a slower rate than the rate at which the price declines. If this is the case, United States imports will rise in terms of physical units but, in terms of debits in the balance of payments, the price decline will more than compensate for this increase. This does not exhaust the number of complicating factors; however it is sufficient to indicate that the rate of exchange is an important determinant of the various items in the balance of payments. This brief discussion suggests to the reader that the rate of exchange may serve as a policy weapon. In Chapter 26, we shall see that it can be effective in this role under certain circumstances.

Rate of Exchange—Determined by the Balance of Payments

We began the discussion of the balance of payments by identifying exports and other credit items as the supply side of the foreign exchange market. Imports and other debit transactions represent the demand for foreign exchange. In the foreign exchange market, traders exchange the monetary units of one nation for those of another country. We noted, however, that it is customary to regard the currency of the nation whose balance of payments is under discussion as "money" and other currency as the commodity offered for sale. In a commodity market free from government controls, the equilibrium price is the rate at which the market is "cleared." That is, all sellers willing to sell at that price find a buyer for their goods, and all buyers willing to purchase at that price are able to secure the quantity of goods they desire. The same principle applies to the foreign exchange market, but it is necessary to emphasize the qualifying phrase, "free from government controls." Thus, the forces of supply and demand determine the exchange rate, but the rate, in turn, is a determinant of the volume of credits and debits. In the foreign exchange market the terminology may lead to more confusion than in the commodity markets since monetary units are present on both sides of the transactions. A person who is speaking of the United States balance of payments and the United States dollar may describe a rise in the rate at which foreign currency exchanges for dollars as an increase in the price of foreign exchange or as a devaluation of the dollar.

In Figure 25–2 we measure the dollar price of foreign exchange vertically and the amount the public is willing to buy or sell on the horizontal axis. The curve DD (a demand curve) represents the volume of foreign exchange the public is willing to buy at varying levels of price. The line SS (a supply curve) denotes the amount of foreign exchange the public is willing to sell at varying levels of price. The point of intersection determines the equilibrium price, p_0, and the volume of transactions, q_0. In this diagram the position and

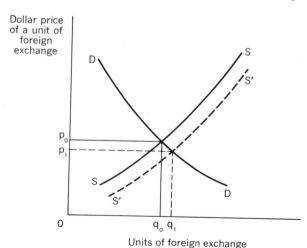

Figure 25-2.   Supply and Demand in the Foreign Exchange
                        Market

the slope of the SS and DD curves are the result of the determinants of the debit and the credit sides of the balance of payments which we have just considered.

When we considered the determinants of the size of several categories of transactions in the balance of payments, we noted that a number of them were subject to frequent change. Consequently, we expect the total volume of credits and debits to be unstable. If we retain our assumption that the market is free of government intervention, we should expect the rate of foreign exchange to fluctuate in response to variations in the debit and credit accounts. For example, the prices of manufactured goods in the United States may fall relative to prices in other countries because of improved methods of production. The lower prices in the United States cause the supply curve in Figure 25-2 to shift from SS to S'S' and the price of foreign exchange to fall from p_0 to p_1. In practice, however, governments intervene in the market to prevent this type of fluctuation. The balance of payments is a useful analytical tool in determining the type and the magnitude of the intervention needed to stabilize the market. It also serves to evaluate the effect of policy.

THE UNITED STATES BALANCE OF PAYMENTS

The United States balance of payments serves as a case study which leads to a better understanding of the relation of these accounts to the rest of the economic system. This study also provides for a discussion of the consequences of a disequilibrium in the balance of payments.

In Table 25-2 we note that the export of goods and services from the United States exceeds imports in dollar value. Since "net exports" is one of its components, this export surplus increases the level of GNP in the United States. This illustrates how these transactions transmit economic fluctuation from one nation to another. In Table 25-2 we also note that all other categories show a net deficit. Consequently, the United States is using its net earnings from exports to finance net private remittances, net government grants and loans, and net private investment abroad. The net deficit on these accounts exceeds the net earnings from the export of goods and services and the result is an overall deficit.[2] This deficit is not a new phenomenon. The total deficit from 1950 through 1964 exceeded $31 billion with the years 1958 through 1964 accounting for $21 billion of

---

[2]Some experts claim that the Department of Commerce overstates the United States deficit on current accounts. They claim that the net credit for "change in liquid assets" (item 11C) should be treated as short-term capital (item 7C). On page 456 we noted that the distinction between categories 7, 8 and 11, 12 was somewhat arbitrary.

this total. Since the United States is the richest nation in the world, it is reasonable to ask why it has not balanced its accounts with other countries.

A comparison with a private household will help us to understand the answer to this question. However, it is dangerous to carry the analogy to extremes. The position of the United States is similar to that of a private household with a high income which is in excess of its cost of living. Because the members of this family are by nature generous, or perhaps because of other motives, the household makes sizable contributions to social and charitable organizations. Furthermore, the household purchases securities and other investment items freely. As a result of all these transactions, payments exceed receipts. The household may draw on its cash balance and it may borrow money to finance the deficit temporarily. In the long run, the household must eliminate the deficit by some combination of (1) an increase in income, (2) a reduction in living costs, (3) a reduction in contributions to social organizations, and (4) a curtailment of its investment program. Failure to eliminate the deficit will lead to a poor credit rating and to eventual bankruptcy. The United States, being in a similar position, can adopt temporary measures which correspond to the household's use of its cash balance and borrowing. Eventually, the nation must eliminate the deficit.

Consequences of the Deficit Position of the United States

For the United States or any other nation, a deficit in the balance of payments leads first to a reduction of its holdings of international liquid assets, such as gold and foreign currency which is generally accepted in international payments. Foreign currency holdings of the United States were not large at any time; hence changes in this item have not been significant. Fortunately, the United States possessed a large stock of monetary gold prior to the 1950's. However, this stock declined from $22.9 billion in 1957 to $13.9 billion in 1965. Presently, United States law requires that Federal Reserve banks keep approximately $8.5 billion in gold certificates as reserves for the Federal Reserve notes in circulation. Accordingly, the United States has only $5.4 billion in "free" gold available for export. Of course, Congress can change the law to free gold held as backing for Federal Reserve notes, but this will only postpone the eventual exhaustion of our gold supply. It will not solve the problem.

Other nations have a balance-of-payments surplus equal to the United States deficit. This surplus permits them to accumulate time deposits and other liquid assets in the United States. This places the

United States in the same position as a bank which finds its deposit liabilities increasing without a corresponding increase in its asset accounts. If the condition continues, the bank must expect that its creditors, losing confidence in the bank's ability to meet its liabilities, will start to withdraw deposits. The United States also must fear a "run on the bank" by the owners of liquid dollar assets. If this occurred the "run on the bank" would take the form of redemption of dollar assets in gold and the export of the gold. The gold outflow could reach crisis proportions very quickly. Hence, one of the consequences of the deficit is the need to take measures to convince the rest of the world that the United States will overcome the difficulty in the near future.

We have arrived at the rather odd conclusion that one consequence of the deficit in the balance of payments is the necessity for eliminating it. We shall consider policies to achieve this objective in a later chapter, but first we must ask, what are the consequences of a failure to overcome the deficit? Continued deficits by a household or private firm lead to bankruptcy. For a nation, a continued deficit in the balance of payments leads to a devaluation of its currency in the foreign exchange market. In the case of the United States, we must assume that in time a continued deficit will exhaust our ability to use balancing transactions (category 11). Applying the principles of price theory, we note that the deficit represents demand for foreign currency in excess of supply at the present exchange rates. Therefore, we expect the price of foreign currency to rise until supply and demand are equal. Devaluation of the dollar is, of course, another way of stating that the price of foreign currency is rising.

In less abstract terms, a chronic deficit in the United States balance of payments will make the dollar less acceptable as payment in international transactions. Persons who normally would accept the dollar anticipate difficulty in spending it. It follows that prices for goods, services, investment items, and other currency will rise if the United States dollar is to be the means of payment. Higher prices if the United States dollar is the means of payment constitutes a devaluation of the dollar.

In a previous section, we noted that the rate of foreign exchange influences the debit and credit items in the balance of payments. Devaluation of the United States dollar would stimulate exports and would discourage imports. Therefore, devaluation is a possible solution to the deficit problem. Unfortunately, devaluation would seriously impair the position of the United States as the economic and political leader of the free world. It would turn the "barter terms of trade" against the United States; that is, cheaper United States dollars (or more expensive foreign currency) would force us to export more in terms of physical units to receive the same volume of im-

usually when imports exceed exports

ports. Also individuals, firms, and foreign governments would be less willing to extend credit and to hold liquid assets payable in dollars if they knew that their value was subject to change. Devaluation, therefore, is an unacceptable solution to the balance-of-payments deficit.

If the deficit were larger and the prospects for overcoming it were less sanguine, we would use the term "potential bankruptcy" to describe the consequence. This is too harsh a phrase to be appropriate for the problem facing the United States. However, other nations have suffered bankruptcy because of a chronic balance-of-payments deficit. For the United States, the problem of the deficit is serious but not critical.

Other deficit nations face consequences similar to those facing the United States. A nation which is not the banker to the free world and which does not have responsibility for economic and political leadership is less fearful of the loss in confidence which accompanies devaluation. On the other hand the exports and the imports of many deficit nations are inelastic with respect to price. In that case devaluation has a more serious effect on the domestic economy.

Consequences of a Surplus
in the Balance of Payments

A nation usually shows little concern over a surplus in its balance of payments. A surplus in the balance of payments creates inflationary pressures according to the "rules of the game" of the international gold standard; however nations no longer abide by these rules.[3] At the present time, nations with a balance-of-payments surplus fear the reactions of nations which have the balancing deficit. Measures which one nation takes to correct its deficit affect the exports and imports of its trading partners.

SUMMARY

Money plays the same role in international affairs that it does domestically. By serving as a medium of exchange and a standard of value, money facilitates international trade and permits a high degree of specialization. However differences exist, the main one is the use of numerous national currencies. The foreign exchange market consists of a communications network and correspondent relations between banks in several countries. This system permits the rapid and easy exchange of one currency for another.

The United States balance of payments is a systematic listing of the types and dollar volume of transactions which cause foreign

[3]See Chapter 26, p. 472.

countries to have a claim upon the United States and those which give the United States a claim against the rest of the world. The dollar volume of the credit and debit sides of the balance of payments depends upon the level of prices, the level of GNP, the rate of return on investment, and consumer preferences in the United States and the rest of the world. The cost of foreign exchange is one determinant of the balance of payments. The balance of payments, in turn, is a determinant of the foreign exchange rate. The balance of payments is in equilibrium when debits equal credits exclusive of gold movements and other balancing items. The United States has had a deficit in its balance of payments for a number of years. Net grants and investments in excess of the export surplus is the cause.

QUESTIONS

1. How would you classify each of the following transactions in the United States balance of payments:
    a. A gift of money by an American to a relative living in Italy?
    b. Expenditures by the United States armed forces stationed in Germany?
    c. Dividends received by an American owner of stock in a Canadian corporation?
    d. The shipment of gold to France?
    e. The sale of United States Government bonds to a bank in Germany?
2. How would a business depression in the United States affect the balance of payments of European nations?
3. How would devaluation of the United States dollar affect the balance of payments of this nation? How would it affect other nations?
4. Is the deficit in the United States balance of payments the result of excessive imports? Discuss.

SUGGESTED READINGS

Balassa, Bela (ed.). *Changing Patterns in Foreign Trade and Payments.* New York: W. W. Norton & Company, Inc., 1964. Part I.

Crutchfield, James A., Henning, Charles N., and Pigott, William. *Money, Financial Institutions, and the Economy.* Englewood Cliffs, N. J.: Prentice-Hall, Inc., 1965. Chapter 12.

Marcus, Edward, and Marcus, Mildred Rendl. *International Trade and Finance.* New York: Pitman Publishing Corporation, 1965. Chapters 5–15.

Snider, Delbert A. *Introduction to International Economics.* 3d ed. Homewood, Illinois: Richard D. Irwin, Inc., 1963. Chapters 8 and 9.

26
EXCHANGE RATES

We have noted that the foreign exchange rate is the price of foreign money. We know also that the forces of supply and demand determine price in a free market. Therefore, we should expect the credit and debit forces of the balance of payments to determine the rate of foreign exchange if the market were free from government interference. Furthermore, since the determinants of the several debit and credit types of transactions are subject to change, we should expect the free market rate of foreign exchange to fluctuate.

This fluctuation of the rate performs a service. It causes adjustments in credit and debit items that keep the balance of payments in equilibrium. This is the same service that changing prices in commodity markets perform. They cause adjustments which bring supply and demand into equality. A fluctuating foreign exchange rate also renders a disservice. Money is useful to mankind because it permits a high degree of specialization. If the value of money fluctuates, its usefulness in this role declines; it does not facilitate trade and specialization to the same extent as does a stable money. For this reason we have stressed the need for stability in the value of domestic money. The same principle applies on the international level.

We need not confine our case against fluctuating rates to this *a priori* reasoning. There have been occasions when nations have permitted the rate of foreign exchange to fluctuate freely. The world discovered that fluctuations were more severe than the imbalance in export-import and other credit-debit items suggested. Speculators anticipating a rise or fall in the exchange rate bought or sold foreign exchange and thus intensified the upward or downward pressure. These pronounced fluctuations and the danger of additional variations discouraged international trade and investment. Because of this adverse effect on international trade, and on occasion for other reasons, nations have not permitted exchange rates to fluctuate freely except for brief periods.[1]

[1] In recent years Canada has permitted rather wide fluctuations in the value of its dollar. This case is an approximation of a freely fluctuating rate. However, there is a limit on the range of these rate changes.

There are many methods by which a nation may intervene in the foreign exchange market to stabilize the rates. Logically, the method used should:

1. stabilize the rate of foreign exchange,
2. provide for equilibrium in the balance of payments,
3. be consistent with the economic philosophy of the nation,
4. be consistent with the objectives of domestic economic policy, and
5. be consistent with the nation's foreign policy.

Point 1 is obvious. Rate stabilization is the primary objective of the policy. Point 2 requires an explanation. We know that a fluctuating price brings supply and demand into equilibrium. If a price is "fixed," there is the danger that supply will consistently exceed or fall short of demand at that price. When a nation stabilizes the foreign exchange rate, the rate can no longer fluctuate to bring the credits and debits of the balance of payments into equilibrium. Therefore, a different means of achieving this equilibrium is necessary.

Point 3 is worthy of mention, although one must admit that a nation is not always logically consistent in developing a group of policies. Nevertheless, a country with the basic philosophy of the United States should adopt policies which influence individual decisions but still permit individual freedom in foreign trade. A collectivist nation may adopt stronger and more direct controls.

We already have some familiarity with points 4 and 5. In an earlier chapter we noted that the gold-outflow problem caused the United States to modify its domestic monetary and fiscal policies. Similar adjustments are necessary in order to co-ordinate a nation's political foreign policy with its foreign economic policy. It is too much to expect that a nation can find the ideal policy that fulfills all these requirements. However, our discussion of the characteristics of an ideal system helps us to understand that policy decisions are not simple. A value judgment is necessary to assign priorities to the several objectives and to compromise between these goals.

Since the exchange rate involves the currency of two countries, we may assume that there is some co-operation between these nations if rate stability exists. This co-operation may be the result of a formal agreement between two countries. Or it may be part of an international agreement designed to promote the stabilization of exchange rates. In still another instance it may involve a tacit rather than a formal agreement. An example of the latter type is the international gold standard.

THE INTERNATIONAL GOLD STANDARD

For many years prior to the depression of the 1930's, the international gold standard was considered the ideal method for stabilizing exchange rates. This international method developed gradually as the nations of the world adopted the gold standard, which we discussed in Chapter 3. By the latter part of the nineteenth century, all but a few nations were on the gold standard and remained on it until the 1930's except for the World War I years.

In Chapter 3 (see page 35) we discussed the method by which the international gold standard stabilized the rates of foreign exchange. The monetary unit of each of the nations was redeemable in a fixed amount of gold. This stabilized the value of each monetary unit in terms of gold. Consequently, the relative value of one monetary unit to another — that is, the rate of exchange — was stable. The ratio of the gold content of the domestic currency to that of the foreign units determined the rate of exchange. For example, the British pound, containing 113.0 grains of gold, exchanged for $4.87 since the United States dollar contained 23.22 gold grains. This rate was known as the *mint par of exchange*. A slight variation in the rate of foreign exchange was possible because of the cost of redeeming currency in gold, shipping the gold to another nation, and converting the gold to the new currency. This variation was so small that we may disregard it in our discussion.

Thus, the international gold standard stabilized exchange rates but what about the other desirable characteristics beginning with point 2, provision for equilibrium in the balance of payments? The gold standard provided a means for keeping the balance of payments in equilibrium. When a debit balance developed, gold exports occurred. If the nation was one in which gold coins circulated freely as money, their export reduced the money supply immediately. It was more likely, however, that the exported gold came from the reserve stock of the central bank or the leading commercial banks. In either case, the outflow of gold served as a signal to the central bank to tighten credit which led to a reduced money supply. If it ignored the signal, the continued drain of gold forced the nation off the standard. Tight credit conditions and a reduced money supply led to lower prices, a smaller national income, and possibly unemployment, which, in turn, tended to encourage exports and to discourage imports. In the nation with a credit balance, an opposite reaction occurred. Gold imports led to easier credit conditions, an expanded money supply, higher prices, a rise in national income, and a consequent increase in imports and decrease in exports. Thus, a disequilibrium in the balance of payments was self-correcting.

The term "self-correcting" is important. The successful operation of the international gold standard did not require discretionary action by the monetary authorities. The government originally established the gold content of the monetary unit, and it freely bought and sold gold at that rate. From then on the government and the central bank simply followed the "rules of the game." Under these "rules" there was an *automatic* tightening or easing of credit in response to gold movements. Furthermore, the policy measures which were used achieved their objectives by indirect methods. They affected the interest rate and the level of prices, but they did not restrict the individual's freedom to export and import and to lend and borrow abroad. Consequently, the gold standard possessed desirable characteristic number 3. It was consistent with the free enterprise and freedom of the individual philosophy which prevailed in the dominant commercial nations.

As long as a nation regarded the danger of inflation as the major economic problem which it faced, the operation of the international gold standard was consistent with the objectives of domestic economic policy. We noted in Chapter 3 that the gold standard placed a physical limit on the expansion of the money supply. However, nations have not regarded the avoidance of inflation as the only or even the chief objective of economic policy since 1930. In its place, full employment and prosperous business conditions have become important objectives. For these objectives, policies necessary to maintain the gold standard are not always appropriate. Note that under the "rules" of the international gold standard the export of gold requires the adoption of tight-money policies. This leads to equilibrium in the balance of payments at the cost of depressed business conditions and unemployment. Therefore, maintenance of the gold standard is likely to call for policies that are not consistent with modern domestic policy objectives.

With respect to foreign policy we should observe that acceptance of the gold standard causes nations to be more closely interrelated economically than is the case with some other systems. All nations use a common money, gold. The international gold standard, therefore, is not consistent with a policy of economic isolation. This is one of several reasons why nations suspend the gold standard in time of war.

The International Gold Standard—an Evaluation

An overall judgment of the system depends upon the relative values one assigns to its several characteristics. For many years the leading countries of the world accepted the international gold standard almost without question. This was an era when the freedom of individuals enjoyed a high priority. There was also a tendency to think that government intervention in the economic system was invariably harmful.

During the worldwide depression of the 1930's, opinion changed. Many nations decided that the need to overcome unemployment was more pressing than the desirability of a stable exchange rate. Furthermore, some nations discovered that an unstable exchange rate was acceptable and even advisable. These nations observed that devaluation of their own currency in the foreign exchange market stimulated exports. At the same time government intervention in the economic system became more acceptable and interference with individual freedom more tolerable. Finally, many nations felt that a system which tied nations together economically reduced the effectiveness of domestic recovery policies. Incidentally, the United States belonged in this latter category in the 1930's. With these changes in opinion and in the sense of values, the international gold standard was no longer an acceptable system.

International liquidity. One more problem which nations on the international gold standard faced deserves comment since it exists today. During the period of universal acceptance of the gold standard, the volume of world business increased rapidly. The increase in the quantity of international money depended on gold production. Since the rate of gold production was less than the growth rate of the world's economy, the danger of a shortage of money existed. Logically, one might suggest that a scaling down of prices would eliminate the problem but this would involve worldwide deflation and probable unemployment. In the absence of a downward movement of world prices, the fear of a liquidity crisis persisted.

Symptoms of an approaching crisis would be a shortage of gold reserves in all countries. One would then expect competitive credit restrictions as nations attempted to attract gold from their neighbors. The crisis itself would be similar to a domestic liquidity crisis. As confidence in the ability of various nations to redeem their money in gold waned, individuals and institutions would redeem the money of those nations in gold and thus would precipitate a massive exchange of credit money for gold. This is the same principle that underlies a run on a bank.

Leading nations attempted to avoid an international liquidity crisis by economizing in the use of gold. The gold bullion and the gold exchange standards, which we discussed in Chapter 3, accomplished this purpose. Unfortunately, using gold efficiently meant that a given quantity of gold as a monetary reserve became the basis for an expanded domestic money supply. When an international "run on the bank" started, this placed additional pressure on the banker nations; that is, the ones holding the gold reserve. This illustrates once again the close relationship of the domestic to the international economy under the gold standard.

The problem is interesting since it points to a fundamental defect in the international gold standard. Gold production rather than the needs of commerce determined the money supply. We have already commented on the lack of logic in such a policy in a domestic monetary system. It is of interest to us also because the danger of an international liquidity crisis exists when nations use a limited gold bullion standard similar to that of the United States today. Currently, the United States is serving as the banker to the free world, and part of our balance-of-payments problems revolves around the chance of a "run on the bank."

A REPLACEMENT FOR THE INTERNATIONAL GOLD STANDARD

The abandonment of the international gold standard required the nations of the world to develop another system. It was most important that the new system provide for reasonably stable exchange rates and for equilibrium in the balance of payments. Of course, after 1930, the economic philosophy, the domestic economic objectives, and the foreign policy of many nations changed. Nevertheless, provision for the other characteristics discussed in this chapter was still considered desirable. To these desirable characteristics, we may add that the system should avoid the danger of international illiquidity. There are two basic methods for achieving these goals. One depends on stabilization funds; the other on exchange controls.

The Exchange Rate for Inconvertible Paper Currency

A nation is on an inconvertible paper standard when it halts the redemption of its currency in gold. When this occurs, money continues to be valuable within the nation's boundaries as long as it is accepted in payment for goods and services. However, the question of its value in the foreign exchange market arises. We answer this in a general way by stating that the domestic currency is worth whatever the owners of foreign currency are willing to give for it. The willingness of holders of foreign currency to part with it depends upon the supply and the demand conditions of the foreign exchange market.

Thus, we return to the credits and the debits of the balance of payments. If the nation allows the foreign exchange value of its money to move in response to the market, we expect an equilibrium rate at which the credit and debit sides of the balance of payments are equal. This condition, in which there is no tendency for exports to exceed imports or *vice versa*, occurs when the purchasing power of domestic currency is approximately the same at home as it is abroad. It is customary to state that the exchange rate in the absence of the gold standard and in a free market is one of *purchasing power parity*. For example, if $4 exchanges for £1, we expect $4 to buy approximately the same amount of goods and services in the United States as £1 does in England. This is the approximate, but not the precise, rate because many goods and services do not enter foreign trade.

Stabilization Funds

The principle of the operation of a stabilization fund is simple. A nation, or more likely the central bank acting as the government's agent, acquires a supply of its own currency in addition to a supply of foreign currency. Using this "fund," it influences supply and demand conditions by buying and selling currency on the foreign exchange market. It is possible to maintain a stable rate for foreign exchange by this method. However, the stabilization fund does not allow a nation to determine *a priori* the rate of exchange. Stabilization is possible only if the nation chooses the long-run equilibrium rate; that is, the rate at which the debits and the credits in the balance of payments are equal. The stabilization fund can overcome short-run inequalities in debits and credits but not a persistent imbalance. A nation may allow the value of its currency to fluctuate freely while the monetary authorities are estimating this equilibrium rate.

The stabilization fund system does not contain an automatic device for achieving equilibrium in the balance of payments. If a nation is fortunate, the exchange rate may lead to deficits in some years and surpluses in others. The balance of payments is in equilibrium over the extended period, and the stabilization fund serves as a temporary or short-run balancing item during times of deficit and surplus. However, if there is a prolonged deficit, the nation will exhaust the supply of foreign exchange in the fund. It follows that the successful use of a stabilization fund involves the adoption of policies to correct disequilibria. These policies are discretionary rather than automatic. They include monetary and fiscal measures to curtail imports and to encourage exports. Or they may be more direct and use import quotas, tariffs, and subsidies for exports. If the disequilibrium is so persistent and so severe that these measures do not correct it, the deficit nation may devalue its monetary unit. In that case the stabilization fund has not "stabilized." However, it has allowed the nation time to try to correct its problems and to make an orderly adjustment in the exchange rate. In summary, stabilization funds cannot receive a perfect rating for characteristic number 2, provision for equilibrium in the balance of payments.

Concerning the other characteristics, the fund method involves government intervention to a certain extent but it leaves the individual free to trade, to loan, and to borrow. This is consistent with the basic economic philosophy of most of the free nations today. One must admit that its use sometimes requires monetary and fiscal policies that are not desirable if one considers only domestic economic objectives. Finally, we must note that it requires a certain degree of co-operation among nations: funds of two nations will not stabilize the rates of exchange unless the nations agree upon a single rate.

Limited Gold Bullion Standard

A limited gold bullion standard, such as the United States employs, may appear to be a minor modification of the international gold standard. This appearance is misleading. In reality, the present system contains major elements of the inconvertible currency-stabilization fund approach. A nation on a limited gold bullion standard buys gold at a fixed rate. It also redeems its currency in gold but for legitimate monetary purposes only. This stabilizes the exchange rate for those nations using the system unless the "limited" feature imposes unreasonable restrictions on redemption. In this characteristic it is similar to the international gold standard. The operation of the system is quite different from the operation of the international gold standard, however, because nations do not allow a deficit or a surplus in the balance of payments to serve as a signal for automatic restrictive or expansionary measures. Instead, the surplus nation simply accumulates gold and financial claims against other countries (balancing items 12A to 12D in Table 25–1). The deficit nation uses balancing items (11A–D) to solve the balance-of-payments problem temporarily. It uses these items to produce the same effect as a stabilization fund. In fact, transactions involving stabilization funds are part of categories 11 and 12 in the balance of payments.

Eventually the deficit nation must take steps to increase receipts and/or to decrease payments. These are discretionary policies like those of a nation with inconvertible currency. In determining policy, the nation will probably place greater emphasis on full employment and other domestic objectives than was the case in the era of the international gold standard. Also, it will be less reluctant to devalue its currency or to suspend redemption in gold. Other characteristics, such as the effect on individual freedom and the need for international co-operation, are the same for a nation on the limited gold bullion and for one on an inconvertible paper standard.

Use of a monetary standard employing a stabilization fund is appropriate for a nation which desires stable exchange rates without subordinating domestic economic objectives to the goal of protecting its gold reserves. It involves a compromise between the extremes of complete control by the government and no government influence. The individual is free to trade, but the government intervenes at its discretion to influence supply and demand conditions in the foreign exchange market. As we have seen, stabilization funds are successful only in the absence of a fundamental disequilibrium in the balance of payments. A fundamental disequilibrium—that is, one whose correction requires drastic changes in the price level or devaluation of the currency—will exhaust the fund. For this reason, nations which normally prefer this method find that they must use a different system in time of war or other crisis.

Exchange Controls

The international monetary systems which we have discussed are consistent with a philosophy which places a high value on individual freedom. Exchange controls, as the term "controls" suggests, are consistent with a different philosophy. The principle underlying this system is a simple one. However, the administration of exchange controls is quite complicated. A nation using exchange controls sets the rate for foreign exchange. As we shall see, this rate need not be the rate which achieves equilibrium in the balance of payments in a free market. To enforce this rate, the nation grants the central bank or the treasury a monopoly of all foreign exchange transactions. Persons who wish to buy foreign exchange can purchase it only from the central bank at the official rate. Likewise, the earners of foreign exchange must sell their proceeds to the central bank. This monopoly power enables the nation to maintain the exchange rate rigidly at the official figure it establishes.

For reasons we shall discuss in a later paragraph, requests to purchase foreign exchange usually exceed the volume of sales to the central bank. Therefore, it is necessary to ration foreign exchange to the applicants with the higher priorities. Because of this lack of balance between supply and demand, there exists a number of unsatisfied applicants for foreign exchange, many of whom are willing to pay a premium rate. This provides an incentive for the earners of foreign exchange to ignore the central bank and to sell directly (and illegally) to the unsatisfied applicants. These earners are generally exporters and the proceeds from the sale of their products usually accumulate as a deposit in a foreign bank. The presence of these foreign exchange balances outside the area of jurisdiction of the control authorities complicates the problem of enforcement. In the absence of vigorous enforcement measures, a "black market" arises where the owners of foreign bank deposits and foreign currency sell these assets. A flourishing black market, of course, destroys the effectiveness of exchange controls. Therefore, a nation which establishes a system to control foreign exchange finds that it must extend the area of its control over other segments of the nation's economic activities in order to prevent the growth of the black market.

Reasons for adopting exchange controls. The most common motive for establishing exchange controls is a desire to maintain an "overvalued" currency in foreign exchange transactions. A currency is "overvalued" if the exchange rate leads to a persistent balance-of-payments deficit in a free market. Correction by means of deflationary domestic policies or by devaluation of the domestic currency in terms of foreign exchange is possible. However, deflation is painful and devaluation turns the barter terms of trade against the nation devaluing its currency. If the demand for exports and/or imports is inelastic with regard to price, severe deflation or devaluation will be necessary. Also, national pride may provide a psychological barrier to devaluation. A nation can avoid the need for either of these policies by using exchange controls. At first, it may regard these controls as a temporary measure; it continues them as a matter of expediency.

The need to ration scarce foreign exchange among the many applicants allows a nation to implement policies its leaders consider desirable. An applicant who receives permission to purchase foreign exchange is the recipient of a valuable privilege. In domestic politics the award or refusal of this privilege can be a means of rewarding friends, applying pressure to neutrals, and punishing enemies. Exchange controls can serve as an implement of domestic economic policy. The central bank may sell foreign exchange to importers of "essential" goods and may refuse to sell for the importation of "non-essentials." The government, of course, determines what is essential and what is nonessential. The definition of terms will be consistent with the nation's domestic economic objectives.

By using exchange controls, a nation can maintain two or more rates of foreign exchange. This is similar to a monopolist who practices price discrimination in selling his product. The use of two rates of exchange allows the nation to be more precise in implementing policies. For example, prior to 1959 Argentina exchanged its peso at the "regular" rate of approximately 1 to 5½ United States cents. There was also a "free" rate of approximately 1 to 2¼ United States cents. The free rate, incidentally, had its origin in an uncontrollable black market. The control authorities could sell United States dollars, or foreign exchange in general, to favored importers at the 5½-cent rate. A less favored importer would receive the free rate, 2¼ cents, for his pesos while still others might be denied the right to purchase foreign exchange. Favored exporters could dispose of their foreign exchange at the free rate while others had to deliver foreign exchange to the central bank at the regular rate. Such a system obviously lends itself to use as a political weapon. It can also serve to promote domestic and foreign economic policy. In the latter respect it achieves the same results as a tariff, a quota on imports, or a series of subsidies and tariffs on exports.

Exchange controls eliminate the free market in which arbitragers operate. Therefore, the cross rates of exchange need not be consistent. By means of exchange controls, a nation can maintain rates that favor imports from certain countries and can discriminate against others. In this fashion exchange controls may serve as an implement of foreign policy.

We have seen enough reasons for imposing exchange controls and the implications of their adoption to know that they are not appropriate for nations dedicated to freedom of the individual. There is an exception to this principle however. In time of war "free" nations have adopted exchange controls along with direct controls over the domestic economy. Exchange controls help to insure that the national resources are making the maximum contribution to the war effort. They are also a useful device to prevent international transactions which aid the enemy.

Exchange controls—consequences. We have considered the possible uses of exchange controls but what about the effect exchange controls have on the nations which adopt them? For nations with a collectivist philosophy, exchange controls are simply a consistent part of an overall economic system. For noncollectivist nations a movement toward a controlled economy and particularly toward controlled or state trading has accompanied the prolonged use of exchange controls. This may not have been the motive for adopting the system, but the need to prevent free trading in foreign exchange leads to this result. Also, there is reason to believe that the use of exchange controls encourages inflation. Controls are not the fundamental cause of inflation but they serve to protect domestic producers from foreign competition and thus reduce the incentives to cut costs. They also protect the nation from the discipline which the balance of payments otherwise enforces on its economic stabilization policies.

Probably the most important consequence of exchange controls is the incentive they provide for bilateral trading. The nation using these controls is in a good position to force its exports upon the countries from whom it buys its imports. When this occurs nations forfeit the advantages of specialization resulting from multilateral trade. Nations cannot buy in the cheapest market. In extreme cases a nation may buy products for which it has very little use because it sells its own products to a nation which has a surplus of these goods. The United States has opposed the use of exchange controls for this reason, and it has attempted to persuade other nations to avoid their use or to discontinue their use if already adopted.

Before ending our discussion of exchange controls, we should summarize the pertinent characteristics. Including the three characteristics described previously, exchange controls:

1. allow a nation to fix and to maintain a stable foreign exchange rate,
2. use rationing techniques to maintain the equality of debits and credits in the balance of payments,
3. are consistent with the philosophy of a "controlled economy,"
4. are consistent with the objectives of domestic economic policy if these objectives require direct government intervention,
5. may serve as a weapon in international politics, and
6. do not promote the optimum allocation of resources if maximum world output is the objective.

EXCHANGE RATES—THE PROBLEM OF THE DOLLAR

In Chapter 25 we noted that the United States has a chronic deficit in its balance of payments. Also, we saw that a balance-of-payments deficit can lead to devaluation of a nation's currency in the foreign exchange market and that this devaluation can be the means of eliminating the deficit. Some economists have recommended that the United States devalue its currency by reducing the gold content of the dollar. They claim that the result would be equilibrium in the United States balance of payments and an increase in international liquidity. This latter phenomenon would occur because the world's stock of gold would be worth more in terms of United States dollars. The United States has rejected these recommendations. It claims that devaluation would weaken the position of the dollar as a "key" international currency with consequent adverse effects on the United States' position as the political leader of the free world. Also, the weakening of the dollar as a key international currency would reduce the supply of international liquid assets and thus would undermine the structure of world payments and trade.

A system of exchange controls or direct restrictions on payments is an alternative solution. However, this method would be inconsistent with United States principles regarding the economic freedom of the individual. In addition, and perhaps of greater significance, restrictions on payments would weaken the status of the dollar as an international currency and would threaten the leadership position of the United States in the free world. Therefore, the nation must solve its balance-of-payments problem without resorting to either devaluation or exchange controls.

United States Policy

The United States has adopted policies which counter the effect of the deficit in the balance of payments as well as measures designed to bring the accounts into equilibrium. In Chapter 24 we mentioned "operation nudge," designed to raise the interest rates on short-term securities. Higher short-term interest rates in the United States encourage individuals to keep their idle funds on deposit in this country rather than abroad (item 11C).[2] The Treasury and the Federal Reserve officials have used moral suasion to influence other central banks to convert dollar assets to United States securities rather than to gold (item 11B). The United States Government has persuaded friendly nations, particularly those with a balance-of-payments surplus, to prepay debts owed to the United States and to pay for military purchases in advance (item 11A).

These measures are palliatives, not cures. They enable the United States to reduce the current outflow of gold by using balancing items other than gold exports. Of course, in time the United States must redeem these securities and other financial assets held by foreigners. In fact the measures are effective only if the creditors believe that the United States will eliminate the payments deficit.

During the time gained by these policies, the United States must bring its balance of payments into equilibrium. To eliminate the deficit, the United States must achieve some combination of (1) an increase in the export of goods and services; (2) a decrease in the import of goods and services; (3) a decrease in net grants, both government and private; and (4) a decrease in net foreign investments. We shall consider policies for each of these categories.

[2] All references are to items in Table 25–1.

　　Increasing the volume of exports is highly desirable but not easy to accomplish. Table 25–2 shows that exports exceed imports including tourist expenditures and military purchases by the United States. The United States, employing both monetary and fiscal policy, aims at a further expansion of this net figure. A relatively low, long-term interest rate encourages domestic investment in new equipment which leads to lower costs of production and a better competitive position for American producers. Fiscal policy employs a lenient income tax depreciation regulation for buyers of plant and equipment. Also, monetary and fiscal policy can assist in preventing inflation so that American products have low prices on the world market. If costs of production and prices in the rest of the world continue to rise, the United States export balance will increase. Obviously, these policies require time before becoming effective.

　　The United States could take immediate action to reduce imports by raising tariff rates. However, this would not be consistent with our foreign policy objective of free trade. Therefore, the United States has confined its policy to a reduction of the value of goods which returning travellers can bring into the country duty free. In addition, the Government has used moral suasion to encourage tourists to travel in the United States instead of abroad, thus reducing the importation of services (item 2D). To a limited extent, the Government has reduced imports by persuading other nations to bear a larger portion of overseas military responsibilities. The United States has also adopted a policy of purchasing a smaller portion of its military supplies abroad.

　　The United States has made no attempt to interfere with private remittances. These are usually contributions to charitable agencies or members of the remitter's family. Government grants present a more complex problem. Since the United States has a deficit, other nations must have a surplus. Therefore, it may appear that the United States deficit is the result of grants to nations with a surplus. The obvious solution appears to be the cessation of the grants. However, the nations with a surplus in their balance of payments are not the recipients of large United States grants. The recipients are in general the underdeveloped nations who also have a balance of payments deficit. Cessation of grants might lead to political instability and is inconsistent with United States foreign policy. The United States is approaching the problem through moral suasion. It attempts to persuade the nations with a surplus to assume a larger part of the burden of the aid to these underdeveloped nations. This policy has had only limited success. Like the other measures we have mentioned, time is necessary before it can become effective.

　　Net private foreign investment is another debit category in

which the choice of a correct policy appears simple. It would appear that a nation operating at a deficit cannot afford foreign investments. Therefore, the United States should adopt policies to restrict the foreign investment activities of American citizens. However, such action would reduce the influence of America in world affairs. Also, some of this investment occurs in underdeveloped countries. It is part of the United States foreign policy to encourage the development of these nations and to supplement private investment with Government grants and loans. More important, foreign investment today leads to dividend and interest income in the future (item 1C). Consequently, the eventual solution to the United States deficit depends in part on the foreign investment programs.

Nevertheless, the United States has used fiscal policy to reduce the volume of private foreign investment. It has imposed a special tax on foreign loans and investments. Since the tax was to be retroactive to the date of the introduction of the bill, it was effective as a deterrent before its enactment by Congress. This serves as an example of the important role of expectations in economic decisions. This tax is to be a temporary measure. In addition, the Government has used moral suasion. The President has urged private business voluntarily to restrict its investments in other countries pending the solution of the balance-of-payments problem.

We have emphasized the problems facing the United States; there is also a bright side to the picture. We should note that the United States consistently had a surplus in the balance of payments from World War I to 1950. This may explain the nation's tardiness in recognizing the deficit as a serious problem as well as its ambitious grant and foreign investment programs. The United States' position contains many sound features. Exports of goods and services exceed imports. Hence, the nation is not living beyond its means in this category. The export surplus also indicates that United States producers are able to compete successfully in world markets. Investment income is large and is rising. This item, plus other adjustments, should bring the accounts into equilibrium. Most experts in international economics expect the United States to solve its balance-of-payments problem without devaluing the dollar.

A new problem is likely to arise when the United States eliminates its balance-of-payments deficit. We observed that United States dollars are an international currency. Therefore, the liquid reserves of the rest of the world consist of dollar holdings plus gold. The United States deficit of approximately $3 billion per year has been a source of additional liquid reserves or international currency for other countries. Consequently, the world has been able to increase the volume of international transactions without a liquidity crisis because of this increase in international money. By solving its balance-of-payments problem, the United States will eliminate this source of international liquidity. Co-operative efforts by the nations of the world will be necessary if they are to avoid an international liquidity crisis. Chapter 27 considers the institutions which can provide this co-operative effort.

SUMMARY

A freely fluctuating foreign exchange rate is one method of achieving equilibrium in the balance of payments. This method permits individuals to trade without government interference. However, experience shows that the risk of loss because of a rate change discourages international trade and international lending. For many years the international gold standard stabilized foreign exchange rates. It also provided for automatic policies which kept the balance of payments in equilibrium. In addition, it permitted free trading and lending by individuals. The nations of the world abandoned this system because they decided that fluctuations in the domestic economy were too high a price to pay for exchange rate stability.

Inconvertible currency standards and limited gold bullion standards use "balancing items" to stabilize the exchange rate. These systems are consistent with the belief in individual freedom, but they do not provide for automatic maintenance of long-run equilibrium in the balance of payments. Discretionary policy measures are necessary to achieve this objective.

Through the use of exchange controls, a nation may establish and maintain a desired exchange rate. This method involves rationing techniques to keep credits equal to debits in the balance of payments and is consistent with an overall system of government control of the economy. A nation may use these controls to maintain an exchange rate that overvalues its currency. Therefore, exchange controls can be implements of policy designed to achieve domestic and international economic objectives. Exchange controls interfere with free multilateral trade and thus prevent the optimum degree of specialization on a worldwide basis.

The United States has rejected both devaluation and exchange controls as devices for the solution of the balance-of-payments problem. Instead, it is employing moral suasion, fiscal policy, and monetary policy to overcome the deficit. When the deficit is eliminated a new problem, international illiquidity, is likely to arise.

QUESTIONS

1. What are the arguments in favor of freely fluctuating rates of exchange? What are the disadvantages?
2. Why is the traditional international gold standard inappropriate in a world which accords a high priority to full employment?
3. Why are stabilization funds likely to be ineffective in the presence of a fundamental disequilibrium in the balance of payments?
4. Can a nation use exchange controls if the domestic economy remains free of government domination? Discuss.
5. What would be the effect of a devaluation of the United States dollar?

SUGGESTED READINGS

Balassa, Bela (ed.). *Changing Patterns in Foreign Trade and Payments.* New York: W. W. Norton & Company, Inc., 1964. Part 3.

Crutchfield, James A., Henning, Charles N., and Pigott, William. *Money, Financial Institutions, and the Economy.* Englewood Cliffs, N. J.: Prentice-Hall, Inc., 1965. Chapter 12.

Lary, Hal B. *Problems of the United States as World Trader and Banker.* Princeton, N. J.: Princeton University Press, 1963.

Snider, Delbert A. *Introduction to International Economics.* 3d ed. Homewood, Illinois: Richard D. Irwin, Inc., 1963. Chapters 10 to 17.

Triffin, Robert. *Gold and the Dollar Crisis.* New Haven: Yale University Press, 1960. Part One.

27

INTERNATIONAL MONETARY ORGANIZATIONS

The need for some form of international monetary co-operation is evident if one remembers that the function of a monetary system is to facilitate trade. In a nation the monetary system achieves this purpose with a common currency and single banking system. Ideally, one might suggest that a common currency and single banking system would be the logical method to achieve this objective internationally. Tradition and a spirit of nationalism are barriers to the establishment of such a system. Other problems would arise. A national monetary policy is necessary to achieve domestic economic goals, and the policies of an international monetary system would not always be consistent with national objectives. If a common monetary system is impractical, however, we can still facilitate international transactions by means of stable exchange rates and a free foreign exchange market. Co-operation is necessary to create these conditions.

The international gold standard provided for stable exchange rates and free markets in foreign exchange. In fact, we may regard gold as the international monetary unit under this system. We have seen that the successful operation of the international gold standard required co-operation between countries. For example, we noted that in 1927 the Federal Reserve System designed an easy-money policy to assist England re-establish the gold standard. Operation of the international gold standard generally involved tacit understandings rather than formal agreements and treaties. Also, the system operated without a formal organization similar to the International Monetary Fund.

THE DEVELOPMENT OF INTERNATIONAL CO-OPERATION

After the collapse of the international gold standard, conditions in the 1930's convinced the leaders of many nations that international co-operation was necessary. As each nation stopped redeeming its monetary units in gold, the value of its currency in the foreign exchange market declined. This devaluation aided its exports temporarily but it encouraged other nations to devalue their currency. In

486

an effort to stimulate their exports, and for other reasons, all nations devalued their currency during this decade. Some writers of this period believed that many devaluations were competitive in nature. Regardless of the motives, the series of devaluations caused constant fluctuations in the rates of foreign exchange and raised a barrier to international trade. Also, severe disequilibria in the balance of payments of many nations led to the use of exchange controls which further restricted trade. These balance of payments difficulties were the cause rather than the result of the abandonment of the international gold standard; nevertheless the exchange controls which followed made the need for a new system of international payments more apparent.

The worldwide depression of the 1930's led to many defaults on international debt. In other instances the debtor paid in local currency, but devaluation and exchange controls reduced the value of these payments to the creditor. The result was the equivalent of at least a partial default. This experience caused investors to be extremely cautious and international investment declined to almost nothing. In the absence of international investment, the world was not allocating its capital resources to the areas where they would be most productive.

World War II led to more exchange controls and the cessation of normal trade relations. It also created a co-operative spirit among the allied nations, especially between the United States and England. As a result representatives of the allied nations met at Bretton Woods, New Hampshire, in 1944, to consider the financial problems which the postwar world would face and to lay plans for a satisfactory international monetary system. To be satisfactory the system should provide for stable exchange rates, the elimination of exchange controls, and a resumption of international investment. Two institutions came into existence as a result of the Bretton Woods meeting. The International Monetary Fund (IMF) was to provide for stable exchange rates and the elimination of exchange controls. The International Bank for Reconstruction and Development (IBRD) was to create conditions leading to the resumption of international investment.

THE INTERNATIONAL MONETARY FUND

The Articles of the Bretton Woods agreement state the general purpose of the IMF:

1. To promote international monetary co-operation through a permanent institution which provides the machinery for consultation and collaboration of international monetary problems.

2. To facilitate the expansion and balanced growth of international trade, and to contribute thereby to the promotion and maintenance of high levels of employment and real income and to the development of the productive resources of all members as primary objectives of economic policy.

3. To promote exchange stability, to maintain orderly exchange arrangements among members, and to avoid competitive exchange depreciation.

4. To assist in the establishment of a multilateral system of payments in respect of current transactions between members and in the elimination of foreign exchange restrictions which hamper the growth of world trade.

5. To give confidence to members by making the Fund's resources available to them under adequate safeguards, thus providing them with opportunity to correct maladjustments in their balance of payments without resorting to measures destructive of national or international prosperity.

6. In accordance with the above, to shorten the duration and lessen the degree of disequilibrium in the international balances of payments of members.

We shall discuss the operation of the IMF first under ideal conditions. Of course, this will be unrealistic since these perfect conditions do not exist. This approach, however, provides us with a clear picture of the principles underlying the organization. Second, we shall examine the actual environment in which the Fund operates and shall note the extent to which it accomplishes its mission.

The IMF is a permanent institution which provides for regular meetings of its members. At these meetings the member nations determine administrative policy for the Fund and discuss international monetary problems and policies. In the ideal environment which we assume exists, the members agree on monetary policies to facilitate the expansion of international trade as well as the other objectives stated in point two of the Articles. More specifically, the members agree on a set of foreign exchange rates. In the ideal world this structure of rates leads to long-run equilibrium in the balance of payments of each nation. A stabilization fund which the IMF operates prevents rate fluctuations in response to short-run disequilibria. In this fashion the system eliminates the need for exchange controls, and the nations with such controls abandon them. Finally, consultation and agreement precede a change in the structure of foreign exchange rates or other adjustments in policy which changing world conditions make necessary. Thus through international co-operation, including the operation of a stabilization fund, the world achieves stable exchange rates and eliminates exchange controls.

The ideal conditions in which such a system could operate successfully did not exist at the time of the Fund's establishment nor do they exist today. Therefore, compromises were necessary. We shall note these compromises with pure principle as we examine the record of the IMF. The creation of the IMF assumed that all nations desired a system of free international payments. In reality, a number of nations preferred a controlled system. Therefore, most collectivist nations did not join, and those that joined did not remain members for long. Presently the IMF operates within the free world only.

Development of the IMF

One hundred two nations are members and their representatives, called governors, meet regularly. Thus the Fund has provided for consultation regarding monetary policy. In addition the Fund has agreed to a "par" value, expressed in terms of gold or United States dollars, for the monetary unit of each member nation. The Fund acquired its capital by setting a quota, in par values, for each member. The prewar national income and the foreign trade of each member were the basis for determining the quota. Each member paid gold into the Fund in an amount equal to one fourth of its quota or one tenth of its reserves of gold and United States dollars, whichever amount was the smaller. The members paid the remainder in either gold or in their own currency — usually the latter. Table 27–1 shows

Table 27–1

QUOTAS OF
INTERNATIONAL MONETARY FUND MEMBERS
as of February 28, 1965

(In millions of U. S. dollars)

Nation	Quota
Argentina	280.0
Australia	400.0
Belgium	337.5
Brazil	280.0
Canada	550.0
China (Taiwan)	550.0
France	787.5
Germany (Federal Republic)	787.5
India	600.0
Italy	500.0
Japan	500.0
Netherlands	412.5
United Kingdom	1,950.0
United States	4,125.0
Remaining 88 nations	3,825.2
Total	15,885.2

Source: International Monetary Fund, *International Financial Statistics* (a monthly), April, 1965, pp. 2–3.

the quotas as of February 28, 1965. The total is the capital of the IMF, and it is also the stabilization fund. Voting rights to control the Fund are roughly proportional to the size of the quota with some preference shown to smaller nations at the expense of larger ones. For example, the United States and the United Kingdom quotas, respectively, account for 26.0 and 12.3 per cent of the total fund; but their voting rights are equal to roughly 25 and 12 per cent, respectively.

The first major problem concerned the determination of par values for 1946. These values should have been the rates of exchange which would have produced long-run equilibrium in the balance of payments. Unfortunately, World War II had disrupted normal trade channels and the widespread use of exchange controls made it difficult to estimate the extent to which the exchange rates then in use differed from the equilibrium rates. Even if the Fund had been able to select equilibrium rates as the par values in 1946, it would have faced the need for sizable changes as postwar reconstruction and adjustments occurred. One approach would have been to

Table 27–2

INTERNATIONAL MONETARY FUND
PAR VALUES OF THE PRINCIPAL CURRENCIES
1946, 1965

(In United States cents)

Nation	Currency Unit	Original Par Value 1946	Par Value 1965[a]
Australia	pound	322.4	224.0
Belgium	franc	2.28	2.282
Canada	dollar	100.00	92.5
France	franc	.839	20.255[b]
Germany (Federal Republic)	deutsche mark	—	25.0
India	rupee	30.225	21.0
Italy	lira	—	.16
Japan	yen	—	.2778
Netherlands	guilder	37.695	27.6243
United Kingdom	pound	403.0	280.0
United States	dollar	100.00	100.00

[a]As of March 15, 1965.
[b]New franc. One new French franc is equal to 100 old francs.
Source: International Monetary Fund, *International Financial Statistics*, April, 1965, p. 10.

wait for a more "normal" period before fixing the par values. This solution, however, would have delayed the operation of the Fund indefinitely. Consequently, the Fund established par values in 1946. Adjustments were necessary in response to changing conditions as Table 27–2 indicates. Of course, adjustments and stability are contradictory terms, at least to some degree. Therefore, frequent adjustments indicate imperfections in the operation of the Fund.

The subscription of members created a stabilization fund for the IMF. Its purpose was to assist members to maintain stable exchange rates without recourse to exchange controls. A member with a deficit in its balance of payments can borrow from the Fund. We use the term borrow but trade or purchase may be more accurate since the deficit nation pays its own currency into the fund and receives the foreign currency it desires in return. For this privilege it pays a service charge of $\frac{1}{2}$ of 1 per cent per year.

At the time of the organization of the IMF, the United States had a large and persistent surplus in its balance of payments. Of course, the rest of the world had a deficit. This deficit probably was unavoidable in the postwar period; however the unrealistic par values increased the seriousness of the problem. We may describe the condition of the balance of payments by stating that United States dollars were scarce and other currency plentiful. If the IMF had operated without restrictions on borrowing, the nations with balance-of-payments deficits would have exchanged their currency for dollars. Since the dollar shortage was sizable and persistent, the Fund's supply of dollars would have disappeared quickly.

The IMF regulations contain safeguards to prevent the exhaustion of the stabilization fund. Normally it expects borrowing nations to repay in three to five years. If a persistent balance-of-payments deficit is the reason for borrowing, satisfaction of this requirement is nearly impossible. Also the Fund may restrict borrowing to one fourth of the borrowing member's quota. By applying the restriction, the Fund held borrowing to a relatively small figure for the first ten years of its existence. This protected the stabilization fund from exhaustion, but it also prevented the IMF from making a significant contribution to the elimination of exchange controls.

Most member nations continued to impose exchange controls because of balance-of-payments difficulties. The Fund permits exchange controls against a "scarce" currency. Of course, in the period when the United States had a massive balance-of-payments surplus the dollar was "scarce." Also, the Fund permits exchange controls which prevent abnormal capital outflows. The early history of the IMF shows that it has the same weaknesses as other stabilization funds. It does not and actually cannot correct a fundamental disequilibrium in the balance of payments. Other measures are necessary to accomplish this purpose.

The IMF's record has improved since the middle of the 1950's. Changed conditions, particularly the reversal of the United States balance of payments from a surplus to a deficit, have relieved the pressure on the balance of payments of other nations; consequently the IMF has been able to relax its restrictions on lending. It now lends up to one fourth of the member's quota automatically and gives

Table 27–3

DRAWINGS FROM THE
INTERNATIONAL MONETARY FUND
Through February 28, 1965
(In millions of U. S. dollars)

Nation	Amount
Argentina	377.5
Australia	225.0
Brazil	478.4
Canada	300.0
France	518.8
India	575.0
Italy	225.0
Japan	249.0
United Kingdom	2,361.5
United States	525.0
Others	3,292.9
Total	9,128.1

KINDS OF CURRENCIES DRAWN
as of February 28, 1965
(In millions of U. S. dollars)

Currency	Amount
Deutsche mark	1,505.9
French franc	856.2
Pounds sterling	638.0
U. S. dollars	4,615.6
Other	1,512.4
Total	9,128.1

Source: International Monetary Fund, *International Financial Statistics,* April, 1965, pp. 4–5, 7.

the member the benefit of the doubt in assessing its request to borrow the remaining three quarters. The IMF will lend in excess of a member's quota if the member presents a valid reason.

Its lending techniques have changed. The IMF will extend a line of credit which guarantees the member's right to borrow up to a certain amount if needed. Table 27 – 3 shows the volume of loans by the Fund as well as the kinds of currency drawn. These measures, combined with an improvement in the balance-of-payments position, have allowed many members to eliminate or at least to reduce the rigor of exchange controls. Thus, the IMF seems to have entered a period when its operations are contributing substantially to exchange rate stability and free foreign exchange markets.

There is a dark cloud in this picture however. The deficit in the United States balance of payments is responsible for the increasing ability of other nations to abandon exchange controls. When the United States eliminates the deficit, problems may arise in other countries.

The IMF and the Future

A number of experts feel that the world is approaching a liquidity crisis of the type we discussed in Chapter 26 in connection with the international gold standard. Currently, international "money" consists of gold and United States dollars which are convertible into gold. The volume of international transactions has been increasing at a more rapid rate than the world's supply of monetary gold. As long as there is a deficit in the United States balance of payments, the United States will pay gold from its reserves or will pay claims payable in United States dollars into the international system. In either case the volume of international "money" increases by $2 to $3 billion per year, the size of the deficit. In this manner, supply has equaled demand. However, the United States must eliminate this deficit in the near future and at that time a shortage may develop in the international means of payment. The consequences would be similar to those described in Chapter 26 and would hinder world trade.

Two proposals for the solution of this problem involve the IMF. The more moderate suggestion calls for an increase in each nation's subscription to the IMF. The enlarged resources would enable the IMF to increase the volume of its loans to members. Nonsynchronization of receipts and payments creates the need for liquidity in international transactions the same as it does on the domestic level. Internationally, nonsynchronization leads to alternate periods of deficit and surplus in the balance of payments. Increased capital would permit larger loans by the IMF and thus would allow for the larger temporary deficits which a nation must expect as its volume of trade grows.

A more radical proposal calls for the transformation of the IMF into a world central bank. Currently, the lending operations of the IMF are similar to the lender-of-last resort function of a central bank. However, the IMF cannot lend in excess of its capital. In fact, it simply exchanges one type of currency for another type. The IMF does not possess the power to create credit which the world accepts as money—the key function of a world central bank. If it were to become a central bank, each nation's quota would become a deposit liability. These deposits would be acceptable in settling international obligations and would be part of the depositor nation's monetary reserve. The IMF then could expand international liquidity by increasing its assets and deposit liabilities as central banks expand the liquidity of the nation for which they are responsible.

The problems of a world central bank become evident as soon as one considers monetary policy. In general terms its monetary policy should ensure the proper degree of international liquidity, but how is the bank to determine how much international money it should create? The most likely answer is that it should stabilize the purchasing power of international money; that is, gold. However, it is unlikely that any single monetary policy is appropriate for all nations. For domestic reasons some nations desire tight- and others easy-money conditions. If the world central bank adopts a tight-money policy, it will create unemployment in the latter nations. If it chooses an easy-money policy, the first group of nations will experience an increase in inflationary pressures. Also, a central bank frequently must adopt policies which are unpopular in certain sectors of the economy. In these instances it is difficult for a central bank to get acceptance of its policies from the single nation to which and for which it is responsible. It is unlikely that an international central bank's decision, made by "foreigners," will be acceptable in all nations.

THE INTERNATIONAL BANK FOR RECONSTRUCTION AND DEVELOPMENT

The basic argument in favor of international investment is the same as the one justifying investment across the regional boundaries of a single nation. It leads to the optimum combination of capital and the other factors of production. Special problems arise in the case of international investment. The nations of the world exhibit great differences in the degree of development and the level of per capita income. The underdeveloped nations are extremely anxious to develop and thus to raise their level of income. This requires capital which they do not possess. The developed nations sympathize with this desire for development because, among other reasons, they feel that it promotes political stability.

The presence of "rich" and "poor" nations and the need for international investment are not recent phenomena. Traditionally, the underdeveloped nations borrowed on the world capital markets or invited direct investment in plant and equipment by foreign firms. That is, they borrowed the savings of individuals and institutions in the developed nations. This system collapsed during the depression of the 1930's. There were several reasons for the collapse. Some ill-advised investment projects could not earn debt service charges. This was an ordinary case of bankruptcy. In other instances, the projects were profitable but exchange controls, currency devaluation, or expropriation caused the creditors to lose their savings. At the end of World War II it seemed likely that these conditions would continue and would prevent an adequate flow of foreign investment to underdeveloped nations. The leading nations of the world have attempted to solve this problem in several ways. Grants, "soft" loans, and technical assistance have satisfied part of the need for development capital. In addition, the Bretton Woods conference led to the organization of the International Bank for Reconstruction and Development.

The IBRD is a companion of the IMF and membership in the latter organization is a requirement for membership in the Bank. Like the IMF the Bank acquired capital by assigning a quota to each member and, also like the Fund, it assigned voting rights that are roughly proportional to the size of a nation's quota, with some favoritism shown to small nations. Table 27–4 shows the quotas and the voting rights. Since the main function of the Bank's capital is to serve as a reserve against bad debt, members need not pay 100 per cent of their quotas into the Bank. In case of need, however, the Bank can demand the entire amount.

Operation of the IBRD

The IBRD is not to compete with private enterprise but is to supply funds where private capital is unavailable. When the IBRD receives an application from a member, it investigates the project. In this respect it acts like an investment bank underwriting a loan. Before extending credit the IBRD must be sure that the project will increase the productivity of the debtor sufficiently to enable it to pay the debt service charges. The IBRD also considers the relationship of the project to the export and import position of the debtor since the debt service charges will increase the total debits in the balance of payments. These investigations frequently involve a thorough study of the economy of small underdeveloped nations. Since the reports of these investigations are valuable, the Bank performs a major service to the nation in advance of any lending activity.

Table 27–4

INTERNATIONAL BANK FOR RECONSTRUCTION AND DEVELOPMENT SUBSCRIPTIONS TO CAPITAL STOCK AND VOTING POWER

as of June 30, 1964

Nation	Subscription to Capital Stock (in millions of U. S. dollars)	Voting Rights (% of total)
Argentina	373.3	1.68
Australia	533.0	2.35
Belgium	450.0	2.00
Brazil	373.3	1.68
Canada	750.0	3.26
China (Taiwan)	750.0	3.26
France	1,050.0	4.53
Germany (Federal Republic)	1,050.0	4.53
India	800.0	3.48
Italy	360.0	1.62
Japan	666.0	2.91
Netherlands	550.0	2.42
United Kingdom	2,600.0	11.06
United States	6,350.0	26.86
Other 88 nations	4,530.4	28.36
Total	21,186.0	100.00

Source: International Bank for Reconstruction and Development, *Annual Report, 1963–1964*, pp. 66–67.

The IBRD may use any of three methods to lend funds to an applicant. It may lend its own capital. The Bank may sell its own debt obligations on the world capital market and lend the proceeds to the debtor. Or the Bank may guarantee the obligations which the debtor sells on the capital market. The Bank usually sells its own bonds and lends the proceeds. This avoids the Bank's calling for the remainder of the members' subscriptions. Creditors seem to prefer this method rather than loan guarantees; however, the IBRD does guarantee loans on occasion. Bank loans may be for five to thirty years' duration. Amortization is usually by installments. The Bank charges the debtor 1 per cent more than it pays on its own bonds and uses the income to create a reserve against loss. In addition, it charges ¼ of 1 per cent to cover administrative costs. The Bank is willing to lend to private firms but the home government must guarantee repayment.

The first IBRD loans were made for the reconstruction of war damage, but that phase of its work is complete. Currently, most debtors are underdeveloped nations who use the proceeds to exploit natural resources, develop transportation systems, construct electric power systems, etc. Table 27–5 shows the debtor nations and the amounts of the loans.

Table 27–5

INTERNATIONAL BANK FOR RECONSTRUCTION
AND DEVELOPMENT
STATEMENT OF LOANS

December 31, 1964
(In millions of U. S. dollars)

Nation	Original Principal Amount[a]	Nation	Original Principal Amount[a]
Argentina	143.5	Netherlands	236.5
Australia	417.7	Nigeria[c]	153.5
Austria	104.9	Norway	145.0
Brazil	267.0	Pakistan	361.2
Chile	136.2	Peru	123.3
Colombia	388.9	Portugal	105.9
Congo[b]	92.5	South Africa	221.8
Finland	187.6	Thailand	186.4
France	250.0	Venezuela	174.0
India	847.1	Yugoslavia	260.8
Iran	212.7	39 other nations	1,788.3
Italy	298.0		
Japan	632.0		
Mexico	439.3	Total	8,174.1

[a]The IBRD granted loans of $8,352.2 million. However, some of the loans have been cancelled. [b]Loan guaranteed by Belgium. [c]Loan guaranteed by the United Kingdom.
Source: International Monetary Fund, *International Financial Statistics*, April, 1965, p. 12.

The IBRD—an Evaluation

The IBRD has an excellent record in terms of the quality of its loan program. This is true if we think of the quality of a loan in terms of a good repayment record or if we adopt a broader human welfare viewpoint. Bank loans have been a means of rehabilitating war damaged areas, and they have aided in the development of resources in capital-scarce areas. The record regarding the volume of Bank loans is less cheerful. Table 27–5 shows total commitments of only $8.2 billion in 18 years (1947–1964). This is slightly less than the United States foreign aid budget for two and one-half years.

The Bank cannot make or guarantee loans in excess of its capital but this is not the restrictive factor. Its capital in 1964 was equal to $21.2 billion; nearly three times the amount of the outstanding loans. The Bank's cautious operation is at least partially responsible for this low volume. Re-establishment of confidence in foreign investment has been one of its objectives. Therefore, it has adopted a conservative attitude in appraising projects and in making guarantees. We must admit also that the Bank's credit terms are not attractive to an underdeveloped nation when compared with a grant. Furthermore, the areas most in need of capital generally have so low a standard of living that their leaders are unwilling to divert a portion of the increased output resulting from development to debt service. Instead, they have sought and have secured grants; thus they avoid the problem of repayment.

Affiliated Institutions

Recognizing that the volume of IBRD loans was not adequate for the needs of underdeveloped nations, the member nations organized two affiliated institutions. They are the International Finance Corporation and the International Development Association.

Formed in 1956 the International Finance Corporation has the same board of governors and executive directors as the IBRD. However, the accounts of the two organizations are separate, and they may not lend to each other. Any member of the IBRD may join the IFC. Each member subscribes to the Corporation's capital in proportion to the member's IBRD subscription, but the IFC has an authorized capital structure of only $100 million. In September, 1964, the IFC had 78 members and capital of $99.0 million.

The IFC promotes economic development through direct investment in private firms. Its criteria for participation are not as rigorous as those of the IBRD. For the most part it provides risk capital and will not provide more than 50 per cent of the cost of an enterprise. By selling its securities, it hopes that its small capital will become a revolving fund. Its investments earn interest and share in the profits of the project. Since it provides risk capital, some losses are inevitable but it hopes that gains will outweigh losses. As of September 30, 1964, it had invested or had committed itself to invest $122.7 million. This is a small amount when measured against the world's needs; however the Corporation is young.

The International Development Association, with an authorized capital of $1 billion, has been in existence since 1960. The system for determining the quotas and the voting rights of the members is similar to that for the IBRD. The Association makes "soft" loans to underdeveloped nations. These are loans which cannot meet the criteria of conservative banking principles. However, they provide for projects that will develop the debtor nation. As of September 30, 1964, ninety-four nations had joined the Association, and its underdeveloped members had received credits of $988 million.

SUMMARY

Some form of co-operation is necessary if money is to perform the same useful service internationally that it does domestically. Traditionally, adherence to the international gold standard provided for co-operation in the form of a tacit agreement to follow the "rules of the game." The unpleasant results in the period following the abandonment of the gold standard demonstrated the need for some form of international co-operation.

At the end of World War II the nations of the world formed the International Monetary Fund and the International Bank for Reconstruction and Development. The purpose of the IMF is to facilitate multilateral exchange. It is to accomplish this objective by providing for stable exchange rates and for the removal of exchange controls. The IMF lends foreign exchange to members with temporary balance-of-payments deficits. It provides for consultation prior to the adoption of policies to correct long-run disequilibria. Fear of an international liquidity shortage has led to proposals to improve the IMF by increasing its resources or by transforming it into a central bank.

The purpose of the IBRD is to channel some of the capital resources of developed nations to underdeveloped countries. The IBRD extends credit only to those projects which it believes will be able to pay for themselves. Because of the high credit standards of the IBRD, the volume of loans has been small. Therefore, two affiliated institutions, the IFC and the IDA, have come into existence to channel resources to projects with lower credit ratings.

QUESTIONS

1. How does the International Monetary Fund resemble a central bank? How does it differ?
2. Why was the International Monetary Fund unable to achieve its objectives in the years immediately following World War II? Does this experience indicate that the IMF is ineffective in times of emergency?
3. How can the International Monetary Fund prevent an international liquidity crisis?
4. How do you explain the relatively small volume of loans made by the International Bank for Reconstruction and Development?

SUGGESTED READINGS

Crutchfield, James A., Henning, Charles N., and Pigott, William. *Money, Financial Institutions, and the Economy.* Englewood Cliffs, N. J.: Prentice-Hall, Inc., 1965. Chapter 12.

International Bank for Reconstruction and Development and International Development Association. *Annual Report 1963 – 64.* Washington.

International Monetary Fund. *Annual Reports.*

Marcus, Edward, and Marcus, Mildred Rendl. *International Trade and Finance.* New York: Pitman Publishing Corporation, 1965. Chapter 16.

Snider, Delbert A. *Introduction to International Economics.* 3d ed. Homewood, Illinois: Richard D. Irwin, Inc., 1963. Chapter 29.

Triffin, Robert. *Gold and the Dollar Crisis.* New Haven: Yale University Press, 1960. Part Two.

INDEX